Other Avon books Edited by
Bill Henderson

THE PUSHCART PRIZE:
BEST OF THE SMALL PRESSES 30270 $5.95

THE
PUSHCART PRIZE, II:
BEST OF THE
SMALL PRESSES

*An annual small press reader assembled with Founding Editors
Anaïs Nin (1903–1977), Buckminster Fuller, Charles Newman,
Daniel Halpern, Gordon Lish, Harry Smith, H.L. Van Brunt,
Hugh Fox, Ishmael Reed, Joyce Carol Oates, Len Fulton,
Leonard Randolph, Leslie Fiedler, Nona Balakian, Paul
Bowles, Paul Engle, Ralph Ellison, Reynolds Price, Rhoda
Schwartz, Richard Morris, Ted Wilentz, Tom Montag, William
Phillips, plus 33 Special Contributing Editors for this edition,
and with the cooperation of the hundreds of small presses
whose names follow . . .*

THE PUSHCART PRIZE, II:

BEST
OF THE
SMALL
PRESSES

Edited by Bill Henderson
with the Pushcart Prize editors

AVON
PUBLISHERS OF BARD, CAMELOT AND DISCUS BOOKS

AVON BOOKS
A division of
The Hearst Corporation
959 Eighth Avenue
New York, New York 10019

Copyright © 1977 by The Pushcart Book Press
Published by arrangement with the Pushcart Press
Library of Congress Catalog Card Number: 76-58675
ISBN:0-380-01895-0

First Avon Printing, March, 1978
Second Printing

AVON TRADEMARK REG. U.S. PAT. OFF. AND IN
OTHER COUNTRIES, MARCA REGISTRADA, HECHO EN
U.S.A.

Printed in the U.S.A.

"The Tennis Game" by Paul Goodman © 1976 by *New Letters*, reprinted by permission of *New Letters* and Mrs. Sally Goodman.
"Arizona Movies" by Michael Van Walleghen, © 1976 by The Review, Inc., reprinted by permission from *The Hudson Review*, Vol. 29, No. 3.
"toussaint" by Ntozake Shange © 1976 by Ntozake Shange, reprinted by permission of *Invisible City* and the author.
"A Woman Waking" by Philip Levine © 1976 by The Modern Poetry Association, first appeared in *Poetry*, reprinted by permission of the editor of *Poetry* and the author.
"The Pure Loneliness" by Michael Ryan © 1976 by *The American Poetry Review*, reprinted by permission of *The American Poetry Review* and the author.
"Zimmer, Drunk and Alone, Dreaming of Old Football Games" by Paul Zimmer © 1976 by Paul Zimmer, reprinted from *The Zimmer Poems* by permission of Dryad Press and the author.
"The Man Who Invented The Automatic Jumping Bean" by "El Huitlacoche" © 1976 by *The Bilingual Review/La revista bilingüe*, reprinted by permission of *The Bilingual Review*, Dept. of Foreign Languages, York College, Jamaica, N.Y. 11451.
"Olympian Progress" by Richard Kostelanetz © 1976 by Assembling Press, reprinted by permission of the author.
"A Garment of Sadness" by Barbara Szerlip © 1976 by Barbara Szerlip and *Gallimaufry*, reprinted by permission of the author and publisher.
"Don't You Ever See The Butterflies" by Ana Blandiana © 1976 by *Invisible City*,

Acknowledgements

reprinted by permission of *Invisible City*.
"A Letter Home" by Adrianne Marcus © 1976 by *Painted Bride Quarterly*, reprinted by permission of the author and *Painted Bride Quarterly*.
"The Deportation of Solzhenitsyn" © 1976 by Amnesty International, reprinted by permission of Amnesty International.
"Another Form of Marriage" by Maxine Kumin © 1976 by The Paris Review Inc., reprinted by permission of *The Paris Review*.
"The Red Cross Night" by Victor Muravin © 1976 by *Confrontation*, reprinted by permission of *Confrontation*, Long Island University.
"Him & Me" by Susan MacDonald © 1976 by Five Trees Press, reprinted by permission of the publisher from *Dangerous As Daughters*.
"Mientras Dure Vida, Sobra El Tiempo" by Carolyn Forché © 1976 by *Dacotah Territory*, reprinted by permission of *Dacotah Territory* and the author.
"In Iowa" by Cinda Kornblum © 1976 by Toothpaste Press, reprinted by permission of the publisher from *Dental Floss*, vol. 1 #2, published by The Toothpaste Press.
"Milk Is Very Good For You" by Stephen Dixon © 1976 by *Quarry West*, reprinted by permission of the author and *Quarry West*.
"The Sleep" by Philip Dacey © 1976 by University of Nebraska Press, reprinted by permission of *Prairie Schooner*.
"Living on The Lower East Side During the Sixties" by Allen Planz © 1976 by Living Poets Press reprinted by permission of Living Poets Press.
"Medicine Bow" by Richard Hugo © 1976 by *Graham House Review*, reprinted by permission of *Graham House Review*.
"The Last Romantic" by Gerald Locklin © 1976 by Duck Down Press, reprinted by permission of the publisher from *The Chase*, a novel by Gerald Locklin, Duck Down Press.
"The Lover" by Eugene Garber © 1976 by *Shenandoah*, reprinted by permission of *Shenandoah*.
"The Party" by James Hashim © 1976 by *Kansas Quarterly*, reprinted by permission of *Kansas Quarterly* and the author.
"The U.S. Chinese Immigrants Book of the Art of Sex" by Opal L. Nations, © 1976 by *Intermedia*, reprinted by permission of Intermedia.
"Crash" by David Cope © 1976 by *Big Scream*, reprinted by permission of the author, previously published in *Big Scream* and *The Stars*.
"Barrett & Browning" by Thomas Lux © 1976 by *Field*, reprinted by permission of *Field*.
"The Station" by Miriam Levine © 1976 by Decatur House Press, reprinted from *To Know We Are Living* by permission of the author and Decatur House Press.
"The Best Ride to New York" by Bob Levin © 1976 by *The Massachusetts Review*, Inc., reprinted by permission of *The Massachusetts Review* and the author.
"We Free Singers Be" by Etheridge Knight © 1976 by *New Letters*, reprinted by permission of *New Letters*.
"Short Stories" by Howard Moss © 1976 by *Shenandoah*, reprinted by permission of *Shenandoah*.
"They Said" by Reg Saner © 1976 by East River Anthology, reprinted by permission of the publisher from *Demilitarized Zones*.
"Going After Cacciato" by Tim O'Brien © 1976 by Tim O'Brien, reprinted by permission of *Ploughshares*.
"Sweethearts," "Under the Boardwalk," "Blind Girls" by Jayne Anne Philips © 1976 by Truck Press, reprinted by permission of Truck Press.
"Cuylerville" by Douglas Crase © 1976 by *American Poetry Review*, reprinted by permission of the author and *American Poetry Review*.
"Song" by James Schuyler © 1976 by James Schuyler, reprinted by permission of The Promise of Learnings, Inc./The Kermani Press, and the author.
"King's Day" by T.E. Porter © 1975 by T.E. Porter, reprinted by permission of Mulch Press.
"Vickie Loans-Arrow, Fort Yates, No. Dak., 1970" from *A Taste of The Knife*, by Marnie Walsh, © 1976 by Ahsahta Press, reprinted by permission of Ahsahta Press.
"Lowghost to Lowghost" by Ross Feld © 1976 by *Parnassus: Poetry In Review*, reprinted by permission of *Parnassus: Poetry In Review*.
"With the Rest of My Body" by Christine Zawadiwsky © 1976 by *Icarus*, reprinted by permission of *Icarus*.
"The Juggler" by Siv Cedering Fox © 1976 by *Kayak*, reprinted by permission of *Kayak* and the author.
"Though It Looks Like a Throat It Is Not" by Patricia Goedicke © 1976 by The Paris Review Inc., reprinted by permission of *The Paris Review*.

8 *Acknowledgements*

"Jimmy Pasta" by Henry Miller © 1976 by Henry Miller, reprinted from *Henry Miller's Book of Friends*, published by Capra Press, by permission of the publisher.
"The Monk's Chimera" by Teo Savory © 1976 by Teo Savory from *A Clutch of Fables*, reprinted by permission of Unicorn Press, Greensboro, NC.
"How It Will Be" by Mary Lane © 1976 by *Lucille*, reprinted by permission of *Lucille*, #7, Spring 1976.
"Return of the General" by Jerry Stahl © 1976 by *Transatlantic Review*, reprinted by permission of *Transatlantic Review*.
"the buickspecial" by Raymond Federman © 1976 by Raymond Federman, reprinted by permission of The Fiction Collective and the author.
"Where The Winged Horses Take Off Into The Wild Blue Yonder From" by Kelly Cherry © 1976 by *StoryQuarterly*, reprinted by permission of *StoryQuarterly*.
"The Fire At the Catholic Church" by John Sanford, © 1976 by John Sanford, from *Adirondack Stories*, published by Capra Press, reprinted by permission of *Capra Press*.
"The New Consciousness, The NEA and Poetry Today" by Felix Stefanile © by Felix Stefanile, reprinted by permission of the author from *Black Rooster, Three*.
"Messinghausen 1945" by Ian MacMillan © 1976 by *TriQuarterly*, reprinted by permission of *TriQuarterly*.
"Laughter and Penitence" by Octavio Paz © 1976 by *Antaeus*, reprinted by permission of *Antaeus*.
"Rabbit Trance" by Jarold Ramsey © 1976 by *Ontario Review*, reprinted by permission of *Ontario Review*.
"Lovers" by Jerry Bumpus © 1976 by *Vagabond*, reprinted by permission of *Vagabond*, originally published in *Vagabond 23/24*.
"The Bank Robbery" by Steve Schutzman © 1976 by *TriQuarterly*, reprinted by permission of *TriQuarterly*.
"The End of Science Fiction" by Lisel Mueller © 1976 by *The Ohio Review*, reprinted by permission of the editors of *The Ohio Review*.
"Theodore Roethke" by James Lewisohn © 1976 by James Lewisohn, reprinted by permission of Greenfield Review Press.
"The Week The Dirigible Came" by Jay Meek © 1976 by Three Rivers Press, Carnegie-Mellon University, first appeared in *Three Rivers Poetry Journal*, reprinted by permission of Three Rivers Press.
"The Boy Scout" by David Ohle © 1976 by *TriQuarterly*, reprinted by permission of *TriQuarterly*.
"Ode To Senility" by Philip Lopate © 1976 by Sun Press, reprinted from *The Daily Round* by permission of the author.
"To My Daughter" by Kathryn Terrill © 1976 by *Poetry Northwest*, reprinted by permission of *Poetry Northwest*.
"Vestiges" by Meredith Steinbach © 1976 by Ploughshares, Inc., reprinted by permission of *Ploughshares* and the author.
"The Family As a Haven in a Heartless World" by Christopher Lasch © 1976 by *Salmagundi* and the author, reprinted by permission of *Salmagundi* and the author.
"The Sage of Apple Valley On Love" by Edward Field © 1976 by *The Texas Slough*, reprinted by permission of the author.
"The Pension Grillparzer" by John Irving © 1976 by *Antaeus*, reprinted by permission of the Harold Matson Agency.
"Lives of the Saints, Part I" by Jon Anderson © 1976 by *Iowa Review*, reprinted by permission of *Iowa Review*.
"The Big Store" by Alan V. Hewat © 1976 by *Iowa Review*, reprinted by permission of *Iowa Review*.
"All Kinds of Caresses" by John Ashbery © 1976 by John Ashbery, reprinted by permission of the author and Georges Borchardt, Inc.
"The Name, The Nose" by Italo Calvino © 1976 by *Antaeus*, reprinted by permission of Sanford Greenburger Agency.
"Mending the Adobe" by Hayden Carruth © 1976 by *The Georgia Review*, reprinted by permission of *The Georgia Review*.
"from The Duplications" by Kenneth Koch © 1976 by Kenneth Koch and *TriQuarterly*, reprinted by permission of Random House.
"Three Day New York Blues" by Jayne Cortez © 1976 by *Yardbird Reader*, reprinted by permission of the author and *Yardbird Reader*. Also © 1973 by Jayne Cortez.
"Preparing to Sleep" by Gregory Orr © 1976 by *Hard Pressed* and Gregory Orr, reprinted by permission of the author.
"The Neighborhood Dog" from *The Intuitive Journey and Other Works* by Russell Edson © 1976 by Russell Edson. Reprinted by permission of Harper and Row, Publishers, Inc.

The book is for Dorothy Galloway Henderson

𝕓 𝕓 𝕓

INTRODUCTION:
About Pushcart Prize II

LAST YEAR PUSHCART PRESS PUBLISHED the first annual *Pushcart Prize: Best of the Small Presses*. The project started as a collector's hobby, something civilized to do on winter evenings—reading the literary presses. And it has evolved this year into a full-time job with a volunteer staff of more than fifty editors and over 3,000 nominations from small press publishers.

The hobby became a job because we imagined that such a collection might be useful for the general reader who couldn't hope to keep up with the authors in the multitudes of small presses. Most of these presses, run from garages, basements, kitchen tables or studio apartments (like Pushcart) or even if affiliated with universities (like *The Iowa Review*, which recently staged a forty-eight hour reading marathon to raise survival funds) have zero budgets for advertising and publicity, lack distribution facilities and face a pervasive apathy from a culture dazzled by conglomerate-controlled publishers and enamored by bestseller noise. We thought presses and their authors might welcome Pushcart's "Prize" as an opportunity to reach a wider audience.

We call the collection a "Prize" in order to offer recognition to writers and also to the literary press movement that in the past nourished Ezra Pound, James Joyce, Upton Sinclair, Carl Sandburg, and Anais Nin, and in earlier centuries Thomas Paine, Edgar Allan Poe, Walt Whitman and Herman Melville, to drop but a few names from a long list. In planning the first *Pushcart Prize* last year we didn't imagine that Pushcart had any authority to issue a "Prize," so we wrote to about 175 small press authors, editors and supporters to ask them what they thought of the idea of an annual collection. Some of them we asked to join us as Founding Editors. Without the backing and judgment on final selections of these

Founding Editors (their names are listed on the masthead) there would be no *Pushcart Prize.*

For this second annual collection, the Founding Editors are joined by thirty-three special Contributing Editors: Allan Kornblum, Allen Ginsberg, Barbara Damrosch, Bob Miles, Carll Tucker, Clarence Major, Elliott Anderson, Erica Jong, Eugene Redmond, Frederick Morgan, George Plimpton, Harold Brodkey, Harvey Shapiro, Herbert Leibowitz, Jerzy Kosinski, John Ashbery, John Gill, Joel Oppenheimer, Lynne Spaulding, Malcolm Cowley, M.D. Elevitch, Mark Strand, Mark Vinz, Mary MacArthur, Michael Hogan, Naomi Lazard, Noel Peattie, Noel Young, Raymond Federman, Richard Kostelanetz, Robie MacCauley, Teo Savory, and William Saroyan.

Like the first edition, this *Pushcart Prize* is just as much a demonstration in democratic picking as it is a book. All of the Founding and Contributing editors were invited to make nominations of their best from calendar year 1976 as were small presses everywhere (six per press). Pushcart did the first reading of the nominations and submitted the list of possible selections to the editorial staff for judgment. Our hope, (and we know it is only a hope), is that we have gathered a fair representation of the best of all sorts of small press writing published in the previous calendar year. With so many smart and cantankerous editors this book is dominated by no individual vision or style. Each of these selections is proof enough that in a publishing community too often sidetracked by commercial ballyhoo, the outstanding literary talent is often found sequestered in the small non-commercial presses.

For talented new writers the small presses almost always offer the only publishing opportunity. Many commercial houses no longer read—let alone publish—manuscripts by unknowns, and only a handful issue poetry. Thus this edition of *The Pushcart Prize,* like the first, is obviously prejudiced in favor of unknown authors, and about half the collection is poetry. But you will find "name" writers here too—John Irving, Howard Moss, John Ashbery, Henry Miller and a few more. They too have turned to small presses.

More than 70 authors from over 60 presses appear in this edition. In the first two editions, 142 authors from over 100 small presses have been represented.

None of the writers were in our first volume—except Octavio Paz. His essay, "Laughter and Penitence," received a record four nominations from editors Harold Brodkey, Nona Balakian, Carll Tucker and *Antaeus.*

We include forty presses that were not in our first volume—from *Paris Review* and *Massachusetts Review* to Truck Press and *Vagabond*—all small, non-commercial and literary and thus meeting the popular definition of "small press."

While we have made no effort to divide the selections into categories, this edition is as varied as the tastes of Pushcart's editors.

In fiction you will discover traditional well-crafted stories such as Tim O'Brien's "Going After Cacciato," nominated by both Joyce Carol Oates and *Ploughshares;* Bob Levin's "The Best Ride to New York"; and Maxine Kumin's "Another Form of Marriage," a favorite of Contributing Editor George Plimpton, and the *Paris Review* staff. We also include two re-discovered short fictions: "The Tennis Game" by the then twenty-one year old Paul Goodman, first small-press-published in 1932, and John Sanford's "The Fire At The Catholic Church" which is prefaced by an account of the author's summer rambles with Nathanael West. We list more personal, autobiographical fictions too such as Kelly Cherry's "Where the Winged Horses Take Off Into the Wild Blue Yonder From" and Raymond Federman's "the buickspecial." Small presses are the only outlet for most of the experimental and/or unusual fiction and this year we include Jerry Stahl's "Return of the General" (winner of *Transatlantic's* "Erotica Award in Fiction"—Stahl's private becomes a general); Steve Dixon's "Milk Is Very Good For You," which might easily have won *Quarry West's* erotica award, if they had one; Italo Calvino's "The Name, The Nose" and three selections from *TriQuarterly's* "Minute Stories" issue by Ian MacMillan, David Ohle, and Steve Schutzman. Then there's Richard Kostelanetz's "Olympian Progress," an experimental literary what-not.

The essays this year also range from the traditional such as Christopher Lasch's "The Family As Haven In A Heartless World" or Ross Feld's "Lowghost to Lowghost"—an examination of the poetry of Jack Spicer, a unique small press and self-published poet—to the personal such as "El Huitlacoche's" "The Man Who Invented The Automatic Jumping Bean," a loving remembrance of the author's father, to the controversial, "The New Consciousness, The NEA and Poetry Today," Felix Stefanile's thoughts on government funding of small presses.

As last year, we include a reprint from the Russian *samizdat* underground, "The Deportation of Solzhenitsyn." Our self-published selection this year is Victor Muravin's memoir of his experiences in a Soviet prison camp "The Red Cross Night" from a portion nominated and featured by *Confrontation*.

It is impossible to sum up the many poems. They are as different as the poets' visions. Special thanks belongs to Poetry editors H.L. Van Brunt and Naomi Lazard and Lynne Spaulding for their help in reading the many nominations. Pushcart's favorites include Douglas Crase's "Cuylerville," Jon Anderson's "Lives of the Saints, Part I," Etheridge Knight's joyous "We Free Singers Be" and Patricia Goedicke's "Though It Looks Like A Throat It is Not" and many more. For every fine poet chosen here we would estimate that a distinguished poet was left out—for reasons of space, editorial oversight, or because the poet was not nominated. In the years ahead we will attempt to make up for the incompleteness of the past so that finally a true "best" of the authors of fiction, non-fiction and poetry will be on record in all our annual volumes.

On behalf of Pushcart and our editors, we hope you will find in the pages that follow a testimony to small press writers, flourishing in 1977 as much as in 1976 and the years before. We invite your suggestions for next year's *Pushcart Prize*.

Bill Henderson

THE PEOPLE WHO HELPED MAKE THIS BOOK

FOUNDING EDITORS—*Anaïs Nin (1903–1977), Buckminster Fuller, Charles Newman, Daniel Halpern, Gordon Lish, Harry Smith, Hugh Fox, Ishmael Reed, Joyce Carol Oates, Len Fulton, Leonard Randolph, Leslie Fiedler, Nona Balakian, Paul Bowles, Paul Engle, Ralph Ellison, Reynolds Price, Rhoda Schwartz, Richard Morris, Ted Wilentz, Tom Montag, William Phillips. Poetry editor: H.L. Van Brunt.*

CONTRIBUTING EDITORS FOR THIS EDITION—*Allan Kornblum, Allen Ginsberg, Barbara Damrosch, Bob Miles, Carll Tucker, Clarence Major, Elliott Anderson, Erica Jong, Eugene Redmond, Frederick Morgan, George Plimpton, Harold Brodkey, Harvey Shapiro, Herbert Leibowitz, Jerzy Kosinski, John Ashbery, John Gill, Joel Oppenheimer, Lynne Spaulding, Malcolm Cowley, M.D. Elevitch, Mark Strand, Mark Vinz, Mary MacArthur, Michael Hogan, Naomi Lazard, Noel Peattie, Noel Young, Raymond Federman, Richard Kostelanetz, Robie MacCauley, Teo Savory, William Saroyan*

DESIGN—*Ray Freiman*

ROVING EDITORS—*Ben Pesta, Bob Seidman, Carole Dolph*

EUROPEAN EDITORS—*Kirby and Liz Williams*

AUSTRALIAN EDITORS—*Tom and Wendy Whitton*

POETRY EDITORS FOR THIS EDITION—*H.L. Van Brunt, Lynne Spaulding, Naomi Lazard*

EDITOR—*Bill Henderson*

CONTENTS

Contents

THE
PUSHCART PRIZE, II:
BEST OF THE
SMALL PRESSES

1977–78 Edition

🔥 🔥 🔥

THE PENSION GRILLPARZER

fiction by JOHN IRVING

from ANTAEUS

nominated by ANTAEUS

M<small>Y FATHER WORKED</small> for the Austrian Tourist Bureau. It was my mother's idea that our family travel with him when he went on the road as a Tourist Bureau spy. My mother and brother and I would accompany him on his secretive missions to uncover the discourtesy, the dust, the badly cooked food, the short cuts taken by Austria's restaurants and hotels and pensions. We were instructed to create difficulties whenever we could, to never order exactly what was on the menu, to imitate a foreigner's odd requests—the hours we would like to have our baths, the need for aspirin and directions to the zoo. We were instructed to be civilized but troublesome; and when the visit was over, we reported to my father in the car.

My mother would say, "The hairdresser is always closed in the morning. But they make suitable recommendations outside. I guess it's all right, provided they don't claim to have a hairdresser actually *in* the hotel."

"Well, they *do* claim it," my father would say. He'd note this on a giant pad.

I was always the driver. I said, "The car is parked off the street, but someone put fourteen kilometers on the gauge between the time we handed it over to the doorman and picked it up at the hotel garage."

"That is a matter to report directly to the management," my father said, jotting it down.

"The toilet leaked," I said.

"I couldn't open the door to the W.C.," said my brother, Robo.

"Robo," mother said, "you always have trouble with doors."

"Was that supposed to be Class C?" I asked.

"I'm afraid not," father said. "It is still listed as Class B." We drove for a short while in silence. Our most serious judgment concerned changing a hotel's or a pension's class standing: we did not suggest it frivolously.

"I think this calls for a letter to the management," mother suggested. "Not too nice a letter, but not a really rough one. Just state the facts."

"Yes, I rather liked him," father said. He always made a point of getting to meet the managers.

"Don't forget the business of driving the car," I said. "That's really unforgivable."

"And the eggs were bad," said Robo; he was not yet ten and his judgments were not seriously considered.

We became a far harsher team of evaluators when my grandfather died and we inherited grandmother—my mother's mother, who thereafter accompanied us on our travels. A regal dame, Johanna was accustomed to Class A travel, and my father's duties more frequently called for investigations of Class B and Class C lodgings. They were the places, the B and C hotels (and the pensions), that most interested the tourists. At restaurants we did a little better. People who couldn't afford the classy places to sleep were still interested in the best places to eat.

"I shall not have dubious food tested on me," Johanna told us. "This strange employment may give you all glee about having free vacations, but I can see there is a terrible price paid: the anxiety of not knowing what sort of quarters you'll have for the night. The Americans may find it charming that we still have rooms without baths and toilets, but I am an old woman and I'm not charmed by walking down a public corridor in search of cleanliness and my relievement. The anxiety is only half of it. Actual diseases are possible—and not only from food. If the bed is questionable, I promise I shan't put my head down. And the children are young and impressionable; you should think of the clientele in some of these lodgings and seriously ask yourselves about the influences." My mother and father nodded; they said nothing. "Slow down!" grandmother said to me. "You're just a young boy who likes to show off." I slowed down. "Vienna," grandmother sighed. "In Vienna I always stayed at the Ambassador."

"Johanna, the Ambassador is not under investigation," father said.

"I should think not," Johanna said. "I suppose we're not even headed toward a Class A place?"

"Well, it's a B trip," my father admitted. "For the most part."

"I trust," grandmother said, "that you mean there is one A place en route?"

"No," father admitted. "There is one C place."

"It's okay," Robo said. "There are fights in Class C."

"I should imagine so," Johanna said.

"It's a Class C pension, very small," father said, as if the size of the place forgave it.

"And they're applying for a B," said mother.

"But there have been some complaints," I added.

"I'm sure there have," Johanna said.

"And animals," I added. My mother gave me a look.

"Animals?" said Johanna.

"Animals," I admitted.

"A *suspicion* of animals," my mother corrected me.

"Yes, be fair," father said.

"Oh wonderful," grandmother said. "A suspicion of animals. Their hair on the rugs? Their terrible waste in the corners! Did you know that my asthma reacts, severely, to any room in which there has recently been a cat?"

"The complaint was not about cats," I said. My mother elbowed me sharply.

"Dogs?" Johanna said. "Rabid dogs! Biting you on the way to the bathroom . . ."

"No," I said. "Not dogs."

"Bears!" Robo cried.

But my mother said, "We don't know for sure about any bear, Robo."

"This isn't serious?" Johanna said.

"Of course it's not serious," father said. "How could there be bears in a pension?"

"There was a letter saying so," I said. "Of course, the Tourist Bureau assumed it was a crank complaint. But then there was another sighting—and a second letter claiming there had been a bear."

My father used the rear-view mirror to scowl at me, but I thought that if we were all supposed to be in on the investigation, it would be wise to have grandmother on her toes.

"It's probably not a real bear," Robo said, with obvious disappointment.

"A man in a bear suit!" Johanna cried. "What unheard-of perversion is *that*? A *beast* of a man sneaking about in disguise! Up to what? It's a man in a bear suit, I know it is," she said. "I want to go to that one first. If there's going to be a Class C experience on this trip, let's get it over with as soon as possible."

"But we haven't got reservations for tonight," mother said.

"Yes, we might as well give them a chance to be at their best," father said. Although he never revealed to his victims that he worked for the Tourist Bureau, father believed that reservations were simply a decent way of allowing the personnel to be as prepared as they could be.

"I'm sure we don't need to make a reservation in a place frequented by men who disguise themselves as animals," Johanna said. "I'm sure there is always a vacancy there. I'm sure the guests are regularly dying in their beds—of fright, or else of whatever unspeakable injury the madman in the foul bear suit does to them."

"It's probably a real bear," Robo said, hopefully—for in the turn the conversation was taking, he certainly saw that a real bear would be preferable to grandmother's imagined ghoul. Robo had no fear, I think, of a real bear.

I drove us as inconspicuously as possible to the dark, dwarfed corner of Planken and Seilergasse. We were looking for the Class C pension that wanted to be a B.

"No place to park," I said to father, who was already making note of it in his pad.

"The Pension Grillparzer," my mother read aloud to us, pointing out the tiny sign.

"What dreadful pretension," grandmother said.

I double parked and we sat in the car and peered up at the Pension Grillparzer; it rose only four slender stories between a pastry shop and a Tabak Trafik.

"See?" father said. "No bears!"

"No *men*, I hope," said grandmother.

"They come at night," Robo said, looking cautiously up and down the street.

We went inside to met the manager, a Herr Theobald who instantly put Johanna on her guard. "Three generations traveling together!" he cried. "Like the old days," he added, especially to grandmother, "before all these divorces and the young people wanting to live in apartments by themselves. This is a *family* pension! I just wish you had made a reservation so I could put you more closely together."

"We're not accustomed to sleeping in the same room," grandmother told him.

"Of course not!" Theobald cried. "I just meant I wished that your *rooms* could be closer together." This worried grandmother, clearly.

"How far apart must we be put?" she asked.

"Well, I've only two rooms left," he said. "And only one of them is large enough for the two boys and their parents. We have some portable cots we can move in, you see."

"We're not usually together," father said.

"And my room is how far from theirs?" Johanna asked coolly.

"You're right across from the W.C.!" Theobald told her, as if this were a plus.

But as we were shown to our rooms, grandmother staying with father—contemptuously to the rear of our procession—I heard her mutter: "This is not how I conceived of my retirement. Across the hall from a W.C., listening to all the visitors."

"Not one of these rooms is the same," Theobald told us. "The furniture is all from my family." We could believe it. The one large room Robo and I were to share with my parents was a hall-sized museum of knick-knacks, every dresser with a different style of knob. On the other hand, the sink had brass faucets and the head-board of the bed was carved. I could see my father balancing things up for future notation in the giant pad.

"You may do that later," Johanna informed him. "Where do *I* stay?"

As a family, we dutifully followed Theobald and my grandmother down the long, twining hall—my father counting the paces to the W.C. The hall rug was thin, the color of a shadow. Along the walls were old photographs of speed-skating teams—on their feet the strange blades curled at the tips like court jesters' shoes or the runnners of ancient sleds.

Robo, running far ahead, announced his discovery of the W.C.

Grandmother's room was full of china, polished wood and the hint of mold. The drapes were damp. The bed had an unsettling ridge at its center, almost as if a very slender body lay stretched beneath the spread.

Grandmother said nothing, and when Theobald reeled out of the room like a wounded man who's been told he'll live, grandmother asked my father, "On what basis can the Pension Grillparzer hope to get a B?"

"Quite decidedly C," I said.

"I would say, myself, that it was E or F," grandmother told us.

My mother ran her hand along the window sill. "Very clean, though," she said.

"I imagine," said grandmother, pulling back the heavy bedspread, "that these things absorb quite a lot."

* * *

In the dim tea room a man without a tie sang a Hungarian song. "It does not mean he's Hungarian," father reassured Johanna, but she was skeptical.

"I'd say the odds are not in his favor," she suggested; she would not have tea or coffee. Robo ate a little cake, which he claimed to like. My mother and I smoked a cigarette; she was trying to quit and I was trying to start, with moderation; therefore, we shared a cigarette between us—in fact, we'd promised never to smoke a whole one alone.

"He's a great guest," Herr Theobald whispered to my father; he indicated the singer. "He knows songs from all over."

"From Hungary, at least," grandmother said, but she smiled.

A small man, clean-shaven but with that permanent gun-blue shadow of a beard on his lean face, spoke to my grandmother. He wore a clean shirt (but yellow from age and laundering), suit pants and an unmatching jacket.

"Pardon me?" said grandmother.

"I said that I tell dreams," the man informed her.

"You *tell* dreams," grandmother said. "Meaning, you have them?"

"Have them and tell them," he said mysteriously. The singer stopped singing.

"Any dream you want to know," said the singer, "he can tell it."

"I'm quite sure I don't want to know any," grandmother said. She viewed with displeasure the ascot of dark hair bursting out at the open throat of the singer's shirt. She would not regard the man who "told" dreams, at all.

"I can see you are a lady," the dream man told grandmother. "You don't respond to just every dream that comes along."

"Certainly not," said grandmother; she shot my father one of her how-could-you-have-let-this-happen-to-me? looks.

"But I know one," said the dream man; he shut his eyes. The singer slipped a chair forward and we suddenly realized he was sitting very close to us. Robo, though he was much too old for it, sat in father's lap. "In a great castle," the dream man began, "a woman lay beside her husband; she was wide awake, suddenly, in the middle of the night. She woke up without the slightest idea of what had awakened her, and she felt as alert as if she'd been up for hours. It was also clear to her, without a look, a word or a touch, that her husband was wide awake too—and just as suddenly."

"I hope this is suitable for the child to hear, ha ha," Herr Theobald said, but no one even looked at him. My grandmother folded her hands in her lap and stared at them—her knees together, her heels tucked under her straight-backed chair. My mother held my father's hand.

I sat next to the dream man, whose jacket smelled like the hay that animals sleep on. He said: "The woman and her husband lay awake listening for sounds in the castle, which they were renting and did not know intimately. They listened for sounds in the courtyard, which they never bothered to lock. The village people always took walks by the castle; the village children were allowed to swing on the great courtyard door. What had awakened them?"

"Bears?" said Robo, but father touched his fingertips to Robo's mouth.

"They heard horses," said the dream man. Old Johanna, her eyes shut, her head inclined toward her lap, seemed to shudder in her stiff chair. "They heard the breathing and stamping of horses who were trying to keep still. The husband reached out and touched his wife. 'Horses?' he said. The woman got out of bed and went to the courtyard window. She would swear to this day that the courtyard was full of soldiers on horseback—but *what* soldiers they were! They wore *armor!* The visors on their helmets were closed and their murmuring voices were as tinny and difficult to hear as voices on a fading radio station. Their armor clanked as their horses shifted restlessly under them.

"There was an old dry bowl of a former fountain, there in the castle's courtyard, but the woman saw that the fountain was flowing; the water slapped over the worn curb and the horses were drinking it. The knights were wary, they would not dismount; they looked up at the castle's dark windows, as if they knew they were uninvited at this watering trough—this rest station on their way, somewhere.

"In the moonlight the woman saw their big shields glint. She crept back to bed and lay rigidly against her husband. 'What is it?' he asked her.

"'Horses,' she told him.

"'I thought so,' he said. 'They'll eat the flowers.'

"'Who built this castle?' she asked him. It was a very old castle, they both knew that.

"'Charlemagne,' he told her; he was going back to sleep.

"But the woman lay awake, listening to the water which now seemed to be running all through the castle, gurgling in every drain, as if the old fountain were drawing water from every available source. And there were the distorted voices of the whispering knights—Charlemagne's soldiers speaking their dead language! And the horses kept drinking.

"The woman lay awake a long time, waiting for the soldiers to leave; she had no fear of attack from them; she was sure they were on a journey and had only stopped to rest at a place they once knew. But for as long as the water ran she felt that she mustn't disturb the castle. When she fell asleep, she thought Charlemagne's men were still there.

"In the morning her husband asked her, 'Did you hear water running, too?' Yes, she had. But the fountain was dry, of course, and out the window they could see that the flowers weren't eaten—and everyone knows horses eat flowers.

"But the woman knew that the good knights would never have let their horses trample the flower beds. She threw open the window and the strong smell of horses was rich in the courtyard—their sweat, their sweet hair, their dung.

"'But look,' said her husband; he went into the courtyard with her. 'There are no hoofprints, there are no droppings. We must have dreamed we heard them.' She did not tell him that she had *seen* them, too, or that there were soldiers; or that, in her opinion, it was unlikely that two people would dream the same dream. She did not remind him that he was a heavy smoker who never smelled the soup simmering; the aroma of horses in the fresh air would, understandably, be too subtle for him.

"She saw the soldiers, or dreamed them, twice more while they stayed there, but her husband never again woke up with her. It was always sudden. Once she woke with the taste of metal on her tongue, as if she'd touched some old, sour iron to her mouth—a sword, a chest plate, chain mail, a thigh guard. They were out there again, in colder weather. From the water in the fountain a dense fog surrounded them; the horses were snowy with frost. And there were not so many of them the next time—as if the winter or their skirmishes were reducing their numbers. The last time the horses looked gaunt to her, and the men looked more like unoccupied suits of armor balanced delicately in the saddles. The horses wore long masks of ice on their muzzles, their breathing (or the men's breathing) was congested.

"Her husband," said the dream man, "would die of a respiratory infection, but the woman did not know it when she dreamed this dream."

My grandmother looked up from her lap and slapped the dream man's beard-grey face. Robo stiffened in my father's lap; my mother caught her mother's hand. The singer shoved back his chair and jumped to his feet, frightened, or ready to fight someone, but the dream man simply bowed to grandmother and left the gloomy tea room. It was as if he'd made a contract with Johanna which was final but gave neither of them any joy. My father wrote something in the giant pad.

"Well, wasn't *that* some story?" said Herr Theobald. "Ha ha." He
rumpled Robo's hair—something Robo always hated.

"Herr Theobald," my mother said, still holding Johanna's hand,
"my father died of a respiratory infection."

"Oh dear," said Herr Theobald. "I'm sorry, *meine Frau*," he told
grandmother, but old Johanna would not speak to him.

We took grandmother out to eat in a Class A restaurant, but she
hardly touched her food. "That person was a gypsy," she told us, "a
satanic being."

"Please, mother," my mother said. "He couldn't have known
about father."

"He knew more than you know," grandmother snapped.

"The schnitzel is excellent," father said, writing in the pad. "The
Gumpoldskirchner is just right with it. But the Bohnensalat is
too wet."

"The Kalbsnieren are fine," I said.

"The eggs are okay," said Robo.

Grandmother said nothing until we returned to the Pension
Grillparzer, where we noticed that the door to the W.C. was hung a
foot or more off the floor, so that it resembled the bottom half of an
American toilet stall door, or a saloon door in the Western movies.
"I'm certainly glad I used the W.C. at the restaurant," grandmother
said. "How revolting! I shall try to pass the night without exposing
myself where every passer-by can peer at my ankles."

In our family room father said, "Didn't Johanna live in a castle
before you were born? I thought she and Grandpa rented some
castle."

"Yes!" mother said. "They rented Schloss Katzelsdorf. I still have
the photographs."

"Well, that's why the Hungarian's dream upset her," father said.

"Someone is riding a bike in the hall," Robo said. "I saw a wheel go
by, under our door."

"Robo, go to sleep," mother said.

"It went 'squeak-squeak,'" Robo said.

"Good night, boys," said father.

"If you can talk, we can talk," I said.

"Then talk to each other," father said. "I'm talking to your
mother."

"I want to go to sleep," mother said. "I wish no one would
talk."

We tried. Perhaps we slept. Then Robo whispered to me that he had to use the W.C.

"You know where it is," I said.

Robo went out the door, leaving it slightly open; I heard him walk down the corridor, brushing his hand along the wall. He was back very quickly.

"There's someone *in* the W.C.," he said.

"Well, wait for them to finish," I said.

"The light wasn't on," Robo said, "but I could still see under the door. Someone is in there, in the dark."

"I prefer the dark myself," I said.

But Robo insisted on telling me exactly what he'd seen. He said that under the door was a pair of *hands*.

"Hands?" I said.

"Yes, where the feet should have been," Robo said; he claimed that there was a hand on either side of the toilet—instead of a foot.

"Get out of here, Robo!" I said.

"Please come see," he begged. I went down the hall with him but there was no one in the W.C. "They've gone," he said.

"Walked off on their hands, no doubt," I said. "Go pee, I'll wait for you."

He went into the W.C. and peed sadly in the dark. When we were almost back to our room together, a small dark man with the same kind of skin and clothes as the dream man who had angered grand-mother passed us in the hall. He winked at us, and smiled. I had to notice that he was walking on his hands.

"You see?" Robo whispered to me. We went into our room and shut the door.

"What is it?" mother said.

"A man walking on his hands," I said.

"A man *peeing* on his hands," Robo said.

"Class C," father murmured in his sleep; he often dreamed that he was making notes in the giant pad.

"We'll talk about it in the morning," mother said.

"He was probably just an acrobat who was showing off for you, because you're a kid," I told Robo.

"How did he know I was a kid when he was in the W.C.?" Robo asked me.

"Go to sleep," mother whispered.

We heard grandmother scream down the hall.

Mother put on her pretty green dressing gown; father put on his bathrobe and his glasses; I pulled on a pair of pants, over my pajamas. Robo was in the hall first. We saw the light coming from under the W.C. door; grandmother was screaming rhythmically in there.

"Here we are!" I called to her.

"Mother, what is it?" mother asked.

We gathered in the broad slot of light. We could see grandmother's mauve slippers and her porcelain-white ankles under the door. She stopped screaming. "I heard whispers when I was in my bed," she said.

"It was Robo and me," I told her.

"Then, when everyone seemed to have gone, I came into the W.C.," Johanna said. "I left the light off. I was very quiet," she told us. "Then I saw and heard the wheel."

"The *wheel?*" father asked.

"A wheel went by the door a few times," grandmother said. "It rolled by and came back and rolled by again."

Father made his fingers roll like wheels alongside his head; he made a face at mother. "Somebody needs a new set of wheels," he whispered, but mother looked crossly at him.

"I turned on the light," grandmother said, "and the wheel went away."

"I told you there was a bike in the hall," said Robo.

"Shut up, Robo," father said.

"No, it was not a bicycle," grandmother said. "There was only one wheel."

Father was making his hands go crazy beside his head. "She's got a wheel or two missing," he hissed at my mother, but she cuffed him and knocked his glasses askew.

"Then someone came and looked under the door," grandmother said, "and that is when I screamed."

"Someone?" said father.

"I saw his hands, a man's hands—there was hair on his knuckles," grandmother said. "His hands were on the rug right outside the door. He must have been looking up at me."

"No, grandmother," I said. "I think he was just standing out here on his hands."

"Don't be fresh," my mother whispered.

"But we saw a man walking on his hands," Robo said.

"You did *not*," father said.

"We did," I said. "And Robo saw him earlier, in the W.C. He was standing on his hands in the W.C."

"We're going to wake up everyone," mother cautioned us.

The toilet flushed and grandmother shuffled out the door with only a little of her former dignity intact. She was wearing a gown over a gown over a gown; her neck was very long and her face was creamed white. She looked like a troubled goose. "He was evil and vile," she said to us. "He knew terrible magic."

"The man who looked at you?" mother said.

"That man who told my dream," grandmother said. Now a tear made its way through her furrows of face cream. "That was *my* dream," she said, "and he told everyone. It is unspeakable that he even *knew* it," she hissed at us. "*My* dream—Charlemagne's horses and soldiers—*I* am the only one who should know it. I had the dream before you were born," she told mother. "And the vile evil magic man told my dream as if it were *news*.

"I never even told your father all there was to that dream. I was never sure that it *was* a dream. And now there are men on their hands, and their knuckles are hairy, and there are magic wheels. I want the boys to sleep with me."

So that was how Robo and I came to share the large family room, far away from the W.C., with grandmother, who lay on my mother's and father's pillows with her creamed face shining like the face of a wet ghost. Robo lay awake watching her. I do not think Johanna slept very well; I imagined she was dreaming her dream of horses, again—reliving the last winter of Charlemagne's cold soldiers with their strange metal clothes covered with frost and their armor frozen shut.

When it was obvious that I had to go to the W.C., Robo's round bright eyes followed me to the door.

There was someone in the W.C. There was no light shining from under the door, but there was a unicycle parked against the wall outside. Its rider sat in the dark W.C.; the toilet was flushing over and over again—like a child, the person was not giving the tank time to refill—and there was quite a terrible stench. I remembered my father saying, as he ushered my mother into Johanna's abandoned room: "If a man tried to pee while standing on his hands, it seems it would go all over his chin."

I went closer to the gap under the W.C. door, but the occupant was not standing on his or her hands. I saw what were clearly feet, in almost the expected position—but *what* feet they were! The feet were shoed with fur—more hair, surely, than the hair on the knuckles grandmother had seen. The feet did not touch the floor; their soles tilted up toward me—dark bruise-colored pads. They were huge feet attached to short, furry shins. They were a bear's feet, only there were no claws. A bear's claws are not retractable, like a cat's; if a bear had claws, you would see them. Here was an imposter in a bearsuit, or a de-clawed bear. A domestic bear? At least—by its presence in the W.C.—a housebroken bear. For by its smell I could tell it was no man in a bearsuit: it was all bear. It was real bear.

I backed into the door of grandmother's room, behind which my father lurked, waiting for further disturbances. He snapped open the door and I fell inside, frightening us both. Mother sat up in bed and pulled the feather quilt over her head. "Got him!" father cried, dropping down on me. The floor trembled; the bear's unicycle slipped against the wall and fell into the door of the W.C., out of which the bear suddenly shambled, stumbling over its unicycle and lunging for its balance. Worriedly, it stared across the hall, through the open door, at father sitting on my chest. It picked up the unicycle in its front paws. "*Grauf?*" said the bear. Father slammed the door.

Down the hall we heard a woman call: "Where are you, Duna?" "*Harf!*" the bear said.

Father and I heard the woman come closer. She said, "Oh, Duna, practicing again? Always practicing. But it's better in the daytime." The bear said nothing. Father opened the door.

"Don't let anyone else in," mother said, still under the featherbed.

In the hall a pretty, aging woman stood beside the bear who now balanced in place on its unicycle, one huge paw on the woman's shoulder. She wore a vivid red turban and a long wrap-around dress that resembled a curtain. Perched on her high bosom was a necklace strung with bear claws; her earrings touched the shoulder of her curtain-dress and her other, bare shoulder where my father and I stared at her fetching mole. "Good evening," she said to father. "I'm sorry if we've disturbed you. Duna is forbidden to practice at night, but he loves his work."

The bear muttered, pedaling away from the woman. The bear had very good balance but he was careless; he brushed against the walls of the hall and touched the photographs of the speed-skating teams with his paws. The woman, bowing away from father, went after the bear, calling "Duna, Duna, Duna. . ." and straightening the photographs as she followed him down the hall.

"*Duna* is the Hungarian word for the Danube," father told me. "That bear is named after our beloved *Donau*."

"*What* bear?" said mother. "I heard a *woman*. Did you drag a bear into our room? Is there another woman here?"

But I left father to explain it all to her. I knew that in the morning Herr Theobald would have much to explain, and I would hear everything reviewed at that time. I went across the hall to the W.C. My task there was hurried by the bear's lingering odor and by suspicion of bear hair on everything; it was only my suspicion, though, for the bear had left everything quite tidy—or at least neat for a bear.

"I saw the bear," I whispered to Robo, back in our room, but Robo had crept into grandmother's bed and had fallen asleep beside her. Old Johanna was awake, however—or she only *appeared* to be: her eyes were open and she turned somewhat in my direction when I whispered to Robo.

"I saw fewer and fewer soldiers," she said. "That last time they came there were only nine of them. Everyone looked so hungry; they must have eaten the extra horses. It was so cold. Of course I wanted to help them, but we weren't alive at the same time; how could I help them if I wasn't even born? Of course I knew they would die, but it took such a long time!

"The last time they came, the fountain was frozen. They used their swords and hatchets and long pikes to break the ice into chunks. They built a fire and melted the ice in a pot. They took bones from their saddlebags—bones of all kinds—and threw them in the soup. It must have been a very thin broth because the bones had long ago been gnawed clean. I don't know what bones they were. Rabbits, I suppose and maybe a deer or a wild boar. Maybe the extra horses. I do not choose to think that they were the bones of the missing soldiers."

"Go to sleep, grandmother," I said.

"Don't worry about the bear," she said.

* * *

In the breakfast room of the Pension Grillparzer—the same room as the tea room, in brighter light—we confronted Herr Theobald with the menagerie of his other guests who had disrupted our evening. I knew that (as never before) my father was planning to reveal himself as a Tourist Bureau spy.

"Men walking about on their hands," father said.

"Men looking under the door of the W.C.," said grandmother. "*That* man," I said, and pointed to the small, sulking fellow at the corner table, seated for breakfast with his cohorts—the dream man and the Hungarian singer.

"He does it for his living," Herr Theobald told us, and as if to demonstrate that this was so, the man who stood on his hands began to stand on his hands.

"Make him stop that," father said. "We know he can do it."

"But did you know that he can't do it any other way?" the dream man asked suddenly, though he was not hostile. "Did you know his legs are useless? He has no shin bones. It is *wonderful* that he can walk on his hands! Otherwise, he wouldn't walk at all." The man, although it was clearly hard to do while standing on his hands, nodded his head.

"Please sit down," mother said.

"It is perfectly all right to be crippled," grandmother said, boldly. "But *you* are evil," she told the dream man. "You know things you have no right to know. He knew my *dream*," she told Herr Theobald, as if she were reporting a theft from her room.

"He is a *little* evil, I know," Theobald admitted. "But not usually! And he behaves better and better. He can't help what he knows."

"I was just trying to straighten you out," the dream man told grandmother. "I thought it would do you good. Your husband has been dead quite a while, after all, and it's about time you stopped making so much of that dream. You're not the only person who's had such a dream."

"Stop it!" grandmother shouted.

"Well, you ought to know," said the dream man.

"No, be quiet please," Herr Theobald told him.

"I am from the Tourist Bureau," father announced, probably because he couldn't think of anything else to say.

"Oh my God," Herr Theobald said.

"It's not Theobald's fault," said the singer. "It's our fault. He's nice to put up with us, though it costs him his reputation."

"They married my sister," Theobald told us. "They are *family*, you see. What can I do?"

"'They' married your sister?" mother said.

"Well, she married me first," said the dream man.

"And then she heard me sing!" laughed the singer.

"She's never been married to the other one," Theobald said, and everyone looked apologetically toward the man could only walk on his hands.

'But one day she will!" he cried. The dream man playfully hit him with a bun. The singer hooted with his mouth full, spraying crumbs.

"I don't think you could catch her!" the dream man hollered, and all three of them burst out laughing.

"Please!" cried Herr Theobald. "What will these people think?" The three misbehavers were sheepish and quiet. Theobald said, "They were once a circus act, but politics got them in trouble."

"We were the best in Hungary," said the singer. "You ever hear of the Circus Szolnok?"

"No, I'm afraid not," father said, seriously.

"We played in Miskolc, in Szeged, in Drebrecen," said the dream man.

"*Twice* in Szeged," the singer said.

"We would have made it to Budapest if it hadn't have been for the Russians," said the man who walked on his hands.

"Yes, it was the Russians who removed his shin bones," said the dream man.

"Tell the truth," the singer said. "He was *born* without shin bones. But it's true that we couldn't get along with the Russians."

"They tried to jail the bear," said the dream man.

"This is partly true," Theobald admitted.

"And we rescued his sister from them," said the man who walked on his hands.

"So of course I must put them up," said Herr Theobald, "and they work as hard as they can. But who is interested in their act in this country? It's a Hungarian thing. There is no *tradition* of bears on unicycles here," Theobald told us. "It means nothing to us Viennese."

"Tell the truth," said the dream man. "It is because I have told the wrong dreams. We worked a nightclub on the Kaerntnerstrasse, but then we were banned."

"You should never have told *that* dream," the singer said gravely.

"Well, it was your wife's responsibility too!" the dream man said.

"She was *your* wife, then," the singer said.

"And she will be mine!" sang the man who walked on his hands.

"Please stop it!" screamed Theobald.

"We get to do the balls for children's diseases," the singer said. "And some of the state hospitals—especially at Christmas. Or for some bigwig's birthday."

"If you would only do more with the bear," Herr Theobald advised them.

"Speak to your sister about that," said the dream man. "It's *her* bear, she's trained him, she's let him get lazy and sloppy and full of bad habits."

"He is the only one of you who never makes fun of me," said the man who could only walk on his hands.

"I would like to leave," grandmother said. "This is, for me, an awful experience."

"Please, dear lady," Herr Theobald said, "we only wanted to show you that we meant no offense. These are hard times. I need a B rating to attract more tourists, and I can't—in my heart—throw out the Circus Szolnok."

" 'In his heart,' my ass!" said the dream man. "He's afraid of his sister; he wouldn't dream of throwing us out."

"If he dreamed it, you would know it!" cried the man on his hands.

"I am afraid of the bear," Herr Theobald said. "It does everything she tells it to do."

"Say 'he,' not 'it,' " said the man on his hands. "He is a fine bear, and he never hurt anybody. He has no claws, as you know, and very few teeth either."

"The poor thing has a terribly hard time eating," Herr Theobald admitted. "He is quite old."

Over my father's shoulder, I saw him write in the giant pad: "An old bear and an unemployed circus act. This family is centered on the sister."

At that moment, out on the sidewalk, we could see her tending to the bear. It was early morning and the street was not especially busy. By law, of course, she had the bear on a leash, but it was a token control. In her startling red turban the woman walked up and down the sidewalk, following the lazy movements of the bear on his unicycle. The animal pedaled easily from parking meter to parking meter, sometimes leaning a paw on the meter as he turned. When he used the meter that way, the woman would scold him and bat at his paw. But the bear got away with what he could. He was very talented on the unicycle, you could tell; but you could also tell that the unicycle was a dead end for him. You could see that the bear felt he could go no further with unicycling.

"She should bring him off the street now," Herr Theobald fretted. "The people in the pastry shop next door complain to me," he told us. "They say the bear drives their customers away."

"But he makes them *come!*" said the man on his hands.

"It makes some people come, and it turns some away," the dream man said. He was suddenly somber, as if this profundity had depressed him.

But we had been so taken up with the antics of the Circus Szolnok that we had neglected old Johanna. When my mother saw that grandmother was quietly crying, she told me to bring the car around.

"It's been too much for her," my father whispered to Theobald. The Circus Szolnok looked ashamed of themselves.

At the door to the elevator grandmother said to Herr Theobald, "You have all gone too far, simply too far." Theobald seemed to accept this judgment; he said nothing. But the dream man was standing unpleasantly close to him, as if he were about to whisper an alarming dream in his ear, and even the usually cheerful singer looked potentially violent. The man who walked on his hands had not come to the elevator to see us off.

Outside on the sidewalk the bear pedaled up to me and handed me the keys; the car was parked at the curb. "Not everyone likes to be given the keys in that fashion," Herr Theobald told his sister.

"Oh, I thought he'd rather like it," she said, rumpling my hair. She was as appealing as a barmaid, which is to say that she was more appealing at night; in the daylight I could see that she was older than her brother, and older than her husbands too—and in time, I imagined, she would cease being lover and sister to them, respectively, and become a mother to them all. She was already a mother to the bear.

"Come over here," she said to him. He pedaled listlessly in place on his unicycle, hanging to a parking meter for support. He licked the little glass face of the meter. She tugged his leash. He stared at her. She tugged again. Insolently, the bear began to pedal—first one way, then the next. It was as if he took interest, seeing that he had an audience. He began to show off.

"Don't try anything," the sister said to him, but the bear pedaled faster and faster, going forward, going backward, angling sharply and veering among the parking meters; the sister had to let go of the leash. "Duna, stop it!" she cried, but the bear was out of control. He let the wheel roll too close to the curb and the unicycle pitched him hard into the fender of a parked car. He sat on the sidewalk with the unicycle beside him; you could tell that he hadn't injured himself, but he looked very embarrassed and nobody laughed. The bear looked like an old man who had taken a clumsy dump in the midst of a sporting event meant for much younger people, and he sat wishing for his dignity back while, in fact, he felt foolish and old and ashamed of his awkwardness, his matted hair, and what terrible vanity had ever made him attempt such a display. "Oh Duna," the sister said, scoldingly, but she went over and crouched beside him at the curb. "Duna, Duna," she reproved him, gently. He shook his big head; he would not look at her. There was some saliva strung on the fur near his mouth and she wiped this away with her hand; he pushed her hand away with his paw.

"Come back again!" cried Herr Theobald, miserably, as we got into the car.

"That bear is just like everyone else," Robo said.

Mother sat in the car with her eyes closed and her fingers massaging her temples; this way she seemed to hear nothing we said. She claimed it was her defense against traveling with such a contentious family.

I steered us off through the tiny streets; I took Spiegelgasse to Lobkowitzplatz. Spiegelgasse is so narrow that you can see the reflection of your own car in the windows of the shops you pass, and I felt our movement through Vienna was superimposed—like a trick with a movie camera, as if we made a fairy tale journey through a toy city.

I did not want to report on the usual business concerning the care of the car, but I saw that father was trying to maintain order and calm; he had the giant pad spread in his lap as if we'd just completed a routine investigation. "What does the gauge tell us?" he asked.

"Someone put thirty-five kilometers on it," I said.

"That bear has been in here," grandmother said. "There are hairs from the beast in the back seat, and I can smell him."

"I don't smell anything," father said.

"And the perfume of that slattern in the turban," grandmother said. "It is hovering near the ceiling of the car." Father sniffed. Mother continued to massage her temples.

On the floor by the brake and clutch pedals I saw several of the mintgreen toothpicks that the Hungarian singer was in the habit of wearing like a scar at the corner of his mouth. I didn't mention them. It was enough to imagine them all, out of the town in our car. The singing driver, the man on his hands beside him—waving out the window with his feet. And in back, separating the dream man from his former wife, the old bear slouched like a benign drunk, his great head brushing the upholstered roof, his mauling paws relaxed in his large lap.

"Those poor people," mother said, her eyes still closed.

"Liars and criminals," grandmother said. "Mystics and refugees and broken-down animals."

"They were trying hard," father said, "but they weren't coming up with the prizes."

"Better off in a zoo," said grandmother.

"I had a good time," Robo said.

"It's hard to break out of Class C," I said.

"They have fallen past Z," said old Johanna. "They have disappeared from the human alphabet."

"I think this calls for a letter," mother said.

But father raised his hand as if his other hand were touching a Bible, and we were quiet. He was writing in the giant pad and wished to be undisturbed. His face was stern. I knew that grandmother felt confident of his verdict. Mother knew it was useless to argue. Robo was already bored, and it was not until later that I read the final entry of the Pension Grillparzer.

Application for a B rating: approved. Father's reason: a lively family with lots of personality. And under the heading "Suspicion of Animals" father wrote (ambiguously): Just like everyone else.

When grandmother was asleep in the car, mother said, "I don't suppose that in this case a change in the rating will matter very much, one way or another."

"No," father said, "not much at all." He was right about that, though it would be years until I saw the Pension Grillparzer again.

* * *

When grandmother died, rather suddenly in her sleep, mother announced that she was tired of traveling. The real reason, however, was that she began to find herself plagued by grandmother's dream. "The horses are so thin," she told me once. "I mean, I always knew they would be thin, but not *this* thin. And the soldiers—I knew they were miserable," she said, "but not *that* miserable."

Father resigned from the Tourist Bureau and found a job with a local detective agency specializing in hotels and department stores. It was a satisfactory job for him, though he refused to work during the Christmas season—when, he said, some people ought to be allowed to steal a little.

My parents seemed to me to relax as they got older, and I really felt they were fairly happy near the end. I know that the strength of grandmother's dream was dimmed by the real world, and specifically by what happened to Robo. He went to a private school and was well liked there, but he was killed by a homemade bomb in his first year at the university. He was not even "political." In his last letter to my parents he wrote: "The self-seriousness of the radical factions among the students is much overrated. And the food is execrable." Then Robo went to his history class, and his classroom was blown apart.

It was after my parents died that I gave up smoking and took up traveling again. I took my second wife back to the Pension Grillparzer; with my first wife, I never got as far as Vienna.

The Grillparzer had not kept its B rating very long, and it had fallen from the ratings altogether by the time I returned to it. Herr Theobald's sister was in charge of the place. Gone was her tart appeal and in its place was the sexless cynicism of some maiden aunts. She was shapeless and her hair was dyed a sort of bronze, so that her head resembled one of those copper scouring pads that you use on a pot. She did not remember me and was suspicious of my questions. Because I appeared to know so much about her past associates, she probably thought I was with the police.

The Hungarian singer had gone away—another woman thrilled by his voice. The dream man had been *taken* away—to an institution. His own dreams had turned to nightmares and he'd awakened the pension each night with his horrifying howls. His removal from the seedy premises, said Herr Theobald's sister, was almost simultaneous with the loss of the Grillparzer's B rating.

Herr Theobald was dead. He had dropped down clutching his heart in the hall, where he ventured one night to investigate what he thought was a prowler. It was only Duna, the malcontent bear, who was dressed in the dream man's pin-striped suit. Why Theobald's sister had dressed the bear in this manner was not explained to me, but the shock of the sullen animal unicycling in the lunatic's left-behind clothes had been enough to scare Herr Theobald to death.

The man who could only walk on his hands had also fallen into the gravest trouble. His wristwatch band snagged on a tine of an escalator and he was suddenly unable to hop off; his necktie, which he rarely wore because it dragged on the ground when he walked on his hands, was drawn under the step-off grate at the end of the escalator, where he was strangled. Behind him a line of people formed, marching in place by taking one step back and allowing the escalator to carry them forward, then taking another step back. It was quite a while before anyone got up the nerve to step over him. The world has many unintentionally cruel mechanisms that are not designed for people who walk on their hands.

After that, Theobald's sister told me, the Pension Grillparzer went from Class C to much worse. As the burden of management fell more heavily on her, she had less time for Duna and her bear grew senile and indecent in his habits. Once he bullied a mailman down the marble staircase at such a ferocious pace that the man fell and broke his hip; the attack was reported and an old city ordinance forbidding unrestrained animals in places open to the public was enforced. Duna was outlawed at the Pension Grillparzer.

For a while, Theobald's sister kept the bear in the cage in the courtyard of the building, but he was taunted by dogs and children, and food (and worse) was dropped into his cage from the apartments that faced the courtyard. He grew devious—only pretending to sleep—and he ate someone's cat. Then he was poisoned twice and became afraid to eat in this perilous enviroment. There was no alternative but to donate him to the Schoenbrunn Zoo, but there was even some doubt as to his acceptability. He was toothless and ill, perhaps contagious, and his long history of having been treated as a human being did not prepare him for the gentler routines of zoo life. His outdoor sleeping quarters in the courtyard of the Grillparzer had inflamed his rheumatism, and even his one talent—unicycling—was irretrievable. When he first tried it in the zoo, he fell. Someone laughed. Once anyone laughed at something Duna did, Theobald's sister explained, Duna would never do that thing again. He became, at last, a kind of charity case of Schoenbrunn, where he died a short two months after he'd taken up his new lodgings. In the opinion of Theobald's sister, Duna died of mortification—the result of a rash that had spread over his chest, which then had to be shaved.

In the cold courtyard of the building I looked in the bear's empty cage. The birds hadn't left a fruit seed, but in a corner of his cage was a looming mound of the bear's ossified droppings—as void of life, and even odor, as the corpses captured by the holocaust of Pompeii. I couldn't help thinking of Robo; of the bear, there were more remains.

In the car I was further depressed to notice that not one kilometer had been added to the gauge, not one kilometer had been driven in secret. There was no one around to take liberties anymore.

"When we're a safe distance away from your precious Pension Grillparzer," my second wife said to me, "I'd like you to tell me why you brought me to such a shabby place."

"It's a long story," I told her.

I was thinking I had noticed a curious lack of either enthusiasm or bitterness in the account of the world by Theobald's sister. There was in her story the flatness one associates with a storyteller who is accepting of unhappy endings, as if her life and her companions had never been exotic to *her*—as if they had always been staging a ludicrous and doomed effort at reclassification.

THE END OF SCIENCE FICTION

by LISEL MUELLER

from THE OHIO REVIEW

nominated by Naomi Lazard

This is not fantasy, this is our life.
We are the characters
who have invaded the moon,
who cannot stop their computers.
We are the gods who can unmake
the world in seven days.

Both hands are stopped at noon.
We are beginning to live forever,
in lightweight, aluminum bodies
with numbers stamped on our backs.
We dial our words like muzak.
We hear each other through water.

The genre is dead. Invent something new.
Invent a man and a woman
naked in a garden;
invent a child that will save the world,
a man who carries his father
out of a burning city.
Invent a spool of thread
that leads a hero to safety;
invent an island on which he abandons
the woman who saved his life,
with no loss of sleep over the betrayal.

Invent us as we were
before our bodies glittered
and we stopped bleeding:
invent a shepherd who kills a giant,
a girl who grows into a tree,
a woman who refuses to turn
her back on the past and is changed to salt,
a boy who steals his brother's birthright
and becomes the head of a nation.

Invent real tears, hard love,
slow-spoken, ancient words,
difficult as a child's
first steps across a room.

CUYLERVILLE

by DOUGLAS CRASE

from AMERICAN POETRY REVIEW

nominated by JOHN ASHBERY

*It will be essential to ruin their
crops in the ground and prevent
their planting more.*
—*George Washington to Gen. John
Sullivan, 1779.*

There's more than one way to look at a place and this
Is one of them: you can imagine the landscape for what
It must have been (*that* feature, *this* one, these same
Horizons were really here, the circumstance of invasion
As it came). That oak was a sapling near their farthest
Town, "a hundred and twenty-eight houses mostly large
And elegant", where the lieutenant like you was getting
His first-hand look for the first time, caught skinning
The Iroquois boys for saddlebags. "The Indians, having
Punished him sufficiently, made a small opening in his
Abdomen, took out an intestine which they tied to the
Sapling, and drove him around it till he had drawn out
The whole of his intestines"—tortures, said the General
In his report, not to be mentioned out of decency
Though it's no secret how important they are to you
In proportion as you break them loose from their first
Dull loyalties. You see, it's partly the place but
Partly the way of discovering it, so these are a good
Illustration of the double-barreled nature of your
Attachment now. The usual gauntlet of preliminaries
Has occurred but you should expect the novelty to increase
As proof of your own similar involvement comes unwound.

One has to marvel at how an intestine could emerge,
Iridescent when you see it in the sun, and be still joined
In rich dark to you at its other end. We don't know
The exact manner of fixing it to this tree but the effect
As you're put through your paces, the eventual unravelling,
That is, will be the same. It's a good lesson in how
Things look from an orbit as it narrows, how things feel
Being reeled in by the bewildering tug of your own insides.
Apparently there's nothing you can do; it's as though
These transplanted membranes move of their own accord
Toward the light, fasten for dear life upon the spot,
Smooth gut devoted to deciduous xylem tube. There's
No way to guess the time each individual case can easily
Involve because of the role intestinal fortitude may play,
But the characteristic responses remain the same and as
Life in the organism erodes away the grass becomes slick
With its visceral wash—irredeemable drift—in a rank
Alluvial fan on the valley floor. It should give you
Something to think about whether you're staying or only
Stopping off to see the place, this clear interior,
So beautiful it turns you inside out to look at it.

GOING AFTER CACCIATO

fiction by Tim O'Brien

from PLOUGHSHARES

nominated by Joyce Carol Oates and PLOUGHSHARES

It WAS A BAD TIME. Billy Boy Watkins was dead, and so was Frenchie Tucker. Billy Boy had died of fright, scared to death on the field of battle, and Frenchie Tucker had been shot through the neck. Lieutenants Sidney Martin and Walter Gleason had died in tunnels. Pederson was dead and Bernie Lynn was dead. Buff was dead. They were all among the dead. The war was always the same, and the rain was part of the war. The rain fed fungus that grew in the men's socks and boots, and their socks rotted, and their feet turned white and soft so that the skin could be scraped off with a fingernail, and Stink Harris woke up screaming one night with a leech on his tongue. When it was not raining, a low mist moved like sleep across the paddies, blending the elements into a single gray element, and the war was cold and pasty and rotten. Lieutenant Corson, who came to replace Lieutenant Martin, contracted the dysentery. The tripflares were useless. The ammunition corroded and the foxholes filled with mud and water during the nights, and in the mornings there was always the next village and the war was always the same. In early September Vaught caught an infection. He'd been showing Oscar Johnson the sharp edge on his bayonet, drawing it swiftly along his forearm and peeling off a layer of mushy skin. "Like a Gillette blueblade," Vaught had grinned. It did not bleed, but in a few days the bacteria soaked in and the arm turned yellow, and Vaught was carried aboard a Huey that dipped perpendicular, blades clutching at granite air, rising in its own wet wind and taking Vaught away. He never returned to the war. Later they had a letter from him that described Japan as smoky and full of bedbugs, but in the enclosed snapshot Vaught looked happy enough, posing with two sightly nurses, a long-stemmed bottle of wine rising from between his thighs. It was a shock to learn that he'd lost the arm. Soon afterward Ben Nystrom shot himself in the foot, but he did not die, and he wrote no letters. These were all things to talk about. The rain, too. Oscar said it made him think of Detroit in the month of May. "Not the rain," he liked to say. "Just the dark and gloom. It's Number One weather for rape and looting. The fact is, I do ninety-eight percent of my total rape and looting in weather just like this." Then somebody would say that Oscar had a pretty decent imagination for a nigger.

That was one of the jokes. There was a joke about Oscar. There were many jokes about Billy Boy Watkins, the way he'd collapsed in fright on the field of glorious battle. Another joke was about the lieutenant's dysentery, and another was about Paul Berlin's purple biles. Some of the jokes were about Cacciato, who was as dumb, Stink said, as a bullet, or, Harold Murphy said, as an oyster fart.

In October, at the end of the month, in the rain, Cacciato left the war.

"He's gone away," said Doc Peret. "Split for parts unknown."

The lieutenant didn't seem to hear. He was too old to be a lieutenant, anyway. The veins in his nose and cheeks were shattered by booze. Once he had been a captain on the way to being a major, but whiskey and the fourteen dull years between Korea and Vietnam had ended all that, and now he was just an old lieutenant with the dysentery. He lay on his back in the pagoda, naked except for green socks and green undershorts.

"Cacciato," Doc Peret repeated. "He's gone away. Split, departed."

The lieutenant did not sit up. He held his belly with both hands as if to contain the disease.

"He's gone to Paris," Doc said. "That's what he tells Paul Berlin, anyhow, and Paul Berlin tells me, so I'm telling you. He's gone, packed up and gone."

"Paree," the lieutenant said softly. "In France, Paree? *Gay* Paree?"

"Yes, sir. That's what he says. That's what he told Paul Berlin, and that's what I'm telling you. You ought to cover up, sir."

The lieutenant sighed. He pushed himself up, breathing loud, then sat stiffly before a can of Sterno. He lit the Sterno and cupped his hands around the flame and bent down drawing in the heat. Outside, the rain was steady. "Paree," he said wearily. "You're saying Cacciato's left for gay Paree, is that right?"

"That's what he said, sir. I'm just relaying what he told to Paul Berlin. Hey, really, you better cover yourself up."

"Who's Paul Berlin?"

"Right here, sir. This is Paul Berlin."

The lieutenant looked up. His eyes were bright blue, oddly out of place in the sallow face. "You Paul Berlin?"

"Yes, sir," said Paul Berlin. He pretended to smile.

"Geez, I thought you were Vaught."

"Vaught's the one who cut himself, sir."

"I thought that was you. How do you like that?"

"Fine, sir."

The lieutenant sighed and shook his head sadly. He held a boot to dry over the burning Sterno. Behind him in the shadows sat the crosslegged, roundfaced Buddha, smiling benignly from its elevated perch. The pagoda was cold. Dank and soggy from a month of rain, the place smelled of clays and silicates and old incense. It was a single square room, built like a pillbox with a flat ceiling that forced the soldiers to stoop and kneel. Once it might have been an elegant house of worship, neatly tiled and painted and clean, candles burning in holders at the Buddha's feet, but now it was bombed-out junk. Sandbags blocked the windows. Bits of broken pottery lay under chipped pedestals. The Buddha's right arm was missing and his fat groin was gouged with shrapnel. Still, the smile was intact. Head cocked, he seemed interested in the lieutenant's long sigh. "So. Cacciato's gone away, is that it?"

"There it is," Doc Peret said. "You've got it now."

Paul Berlin smiled and nodded.

"To gay Pareee," the lieutenant said. "Old Cacciato's going to Paree in France." He giggled, then shook his head gravely. "Still raining?"

"A bitch, sir."

"You ever seen rain like this? I mean, ever?"

"No, sir," Paul Berlin said.

"You Cacciato's buddy, I suppose?"

"No, sir," Paul Berlin said. "Sometimes he'd tag along, but not really."

"Who's his buddy?"

"Vaught, sir. I guess Vaught was, sometime."

"Well," the lieutenant said, dropping his nose inside the boot to smell the sweaty leather, "well, I guess we should just get Mister Vaught in here."

"Vaught's gone, sir. He's the one who cut himself—gangrene, remember?"

"Mother of Mercy."

Doc Peret draped a poncho over the lieutenant's shoulders. The rain was steady and thunderless and undramatic. Though it was mid-morning, the feeling was of endless dusk.

"Paree," the lieutenant murmured. "Cacciato's going to gay Paree—pretty girls and bare ass and Frogs everywhere. What's wrong with him?"

"Just dumb, sir. He's just awful dumb, that's all."

"And he's walking? He says he's walking to gay Paree?"

"That's what he says, sir, but you know how Cacciato can be."

"Does he know how far it is?"

"Six thousand eight hundred statute miles, sir. That's what he told me—six thousand eight hundred miles on the nose. He had it down pretty well. He had a compass and fresh water and maps and stuff."

"Maps," the lieutenant said. "Maps, flaps, schnaps. I guess those maps will help him cross the oceans, right? I guess he can just rig up a canoe out of those maps, no problem."

"Well, no," said Paul Berlin. He looked at Doc Peret, who shrugged. "No, sir. He showed me on the maps. See, he says he's going through Laos, then into Thailand and Burma, and then India, and then some other country, I forget, and then into Iran and Iraq, and then Turkey, and then Greece, and the rest is easy. That's exactly what he said. The rest is easy, he said. He had it all doped out."

"In other words," the lieutenant said, lying back, "in other words, fuckin AWOL."

"There it is," said Doc Peret. "There it is."

The lieutenant rubbed his eyes. His face was sallow and he needed a shave. For a time he lay very still, listening to the rain, hands on his belly, then he giggled and shook his head and laughed. "What for? Tell me—what the fuck for?"

"Easy," Doc said. "Really, you got to stay covered up, sir, I told you that."

"What for? I mean, what for?"

"Shhhhhh, he's just dumb, that's all."

The lieutenant's face was yellow. He laughed, rolling onto his side and dropping the boot. "I mean, why? What sort of shit is this— walking to fucking gay Paree? What kind of bloody war is this, tell me, what's wrong with you people? Tell me—what's *wrong* with you?"

"Shhhhhh," Doc purred, covering him up and putting a hand on his forehead. "Easy does it."

"Angel of Mercy, Mother of Virgins, what's *wrong* with you guys? Walking to gay Paree, what's *wrong*?"

"Nothing, sir. It's just Cacciato. You know how Cacciato can be when he puts his head to it. Relax now and it'll be all fine. Fine. It's just that rockhead, Cacciato."

The lieutenant giggled. Without rising, he pulled on his pants and boots and a shirt, then rocked miserably before the blue Sterno flame. The pagoda smelled like the earth, and the rain was unending. "Shoot," the lieutenant sighed. He kept shaking his head, grinning, then looked at Paul Berlin. "What squad you in?"

"Third, sir."

"That's Cacciato's squad?"

"Yes, sir."

"Who else?"

"Me and Doc and Eddie Lazzutti and Stink and Oscar Johnson and Harold Murphy. That's all, except for Cacciato."

"What about Pederson and Buff?"

"They're the dead ones, sir."

"Shoot." The lieutenant rocked before the flame. He did not look well. "Okay," he sighed, getting up. "Third Squad goes after Cacciato."

Leading to the mountains were four clicks of level paddy. The mountains jerked straight out of the rice, and beyond those mountains and other mountains was Paris.

The tops of the mountains could not be seen for the mist and clouds. The rain was glue that stuck the sky to the land.

The squad spent the night camped at the base of the first mountain, then in the morning they began the ascent. At mid-day Paul Berlin spotted Cacciato. He was half a mile up, bent low and moving patiently, steadily. He was not wearing a helmet—surprising, because Cacciato always took great care to cover the pink bald spot at the crown of his skull. Paul Berlin spotted him, but it was Stink Harris who spoke up.

Lieutenant Corson took out the binoculars.

"Him, sir?"

The lieutenant watched while Cacciato climbed towards the clouds.

"That him?"

"It's him. Bald as an eagle's ass."

Stink giggled. "Bald as Friar Tuck—it's Cacciato, all right. Dumb as a dink."

They watched until Cacciato was swallowed in the rain and clouds.

"Dumb-dumb," Stink giggled.

They walked fast, staying in a loose column. First the lieutenant, then Oscar Johnson, then Stink, then Eddie Lazzutti, then Harold Murphy, then Doc, then, at the rear, Paul Berlin. Who walked slowly, head down. He had nothing against Cacciato. The whole episode was silly, of course, a dumb and immature thing typical of Cacciato, but even so he had nothing special against him. It was just too bad. A waste of time in the midst of infinitely wider waste.

Climbing, he tried to picture Cacciato's face. The image came out fuzzed and amorphous and bland—entirely compatible with the boy's personality. Doc Peret, an acute observer of such things, hypothesized that Cacciato had missed Mongolian idiocy by the breadth of a single, wispy genetic hair. "Could have gone either way," Doc had said confidentially. "You see the slanting eyes? The pasty flesh, just like jelly, right? The odd-shaped head? I mean, hey, let's face it—the guy's fuckin ugly. It's only a theory, mind you, but I'd wager big money that old Cacciato has more than a smidgen of the Mongol in him."

There may have been truth to it. Cacciato looked curiously unfinished, as though nature had struggled long and heroically but finally jettisoned him as a hopeless cause, not worth the diminishing returns. Open-faced, round, naive, plump, tender-complected and boyish, Cacciato lacked the fine detail, the refinements and final touches that maturity ordinarily marks on a boy of seventeen years. All this, the men concluded, added up to a case of simple gross stupidity. He wasn't positively disliked—except perhaps by Stink Harris, who took instant displeasure with anything vaguely his inferior—but at the same time Cacciato was no one's friend. Vaught, maybe. But Vaught was dumb, too, and he was gone from the war. At best, Cacciato was tolerated. The way men will sometimes tolerate a pesky dog.

It was just too bad. Walking to Paris, it was one of those ridiculous things Cacciato would do. Like winning the Bronze Star for shooting a dink in the face. Dumb. The way he was forever whistling. Too blunt-headed to know better, blind to the bodily and spiritual danger of human combat. In some ways this made him a good soldier. He walked point like a boy at his first county fair. He didn't mind the tunnel work. And his smile, more decoration than an expression of emotion, stayed with him in the most lethal of moments—when Billy Boy turned his last card, when Pederson floated face-up in a summer day's paddy, when Buff's helmet overflowed with an excess of red and gray fluids.

It was sad, a real pity.

Climbing the mountain, Paul Berlin felt an odd affection for the kid. Not friendship, exactly, but—real pity.

Not friendship. Not exactly. Pity, pity plus wonder. It was all silly, walking away in the rain, but it was something to think about.

They did not reach the summit of the mountain until mid-afternoon. The climb was hard, the rain sweeping down, the mountain oozing from beneath their feet. Below, the clouds were expansive, hiding the paddies and the war. Above, in more clouds, were more mountains.

Oscar Johnson found where Cacciato had spent the first night, a rock formation with an outcropping ledge as a roof, a can of burnt-out

Sterno, a chocolate wrapper, and a partly burned map. On the map, traced in red ink, was a dotted line that ran though the paddyland and up the first small mountain of the Annamese Cordillera. The dotted line ended there, apparently to be continued on another map.

"He's serious," the lieutenant said softly. "The blockhead's serious." He held the map as if it had a bad smell.

Stink and Oscar and Eddie Lazzutti nodded.

They rested in Cacciato's snug rock nest. Tucked away, looking out on the slate rain toward the next mountain, the men were quiet. Paul Berlin laid out a game of solitaire. Harold Murphy rolled a joint, inhaled, then passed it along, and they smoked and watched the rain and clouds and wilderness. It was peaceful. The rain was nice.

No one spoke until the ritual was complete.

Then, in a hush, all the lieutenant could say was, "Mercy."

"Shit," was what Stink Harris said.

The rain was unending.

"We could just go back," Doc Peret finally said. "You know, sir? Just head on back and forget him."

Stink Harris giggled.

"Seriously," Doc kept on, "we could just let the poor kid go. Make him MIA, strayed in battle, the lost lamb. Sooner or later he'll wake up, you know, and he'll see how insane it is and he'll come back."

The lieutenant stared into the rain. His face was yellow except for the network of broken veins.

"So what say you, sir? Let him go?"

"Dumber than a rock," Stink giggled.

"And smarter than Stink Harris."

"You know *what*, Doc."

"Pickle it."

"Who's saying to pickle it?"

"Just pickle it," said Doc Peret. "That's what."

Stink giggled but he shut up.

"What do you say, sir? Turn back?"

The lieutenant was quiet. At last he shivered and went into the rain with a wad of toilet paper. Paul Berlin sat alone, playing solitaire in the style of Las Vegas. Pretending, of course. Pretending to pay thirty thousand dollars for the deck, pretending ways to spend his earnings.

When the lieutenant returned he told the men to saddle up.

"We turning back?" Doc asked.

The lieutenant shook his head. He looked sick.

"I knew it!" Stink crowed. "Damn straight, I knew it! Can't hump away from a war, isn't that right, sir? The dummy has got to learn you can't just hump your way out of a war." Stink grinned and flicked his eyebrows at Doc Peret. "I knew it. By golly, I knew it!"

Cacciato had reached the top of the second mountain. Standing bareheaded, hands loosely at his sides, he was looking down on them through a blur of rain. Lieutenant Corson had the binoculars on him.

"Maybe he don't see us," Oscar said. "Maybe he's lost."

"Oh, he sees us. He sees us fine. Sees us real fine. And he's not lost. Believe me, he's not."

"Throw out smoke, sir?"

"Why not?" the lieutenant said. "Sure, why not throw out pretty smoke, why not?" He watched Cacciato through the glasses while Oscar threw out the smoke. It fizzled for a time and then puffed up in a heavy cloud of lavender. "Oh, he sees us," the lieutenant whispered. "He sees us fine."

"The bastard's *waving!*"

"I can see that, thank you. Mother of Saints."

As if stricken, the lieutenant suddenly sat down in a puddle, put his head in his hands and began to rock as the lavender smoke drifted up the face of the mountain. Cacciato was waving both arms. Not quite waving. The arms were flapping. Paul Berlin watched through the glasses. Cacciato's head was huge floating like a balloon in the high fog, and he did not look at all frightened. He looked young and stupid. His face was shiny. He was smiling, and he looked happy.

"I'm sick," the lieutenant said. He kept rocking. "I tell you, I'm a sick, sick man."

"Should I shout up to him?"

"Sick," the lieutenant moaned. "Sick, sick. It wasn't this way on Pusan, I'll tell you that. Sure, call up to him—I'm sick."

Oscar Johnson cupped his hands and hollered, and Paul Berlin watched through the glasses. For a moment Cacciato stopped waving. He spread his arms wide, as if to show them empty, slowly spreading them out like wings, palms up. Then his mouth opened wide, and in the mountains there was thunder.

"What'd he say?" The lieutenant rocked on his haunches. He was clutching himself and shivering. "Tell me what he said."

"Can't hear, sir. Oscar—?"

There was more thunder, long lasting thunder that came in waves from deep in the mountains. It rolled down and moved the trees and grasses.

"Shut the shit up!" The lieutenant was rocking and shouting at the rain and wind and thunder. "What'd the dumb fucker say?"

Paul Berlin watched through the glasses, and Cacciato's mouth opened and closed and opened, but there was only more thunder. Then his arms began flapping again. Flying, Paul Berlin suddenly realized. The poor kid was perched up there, arms flapping, trying to fly. Fly! Incredibly, the flapping motion was smooth and practiced and graceful.

"A chicken!" Stink squealed. "Look it! A squawking chicken!"

"Mother of Children."

"Look it!"

"A miserable chicken, you see that? A chicken!"

The thunder came again, breaking like Elephant Feet across the mountains, and the lieutenant rocked and held himself.

"For Christ sake," he moaned," "What'd he say? Tell me."

Paul Berlin could not hear. But he saw Cacciato's lips move, and the happy smile.

"Tell me."

So Paul Berlin, watching Cacciato fly, repeated it. "He said goodbye."

In the night the rain hardened into fog, and the fog was cold. They camped in the fog, near the top of the mountain, and the thunder stayed through the night. The lieutenant vomited. Then he radioed that he was in pursuit of the enemy.

"Gunships, Papa Two-Niner?" came the answer from far away.

"Negative," said the old lieutenant.

"Arty? Tell you what. You got a real sweet voice, Papa Two-Niner. No shit, a lovely voice." The radio-voice paused. "So, here's what I'll do, I'll give you a bargain on the arty—two for the price of one, no strings and a warranty to boot. How's that? See, we got this terrific batch of new 155 in, first class ordinance, I promise you, and what we do, what we do is this. What we do is we go heavy on volume here, you know? Keeps the prices low."

"Negative," the lieutenant said.

"Well, geez. Hard to please, right? Maybe some nice illum, then? Willie Peter, real boomers with some genuine sparkles mixed in. We're having this close-out sale, one time only."

"Negative. Negative, negative, negative."

"You'll be missing out on some fine shit."

"Negative, you monster."

"Okay," the radio-voice said, disappointed-sounding "but you'll wish . . . No offense, Papa Two-Niner. Have some happy hunting."

"Mercy," said the lieutenant into the blaze of static.

The night fog was worse than the rain, colder and more saddening. They lay under a sagging lean-to that seemed to catch and hold the fog like a net. Oscar and Harold Murphy and Stink and Eddie Lazzutti slept anyway, curled around one another like lovers. They could sleep and sleep.

"I hope he's moving," Paul Berlin whispered to Doc Peret. "I just hope he keeps moving. He does that, we'll never get him."

"Then they'll chase him with choppers. Or planes or something."

"Not if he gets himself lost," Paul Berlin said. "Not if he hides."

"What time is it?"

"Don't know."

"What time you got, sir?"

"Very lousy late," said the lieutenant from the bushes.

"Come on."

"Four o'clock. O-four-hundred, which is to say a.m. Got it?"

"Thanks."

"Charmed." His ass, hanging six inches from the earth, made a soft warm glow in the dark.

"You okay, sir?"

"I'm wonderful. Can't you see how wonderful I am?"

"I just hope Cacciato keeps moving," Paul Berlin whispered. "That's all I hope—I hope he uses his head and keeps moving."

"It won't get him anywhere."

"Get him to Paris maybe."

"Maybe," Doc sighed, turning onto his side, "and where is he then?"

"In Paris."

"No way. I like adventure, too, but, see, you can't walk to Paris from here. You just can't."

"He's smarter than you think," Paul Berlin said, not quite believing it. "He's not all that dumb."

"I know," the lieutenant said. He came from the bushes. "I know all about that."

"Impossible. None of the roads go to Paris."

"Can we light a Sterno, sir?"

"No," the lieutenant said, crawling under the lean-to and lying flat on his back. His breath came hard. "No, you can't light a fucking Sterno, and no, you can't go out to play without your mufflers and galoshes, and no, kiddies and combatants, no, you can't have chocolate sauce on your broccoli. No."

"All right."

"No!"

"You saying no, sir?"

"No," the lieutenant sighed with doom. "It's still a war, isn't it?"

"I guess."

"There you have it. It's still a war."

The rain resumed. It started with thunder, then lightning lighted the valley deep below in green and mystery, then more thunder, then it was just the rain. They lay quietly and listened. Paul Berlin, who considered himself abnormally sane, uncluttered by high ideas or lofty ambitions or philosophy, was suddenly struck between the eyes by a vision of murder. Butchery, no less. Cacciato's right temple caving inward, a moment of black silence, then the enormous explosion of outward-going brains. It was no metaphor; he didn't think in metaphors. No, it was a simple scary vision. He tried to reconstruct the thoughts that had led to it, but there was nothing to be found—the rain, the discomfort of mushy flesh. Nothing to justify such a bloody image, no origins. Just Cacciato's round head suddenly exploding like a pricked bag of helium: boom.

Where, he thought, was all this taking him, and where would it end? Murder was the logical circuit-stopper, of course; it was Cacciato's rightful, maybe inevitable due. Nobody can get away with stupidity forever, and in war the final price for it is always paid in purely biological currency, hunks of toe or pieces of femur or bits of exploded brain. And it *was* still a war, wasn't it?

Pitying Cacciato with wee-hour tenderness, and pitying himself for the affliction that produced such visions, Paul Berlin hoped for a miracle. He was tired of murder. Not scared by it—not at that particular moment—and not awed by it, just fatigued.

"He did some awfully brave things," he whispered. Then realized that Doc was listening. "He did. The time he dragged that dink out of his bunker, remember that."

"Yeah."

"The time he shot the kid in the kisser."

"I remember."

"At least you can't call him a coward, can you? You can't say he ran away because he was scared."

"You can say a lot of other shit, though."

"True. But you can't say he wasn't brave. You can't say that."

"Fair enough," Doc said. He sounded sleepy.

"I wonder if he talks French."

"You kidding, partner?"

"Just wondering. You think it's hard to learn French, Doc?"

"Cacciato?"

"Yeah, I guess not. It's a neat thing to think about, though, old Cacciato walking to Paris."

"Go to sleep,," Doc Peret advised. "Remember, pal, you got your own health to think of."

They were in the high country.

It was country far from the war, high and peaceful country with trees and thick grass, no people and no dogs and no lowland drudgery. Real wilderness, through which a single trail, liquid and shiny, kept taking them up.

The men walked with their heads down. Stink at point, then Eddie Lazzutti and Oscar, next Harold Murphy with the machine gun, then Doc, then the lieutenant, and last Paul Berlin.

They were tired and did not talk. Their thoughts were in their legs and feet, and their legs and feet were heavy with blood, for they'd been on the march many hours and the day was soggy with the endless rain. There was nothing symbolic, or melancholy, about the rain. It was simple rain, everywhere.

They camped that night beside the trail, then in the morning continued the climb. Though there were no signs of Cacciato, the mountain had only one trail and they were on it, the only way west.

Paul Berlin marched mechanically. At his sides, balancing him evenly and keeping him upright, two canteens of Kool-Aid lifted and fell with his hips, and the hips rolled in their ball-and-socket joints.

He respired and sweated. His heart hard, his back strong, up the high country.

They did not see Cacciato, and for a time Paul Berlin thought they might have lost him forever. It made him feel better, and he climbed the trail and enjoyed the scenery and the sensations of being high and far from the real war, and then Oscar found the second map.

The red dotted line crossed the border into Laos.

Farther ahead they found Cacciato's helmet and armored vest, then his dogtags, then his entrenching tool and knife.

"Dummy just keeps to the trail," the lieutenant moaned. "Tell me why?" Why doesn't he leave the trail?"

"It's the only way to Paris," Paul Berlin said.

"A rockhead," said Stink Harris. "That's why."

Liquid and shiny, a mix of rain and red clay, the trail took them higher.

Cacciato eluded them but he left behind the wastes of his march—empty tins, bits of bread, a belt of golden ammo dangling from a dwarf pine, a leaking canteen, candy wrappers and worn rope. Clues that kept them going. Tantalizing them on, one step then the next—a glimpse of his bald head, the hot ash of a breakfast fire, a handkerchief dropped coyly along the path.

So they kept after him, following the trails that linked one to the next westward in a simple linear direction without deception. It was deep, jagged, complex country, dark with the elements of the season, and ahead was the frontier.

"He makes it that far," Doc Peret said, pointing to the next line of mountains, "and we can't touch him."

"How now?"

"The border," Doc said. The trail had leveled out and the march was easier. "He makes it to the border and it's bye-bye Cacciato."

"How far?"

"Two clicks maybe. Not far."

"Then he's made it," whispered Paul Berlin.

"Maybe so."

"By God!"

"Maybe so," Doc said.

"Boy, lunch at Tour d'Argent! A night at the old opera!"

"Maybe so."

The trail narrowed, then climbed, and a half-hour later they saw him.

He stood at the top of a small grassy hill, two hundred meters ahead. Loose and at ease, smiling, Cacciato already looked like a civilian. His hands were in his pockets and he was not trying to hide himself. He might have been waiting for a bus, patient and serene and not at all frightened.

"Got him!" Stink yelped. "I knew it! Now we got him!"

The lieutenant came forward with the glasses.

"I knew it," Stink crowed, pressing forward. "The blockhead's finally giving it up—giving up the old ghost, I knew it!"

"What do we do, sir?"

The lieutenant shrugged and stared through the glasses.

"Fire a shot?" Stink held his rifle up and before the lieutenant could speak he squeezed off two quick rounds, one a tracer that turned like a corkscrew through the mist. Cacciato smiled and waved.

"Look at him," Oscar Johnson said. "I do think we got ourselves a predicament. Truly a predicament."

"There it is," Eddie said, and they both laughed, and Cacciato kept smiling and waving.

"A true predicament."

Stink Harris took the point, walking fast and chattering, and Cacciato stopped waving and watched him come, arms folded and his big head cocked as if listening for something. He looked amused.

There was no avoiding it.

Stink saw the wire as he tripped it, but there was no avoiding it.

The first sound was that of a zipper suddenly yanked up; next, a popping noise, the spoon releasing and primer detonating; then the sound of the grenade dropping; then the fizzling sound. The sounds came separately but quickly.

Stink knew it as it happened. With the next step, in one fuzzed motion, he flung himself down and away, rolling, covering his skull, mouth open, yelping a funny, trivial little yelp.

They all knew it.

Eddie and Oscar and Doc Peret dropped flat, and Harold Murphy bent double and did an oddly graceful jackknife for a man of his size, and the lieutenant coughed and collapsed, and Paul Berlin, seeing purple, closed his eyes and fists and mouth, brought his knees to his belly, coiling, and let himself fall.

Count, he thought, but the numbers came in a tangle without sequence.

His belly hurt. That was where it started. First the belly, a release of fluids in the bowels next, a shitting feeling, a draining of all the pretensions and silly hopes for himself, and he was back where he started, writhing. The lieutenant was beside him. The air was windless—just the misty rain. His teeth hurt. Count, he thought, but his teeth hurt and no numbers came. I don't want to die, he thought lucidly, with hurting teeth.

There was no explosion. His teeth kept hurting and his belly was floating in funny ways.

He was ready, steeled. His lungs hurt now. He was ready, but there was no explosion. Then came a fragile pop. Smoke, he thought without thinking, smoke.

"Smoke," the lieutenant moaned, then repeated it, "fucking smoke."

Paul Berlin smelled it. He imagined its velvet color, purple, but he could not open his eyes. He tried, but he could not open his eyes or unclench his fists or uncoil his legs, and the heavy fluids in his stomach were holding him down, and he could not wiggle or run to escape. There was no explosion.

"Smoke," Doc said softly. "Just smoke."

It was red smoke, and the message seemed clear. It was all over them. Brilliant red, thick, acid-tasting. It spread out over the earth like paint, then began to climb against gravity in a lazy red spiral.

"Smoke," Dock said. "Smoke."

Stink Harris was crying. He was on his hands and knees, chin against his throat, bawling and bawling. Oscar and Eddie had not moved.

"He had us," the lieutenant whispered. His voice was hollowed out, senile sounding, almost a reminiscence. "He could've had all of us."

"Just smoke," Doc said. "Lousy smoke is all."

"The dumb fucker could've had us."

Paul Berlin could not move. He felt entirely conscious, a little embarrassed but not yet humiliated, and he heard their voices, heard Stink weeping and saw him beside the trail on his hands and knees, and he saw the red smoke everywhere, but he could not move.

* * *

"He won't come," said Oscar Johnson, returning under a white flag. "Believe me, I tried, but the dude just won't play her cool." It was dusk and the seven soldiers sat in pow-wow.

"I told him it was crazy as shit and he'd probably end up dead, and I told him how his old man would shit when he heard about it. Told him maybe things wouldn't go so hard if he just gave up and come back right now. I went through the whole spiel, top to bottom. The dude just don't listen."

The lieutenant was lying prone, Doc's thermometer in his mouth, sick-looking. It wasn't his war. The skin on his arms and neck was loose around deteriorating muscle.

"I told him—I told him all that good shit. Told him it's ridiculous, dig? I told him it won't work, no matter what, and I told him we're fed up. Fed up."

"You tell him we're out of rations?"

"Shit, yes, I told him that. And I told him he's gonna starve his own ass if he keeps going, and I told him we'd have to call in gunships if it came to it."

"You tell him he can't walk to France?"

Oscar grinned. He was black enough to be indistinct in the dust. "Maybe I forgot to tell him that."

"You should've told him."

The lieutenant slid a hand behind his neck and pushed against it as if to relieve some spinal pressure. "What else?" he asked. "What else did he say?"

"Nothing, sir. He said he's doing okay. Said he was sorry to scare us with the smoke."

"The bastard." Stink kept rubbing his hands against the black stock of his rifle.

"What else?"

"Nothing. You know how he is, sir. Just a lot of smiles and stupid stuff. He asked how everybody was, so I said we're fine, except for the scare with the smoke boobytrap, and then he said he was sorry about that, so I told him it was okay. What can you say to a dude like that?"

The lieutenant nodded, pushing against his neck. He was quiet awhile. He seemed to be making up his mind. "All right," he finally sighed. "What'd he have with him?"

"Sir?"

"Musketry," the lieutenant said. "What kind of weapons?"

"His rifle. That's all, his rifle and some bullets. I didn't get much of a look."

"Claymores?"

Oscar shook his head. "I didn't see none. Maybe so."

"Grenades?"

"I don't know. Maybe a couple."

"Beautiful recon job, Oscar. Real pretty."

"Sorry, sir. He had his stuff tight, though."

"I'm sick."

"Yes, sir."

"Dysentery's going through me like coffee. What you got for me, Doc?"

Doc Peret shook his head. "Nothing, sir. Rest."

"That's it," the lieutenant said. "What I need is rest."

"Why not let him go, sir?"

"Rest," the lieutenant said, "is what I need."

Paul Berlin did not sleep. Instead he watched Cacciato's small hill and tried to imagine a proper ending.

There were only a few possiblities remaining, and after what had happened it was hard to see a happy end to it. Not impossible, of course. It could still be done. With skill and boldness, Cacciato might slip away and cross the frontier mountains and be gone. He tried to picture it. Many new places. Villages at night with barking dogs, people whose eyes and skins would change in slow evolution and counterevolution as Cacciato moved westward with whole continents before him and the war far behind him and all the trails connecting and leading toward Paris. It could be done. He imagined the many dangers of Cacciato's march, treachery and deceit at every turn, but he also imagined the many good times ahead, the stinging feel of aloneness, and new leanness and knowledge of strange places. The rains would end and the trails would go dry and be baked to dust, and there would be changing foliage and great expanses of silence and songs and pretty girls in straw huts and, finally, Paris.

It could be done. The odds were like poison, but it could be done.

Later, as if a mask had been peeled off, the rain ended and the sky cleared and Paul Berlin woke to see the stars.

They were in their familiar places. It wasn't so cold. He lay on his back and counted the stars and named those that he knew, named the constellations and the valleys of the moon. It was just too bad.

Crazy, but still sad. He should've kept going—left the trails and waded through streams to rinse away the scent, buried his feces, swung from the trees branch to branch; he should've slept through the days and ran through the nights. It might have been done.

Toward dawn he saw Cacciato's breakfast fire. He heard Stink playing with the safety catch on his M-16, a clicking noise like a slow morning cricket. The sky lit itself in patches.

"Let's do it," the lieutenant whispered.

Eddie Lazzutti and Oscar and Harold Murphy crept away toward the south. Doc and the lieutenant waited a time then began to circle west to block a retreat. Stink Harris and Paul Berlin were to continue up the trail.

Waiting, trying to imagine a rightful and still happy ending, Paul Berlin found himself pretending, in a vague sort of way, that before long the war would reach a climax beyond which everything else would become completely commonplace. At that point he would stop being afraid. All the bad things, the painful and grotesque things, would be in the past, and the things ahead, if not lovely, would at least be tolerable. He pretended he had crossed that threshold.

When the sky was half-light, Doc and the lieutenant fired a red flare that streaked high over Cacciato's grassy hill, hung there, then exploded in a fanning starburst like the start of a celebration. Cacciato Day, it might have been called. October something, in the year 1968, the year of the Pig.

In the trees at the southern slope of the hill Oscar and Eddie and Harold Murphy each fired red flares to signal their advance.

Stink went into the weeds and hurried back, zipping up his trousers. He was very excited and happy. Deftly, he released the bolt on his weapon and it slammed hard into place.

"Fire the flare," he said, "and let's go."

Paul Berlin took a long time opening his pack.

But he found the flare, unscrewed its lid, laid the firing pin against the primer, then jammed it in.

The flare jumped away from him. It went high and fast, rocketing upward and taking a smooth arc that followed the course of the trail, leaving behind a dirty wake of smoke.

At its apex, with barely a sound, the flare exploded in a green dazzle over Cacciato's hill. It was a fine, brilliant shade of green.

"Go," whispered Paul Berlin. It did not seem enough. "Go," he said, and then he shouted, "Go."

ZIMMER DRUNK AND ALONE, DREAMING OF OLD FOOTBALL GAMES

by PAUL ZIMMER

from THE ZIMMER POEMS (Dryad Press)

nominated by Harvey Shapiro and Mary MacArthur

I threw the inside of my gizzard out, splashing
Down the steps of that dark football stadium
Where I had gone to celebrate the ancient games.
But I had been gut-blocked and cut down by
A two-ton guard in one quarter of my fifth.
Fireflys broke and smeared upon my eyes,
And the half-moon spiraled on my corneas.
Between spasms the crickets beat halftime to
My tympanum, and stars twirled like fire batons
Inside the darkness. The small roll at my gut's end,
Rising like a cheer, curled up intestine to my stomach,
Quaking to my gullet, and out my tongue again.
Out came old victories, defeats and scoreless ties,
Out came all the quarters of my fifth,
Until exhausted, my wind gone and my teeth sour,
I climbed the high fence out of that dark stadium,
Still smarting from the booing and hard scrimmage
I zigzagged down the street, stiff-arming buildings,
And giving flashy hip fakes to the lampposts.
I cut for home, a veteran broken field drunkard,
With my bottle tucked up high away from fumbles.

LIVES OF THE SAINTS, PART I

by JON ANDERSON

from THE IOWA REVIEW

nominated by THE IOWA REVIEW

This is the rain on Mozart's grave,
Shearing to glissandi.
Where do you little lie, exhausted, whole,
& wholly done?
Sweet Amadeus,
When I sip my bourbon,
Weaving myself toward pure abstraction—
The recollection
Of emotion without the tired events—
I'd trade my part in this to bear your song:

Even the most,
Last, broken, Wolfgang, human moan.
You are so friendly & your pillow was a stone.

This is Mozart:
A curtain of rain,
The turning heads of certain women,
The sweetness of bourbon,
Sweetness of music,
the poor politeness of oblivion.

*

"Dear Sir
I am in a Madhouse & quite
Forget your Name or who you are
You must excuse me
For I have nothing to communicate
Or tell & why
I am shut up I don't know
I have nothing to say so must conclude
Yours respectfully
John Clare"

Was this his letter into the earth?
Was it wholly composed
Of solitude?
It was wholly composed.
Did he bear extravagant pain,
Whose poems, of such light fragrance
As to be
(Dear Sir, forgive us) small?
You are minor, Sir, & would not offend.
I am, respectfully,
Yours.

*

Under the gathering, luminous clouds
He walked his grounds, thought:
Another reigns:
I must not (Tolstoy) be myself!
& fled from home.
We have the early flickering films,
The mourning strangers, waving.

All day
He lay at Astapovo Station,
Over & over: "I do not understand
What it is I have to do!"

"Yes, one good deed,
A cup of water, given . . ."
Prevailed: his gentleness, his pride,
Who would not bow.
(The light: a small tin lamp w/o a shade)
To read himself:
"I have no passport.
I am a servant of God."

*

The age demanded acquiescence.
Stalin's cock, a stone.
The heart
of Mandelstam, in exile, pumps & dries.
The bells of Petrograd,
The bells of Leningrad,
Limed with ice,
Are hollow;
Silence stalks the frozen snow.

We threw our matches
Three times in our Yankee vodka,
Hoping for a conflagration—
Anger!
For Mandelstam, for Mayakovsky,
Anna Akhmatova!
For timid Mandelstam, three times a fool,
Accused & blessed:
Poet! Russian! Jew!

*

I am Chopin,
I enclose a little time,
I bow & play:
The sea, the chandelier, this room, the sky,
The cliffs at Sourash,
Even the whole of Europe,
Blown black, spin—
The music speeds . . . retreats . . .
& I am Robert Schumann,
Mad & done,
Yet must, a little time, go on.

Now
At the hour we lately lie awake,
Give us that surety
On which our fragile art depends.
I am Robert Schumann,
Bewildered, woken
By a strange sonata in a foreign bed
Give me a little time,
Eternity,
↳ I will mend.

THE RED CROSS NIGHT

memoir by VICTOR MURAVIN

from CONFRONTATION

nominated by CONFRONTATION

EDITOR'S NOTE: *The following excerpt is from "Aurora Borealis," a privately printed book. It is the second part of a trilogy, which in the words of its author, Victor Muravin, tells the "life story of a Russian merchant marine captain on the background of events which were partly described by Mr. A. Solzhenitsyn. My books are less political, but more personal and pyschological."*

Mr. Muravin was a University lecturer in American Studies in the U.S.S.R., and he has worked as a merchant marine officer and seaman. He came to the United States a short while ago. . . . It is of some comment (and concern) that the author, at this juncture, has had to resort to private publication in the U.S. as well.

The excerpt below describes the visit of a Red Cross team to a Siberian labor camp. The action of the entire second book is set in this camp. Vikenty, who has been imprisoned for 10 years, is the central character in the narrative, and the narrative point of view may be presumed to be his. —

Martin Tucker—
editor, *Confrontation*

A MONTH HAD PASSED since they had buried Dummy when rumors spread through the camp about the imminent arrival of a delegation from the American Red Cross. It was March. There were still hard frosts, and almost every week a blizzard would blow up, burying the camp and its chimneys in six feet of snow. Work would then cease and the men would stay in the huts, taking turns to dig trenches through the snow to the huts and the kitchen. Without work life was even worse. There was no radio or newspapers; there was nothing except the bunks, the men on the bunks and their sick, mutilated souls.

The news about the Red Cross delegation was received like the announcement of an imminent revolution. The men talked of nothing else for a week, and then it was all forgotten. One day at the beginning of April Major Sinichkin's car stopped suddenly at the door of the hut. He emerged from the vehicle, chewing his thin lips contentedly, and watched as two soldiers unloaded some cans, brushes and sacks and carried them into the hut past the puzzled zeks.

Sinichkin followed them and gazed proprietarially around the hut, which had frozen in anticipation. "Here you are, lads," he said affably, "soap, paint, brushes. They're just bringing the linen, what! Wash and clean the hut. Put new sheets on the bunks. There's a celebratory dinner today to mark the arrival of the delegation from the American Red Cross. They'll be here tomorrow. In the morning, when the whole hut will be bright as a new penny, you're all to go into the forest to cut fir trees. Decorate all the walls and the whole yard with firs so that it looks pretty and smells good. And you'll get a good dinner today—I'm feeding you up for the inspection, what!" He guffawed and went back to his car.

The men rushed excitedly to the cans and bundles of linen. The dust rose in clouds in the hut as they swept out the ten years of dirt. They brushed down the cobwebs and dragged the mattresses out into the frost, colliding with each other and falling down, their faces shining with delight. The hut resembled a battlefield. Two hours later the accurately drawnup rows of snow-white bunks and the shining-clean wooden walls and floor looked more like a military summer camp than the last refuge of the prisoners of the Tishina gold mine. Towards dinner time a mobile kitchen arrived with two steaming coppers. This time the cook himself—one of the guards— served the food. The aroma of real meat borshch had a stupefying effect. In a funereal silence the whole hut lined up at the mobile kitchen. The soldier sat between the coppers in his sheepskin coat and handed each man half a loaf of tasty wheat bread and ladled out a full mess-tin of borshch. They could have as much of it as they wanted.

Vikenty could hardly prevent himself from pouring the whole mess-tin of borshch straight down his throat. He sat on his bunk hastily gulping it down, and he had half of the unexpected bread ration under the mattress. Then he joined the line again and received another helping of borshch. He broke out in a sweat as he forced himself to finish it. He looked around at the other zeks chomping away against a background din of spoons and belches.

They served only one helping of pearl-barley *kasha*. When both coppers had been emptied, the cook took the wheel of the supply vehicle which housed the mobile kitchen and drove off to the guard building at the other end of the camp. Dinner for all three huts was being cooked there that day.

The starved men reacted to the satisfying meal in various ways. Some lay back contentedly on the white line, their beards turned upwards, belching noisily as they digested the food. Others sat or lay about, holding their stomachs. By evening several men had died and a dozen had gone to sick-bay as a result of the heavy meal.

Vikenty had listened to Sinichkin's speech that morning with a feeling of alarm. And the feeling had stayed with him all day. He believed that the Americans really were coming: Sinichkin would not have excited the men for no purpose. But the news of the expedition into the forest to cut fir trees had shocked him by its patent stupidity and deceit. There were as many firs as anyone could want right outside the huts. Why go into the forest? His anxiety increased when he left the hut after the meal. "We haven't had a blizzard for some time now," he thought suddenly. On the horizen the edges of the pale-blue sky were covered with broken cloud— that meant a wind was blowing somewhere. In the old days at sea such clouds in the evening had indicated a typhoon by morning.

Where had Sinitsa decided to hid them? Was he afraid to show them to the Americans? That was understandable! But it wasn't worth it to him to bury the whole camp. Vikenty was already in his third year in the camp and he still had half his time to serve. But he had a chance of surviving and getting out. With so much time already served, behind him! And not this visit. He was sure his intuition was not mistaken. Sinitsa was sending the whole camp into the forest away from the visitors, who would meet with the soldiers. But what would happen to the prisoners? Even if he didn't have them all shot there in the forest, they might still die in a blizzard. Because a blizzard was certainly on the way.

With sinking heart he watched some unfamiliar birds swoop out from behind the roofs and fly off almost hugging the ground. Pressure! That was how birds behaved when the barometer was falling. Should he tell Sinitsa? No, that would be fatal. It would cost him nothing to kill a man, or rather to have others kill him. If he spoke up, Sinista would not let him live. All these years they had never sent the zeks out to work before a blizzard; the guard received a weather report from Magadan. What would happen now? Either Sinichkin had gone out of his mind with joy or he had forgotten about the forecast. What should he do?

He went back to his bunk, exchanging winks on the way with a few of the men he knew best by sight. He lay down and pulled the blanket over his head out of habit. The others suspected nothing! And he couldn't tell anyone. What was he to do?

Vikenty lay on the bunk thinking furiously, as he used to have to think on the bridge when his clarity of mind determined whether the ship would cope with the raging sea or go to the bottom.

Feverishly he turned over in his mind all the possible options, but he could find no solution. He had never known himself to be in such a state of alarm before. Even in the summer of 1936, when his icebreaker *Arktika* had lost the screw off Cape Shmidt, in the eastern sector of the Arctic, even then he had not lost his presence of mind and had brought the vessel out into the open sea under sail. And there had been many other dangerous moments in this life. But he had always been confident, sensing that fate and fortune would leave him an outlet somewhere, a chance of surviving the storm.

Now for the first time in his life he felt condemned to death: he was waiting for the sentence to be carried out and had no means of changing or preventing it.

The delegation's visit was an accident. It could have arrived at any time. That he could believe. Sinichkin's desire to clear everyone out of the way and clean up the camp for the duration of the delegation's visit was also natural and understandable. And now Vikenty was beginning to comprehend the final detail—the major had obviously been carried away by events and had forgotten about the weather forecast. Vikenty no longer doubted that a blizzard was on the way. In such weather, when fifteen degrees of frost were still nipping your nose, a blizzard meant a quick death; even if you dug yourself into the snow, this treacherous light frost would reach you and turn you into an icicle in half an hour. In Kolyma an April blizzard was dangerous.

He lay until morning tormented by his thoughts. He went out into the yard with the others. They lined up in a festive mood: they had a walk to look forward to and later a meeting with representatives of the American Red Cross: Sinichkin had promised that they would be able to ask questions about the international situation.

Still undecided what to do Vikenty glanced once more up at the sky, a morbid anxiety in his eyes: in the west the cloud cover had increased almost imperceptibly. But the air had not grown warmer, as it usually did before a blizzard. The men, distracted by the prospect of such an unusual visit, seemed to have forgotten about nature and its laws.

Ten soldiers with submachine guns stood in a chain alongside the column. "Atten . . . shun!" The voice of the officer commanding the detachment rang out at the head of the column. Without realizing what he was doing or why, Vikenty went behind the hut to the place where firewood for the stoves was always chopped. It was as if he was in an hypnotic trance, acting not according to the dictates of reason, but instinctively. He gave one last misty glance around him, picked up an ax, laid his left arm on the scarred tree stump and chopped through his wrist. His left hand flew off and lay in the snow like a red pancake. Dark red blood was spurting from the stump of his left arm. He gripped it with his right hand and staggered out from behind the shed. He caught a glimpse of the astonished faces in the gray column of men, then crashed onto the snow.

"It's a bad sign!" the major thought irritably as he watched the column of prisoners and guards march away. "A bad sign!" He glanced angrily at the bloody zek lying in the snow and the medical orderly kneeling beside him. Two solders had quickly brushed away the strip of bloodstained snow.

"How is he—is he going to die or not?" he asked the medical orderly.

"No, Comrade Major, he should live. He's a strong fellow, although he's lost a lot of blood. What do you want done with him?"

"What can we do!" Sinichkin shrugged in perplexity, alarmed at the thought that such a strange incident might reach the ears of his enemies in the MVD Camps' Authority at Magadan. "Get him to the sickbay, and make sure he doesn't die. What was he up to there— chopping wood? Or did he do it on purpose?"

"On purpose?" The soldier rose to his feet and shook his head. "Hardly on purpose, Comrade Major! He'd have to be an aminal to do that!"

"Ye-es. Put him in the soldiers' sickbay and feed him up so he doesn't die. I'll have a chat with him later!" He turned away abruptly and went towards the duty office. His premonition proved correct—a telephonist rushed out of the door to meet him rattled.

"What's up with you! Lost your prick?" the major blurted out in amazement, rubbing his bruised chin.

"Yessir, Comrade Major!" The soldier came to attention.

"What do you mean 'Yessir'?"

"Yessir, lost my prick!" the terrified soldier gasped.

"To hell with you!" the major cursed. He had quite forgotten the joyful mood which had possessed him in recent days. He went into the duty office, picked up the receiver and broke into a smile.

"Yes, Comrade General, I hear you!"

"Sinichkin!" The voice of the general commanding the Authority came hoarsely from the receiver. "Is everything ready there, as I ordered? The huts must be sparkling, and keep the men away in the forest till evening. I'm sending some more soldiers today. They're experienced men, they'll know what to do. And two photographers are coming, from our paper. Well?"

"It's all right, Comrade General." Sinichkin coughed into the receiver. "Everything's ready. When can we expect them? In an hour? Yes, sir, I'll see to it all, Comrade General. Goodb . . . Thank you! All the best.'"

An hour later two green broad-wheeled cross-country vehicles drew up in the camp, which there had never been any need to surround with wire. A group of well built soldiers climbed out of them.

At noon the line of vehicles at last appeared: the general's green car was followed by a long black ZIA-101 carrying the visitors. A closed truck with a platoon of guards and MGB men brought up the rear of the cavalcade. In the yard, near the camp office, stood Major Sinichkin and a few soldiers; behind them steam rose from the kitchen where a tasty dinner was being prepared for the prisoners working in the pits two kilometers away from the camp.

The major ran briskly up to the car, opened the door and came rigidly to attention.

"Well, well, hello there, old chap!" the fat general bellowed affably. He was wearing his general's overcoat with the astrakhan collar, a tall astrakhan hat and felt boots. There was a single big star on his epaulets. "Here we are then, and we've brought our visitors from across the ocean. They want to acquaint themselves with your establishment, with our system of re-education!"

"I serve the Soviet Union!" Sinichkin rattled off as he saluted.

"Good man, you serve well!" The general reached out to shake his hand. The major almost fell down from joy and astonishment. It was the first time he had shaken a general's hand. He gave the two women and two men a look of curiosity and gratitude. They were wrapped up in fur coats and hats and were listening attentively to the interpreter, an MGB captain dressed in an expensive fur coat, a musquash cap and felt boots. These boots were cut in a distinctive big-city style: narrow, and of a beautiful grayish color.

"Welcome, comrades ladies and gentlemen!" Sinichkin ran up to the group and clicked his heels.

"Dis iss head of de kemp, medjor Sinichkin," the interpreter said quietly.

"Oh! Very good!" One of the men held out his hand. The major shook it vigorously, then stepped back and listen attentively to his visitor's long tirade.

"Mr. Cherston, the head of the delegation," the interpreter translated, "is glad to say hello to the major and all the soldiers in the camp on behalf of the delegation. Now they would like to learn something about the prisoners' routine and work and take a few photographs, if it's not prohibited. The press of free America will be delighted to have some shots taken in cold remote Siberia."

"Yes, of course." The major waved his hand. "Please follow me!"

"But where are all the men?" The captain translated the questions of the members of the delegation as they moved slowly down the central aisle in hut No. 1, feeling the freshly-laundered crisply-starched sheets in surprise.

"They're all at work just now. Their dinner has been taken to them. They'll be back this evening. With us, gentlemen, work is a matter of honor, valor and heroism!" Sinichkin smiled radiantly at his own fluent utterance and noticed the general's ironic but approving glance.

"Mrs. Brady," the interpreter said, "is pleasantly surprised. She had heard a lot of critical reports about the living conditions of Soviet prisoners and suddenly—such a pleasant surprise! Of course you Bolsheviks, she says, have many enemies in the world who either do not know the true state of affairs or make a point of not knowing."

Mrs. Brady took a few photographs.

A minute later the delegation was already driving in a crosscountry vehicle towards the pits, where Petka the former Vlasov man was buried.

"Where is the gold mined here?" the other American, who had said nothing so far, asked in a puzzled voice.

"You'll soon see!" The general roared, without giving Sinichkin a chance to open his mouth. "Right here. The gold is mined in these pits in the sand. We don't build underground shafts because it's too dangerous for the men—sand is an unstable substance, gentlemen. Come with me, please!" He jumped out into the snow and offered his hand to one of the women.

The car had stopped on the side of a small hill. The visitors climbed out into the hard crunchy snow. They were smiling happily, either because of the fresh frosty air, or simply at the thought that they were at the very center of the Soviet hell and were now about to see things that their colleagues back home in the States had never even dreamed about.

From the hill they could see spread out below them like a cupped palm a broad valley, several square kilometers in size hemmed in on all sides by identical hills with their growth of stunted firs and gray bushes. The white blanket of snow covering the valley was studded with yellowish mounds of sand, beyond which, they supposed, lay the pits.

The visitors were chatting animatedly about something and gesticulating towards the valley.

"They say this valley reminds them of a battlefield," the MGB captain said, '—trenches and earthworks. They ask where we've brought them!"

"A battlefield! That's very witty!" MVB Major General Vasily Zakharovich Nikonov gave the visitors a relaxed smile and invited them to follow him with a broad proprietarial gesture. "In fact this is a battlefield—the battle is for the establishment of the material and technological base of communism in our country and for the reeducation of man! We reeducate by labor. Nothing but labor, ladies and gentlemen! This way, please."

The group began to descend the hill towards the first trench. The sheepskin-coated soldier standing watch on a nearby mound came to attention and saluted. Vasily Zakharovich, his face red from the cold, waved affably at the soldier, and led the visitors to the edge of the trench. Far below three men in quilted clothing were wielding their spades.

"Is this where you mine the gold?" The second woman, Mrs. Morrison, was genuinely astonished. "I would like to see how they do it. If the general would be so kind?" The interpreter could hardly translate her throaty gurgling.

Sinichkin glanced at the general and made a sign. The soldier dropped his submachine gun and ran to help. The three gray-clad zeks received the men and women at the bottom of the pit. The four-yard descent down the steep ramp was accomplished successfully, and the visitors crowded round the iron sieve, under which a sprinkling of large and small nuggets and a layer of gold dust gleamed yellowly on the wide strip of tarpaulin. The husky well-fed prisoners, with only a day or two's stubble on their faces, smiled shyly at the visitors. The guards and the MGB men crowded round the top of the pit, and the two special correspondents from the MVD Authority, who looked like foreigners, clicked their cameras.

The visitors stood round the tarpaulin in silence, examining the precious metal which gleamed with an even dull color.

"Can we touch?" asked Mr. Cherston, the head of the delegation. The general and the major nodded simultaneously. Cherston squatted down, tossed aside his black fur gloves and buried his hands in the gold. He stared at the beauiful cold nuggets cupped in his hands and became oblivious of all else. His three companions also scooped up handfuls of nuggets and stood gazing at the gold as if they were bewitched. Silence reigned for several moments.

"Ahem," Vasily Zakharovich coughed. "Perhaps the visitors have some questions?"

"Oh, yes, a lot of questions!" Cherston gave a start and poured the gold back onto the tarpaulin. He stood up and smiled in embarrassment. "I'm sorry, but I've never seen such wealth in all my life, if you don't count movies about Aladdin's cave! What riches you have, gentlemen! This is high quality gold, of course, I know something about this business! How much gold do you have here?" He glanced questioningly at the officers.

"We, Mr. Cherston," Sinichkin answered, after his chief had nodded for him to go ahead, "We have enough of this gold to last a thousand years. And this is only one field! We have hundreds of fields like this," he continued, watching the visitors' faces grow long. "We are the richest country in the world!"

"Oh, yes?" the second man asked ironically, coming to himself after his contemplation of the gold. "But this wealth doesn't prevent you having a very low standard of living, gentlemen. We in America are convinced that you do not know how to exploit your wealth correctly."

"And you want to help us?" The captain hastily translated the general's mocking retort.

"Well why shouldn't we help you?" Mrs. Brady gave the general a hard look.

"All right, ladies and gentlemen." Vasily Zakharovich yielded. "We're not against help, but unfortunately my rank does not permit me to decide such questions. They are decided only in Moscow, and anyway I think we'll manage to cope with our gold ourselves and with our other problems. But thanks for the canned meat all the same. And for the military supplies and the rest of it. You certainly helped us out in the war. And in exchange we'll give you gold. We're not greedy people . . . Well, then, ladies and gentlemen." Nikonov had decided to change the subject. "There are three of our prisoners. Please question them, if you wish."

The three zeks came closer. Their clothes were old but still sound.

"Can I snap them?" Mrs. Morrison pushed the man's fur cap which she had acquired in Moscow onto the back of her head, letting her beautiful blonde hair flow down onto the expensive dark-red fur coat, and took her camera from its leather case.

"Of course!" Vasily Zakharovich smiled at her amiably. "Take any pictures you want."

"Will one of them take off his jacket?" Mrs. Morrison asked, blushing. At a sign from Sinichkin one of the zeks stepped forward, quickly removed his quilted jacket, then his old but clean army shirt, and gray woolen undershirt. He stood in front of the group, smiling in embarrassment.

"What a man! What do you feed them on?" Mrs. Brady asked in astonishment as she examined the gold miner's hairy chest and powerful muscles.

The other two zeks also stripped to the waist. The delighted visitors clicked their cameras with gusto, taking shots of each zek separately, then all three together, now holding their spades, now with handfuls of gold.

"They eat the same as we do, dear visitors," Vasily Zakharovich explained in a businesslike manner. "With us, the men come first. Our system of reeducation is the most human in the world. The guards are absolutely forbidden to lay their hands on the men. It's

true, we do have some difficulty with provisions, after the destruction we suffered in the war, but we see that the prisoners working in
the gold mines get the best of everything."

"Yes, of course, that's perfectly natural." Mr. Cherston nodded.
"After all, they pay good money for it!"

"Exactly! Good money!" The general laughed cheerfully.

"And why are you here?" Mrs. Morrison asked one of the prisoners timidly.

The zek listened to the translation and blushed. He glanced
anxiously at the officers, then said in a firm voice, "I collaborated
with the fascist army against my own people."

"You must be sorry for what you did?" Mrs. Morrison gave him an
anxious and pitying look.

"I'm very sorry about everything. Now I'm expiating my guilt. I
have no complaints against anyone."

"And why are you here?" Mr. Cherston turned to one of the other
zeks.

"I killed my wife, out of jealousy."

"Heavens!" Mrs. Morrison looked fearfully at their companions.
"And you're in a camp for what? I suppose you were an honest man
before the murder? You killed her out of jealousy, for innocent
motives, didn't you?"

"Of course. I loved her very much. I could not bear to see her with
another man," the zek answered in a loud voice, squinting at the
tense faces around him.

"How cruel your country is!" Mr. Morrison exclaimed to the
general. "How can you punish people so cruelly for committing
murder for innocent motives?"

"It can't be helped, dear visitor." The general shrugged his shoulders. "We have our laws. Human life is sacred for us. Taking
somebody else's life carries a heavy penalty. In this respect our
legislation is more humane than yours. In your country you can
murder as many people as you like and remain at liberty. We isolate
such people and make them expiate their guilt through work. Our
laws are socialist laws, more advanced than yours. It's quite possible, ladies and gentlemen, that the time will come when you will
have to learn from us how to organize people and society . . . And
now please follow me."

He held out his hand to the first of the soldiers forming a chain up the ramp. The three zeks quickly put their clothes back on, while the men boisterously hauled the two furiously blushing women out of the pit.

"What is it?" Sinichkin went anxiously to meet the signalman from the camp guard who was hurrying towards them. The official camp car had stopped a short distance away.

"Here, Comrade Major, it's urgent!" The soldier handed him a white message form. He was breathing heavily and had forgotten to salute.

"What's wrong Major?" The general hurried up to him, sensing bad news.

"A b-blizzard!" The major handed him the message. His face as he looked at the general was just as white as the paper.

"Ladies and gentlemen!" Nikonov turned abruptly to the visitors. "We have received an emergency weather report. A heavy snowstorm is on the way. Please get back to the car immediately. We're returning to the camp. Quickly!"

The soldiers ran to the cars, dragging the bewildered visitors with them. On the way the interpreter explained to them hastily what a blizzard in Kolyma meant.

Sinichkin spoke right into the face of one of the soldiers, making him recoil. "Tell everyone to get back inside the camp immediately! Immediately! At the double!"

"Send a truck for the men from the camp!" He shoved the signalman in the shoulder. "And have it here in fifteen minutes!"

The guard ran towards the pits and the signalman to the car, which disappeared with a roar over the top of the hill. Two men were left on the hillside—the general and Sinichkin. Nearby stood the general's car with an army driver at the wheel.

"Well, what happened to you? Fell asleep, eh?" Vasily Zakharovich said coldly, watching the major's pale face. "In our job you can't afford to miss anything, Comrade Sinichkin. Will you have time to get the men back?" General Nikonov continued his interrogation as he got into the rear of the car and sat down in the corner, gesturing for the major to sit beside him.

"I h-hope so!" Sinichkin answered hoarsely. Forgetting the general, he took the driver by the shoulder. "Back to the camp, please. And step on it!"

The car roared off along the bumpy frozen road. Just outside the camp the driver turned sharply aside to leave room for the crosscountry vehicle that was speeding towards them on its way to pick up the men from the work site, who were already running helter-skelter along the road towards camp.

translated from the Russian by Alan Thomas

THOUGH IT LOOKS LIKE A THROAT IT IS NOT

by PATRICIA GOEDICKE

from PARIS REVIEW

nominated by Mark Vinz

The shape of loneliness is a hole
By definition, to be filled.

At the outer edges of the hole
The lizard of jealousy sits
Licking his cold lips

For the shape of loneliness is a hole
With teeth on either side.

In the middle of everyone's body
Like an empty house, like a coffin

Though it looks like a throat it is not,
Though it looks like a cunt it is not,

Nothing glows in it but heartburn,
Nothing lives in it but hot air,
Gulps of it, rushing through the passages

Occasionally a sigh hurtles through it
Like the roar of a buffalo in a wind tunnel

So that the thin shell of self pity all around it
Shivers a little, and whines

So that it develops a red nose
Complaining to itself, and muttering
Gradually its conversations become more boring

So that everyone walks right by it without looking,
Nobody even bothers to fall in it
By accident,

Tears water it, profusely
Eventually sadness swamps everything,

Out there among the stars
And the light years between stars

Even the last tiny pinprick of fire at the bottom
Soggy as a landslide sloughs away
To the other side of space

For the shape of loneliness is a hole
Without any edges, finally

The entire universe whistles through it.

WE FREE SINGERS BE

by ETHERIDGE KNIGHT

from NEW LETTERS

nominated by Herbert Leibowitz

> *If we didn't have the music, dancers*
> *would/be soldiers too, holding guns*
> *in their arms, instead of each/other.*
> *–Fr. Boniface Hardin*

We free singers be
sometimes swimming in the music,
like porpoises playing in the sea.
We free singers be
come agitators at times, be
come eagles circling the sun,
hurling stones at hunters, be
come scavengers cracking eggs
in the palm of our hands.
(Remember, oh, do you remember
the days of the raging fires
when I clenched my teeth
in my sleep and refused to speak
in the daylight hours?)
We free singers be, baby,
tall walkers, high steppers,
hip shakers, we free singers be
still waters sometimes too.
(Remember, oh, do you remember
the days when children held our hands

and danced
around us in circles, and we laughed
in the sun, remember
how we slept in the shade of the trees
and woke, trembling in the darkness?)
We free singers be
voyagers
and sing of cities
with straight streets
and mountains piercing the moon—
and rivers that never run dry.
(Remember, oh, do you remember
the snow
falling
on broadway
and the soldiers marching
thru the icy streets
with blood on their coat sleeves.
remember how we left the warm movie house
turned up our collars
and rode the subway home?)
We free singers be, baby,
We free singers be.

☾ ☾ ☾

THE BIG STORE

fiction by ALAN V. HEWAT

from THE IOWA REVIEW

nominated by THE IOWA REVIEW

THROUGH THE OPEN DOOR of the Detention Room I could see the girl sitting tensely erect in the straightbacked chair. I beckoned Odile-Odette, the matron, out into the corridor. "What's the story?" I asked.

"She say she weel talk with no one but you, Alain," the matron answered. "*Alors*, I . . ." she shrugged piquently. *Toujours gai*, I thought. Fifteen years of rousting, strip-searching and mother-henning every species of booster, junkie, con *artiste* and street harpy, and not an ounce of rich Gallic *crème* had been skimmed from her Parisian soul.

"Okay, *copain*," I said, "I'll take it from here. *Merci*."

"*Euhhh* . . ." she shrugged.

I unbuttoned my trench coat and half-sat on the edge of the desk, facing the girl. "Hello, Louise," I said. "Pretty early in the day for this kind of rendezvous, isn't it?" I pushed my fedora up on my forehead and rubbed my eyes. The dregs of sleep still stuck to me like ticks in the creases of an old dog's hide.

"Early for you maybe," she said with a weak half-smile. Fatigue and fear had carved their tracks on what would otherwise have been a pretty face. "Are you the one called Al?"

"Some call me that," I acknowledged. I let my eyes do a recon on her body; they reported lush terrain.

She tried another, brighter smile and brushed a lank strand of blonde hair away from her eyes. The night shift had busted her red-handed in Ecclesiastical Supplies, trying to slip a seven-hundred dollar jewelled bishop's miter (Anglican) into a false-bottomed box, and had slapped her into the little grey room to sit alone for five hours. According to her printout it was her first offense, so she had every reason to be one step from gonzo, but she still had the presence of mind to try to assert some style. I found myself liking her for that.

"They said you weren't any ordinary copper, Al. They said your solitude clothes compassion. Even tenderness." As she spoke, her eyes locked onto mine. Hers were green, and they softened as the boldness of her words melted away some of the glazing of fright on them. Mine are brown.

"People always talk," I said. "They want to shape you to the dimensions of their own sentimentality, fit themselves to you where you don't fit them. It's a cockamamie world, kid." I kept my voice neutral. The day was just beginning, and I had a hunch that more expert hands than Louise's would be tugging at my ego before it ended. "Let's get something straight," I said. "I'm no copper, Louise. I'm a dick. And you're no oasis on the endless desert of my alienation. You're a booster. That lays out the whole *corrida*, game, set and match. You could've saved yourself some seat-squirming, because I'm not going to tell you anything the others couldn't have told you five hours ago."

That shook her. Fear fell over her face again like a vulture's shadow. In a way, I was sorry to see her let go so fast, but it didn't surprise me. Confront Louise's type with the ineluctible modality of their situation and they change feelings the way a hypochondriac changes doctors: fast and often.

She looked down at her hands, trembling in her lap. "Don't you want to know why I did it?" she asked softly.

"I suppose it's the Rogation Days." Her head snapped up, but before she could say anything, I went on: "Not that it matters. You were apprehended in contravening the Property Laws, an objective fact which entails two options upon you. You may accept prosecution, for one. That's detention without bail, conviction without appeal, incarceration without parole, rehabilitation and stigmatization. That's the hard way." She opened her mouth to speak, but I cut her off with a gesture. "The other way is this," I said. "You sign the Culpability Forms here and now, the matron takes you upstairs and you can be stigmatized and on your way home within the hour. You want to flip a coin?"

She wanted to sneer, but her lips wouldn't support it. "Fancy words for a tattoo," she said, a half-beat ahead of a sob.

"Brass isn't your substance, Louise," I snapped. "If this were New York, you'd lose your right thumb and do hard time besides. I'd say a couple of letters tattooed on the back of your hand isn't that high a price, compared. Anyway," I said, letting my voice soften—I still hadn't given up on liking her—"Anyway, the needles here are sterile and almost painless, and Sailor Vincent'll even let you pick your color and lettering style. He takes pride. Not like those graffitists at Rehab. You shouldn't have to think twice, Kid. It's night and day." I watched her, knowing what was coming next.

It came. She slid forward in the chair so that her skirt rode up under her bottom and let her hands play her bare thighs. She drooped her eyelids and slid her tongue slowly across her lower lip. It was sexual invitation as it existed in some man's fantasy of some woman's fantasy of some man's fantasy of some woman's fantasy, *ad infinitum;* a Moebius track I'd long since given up jogging on. "Can the wearisome burleycue," I snorted, stifling a yawn.

"But they said—"

"Sign the paper, Louise."

She learned toward me, staring intently as though my eyes bore a message written in a half-forgotten language. "You've been wounded in your heart, haven't you?" she breathed. "They were right. Your solitude wafts like an after-shave scent."

I grinned away my mounting annoyance. "There's a brand of stinkum that's even cheaper," I said. "It's called cursory intimacy, and it smells like dogsbreath."

She touched her breasts, offering them. "Woof, Al," she said. "Arf, arf," I answered for the sheer crazy hell of it, and rang for the matron. In my line temptation comes at you from a thousand directions, wearing a thousand faces, all trying to push you off the wire you walk every day, all by yourself; I'm a dick, at the Big Store.

The name of the shop is Griffin and Bludgin, and it occupies the first forty-eight levels of the two-hundred-and-twelve-level Northeast Vertical Arcopolis (West Bank). My office is on forty-six. I was about to hop onto the paternoster when the next tender was announced.

"Psst. Hey, Al. *Al.*"

I turned toward the voice. Its generator was lurking in the recessed doorway that led to the fire stairs, a tall, lean gent in a double-breasted Chesterfield and bowler hat. His closely trimmed hair was greying at the temples and there was salt and pepper in his eyebrows and his pip-pip mustache. I leafed through my memory and came up empty on the name, but my instinct had already filled in the species tag: hophead.

As I approached, he beckoned with furtive impatience, ducking his head from side to side and jerking his body around as if his underwear were wired to some treadmill dynamo propelled by spastic kangaroo rats. It was true that his appearance suggested a newly retired Brigadier, but his demeanor bore the hashmarks of service in an army whose doom was preordained.

"What's the pitch?" I said, keeping my distance.

He grinned with twitchy imprecision. "I have it that you're the dude they call Al," he said. His voice surprised me; it was deep and smooth, controlled. I said nothing. "They say you're a hip dude, Al," he continued. "And I say that's cool, because I have the sort of proposition for you that a really hip dude can dig on, don't you know? Huh. Look here—"

"Drugs," I said.

His pale-lashed blue eyes widened, and he stared at me with forced amazement, then turned away and bent double in silent laughter. "*Drugs!*" he said to no one in particular, then straightened suddenly and faced me again, this time with a menacing scowl. "If I want *drugs*," he said, "I visit the chemist. Don't jive me, Al my man. Here's my card." From between his fingers he produced a calling card, bearing the name LORD PETER LORD and a London address (West End). "Lord Peter is not to be jived," he admonished with a flick of his hand. "Lord Peter is no chemist, no drug merchant and no dope pusher, do you dig? No. The commodity here is what you might want to call sweet and bad. Say candy. Uh-huh, *nose* candy. Look here." He ducked away and came back with a sapphire-lidded snuffbox which he opened, revealing a crystalline white powder within. "Go ahead, Al," he said. "Slide some of that into your septum, brother. They say you're the Lone Ranger, here, my man, and I say powder your nose with this shit, and you can ride off into the golden sunsets of your mind. It's super-clean and super-fine. It's *organic*, Jim, and there is lots more where that came from. They say you're ripe for some discreet thrills, Al, and I can proffer the franchise. Yes. Now dig this proposition . . ."

I tuned out his babbling while my mind sifted the data. Before I'd even had a chance to get to the office I'd had sex and chemical nirvana thrust at me. What next, I wondered, flowers? I could feel myself getting edgy. You'd think that "They"—whoever "they" were—would have learned by now, but maybe it was just as well that they never had; when they did, I might be out of a *raison d'être*.

I might have saved myself a lot of trouble if I'd been more attentive to Lord Peter, but the nattering snowbird was getting on my nerves, so I gave him a chop under the ear and tossed him down the fire stairs. I didn't stay around to watch him land; I was already late for work.

Emma was waiting at the door of the outer office. "Hi, toots," I said, brushing past her. I stopped short, arrested by something flickering beneath the surface of her calm, dark eyes, something I'd almost missed. Almost. "What's up?" I said. Emma and I had been a team for seven years. We knew each other's signals.

She nodded toward my inner office. "Company, Alejandro," she said. "A couple of hundred-twenty-seventh-level types."

"North side?"

"My guess," she nodded.

I grinned. "When was the last time you were wrong?" She'd come in as a secretary, even though I hadn't asked for a secretary. Hell, nothing undermines your independence like a hierarchic relationship, I'd told them. The T.O. calls for it, they said. Some T.O., I said. As soon as she'd learned the ropes, I'd made her my associate, without benefit of T.O. It had been a right move. Emma was as tough as I was, as competent and almost as independent. She ran her own cases, carried her own passkeys. She looked out for herself. We

took turns at playing gofer, alternating weekly. "Anything else?"
I said.

"What do you mean?"

"Something in your eyes."

"Look again."

She had me. Whatever I'd reacted to was gone now, and I didn't
have time to try to reconstitute it. I had company.

They were standing in the center of the room, four feet from the
front of my desk. Side by side, like mismatched andirons. They wore
their hats low on their foreheads and their hands in the pockets of
their overcoats.

I scaled my fedora onto a peg and tossed my trench coat over the
top of the filing cabinet, without attracting any noticeable attention.
"*Buon giorno,*" I said. No fires of amenity were lit from my spark. I
began to wonder if the decorators might have installed the two
figures on my carpet as an amusing new kind of semi-kinetic
sculpture. Given the choice, I'd just as soon have taken a model
railroad. I sat at the desk and pressed Emma's button on the inter-
com. "Hey, I forgot," I said. "Prune Danish this morning, okay?" It
was her week.

"Anything for the company?" she answered.

With my eyes I inquisited the company. "Gentlemen?" I said.
The word fluttered around the room in confusion, like a one-eyed
sparrow in hall of mirrors.

The short, fat half of the asymetrical tandem shrugged."Eh,
shoo," he said. "Habatta hot chawklit, eh? Anna cannoli? Nice." He
licked his thick, purple lips. The gesture created a visual effect only a
deviate could appreciate.

"Dieting, are you?" I said blandly. He looked like ten gallons of
spumoni in a five-gallon container. As soon as my words sank in,
great shifting forces began to labor at rearranging his face into a
sheepish smile, but before they could complete the task his companion reached over and grabbed a handful of cheek and twisted, hard.

"Sharrup," the companion snarled. His hand snaked back into his
coat pocket. "My associate change his mine," he explained to me.
"We catch a bite onna way over." He was tall and as stark as a bicycle
chain, with a complexion like minced *weisswurst.*

The fat one kneaded his cheek like Goodyear smoothing a wrinkle
on his blimp. "Yeh," he said thickly. "Wharra you thin, it's a tea
potty?"

"Suit yourself," I said. "That's all, toots."

"*Zu befehl*," Emma answered.

"Anyways," the fat one sneered. "You get from Cohen's, don't ask how we know, eh?" He was trying to salvage some self-respect. "I like from Cohen's," I said.

"*Immondizie*," he spat, shifting a few pounds of lip this way, a few more pounds that. "Gobbidge, knowwottamean? You likea nice *cappucino* anna bitea pastry—nice—you go Vito's, up hunnerd-twenny-sev', hah? I—"

"Sharrup," the tall one interrupted, this time without the pinch. "We he' on bidniz."

"Ass ri'," the fat one affirmed.

"You don't say," I said. "I thought maybe you'd stopped in to compare recipes. Now me, I've found I can make my *involtini* come alive by adding just a suggestion of tarragon to the broth."

The fat one sputtered like a sucking chest wound. "Wharra you, crazy?" he cried.

"Sharrup," the tall one inserted. He regarded me with eyes you could smash diamonds on. "We gotta proposish'," he said. I nodded. I wasn't surprised. Not today. "Yudda one calt Al," he said. "To you we come in respeck." As a signal of his respect he lifted his upper lip in a vulpine grin. His teeth looked as though they'd been marinating in hot root beer for a generation or so. "We reppasent someone that if I tolya the name you'd shitchersef."

"Try me," I said. "It might clear the air in here."

"Gahead," he said with cool menace. "Smott awf."

"Yeah," the fat one echoed, "gahead. See iffa you so smott when you walkin' backward onnacounta you knees benda wrong way." He flexed his shoulders. It may have been my imagination, but I thought I heard some seams protest.

"Sharrup," the tall one said.

"Who are you?" I said. Though their timing was great, the repartee was starting to cloy.

"Ossa," he said, with a short bow.

"Peglioni," said the fat one. "Pasquale. Hawwaya?"

"Who sent you Knights of Columbus and what are you pushing, fun, money or merchandise?" It was time to take control.

Ossa squinted closely at me, as though counting the bones in my inner ear. "Howa you like to be rich, Al?" he said. "Plenty rich? They sayin', the sex thing don't get t'rough to Al. No offense, it's what they sayin'. They sayin', you don't score Al witha pills an' powders. Again, no offense, eh? Word is, they sayin' that Al, he—— *come si dice*—he dwell ascetical inside a basilica of solitude. Pleasure don't tempt, they sayin'. It'sa pattern like anxiety, eh? So you ask, wheresa source of anxiety inna modern life, eh? Anna supposish' is: money. Wharra you thin'?"

"We talkin' fi' figures atcha, Al, openers," the fat one said. "That's some kinda K."

Things were clicking in the back of my brain, forming into a pattern. I wasn't being tempted today; I was being set up. Real temptation is spontaneous, serendipitous, but all three of the siren songs I'd heard this morning were piping the same tune. Before things went any further, I had to find out who the composer was.

I leaned back in my chair as nonchalantly as I could. "Before I punch up a No Sale," I said, "there are a few things I'd like to know. And you're going to enlighten me." I let my jacket fall open to give them a look at the .38 Police Special on my belt.

"Yah yah yah," Ossa barked. "Wharra you afraid?"

I shrugged. "Prolonged pain," I said, "wasting disease, the unhappy moments when you see love becoming indifference, poisonous reptiles. The usual."

"Spoze," he said. "Spoze I say this izza nawffa——"

"Don't say it and you won't be sorry," I riposted.

For a tense moment we all stared sulphurously at each other. Then Ossa shook himself lightly like a duck coming in out of a thin mist and tapped Peglioni on the shoulder. "Camawn, 'Squale," he said. "I treatcha piecea pie."

"Wait a minute . . ." I started to say, but Ossa's words had been a signal. As soon as they were spoken, points appeared in the fabric in front of the left-hand pockets of both men's coats, points which began to spew soft lead. I kicked my chair away from the desk, drawing my .38 as I rolled out of the line of their fire. I took Ossa first, through his eye; it seemed it wasn't unbreakable after all. Then Peglioni, who had hesitated just long enough to even up the odds. Perhaps the word "pie" had distracted him; at least it was nice to think so. After all, gluttony is one of the deadly sins. They fell together in a pile, Peglioni on Ossa. Or maybe the other way around. I didn't particularly care; they had already ceased to exist for me.

Reholstering the .38, I stepped around them and out to the outer office. Emma hadn't come back with the coffee yet, but I didn't have time to wait. Someone was making a determined effort to get at the substance of my ego, and I couldn't afford just to sit around waiting for the next attempt. At Emma's desk I put a quick call to the cleanup boys and asked them to get the mess off my carpet. As I was getting up to leave, the phone rang. On my line.

I hesitated. My adrenaline had me as nerved up as a fire-walking fakir with athlete's foot. What now? I wondered. I lifted the phone with caution that would have done credit to a bomb-disposal expert. "Yeah," I said.

"Albie?" said the dick on the other end. "It's Jerry. I'm in Pets."

I forced myself to breathe. "What's up, Jer?" I said, listening carefully.

"There's a bunch of kids from the Neo-Pan-African Directorate down here trying to get into the lion cage," he reported. "They say they have to dance with Simba before the sun warms the topmost branches of the fever tree today. They say if they don't famine is gonna dry up the dugs of our mothers and pestilence will blind our eyes with scabs. It's got a touchy feel to it, Albie. I may need some help."

I replayed the report in my head, probing for traps. It sounded straight, but just to be sure I asked: "Did anyone ask for me personally, Jer?"

"Huh? No, I just thought you oughtta know."

"Fair enough," I said. Jerry was a person I could trust; a good dick. "Call Negotiations on one-five and have them send one of their people. No, better make it two: one cultural and one religious. That'd be Doctor Fred and The One Who Swallows Like a Giraffe (Slowly). Clear the area and don't be afraid to do some dealing yourself, until the others get there. Give 'em a couple of crocs if you think you need to buy time; I'll square it with the Merchandise Manager. The main thing is, don't let them get a hand on Simba. That's an order, Jer."

"Roger, Albie."

"Good dick." I hung up, feeling better. It was a nice, restorative slug of down-to-earth reality: the first routine event of the day.

Emma ankled in with the coffee and pastries. "All yours, toots," I said. "No breaks for the wicked today." She seemed to start at the sound of my voice, and when I looked that something I'd seen before was back in her eyes.

"Holy Toledo," she cracked. "Another day at the Big Store, eh?"

"Unh-huh," I said. Now it was gone again, leaving behind only a faint, warning tingle on my nerve endings, as nebulous as an echo. I let it pass. How do you figure a dame anyway?

"By the way," Emma said, "I passed Harry on the escalator just now. He was on the way to Pharmaceuticals. Some geek's loose down there with a vial of VH 79/80."

"The lupus culture?"

She nodded. "The one that's on special this week. He used a micro-charge to blow a hole in the ventilation shaft and now he says he'll dump the germs in unless the store hires no fewer than four hundred ethnic Taiwanese in positions of Assistant Buyer and above."

"Jesus," I said, "if he does, there won't be a nose left in the whole Arcopolis by Thanksgiving. What's Harry doing?"

"Negotiating, what else?"

I couldn't let it go by. "Did anyone ask for me personally?" I asked.

She flashed me a look I couldn't interpret. "No," she answered. "All Harry said was, 'Tell Alf if you see 'im.'" Her imitation of Harry's brisk drawl was exquisite; but then, everything Emma did was exquisite.

"Harry's a good dick," I said. "Anything else?"

Some sudden impulse seemed to press her mouth open, but she caught it and shrugged it away. "I guess not," she said.

"Okay," I said, heading for the door. "Ciao." I didn't have time to harvest ambiguities; for better or for worse, I had a caper to track.

I didn't have to wait long for the break. I was approaching the down escalator on forty-five when a voice somewhere in the neighborhood of my left elbow rasped out, "Well well well, Aloysius my lad. How's your goodself this fine business day?" I turned to face the shriveled bonhomie of George (Yankee) Dougal Bludgin himself, the oldtime drygoods merchant who, more than two-thirds of a century earlier, had joined up with the late J.H.S. Griffin to found the Big Store. Though officially retired, Bludgin continued to visit the premises daily, a wire-rimmed, sleeve-gartered wraith who doddered about the shop annoying the employees with his platitudes and kibitzing. Still, he was a spunky old jasper, and I rather liked him, though I didn't have time for his digression today. I bade him Good Morning as noncommittally as I could and hastened on toward the escalator.

He wasn't going to let me pass that easily. "There there," he croaked heartily, hooking a claw into my sleeve. "None of that Mister Bludgin stuff with us, Aloysius. The name's Yank, to you. Call me anything but don't call me late to supper, eh?" He winked stickily up at me and spread his wattles in a grin. "You're just the feller I was looking for, by golly, and with your kind indulgence I'll just perambulate along with you for a quick nonce. After you, sir. After you." He shooed me ahead of him onto the escalator and sidled on three steps behind, which put our heads at the same level as we descended. "Yes sir," he said, "just the feller. I come to you with a proposition, Aloysius, and I'd wager cheese against chalk it'll be manna to your ears. But don't let me entice you; the product has to sell itself, whether it's birdseed, barley or buttonholes. Are you game, sir?" His head bobbed toward me like an egg in boiling water. I kept my face straight to hide my impatience. "Fair enough," Bludgin continued. "grant him the open door and the crackerjack salesman can find his own way into the parlor. I won't mince words now. The nut of it is—oh here, let's go around again, what say?"

We had reached the bottom of the escalator, and he scuttled around and mounted the adjacent, ascending stairs. I tagged along, wondering where he was leading me. "Up up, eh?" he beamed moistly. "The appropriate direction for positive cogitation. You know the expression, up and coming? The ambitious man builds his house on the hilltop, to show the world his eye is on the heights. Ha. Sleep with a pillow, lad. The sludge won't collect in your cranium while you're banking your fires. Up up. Where was I?" He tapped his temple with an index finger you could clean pipestems with. "Ah yes," he said. "We've had our eye on you for some time. Aloysius. We've observed your *modus operandi* and perused your *curriculum vitae*. By the bye, you're not Italian, are you?"

I felt myself draw a sharp breath. The familiar tune was sounding in my head again, with a variation that made my suspicions dance: the *they* employed by the others—Louise, Lord Peter, Ossa—had become *we* in Bludgin's gummy ramblings. If the transition was true, it could be my chance to unlock the libretto and see how the final scenes were writ, and in whose hand. I listened as the old drummer rattled on.

"Back in my day," he said, "all the ace dicks were Irish. Nowadays any jackanapes with a taste for the iron figures he has the stuff. Takes more than that, as you well know. You're a man who knows how to

keep his bib and tucker shiny. I'll talk turkey with you, Aloysius. I'm
an octogenarian, but if I was in your shoes I'd grab temptation by the
throat and waltz her into the boudoir. Here here, after you."

We made the turnaround and got back onto the down escalator.
Bludgin's breathing had become slightly labored, but his words hit
me like darts from a blowgun. It was all I could do to keep from
grabbing him and shaking the punchline from him. "We've got plans
for you, lad," he said. "We know you work alone and keep your own
counsel, and that's a fine thing. Self-reliance is something they used
to teach in the old school, but it seems to be something they've
dropped from the syllabus since I took my BHK—that's Bachelor of
Hard Knocks. Nevertheless, the solitary man is vulnerable. You
march too long to your own drummer and pretty soon you're out of
step. Mrs. Bludgin—God rest her—used to say to me, she'd say . . .
herrk . . ." He gasped and began to change color. His hands made a
couple of weak forays against his stiff collar, like mice trying to climb
out of a cast-iron bathtub. He fell forward into my arms.

I carried him off the escalator and laid him on the floor, cradling
his head in my hands. His breath was misfiring and his eyes were
rolled up under their lids. Life had already decamped from his old
carcass and death was installing its own effects. "Yank," I said, "tell
me, quick. Who's behind you? What's the caper? Why me? Who's
offended?" I bent my ear to his mouth but there was no sound there
except the wintry sussurrus of his failing breath, sweetened by
Sen-Sen. "*Yank,*" I cried, shaking the old egg. His lips moved.
"Blueballs," he gasped, and died.

As a crowd gathered around us, I crouched over the corpse and
tried to assess my situation. It was no surprise that I was up against
collective opposition. Hell, you might say that's the story of post-
industrial society. But what did they want? Unless I could answer
that, my chances of thwarting their caper were no better than the
odds on a one-legged man in an asskicking match. So far they'd tried
to bribe me and buy me, and all I'd learned from it was that I was a
target. "They"—or "we"—were after *me*. Or were they? The only
real proof was in my own feelings, which were real enough to me, all
right, but so what? Subjective reality won't even buy you a cup of
ersatz java, at the Big Store. I could feel the sweat breaking out on
my brow, and my head began to swim. This was like trying to
arm-wrestle with a *Zeitgeist*. I had to get someplace where I could
think.

I stood and muscled my way out through the crowd. I grabbed a house phone and told the operator to send a cleanup crew. The operator told me to hold on; someone was trying to reach me. I would have hung up, but the connection was already made and a familiar voice was hissing in my ear.

"Mister Alphonse?" the voice said, with a whistle around the esses.

"Is that you, Roy?"

"It's me, Mister Alphonse," he said. "Roy, the elevator boy." All the way down at the bottom of the Arcopolis, beneath the automatic high-speed elevators, paternoster, pneumotubes, moving ramps escalators, funiculars, tracked vehicles and molecular transit cabins that held the place together, was the solitary Otis elevator which Roy had been driving for more than sixty years. It lurched and wheezed like an asthmatic acrobat and reached no higher than the sixteenth floor of the Big Store, and its continued service could be explained only as an uncharacteristic gesture of sentiment by management to Roy and to the stores oldest customers, for whom there was also maintained a token stock of goods in whalebone and genuine leather.

"How's life, Roy," I said, "still got its ups and downs?" If I hadn't said it, he would have.

"I'm stuck, M-mister Alphonse," he croaked. The catch in his voice could have been fear, fatigue or famine, but it was somehow familiar enough to force caution on me.

"I'll bite," I said. "What's holding you up?"

"M-me and the Otis, we're jammed, M-mister Alphonse," he said. His voice dropped to a whisper. "And get this one: I d-don't even know where. Hell's bells. I got to keep my voice down, so as not to spread any doom amongst the passengers, b-but I'm making no secret of the fact this is a new one on m-me. Sixty-two years and you see a lot. M-malfunction, sure. Even a streamline rig like the Otis gets weary. Who don't? P-perfection's the dream of youth. Jesus, can you f-figure it? I'm luh . . . I'm luh . . . I luh . . ."

"Roy?"

"I'm *lost*, Mister Alphonse."

"Who isn't," I said, only half to myself. My heart went out to the old boy. Like me, he was a loner, a free-lance. It was a bad day for our kind.

"Mister Alphonse," he whispered, the fear rustling in his voice

like a black widow spider in a cellophane bag, "I'm on thirteen."
My ear did a double-take. "But Roy—" I started to say.

"M-mister Aphonse," he interrupted, "THERE IS NO THIR-
TEENTH FLOOR!" As his voice rose, it was joined in its ascent by a
crescendo of muttering in the background. I heard: "How's that?"
and "Queen? Queen?" and then Roy, saying "Face the front of the
car, please." The background noise died away.

"Roy," I said, "are you sure?"

"Mister Alphonse," he answered with weary dignity, "I've been
squeezing up and down the same shaft for sixty-two years, like the
senior citizen said to his childhood sweetheart. Now all of a sudden
there's a set of doors with a big red thirteen on them that was never
there before. You tell me."

"Well, why don't you—"

"Open them? Look here, young man, I've got passengers aboard.
All right, if it was me alone, I'd say, well Roy, this is it. You overshot
a few, you shortstopped some more, and now you made it square to
thirteen, everybody out. That's what I'd say. But Mister Alphonse,
some of these poopsies have been riding with me for a golden half a
century. They trust me like the church or synagogue of their choice.
I ask you, how can I discharge them here, where every elevator boy
ever born of woman knows your thirteenth floor is the horizontal
shaft that runs right off the edge of life. It's the last stop, all off, don't
crowd. It's your coffin, Mister Alphonse. Your coffin. I'd sooner
strap them to my back and go hand over hand up the cable to safety,
like I did in thirty-three, before you were even whelped. Yes, by
Jesus, I would. But you know," he added, his voice tightening, "I
don't think I got a cable any more. I think I'm in the wrong hole. I
think—hell's bells, I don't know what to think, Mister Alphonse. I
need help."

I didn't hesitate. I couldn't, even though suspicion was hammer-
ing on me with a stroke that said: set-up. "Hang on, Roy boy," I said.
"We'll find you and get you home safe." I didn't know how I'd do it,
but I knew I had to; that proud old man was my ticket to self-respect.

"Mister Alphonse," his voice rose and scolded, "I didn't ask for no
we. I wanted a *we*, I'da called up Jack over at maintenance and then
sat around three days while him and that Franco formed up a
committee and took a vote on what to do. You can't get piss poured
out of a boot nowadays until you've got consensus and social
guidelines. I know about that. I called *you*, Mister Alphonse, 'cause

I need action, fast and independent, and that's your style. Don't let me down son, or . . ." His voice trailed off in a sigh that held every one of his years.

My ears sizzled. I hadn't heard it myself, but the old fox had pounced on the collective pronoun as if I'd tied bright feathers to it. "*Touché,*" I growled. "You just keep your passengers sweet until I get there."

"Yes *sir,*" Roy fluted. "We'll get going on a word game, maybe a song-sing. I dunno; sometimes *in extremis* a group'll take to confessional reminiscence. Sometimes a star is born. We'll see. Leave it to me, Mister Alphonse." There was a new lilt in his voice which struck me as somehow incongruous; it was almost feminine.

"Good man," I said, and hung up. A vagrant impulse scratched at the back door of my mind: to call Emma with a quick fill-in. I shut it out in an instant. This was no time to play footsie with organizational responsiblity. I had to play the hand I held or fold the game.

I used the bypass key to unlatch the elevator doors on fifteen and leaned into the shaft, beaming my flashlight down into the gloom. The hole was as bleak as an amputee's sleeve, with no sign of Roy's car or even the cable on which it depended. The guide rails were dull and fuzzy with dust and two stories overhead the pulleys and drive wheels sat uselessly, like teeth on a dresser. Spider webs festooned the counterweight track on the facing wall. I might have been a relic hunter unsealing a Biblical-era catacomb, except that the old sarcophagi don't sing and from somewhere below me I could piece out the sounds of a measly chorus. It was barely audible in the tumult of the Big Store, but there it was, a thin quavering "Nearer My God to Thee." It was all the invitation I needed.

Two feet to the left of the doors, a narrow iron ladder was set into a recessed channel in the wall of the shaft. I swung aboard and kicked the doors closed. The noise of the store faded and the singing became more distinct, changing now to "Row Row Row Your Boat," as a three-part round. I switched off the flashlight and stuck it in my pocket, and began to hum along, adding a fourth part. As my eyes became accustomed to the darkness, I started down.

At first I lowered myself with exaggerated caution, as though slipping into bed with a couple of scorpions, but then I found a rhythm of descent that soothed me. When he's on a caper, a good dick is like a good reporter; all of his senses are focused on the who, what, when, where, how and why. But when the action starts, the dick shuts off the distractions and concentrates on his body, and that's what I did now. Let my unfathomed adversaries do the puzzling for a change; I was alone, the way I liked it. No phantoms for me; just the rusty grit on the ladder rungs, the pleasant muscle straining in my shoulders and forearms, the pressure of my .38 against my thigh, my animal motion. And somewhere in the background a song: *Hare Krishna, Hare Krishna, Krishna Krishna, Hare Hare,* to let me know that Roy was keeping up his end of the bargain.

Then, without warning, my foot hit the roof of the elevator car.

As if a plug had been pulled, the singing stopped in mid-phrase. I tested my weight on the roof and found it would hold me. "Roy?" I called, letting go of the ladder.

"Mister Alphonse?" came the answering shout from below.

"Everything's jake," I shouted, and it was, too, for just about as long as it took to say so, until another voice—not Roy's, but a voice even more familiar than Roy's—said, "Wait a sec," and something happened under my feet.

I once knew an old dick named Hartman, who used to say, "Some days you crack the case, and some days the case cracks you." He left out those days when it all happens at once. Like today.

A hatch in the roof of the elevator car swung open beneath me and I found myself on top of ten feet of open space. On my way through it, I extemporized some maneuvers for which the Olympic free-diving judges have no grades, with a boffo finale that consisted of landing on the back of my neck with all of my hundred and ninety-seven heavier-than-air pounds. As the roar of an appreciative crowd thundered in my ears, I gracefully lost consciousness.

Some time latter the rabble got whipped into line and began chanting my name. *"Per-ry Per-ry Per-ry,"* they chorused, which was puzzling; nobody had called me Perry for years. I'd even managed to break my mother of the habit, though she slipped once or twice at the end. I raised up on my elbows to try to get a better perspective on the testimonial, and as I did the audience dispersed into an invisible distance, leaving behind a solitary cheerleader who bent over me and said, "Perry? Are you all right? Perry?"

It was Emma.

"Toots," I said, shaking my head.

"Are you all right?"

"Copacetic," I managed, but I had to close my eyes again. What in the name of Spade was going on? This was no elevator car I found myself in; it was a green, grassy field dappled with white flowers. Nearby, birds sang in a leafy shade tree which had a swing hanging from one of its lower branches, and on the other side of the house a creek burbled merrily. The house! It gleamed like a peeled egg beneath the cloudless sky, and through an open upstairs window a lace curtain, tickled by the warm breeze, beckoned to me with a gesture that I recognized as concupiscent. That would be our bedroom, I realized.

Emma touched my face. "Poor baby," she said. "That was quite a tumble. If you don't feel up to it, we can just lie quietly and be close. The kids won't be home until suppertime." As if cued by her words, a sweet scent tweaked my nostrils: apple pie, cooling on a kitchen windowsill. "Your favorite," Emma whispered. She kissed my ear. "Let's go inside," she purred.

I shook her off and stumbled to my feet, holding my head. I needed to think, to evaluate the situation, but all that occurred to me were the sensations of this place. "Just feel it," said Emma. "Isn't it ideal?" "Ideal?" I said. "I don't know." For no reason I was smiling. I put my hand over my mouth. Confusion lashed around inside me like the tail of a giant lizard beset by fire ants. "What an ugly image," Emma said, making a face. I registered the face; it was a mock expression of fear. Fear. That seemed right. I felt afraid. "You don't have to be," Emma said. How did she know? Unless . . .

I closed my eyes again, but nothing went away. I was shorn of my own reality, straining to find a handle, a tool, something . . .

"Perry, don't," Emma said gently.

A word jumped to my lips and I snapped at it like a trout rising to a fly. "Al," I said.

A sudden, small chill fluttered in the breeze.

"Perry, *darling.*" Her arms went around me and her lips found the side of my throat.

"Al," I said, louder this time. "I'm the one called Al." It raised gooseflesh on her bare arms. "Yeah," I said, "Al. The dick. The solo operator." It started to get easier, as one word drew another behind it. "The shamus," I said, as a cloud passed in front of the sun.

"No," Emma cried, grinding her body against me. "Look at me, Perry. You mustn't. You don't know—"

I twisted away from her. "Ixnay, toots," I said. "You got the wrong patsy. If you want Perry, look in the herd where the rest of them are: the Perrys, the Barrys, the Jerrys, the Carys, the Larrys, the organization types. But don't look for me, there, because I'm my own organization, baby, overlord and underling, the whole lineup complete in one slightly shredded package, but free to roll like a billiard ball, to carom and kiss and roll away. . . ." I was babbling now, because I knew I had to. I had to keep my thoughts obscured, and inane spontaneous verbiage was the nearest opaque material at hand. So I kept on talking, tough and sassy the way a dick talks, because now I knew where I was.

"You're *home*," Emma pleaded. "Where you *belong*. Where you're loved and needed and—"

"Put a belt on it, sister," I snarled. "You don't have to tell me where I am. Roy gave me that much. Thirteen, he called it, and now it's coming back like a song. Thirteen. In the old days they called it Notions. Counters stacked high with ideals, promises, humours, hot flashes, aspirations, hobgoblins, the whole *megilleh*. In the Thirties the big item was Pie in the Sky. In the Forties, Doing Your Part was a sellout, and there were always specials on things like Zip Your Lip and Four Freedoms for the price of three. Get the picture? The old-timers'll tell you the Big Store was never bigger than it was then.

"But something queered the deal. The department got overbought in imports, and the goods went stale on the shelves, and before they knew it every corner stunk of Red Menace and a Doomsday Culture got into the carpeting. You couldn't bring the customers in with grappling hooks; they were wary as a turkey the day before Thanksgiving. So management did the only sensible thing. They closed down the department and sealed off the floor. Sure, some of the goods were still salable—things like Pressure to Conform, and Getting in Touch with Your Feelings—so they spread them around in little boutiques all over the Arcopolis. Funny how I forgot about it, or maybe not so funny. I'd guess you had it figured pretty close. All those mugs of yours throwing around the 'theys' and 'wes'—just the thing to fire up the gas under my paranoia. Everything pointed to a collective enemy.

"Then you hit me with Roy, and you knew I'd jump. Hell, he's as real as they come, one of those spunky old loners they just don't make any more, all spit and elbow grease. If he said there was no thirteenth floor, I was primed to buy it without question. It never occurred to me that not only was there a thirteenth floor but by now all the old virulent strains would have died off, and anyone with a passkey could move in and set up shop with his—or her—own fantasies. It was slick, toots. Damn slick."

Emma sobbed once. "I think your word was 'exquisite,' Alejandro," she said. "I appreciated that coming from you. I really did."

I opened my eyes.

The country of Emma's fantasy had disappeared and we were back inside an elevator car. Emma stood against the back wall, wiping away the tears. At my shoulder were two steel doors, closed tight. A big red 13 was painted across them.

"You ought to know," Emma said, "that Roy wasn't in on it. He got fifty dollars and a ticket to the dog track delivered with his milk this morning." She switched into Roy's voice. "He's gone to the doggies, Mister Alphonse," she wheezed. I grinned, this time because I felt like it.

"What about the rest of your little repertory company?" I said. "I can figure Louise and the junky and those two goombahs—they were all fresh out of the plea-bargaining tank—but what about old Bludgin? Was he terminal or something?"

"Just an old drummer making his final pitch," she said. She smiled sadly. "He was so tickled to get a chance to push something he really believed in again, that . . . well, I guess he didn't mind giving it everything he had. He really admired you a lot."

"What are you talking about?" I said.

Her eyes flashed angrily. "You fool," she said. "Why do you think I dragged you down here?"

"Never mind that," I said. I knew why. The scent of the apple pie was still fresh in my nose, to remind me how compelling Emma's ideal of romance was to me. No use retracing that ground, or I might get sucked in for good. After all, people are forever trying to wrap you in the cloak of their own sentimentality; who's to say that just one time it might not fit?

"You're wrong," Emma said. "Oh, I had my own reasons for doing it this way. Hell, I know what's beneath your shell of solitude, toots. I know there's compassion there, and tenderness, and heaven knows I can always use a little more of that. But that's not why I did it."

"Okay," I said. I could accept the correction, because it didn't matter. I leaned against the doors and lipped a Camel out of the pack, while Emma kept on talking. They were going to get me, she said. I snapped a Blue Tip into flame with my thumbnail. She just wanted to get me out of their sight for a while, she said. I pulled my fedora low on my forehead. The smoke rasped across my eyes like emery board. They wanted to promote me, she said. Or maybe it was demote me? The wanted me to be Perry again. Or maybe not. It was like the old song. Tulip or Turnip. Rosebud or Rhubarb. I could be either; I could be both. Whatever, it would still be me. I flipped up the collar of my trench coat and tugged the belt tight.

I opened the doors.

Outside, the dark streets glistened, their puddles reflecting the halos gathered by the streetlights in the evening fog. The only sounds were the muffled peals of the buoys in the harbor, and the mournful hoot of a ship's horn somewhere out on the bay.

Emma touched my sleeve. "Al," she said, "let me . . ."

I tapped her under the chin, gently. "Sorry, kid," I said.

"Can't take the sunshine, huh?" Her smile flickered like a candle in a birdcage, but she managed to hold onto it. She had that kind of style.

"Maybe next time," I said. I owed her that much.

Her lips brushed my cheek. "So long sucker," she said. "See you in the funny papers." She turned away.

"Ten-four," I answered softly. And as the elevator doors eased shut behind me, I stepped out into the hostile night, back on the wire I walk all the time, all by myself. It's the only way for me. I'm a dick, at the Big Store.

THE BEST RIDE TO NEW YORK

fiction by BOB LEVIN

from THE MASSACHUSETTS REVIEW

nominated by THE MASSACHUSETTS REVIEW

THE FIRST TEAM I WAS EVER ON that won anything, the guy that won it for us was a skinny spade forward, Irving Ballard, with a funny weird jumpshot where he held the ball out to the side, like a waiter with a tray, and slid under it kinda and pushed real sweet. He hit four in the last two minutes, and I hit a couple, and we beat Bonner for the Valley title 12 years ago; and I don't think I ever felt so boss. Most of the guys off that team went on to college, and I remember asking Irving Ballard one night where he was going. He wasn't any street nigger, his folks worked, and he played good jazz piano—he played the best "Soul Sister" I ever heard—and I figured he'd go to music school at least. We were out at the Center, waiting on winners, a couple beers gone; and Irving Ballard just lay back on the grass, looked up the moon, and said, "Shit, man. You mean be a everybody."

I went down to Temple, and we won a lot. We won the Big Five and the MAC twice and a Holiday Festival. I'd come home summers and go to the Center, and Irving Ballard'd be around. I'd say how you doing and he'd say good and I'd say I was doing good, and we'd play some three on three and have some beers. He still had that funny shot and he didn't miss from 15 feet. He was playing in a trio, local gigs, he said, with Jimmy Horse who worked at the post office, and a white drummer who sat in once with Cannonball at Peps. Irving Ballard was doing Robe then and he was the first guy I knew to be smoking too and after a while everybody heard he was doing hard drugs; and then he didn't come around the Center any more and there were stories about him being busted and then he wasn't anywhere anymore and there weren't even stories.

After finishing school I went over to Spain and played two years there, a good scene. Then I came back and figured to keep playing. I enjoyed ball, and I enjoyed the life a whole lot. I was good. There wasn't anything I did any better, and I just figured I would do it. I was a late cut by the Knicks that fall, '66. They had a couple no cuts signed, but to keep me available McGinty lined me up a deal with the Gorgetown Ghosts in the Allegheny Assoc. It was small time, but it was cool. I just wanted to play and there would be next year. In the Assoc. you played weekends all across Pa., going down to Jersey, Delaware, sometimes DC. I had a good year, was all-league; but in the fall the Knicks had everybody back, plus two first round picks, and I didn't even make camp. I was too small to play forward and too slow for guard in the bigs, and I knew it by then. But it was cool. I was doing what I wanted, playing ball, living the life, and I stuck with the Ghosts.

Now on the road with the Ghosts I'd run into a lot of guys I knew or played with or against in high school or college or someplace. They'd come up before a game, say hi, how you doing, ask me over. I never did run into Irving Ballard though. Guys from the Valley'd remember that jumpshot, some'd even remember "Soul Sister," but nobody knew what happened to him personally.

That was a very good line, you know. It was one of the great ones that said a whole book about time and place and how you live. You never forgot it. Irving Ballard, lying there on the grass, sweating, a quart of Schmidts. "You mean be a everybody." Over the years I used that line a lot. It said it just right for anybody I'd be hanging with, having a beer with, screwing around with. Those were the choices all right. Be an everybody. Not be one. All I could figure was maybe Irving Ballard took it to extremes.

Anyway, there I was 12 years later, far from Irving Ballard and the Center with another big game coming up. Us and the Suns. The play-offs three and three, the crunch coming. I had woke up in the middle of the night right in the blackest part and lain there for the longest time. It can be rough when you're half asleep like that. Your guard's down, and the doubts creep in like rats and gnaw at your weak spots. It wasn't the game that had me spooked, you understand. I had been through plenty of those. It was my roomie, Jojo, and his fucking robbery trip had me like that. That was where the weak spot was. It wasn't every night your roomie gets arrested for robbing some grocery and beating up an old man. It wasn't every night the cops are by, pawing through his room, tossing in a pile his cowboy boots, his Auto-Bar T-shirt, his Dylan, everything he had. I lay there on my back, rigid, eyes on the ceiling, hands behind my head. The blacks turned to greys and the greys to whites and other colors. I thought about the game—about Irving Ballard—about Joj, caught, facing time, pinned against it like a bug. Sometimes I thought it all must be a dream and that it must be coming to an end.

Leaving our bathroom you look down a narrow hall that opens into the living room. I walked down it, a towel wrapped around me, walking slow, sighting down the hall, the living room shaking at the end, getting bigger as I walked. We'd had a party after we'd beat Sunbury to tie the series, and we still hadn't cleaned. Scattered around the living room were pizza cartons with crust still in them and beer cans and a ton of butts and matches. Above it all, hanging limp, was a satin sheet on which some stews from Allegheny had stitched GO GHOSTS SPOOK THE SUNS. It was a mess, but I dug it. I dug the look of old parties and the smell. So much good energy went into getting it like that. I thought about Joj again and the old parties. Teardrop Lake Staffies. The Party the Beatles Didn't Come To. I remembered a lot of old parties and a lot of different people I had a lot of fun with, and damn if they all weren't someplace else.

I needed noise. I put the closest album on the stereo and floored the volume:

Let's spend the night together
For I need you more than ever.
Let's spend the night together, yeah.

It helped. The Stones scared the rats. I went into the kitchen and put on coffee. By the time it finished dripping, the phone was ringing. I thought about it, but I let it ring.

II

Visiting at the jail wasn't until afternoon. I didn't feel like hanging around our place so I took a ride into town. It wasn't a bad day. Bright and clear and crisp enough to bite. I was wearing a tan zipper jacket and an old red sweater and black levis and black Converse low cuts, taped to hold at the heels, and that cold just cut right through. I stalled through the ride down the Pike, not moving off the slow lane, not racing after green lights. I let the flow nibble away the time. I kept the radio loud so it filled my head.

I parked downtown and walked around a bit. I stared in the window of the second-hand store over behind the court. It was a place I liked, sitting in the shade of two tall elms, dark and calm and quiet. Me and Joj'd bought a black leather sofa there, and I'd bought a pepper mill and just last week a 78 of Louis Jordon and his Tympany Five doing "Open the Door, Richard:" but there were people inside so I didn't go in. Everything there was old and used and from somebody's life before, and I could feel kind of odd holding on, knowing that, feeling maybe I wanted it too. Sometimes when I found something I had long ago or that my folks did I felt really weirded out, and I just didn't like there being other people there to see.

I bought mustard pretzels off the guy at the corner, salty, lots of mustard, and I finished them off walking, wiping my fingers inside my pockets where it didn't show. I killed some time jiving a couple chicks outside the beauty college, bummed the Gazette off one of them, and looked through it for a story on the robbery; but there wasn't much. The sports section had a big spread on the game though. There were rosters and color and interviews with each coach. There was an old picture of me, palming two balls, and one of Chrispie, the Suns' top scorer. "NOAH RAEZOR LEADS GHOSTS," it said under mine. His just had his name and average.

I stopped by the porno store after that and looked at a couple of stroke books, half-wondering if somebody I knew from the road or someplace was gonna show up in the pictures, and then I walked around some more, and about noon I fell by Rover's. Tony Fish was behind the bar. "Hey, Raez," he yelled when I come in. "You gonna whip them bastards?"

"Ice cream, baby." I gave him a clenched fist. The old men at the bar nodded and smiled. I went into the back room. The Ghost's Tomb they called it. It was all fixed up with Gorgetown Ghost stuff. Gorgetown Ghost clippings and programs on the walls. Gold Ghost trophies and unies and scuffed balls signed by the guys who'd been big here once. Gorgetown was way up in the Poconos, a couple hundred miles from Pittsburgh and Philly, further from New York, and it didn't have much. Nobody in Gorgetown cared about football or baseball or the NBA or colleges. All they cared about was us. As heroes went, we were it, and the Tomb was the special place they gave us.

My hamburger came back extra thick, burnt on the outside, raw in the middle. I put on a lot of salt. I put salt and pepper on the fries and a lot of sugar in the coffee. People came over and said they felt bad about Jojo. I said thanks. They wished me a lot of luck with the game and told me not to let it get me down.

I had been there about a quarter hour when Rover, himself, sat down. "Raez," he said. "A real shame about Joj."

"Yeah. Say, when you gonna start putting meat in these things?"

"Up yours."

"I think I went through last night's *News*, and I still got half of it left."

"Listen, hot dog, I been talking to some of the boys at the station and just wanted to let you know your pal's ok."

"Thanks." I put down the rest of the burger. "I was going over there anyway."

"Well, while you were waiting so you don't worry. I figured you should know."

"Thanks a lot."

"Yeah, well, anything I can do, you know." He snapped his fingers, and one of the waitresses brought him coffee. She refilled mine. Rover watched me eat over the top of his cup. I didn't really feel like eating, but I figured the more I could do of what I usually did the better. "He really did it, huh?" Rover said. "Confidential, I mean."

"Far as I know."

"Crazy bastard. What, he need the money, huh?"

"No. He didn't need the money."

"Not the money." He thought about that. "What then?" I shrugged.

"Must of been something. He had to have a reason. I mean, hell, it's not like something you do for no reason. It's not farting up the wind for christsake."

"Yeah."

"The man robbed a fucking store."

I didn't say anything. I just repeated the words to myself all together and then one at a time. The Man Robbed A Fucking Store. The words appeared on the screen in my head, then puffed apart and blew away. It was sinking in.

"You ok? You look a little spacey."

"No. I'm cool."

"Terrific. It's a big one, right? Who knows. Maybe you win this one the town goes so fucking crazy the mayor pardons Jojo or something."

"Who knows."

"It could happen, right?"

"I kinda doubt it."

"Well, like you say, it could happen. It's worth thinking about. It sure beats the hell going out there all down and fucked over and getting your fucking ass whipped."

"Look," I said. "Nobody's planning on getting his ass whipped. You got a lot of bread on this or something?"

"Take it easy. I'm just rooting is all."

"Freddy Fan."

"Come on. You know me. Trying to pick you up is all."

"I mean what the fuck is going on. What the hell's everybody expect me to do. It's not just fucking everyday, is it?"

"Yeah. Sure. C'mon. Nobody meant nothing."

"Yeah," I said. "Christ, you'd think I was gonna blow up the fucking jail or throw the fucking game or I don't know what the fuck else. Man, I'm just trying to fucking deal with it, you know."

"Listen, I was wrong. Out of place."

"He was my friend, right?"

"Right."

"Well, ok, water over the dam. Beat the Suns, right?"

"Sure. Beat 'em." We shook hands. "See you later," Rover said. "Gotta see a man." He waved at two couples in a corner and headed back to the kitchen. I called the girl over to put some more hot in my cup.

I sipped my last cup of coffee and thought about it. It seemed right he had a reason. I sat there a long while, and then I remembered the Jersey turnpike and how I hate that fucking road. It's so dull, so all the same, and I been down it so many times I know every building I'll pass, every plant even. Last year we had this big snow, and Joj and I were sitting around, not knowing what to do, drinking some; and he said, "Hey, man, let's drive to New York." And we did. We stocked up on pills and six packs, and we drove to New York; and it was the best fucking trip I ever took. We couldn't do over 35, and we slipped all over the road, and sometimes when the wind shifted and blew across the road we couldn't see. But we made it all the way, and it was the best ride to New York ever. The more I thought about it, the more I figured he was after something like that.

III

The cell was 8 foot high and 8 foot deep and maybe 8 foot across. It was painted grey, all grey, one big prism of grey. You could smell that grey. You could taste it. It was fresh paint but already scarred by the bids for fame of its most recent inhabitants. I STUK IT UP DALE'S ASSHOLE, said the biggest.

In the back of the cell was a toilet with no lid. Riveted to the left hand wall were two steel slabs upholstered with thin mats. Jojo lay on the low one, his good suede jacket balled up for a pillow. The bulb in the walkway behind me threw the shadows from the bars against him. It threw them hard. "Hello, John Dillinger," I said. "How you doing?"

"Hey, Raez, how you been?" He rolled onto his side and rubbed his eyes. "Looks like I'll live."

"Terrific."

"Yeah. Me reign of terror's over." He shrugged and lit a smoke. "Yeah. They asked me some questions. I gave them some answers. Then we shot the shit about ball. Can you dig it? The crisis of me young life, and I'm talking ball. You got a lot of fans here, you know that? You are very well regarded."

"That's good to know." I watched him constant, like some part of me thought it wasn't going to be really Joj. Well, there was the brown hair and the smile and busted nose and all of him, I guess, I ever seen. Only the shadows from the bars were new.

"It was a slow night mostly," Joj said. "Besides me they only booked two drunks. I tried organizing some bar rattling, tried a little "'Nother Man Done Gone," but the drunks couldn't get it together. The guards said it was slow. They said they do better when it's hot or when there's a full moon. They were serious about the full moon shit. Something about the tides and body fluids." He took another hit on his cigarette. We both watched the smoke disappear.

There was a lot to talk about but nothing I could say. I walked down the walkway to the end. It wasn't far. One cell was empty. The drunks were in another, their belts curled like snakes on the walkway floor. At the end was an empty wall socket with cobwebs spun off it. In the web were dead husks of bugs and dust, just dust.

When I came back, Joj was sitting on the edge of the bunk. He licked his fingertips and ran his thumb across them Jerry Lucas-style. "What do you think, man?"

I laughed sadly. "I hate those fucking open questions."

"I know, man, but what do you think?"

"What can I say? I hate to see you in there like that."

He licked his fingers again. "I figure all I got to do is not let it get to me. Just keep my head someplace else and not let the fuckers run their trip on me. It don't have to go like they expect, you see what I mean?"

I nodded. I was thinking he was taking it pretty good. Better than me. It was bad seeing him there and not being able to do nothing.

"Yeah. It's just where your head's at. I mean, I can't pull much time. Christ, I'm a fucking first offender. Just a young boy led astray. I'll be out quick, Raez. I knew you'd see it, man. A lot of guys wouldn't, but I knew you would."

I still didn't say anything. My hands were on those bars, testing hard against them like I was doing isometrics. The bars were thick and stiff and damn cold, and there wasn't any give. Not one inch. "What the hell are you doing in there?" I said. I must of said it funny.

Jojo looked at me like he'd been hit. I don't know if how I sounded scared him for himself or it just put him off, me coming on like Johnny Judgment. I wasn't going to ask though. I already asked what I had to even if he couldn't tell me.

Jojo came over and stood by the bars. He put his hands on them over mine like we were two kids choosing up for first pick. "Look, man," he said. "It's gonna be all right. Same as always. What happens, happens; and it's no big thing."

"It shouldn't of happened, Joj," I said. "Shit, something's wrong. You shouldn't be there, man. It's fucked. It's fucked, that's all."

"Come on now, be cool. It ain't the end, man. Life ain't no book. If it is hell, I got plenty pages left."

"OK," I said after a minute. "I guess there's just lots I don't figure to happen, and this, sure as shit, is one."

Jojo smiled. "You'll be all right. Me too. Listen, there any of the good Panamanian shit around?"

I shrugged like I didn't know.

"See if you can score some. Bake it in a pie, man. Fuck that saw shit."

I said all right. I still felt bad though. There he was: my roomie, my friend. We'd been through all this shit together. We dug the same scenes; we hated the same too. I knew Joj was boss. I knew it, man. There were all these ass holes around, and Jojo wasn't one, and now, what the fuck, there he was, where he was; and they weren't; and if it meant anything at all it was like I said. Things were fucked.

I rode out to town to where you could see across the flats to the Poconos climbing through the haze. I sat there a while, looking at them, seeing where the mines had been cut in and the timber strippped. The timber was coming back though, and nobody expected the mines to last the decade. Already the town was getting shaky-crazy thinking about it. Every week, it seemed, somebody shot somebody down or ran a car off a road and down a gulch like nothing mattered. The people'd been born here and stayed without thinking, and now the mines where they mostly worked were going and with them most of their reasons. The timber was creeping back and deer were feeding in backyard gardens, and the people wondered about wolves coming and bears and who knew what. Indians, maybe, scalping settlers and eating hearts.

Being a Ghost, I usually didn't care. I played some ball, rode my bike, smoked a little this and drank a little that. I partied. I hiked into the woods. I never figured I'd end up any place like Gorgetown. Shit, I never figured I'd end up. A little more speed, a couple more inches, it might of been different. But what the hell. I knew who I was and what I had. In the league I was in I was a draw. The refs gave me the extra step and let me grab.

I sat there and watched the sun move across the mountains. Seeing mountains felt good. It felt solid. You could count on them being there for you. I'd hike into the mountains a lot and sit. It was cool and quiet, and in the pines I was the smallest thing around. After a while I put Jojo out of my mind. I had that game to think about.

IV

Our home court was in an old armory across from the bus depot. I got there early, parked out back, and changed. I wanted to beat the crowd and the noise and all the build up. I like it that way. It meant it would grow up around where I already was. I wouldn't be plunging into it from someplace else. I laced my sneakers tight and pulled the grey Ghost t-shirt over my head. The red 13 rode my front and back.

The floor had its dead spots, and there was always a chance the balcony overhang would slap down a shot from too deep in the corner; but I was alone, and the feel was nice. I jogged a couple laps to loosen up. I went around and around, stretching out, my sneakers squeaking on the boards, my feet smacking the floor; and not one other sound.

I moved out onto the court, booming my dribble through the empty hall. There was no one else. There was everything I needed though: me and the ball and a hoop to put it through. It was simple. It was beautiful. Some guys dog it when they're alone. Not me. No sense making it easy for yourself. You've got to toughen up. You've got to get it all going. You get it going, and it keeps on coming. You get it all going, and it keeps on coming, and you keep it on going, pushing it, driving it, doing it like there's nothing else. You know what you're doing and how to do it and when it's done. You're jumping, bouncing all the time; you're driving and crashing hard; and your hair's down your forehead, and your sweat stings your eyes, and your breath rips your lungs. But you do it. You do it hard enough and often enough, and you win. Get it on, and, man, nobody can stop you but you.

I lobbed in one-handers and tapped in follows. I kicked in jumpers, pushed in hooks, swept in shovel shots. I had it all. I moved into the corner, rocked back off a shoulder fake, and swished a one hander. I moved out a little further, faked left, dribbled once right, and banked a jumper. I went back into the corner, faked to the base line, and drove toward the key, hooking off the drive. I had it all.

In time the armory began to fill. The kids arrived, the old men, the couples. At first they were drops, then patches, then great globs of color across the stands. Smoke began to drift toward the ceiling, hover around the lights, and sift between the banners that hung straight down. The armory began to warm and buzz, to almost move. I was still alone on the court. I took my shots. I followed them up. Each time I hit an air horn blasted. A colored kid came out of the stands and stood under the basket and fed the ball back to me.

"Bet you can't make it from there, man," he'd say.

I'd hit it.

"Bet you can't make three in a row."

I'd do it.

"You ain't no Dr. J., man."

"Shit, he ain't me."

When I was stoked up so good it couldn't burn out, I ambled off the court and stood in the runway near the locker room door. The light caught columns of the rising-falling-turning dust and made them glitter like even they were valuable. The court floor shone like a field of gold. And the glow in me seemed its mate.

I joined the team's charge out of the locker room, and we split into two lines for lay-ups. The Suns were already out, running a four line drill off a double post in their yellow sailor boy warm-ups, lots of chatter, lots of behind the back and between the legs. We just did our two lines. The guys who could stuff, stuffed; the guys who couldn't, didn't. We took our lay-ups from the right, from the left, then down the middle. We took jumpshots from the line. We made a semi-circle around the basket, 20 feet out, and shot, alternating two guys under to 'bound, switching guys onto the line to shoot fouls. Funny, but I never been in one of those fancy drills. Ever since junior high my teams did it this way. Counting summer leagues, it must of been a million times I've done it. I still always looked to see if my shot went in. I still got pissed if it didn't.

All the while the excitement built. The place would sell out for sure. Three thousand three oh three, the announcer would say. They would applaud themselves. They were clapping now. They were stamping on the wooden stands. GO. GO. GO. GO. GO. GO. GO. The organist ripped into an up-tempo "Ghost Riders in the Sky." The guy in the white sheet raced up and down along the edges of the court, shrieking and ringing his bell. The cheerleaders in the

Ghost sheet mini-skirts jumped up and down, did splits and hand stands. GO. GO. GO. GO. GO. GO. GO. A big bass drum went boom, boom, boom.

I came out for my turn at the line and saw the five Sun starters. They had pulled out of their drill and were standing at mid-court staring at us real hard. A psych job. What jive. Whatever they were trying got buried by the drum and air horns and the chanting, stomping crowd. GO GHOSTS GO. GO GHOSTS GO. I hit five-for-five. The buzzer sounded, clearing the court.

The coach called us together. He said some words. He didn't have to say anything. We'd split ten games with the Suns this year. The playoffs were three and three. Everybody knew everybody. Some of those guys I'd played one thousand one times. Fitch would muscle underneath. Chrispie'd cheat off early on the break. Gort looked for the drive. We would run and they would run and everybody'd hit the boards and go for the ball. Even our out-of-bounds plays were the same. There was nothing to say about it. All we had to do was win. That was all we had to do.

They announced the line-ups. We slapped hands and asses and said go get'em. So'd the Suns. A recorded anthem played.

At the tap I lined up against Juicey Fitch, a black guy with a shaved head, goatee and muscles in his arms like melons in a sock. He started muscling me already, fighting over who stood where on the circle.

"Be serious," I said.

"Too bad 'bout your chicken shit buddy, mother," said Fitch.

We got the tap. We started moving back and forth on the shiny floor between the red and blue lines. The familiar patterns formed. The criss-crossed forwards. The double picks. The rolls toward the hoop. The channeled movement without the ball. I put myself into the flow, the loops, the arcs, the circling, the straight, charging drives. I ran the patterns for the millionth zillionth time, feeling absolutely perfect, trying to make number one million one zillion and one the best I'd done it ever. I was doing what I wanted and there were people trying to stop me and most of the time they didn't. Most of the time they couldn't. We went back and forth. We went up and down. Full speed. The whole world was in those red and blue lines. All of it. The crowd's roar was as constant and unnoticed as air. The horns and the drum were far away. I moved in my own familiar, chosen, vital world, and nothing else mattered.

"Too bad about your buddy, man," Juicey Fitch said. "I hear the fucker's done it this time."

"You want to suck my what?"

We went up and down the court, giving the ball up, getting it back, taking the good shot. Fitch was using his muscle a lot. He was using his mouth too. "He wasn't much good anyway. I hear they only kept him on account of you. They got somebody cuter for you now, punk?"

The first quarter ended quick. It had started, and then it was done. The buzzer caught me blind. I had forgot they had them, I was that into the play. I couldn't believe it. I had hit some jumpers and scored some underneath, but there was so much else I could of done. I was still wondering what happened to the fucking first quarter when I noticed the second one was half gone. I called for the ball. I didn't get it. Shit, give me the ball. I was still thinking about it when Fitch blew by me, driving, which he never did. Gort stole the in-bounds pass, missed the cripple, and Fitch, the fucker, stuffed the follow-up while I stood there cursing. Next time down I threw up a one-hander that almost missed the gym. The Suns scored again, cutting our lead to one, and I tried dribbling through two guys and ended up kicking the ball out of bounds off my knee. The coach called time.

"You ok, Raezor?"

"Terrific, man."

"You look terrific."

I wiped the sweat away with a towel. A couple little fuckups and he was coming apart. Move the ball was what he knew. Hit-the-open-man shit. I walked away, back onto the court. Let's get it on, I thought. Come on. Come on. I stood in the center circle, staring up at the lights. The crowd roar began to build. I was in the exact center. The coach had the four other guys around him, but he was just standing there with his hands loose at his sides. The Suns were in a little ring around their coach's waving finger. Everybody was waiting for something, but, man, I was ready. I was in the center, bouncing on my toes. I thought I'd do a handstand. I thought of playing the whole game on my hands. The ghost flapped around and around, clanging his bell.

Fitch picked me up in back court. Stuck his chest right into me. "Any word on your buddy? They get Melvin Belli for the sucker? Who you get to wipe your ass now?"

It was a good game. It had all you want. Good pace. Good contact.
Both teams were working good. Everybody out there was playing,
and the refs were letting us play. I was playing good. Fitch too. We'd
go up three or four. They'd bring us back to one. They never got it
even, and they never got ahead. We went up and down, moving the
ball, switching, playing the good D. It seemed there was no reason
not to go on like that forever. Except the clock. Overhead it was
running down.

The heat I'd stoked in warm-ups was still with me. It was my fuel.
It had me pushing off a little stronger, grabbing harder, putting out
more totally than I ever had before. I couldn't of done more. It was
perfect, so perfect. I felt so good, slid along the good goody goodness
of it all. And suddenly, at some point, I don't know when, I'm not
sure why, it had me someplace I had never been. I was still in the
game, isolated from what was outside it, but I had gone one step
more—I was isolated in it. I still made the right moves, still executed as I wished, but I was some place else. While the crowd
roared, the drum banged, the ghost flapped, I slipped away. The
effort in the game didn't matter. The pain didn't. I left the pace and
the noise and the smoky arena. I could still see people, see the ghost,
the coach. Juicey Fitch still guarded me. I felt his body against mine.
I heard its words. But it all was distanced. I was up in the lights with
the smoke. I hung on the back walls and twisted in the air with the
dust. I was everywhere, and I was, too, encapsulated, contained,
removed.

We went up and down the court. I kept calling for the ball. I'd put
it on the floor and go to the hoop. I'd call for it and do it again. Fitch
kept trying to hold me out. He used his hands. He leaned. He gave
me a knee. He still thought he was right there. He still thought he
was guarding me. He was going crazy that he couldn't.

I turned my mind on Fitch. I zeroed in on him like some death ray
and waited for him to crumple, char, dissolve. I turned the dials with
words. You prick. He fucking thought he was still guarding me.

The air horns shrieked. The drums banged out of control. The
mascot ghost ran and waved his arms into a whitish blur. The crowd's
noise swelled past all restraint. It did not leap from lungs. It dangled
bodies beneath it. Fitch and I banged together. We pounded elbows
and knees. He'd push me when I'd go up for a shot and try to
submarine me. I ran him into a basket support on a drive. We went
up and down.

Coming out of a scramble for a loose ball I felt my arm sting. I looked. Red lines. I wiped my arm on my shorts. The line refilled. I licked them clean. I licked them again. Fitch grinned, fist clenched. The blood dripped off me and fell on the floor. Somebody else ran through it. That was me down there. The prick'd torn me up. With us up one, Fitch picked off an offensive rebound and spun to go back up. He was inside and going up, but I got there. I got up there. I got my hand on the ball, solid, for the stuff. Our muscles locked, and we froze, suspended in the air at the height of our jumps, each with one hand on the ball, the ball pinned between us, holding us together. We fell back to earth, Fitch first. The whistle blew to end the play and start another jump, but as Fitch relaxed, I didn't. My arm followed through, drove down, came off the ball, and crashed into his black face below his eye. Fitch fell hard. I watched him, heard him hit, heard the wild yells build. Fitch got up. He charged. I hit him full in the face with the ball from two feet, and he fell again and slid sillily across the hardwood floor in his satin undershorts. I was about to find out how hard I could kick with sneakers on when a couple guys grabbed me and pulled me away.

I took a last look around at it all. The teams swirled together, grey and gold. The coach was on his feet, red-faced, going ashy grey. I was still looking when the ref, a skinny guy with acne, threw me out. Stuff was coming from the balcony. An egg came out of the lights and landed near Fitch, splattering him. I wanted no trouble. I was done. The ref was right. They always were. I shouldn't play any more. I went down the runway to the locker room. Here came another egg.

The locker room was cold. I sat on the hard bench between two damp towels, my uniform on the floor in a pile. My breathing racked my chest. My muscles shook with tiny shudders, fairy wings. Sweat poured off me and dropped to the floor. I licked the red streaks on my arm. If I drank enough water, I would get back the sweat. If I ate, I'd get the blood. I could put on my clothes. Overhead the feet pounded on the floor. The half was almost over. I didn't know the score.

V

I went out the side door into the alley without looking back. It was very dark. A cat on a garbage can hissed. Fuck you, cat. Just fuck you.

There was a Howard Johnson's on the corner with a counter up front and dining room behind. I took a booth in the dining room and leaned back against the wall, my feet on the booth. I thought a lot. About the game. Joj. It meant a lot, you know, having somebody you could look at every day and see they were ok, and read there you were too because you did it all the same. There's a power there from being so and saying fuck the rest. It can go on like that a while, maybe longer. Then, say, somebody eats too much acid and turns their head to mush and somebody else gets shit face and dead in a wreck and, say, just say, your roomie, the best one, the last one, you and him drawn up like wagons in a circle, gets busted for something so crazy and weird and small it's fucking nothing at all. All of a sudden you start remembering you own ankles you tore up and your skids, and you know, you just know, it's not going to work out, it's over, and that it never does for no one.

I had two cheeseburgers, french fries, coffee. When I finished I remembered something we used to do in junior high. I put the check in my pocket and walked by the cashier to the counter. I ordered a double-decker chocolate cone and went back to her. I gave her the stub for the cone and paid for it. Outside, I threw it and the other check away.

Then I went home, the mountains a huge, dark backdrop for the ride. Maybe I would go up there tomorrow. Maybe the day after. Mist floated in the air. As I moved, it brushed my face like tears. At the front door I thought I heard somebody. "Hello," I called. "Hello. Anybody there?" There wasn't anybody there. I hadn't thought there would be. All there was were the remnants of the party, us, ticked one day closer to the end.

ODE TO SENILITY

by PHILLIP LOPATE

from THE DAILY ROUND (Sun Press)

nominated by Sun Press

The ultraviolet night-light in the florist's
seen from a bedroom window, 6:15
Hour of furry dawn, no one is up yet
I leave the woman's house before her daughter wakes up
I wish I could tell this girl I mean her mother no harm
The woman goes back to sleep, I close the latch behind me
I am old, old, old
I start to fall asleep in the taxi
I climb the brownstone steps with a full bladder
With one gesture I fling off my coat and open the door
I am tired and curl up on my bed
I am realizing my lifelong ambition, to grow old

I want to be eighty and have people whisper about me
in gatherings: He was a Communist,
he was the first to take acid
the earliest to recognize the System was rotten
And look how serenely he carries himself
such vibrant eyes   how well-preserved
these men of conviction remain!

Let them think I had a crazy youth
that blondes in furs beat down my door

I want to be eighty and tell anecdotes
the same five anecdotes
about the time I outwitted the tax service

I want to be old and tiresome and able
to forget those caresses
turning self-reflective on the thigh
forget the daughter in the next room

I know enough about the light behind the shadow behind the light
behind the marble on the terrace in the morning
and on everyone's faces

let me grow senile enough to watch
with gumless charity the pretty woman
squirming on a man's lap in the empty bus—
thinking,
Who are all these children who call me grandfather?
I don't remember marrying.
Which one of them did I finally love now,
Which one of them decided to put up with me?

VESTIGES

fiction by MEREDITH STEINBACH

from PLOUGHSHARES

nominated by PLOUGHSHARES

It is an early autumn sunday evening. Still warm and Michael has not made love to me since August. Each night he sleeps as he sleeps tonight, facing the window with his knees drawn up away from me. This lack of attention is not, he says, because he doesn't want me; it is, he says, because he can't.

In the dark I bend my body around him, listening to the yellow leaves curling against the window screen. His buttocks are warm against my thighs and pelvis. My face rests between his shoulder blades, the cotton cloth of his pajama fluttering against my mouth each time I breathe. I put my arm around him; he clutches my fingertips while he sleeps.

Together we have grown self-conscious. We worry together and separately. I ask myself: What changes passion to impotence? What changes it back again?

Last week Michael thought he had an answer. Wednesday evening at the theatre he invited two strangers to our house for dinner. I told him I wasn't interested in anyone else.

"Stop thinking about yourself," he said. "You have to think about me now. Think about me."

I think about him all the time. I remember the day when we were late for dinner, tacking back and forth across the channel, waiting for the man in the red hat to raise the bridge over Hood Canal. Michael used to drop anchor every time we came in sight of him, whether we had passage through the bridge or not. "It's the Hood Canal Lust," he said.

I wondered if the bridgemaster would be disappointed now to see our boat in motion, no longer floating captainless while we went below into the cabin. I watched the cars from the Bremerton ferry snake over the span and into the forested hills.

"It's times like this I want to chop down that mast," he said, scowling at the speck of red in the arched stone tower.

"I'll get you a canoe for Christmas."

"You do and you'll paddle it." He wrapped a piece of rope around his hand.

"I like the waiting just fine." I said. "You're the man in the rush."

"Dr. DiCori will be holding dinner again."

"He knows how long it takes us to get there," I said. "Why don't you read if you can't enjoy me or the scenery."

"Next time, we drive," he said. His fingers tensed, released, gripped the tiller again, turning white against the grain of the wood.

"Fine. *You* drive. I've had better company on a bus."

"Take the tiller," he said and went below to get his book. "Listen to this," he said, reading from one of his medical texts. "Terratoma—"

"I don't want to hear about those tumors again."

"You do this one. It's just gruesome enough. This tumor starts in the ovary all by itself. When they remove it, guess what they find. Teeth. Spontaneous generation of cells. They've found full sets of teeth in women's ovaries. And hair."

I've got teeth in my belly too, I thought. Look what happens to a woman without sex in her life. I was thinking about asking Dr. DiCori about it. He was not a young man but he took an interest in the interns that was uncommon among the deans at the medical college. Michael liked him; he called him The Sage.

"Why don't you tell Dr. DiCori about it?" I asked him.

"I'm sure Dr. DiCori knows all about terratomas, Zara."

"Michael, I'm talking about—"

"That's just what I want, Dr. DiCori taking me into the conference room each morning to say, 'Well, Dr. O'Dea, did you get it up?' "

I reached for his hand but he moved it away, running it along the guyline.

"It couldn't hurt to consult someone, Michael. I don't like us being so nasty to each other."

"I already did, Zara."

I waited.

"I will not see a psychiatrist."

In a tavern six months later, Michael confided in someone else. After five margueritas, he told the whole bar. We had been sitting in the corner, Michael touching my hair. As I went into the bathroom, I saw him stand up, pushing his way to the front. When I closed the door, he began to shout: "Hey there, you drunken anemics! Listen up!" The room fell into silence. I cowered; I ran the water so no one would come in. "I'll give you a guess how long it's been since old Doc here could get it up." When I came to fetch him off the top of the bar, they were all offering to accompany me home.

In the car I cried, humiliated.

"How do you think I feel," he said.

"Let me hold you," he says when we get into bed. Still he says these things. "Let me touch you." When I am ready for him, fear gnaws him like an animal, devours his confidence from the inside out. "Not tonight," he says abruptly. He doesn't need to say these words.

"You're tired," I said the first few times. "Get some sleep." I said it nervously, embarrassed for us both.

"Don't worry," I tell him whenever he mentions it. "Everything will be all right before you know it." But there is no end: every action, every item of apparel seems a lure or some form of denial. Everything I say spins carefully away from this.

I am growing ragged with these changes, questioning now my own body and my mind, wondering if this could be my fault. Everyone must notice it. Even the man at the soda fountain commented on my state. He set my lime phosphate on the counter and looked at me. "Hey, you don't look so plucky tonight." He wiped his hands on his stained white apron. "In the afternoon you should lie down with your feet up and savor your sleep. Elevating your paddies keeps the swelling out of those ankles, puts the blood in your brain."

"Thanks," I said. "I'll try that." I took a newspaper from the rack and pretended to read.

"You've got wear and tear marks under your eyes. Bad circulation, exhaustion contribute to that."

The blond boy, who sits at the far end of the counter each night reading his French, looked over at me and winked.

When Father asked us to move inland and live with him at the lake, Michael was determined. "Are you sure?" I asked. "We could stay here and buy our own house. You could start your own practice."

"No," he said. "Someday the house will be ours anyway. And your father needs company."

I liked to watch them going off to the clinic together, coming home again to work outside: Father, in the garden, hoeing and stooping over weeds, digging furrows around them, twisting them meticulously from the soil, careful not to leave any roots behind; Michael climbing ladders and painting window trims, while Father stood below, directing.

At night they sat in the den at opposite ends of the horse-hair sofa, drinking brandy and listening to the waves. "To catch a wall-eyed pike the right way," Father said one evening after dinner, "you must have caught one before. The eyes are the secret. Catch your first one with some ordinary bait, remove its eyes, and you've got it made."

I remembered Father holding the eye of the pike, hooking the small black elipse with a quick jab as if he were suturing a wound. "You have to be careful not to puncture the pupil," he said, "or the silver will run out."

"Those eyes are like ornaments on the bottom, Michael," Father said, studying his face. He filled his glass again. "The other pikes go wild."

When I was small, I asked Father what happened to the fish, the ones without eyes.

"Oh, those." His fishing line whined as he reeled the slack out of it. "I swear it doesn't hurt the fish, Zara," he said.

Father feels this tension now between Michael and myself. He is uncomfortable, afraid that we will end our marriage and leave him alone again. Everytime we take the boat out, he moves in his round aging way down to the dock in time to ask. "Think you'll catch your wild-eyed phantom today?"

"The only wild-eyed phantom I've had anything to do with this summer," Michael said last time with a discernible note of betterness, "is your daughter." Then he pushed off from the landing and began to fume, "Won't he ever stop asking about that God damn fish?"

Still we are attempting our diversions, our small recreations, pretending everything is the same. Monday I laid out the table cloth in the sand beneath a scrubpine. I set out the things from the basket. "We're going to have a good time," I had told Mrs. McGehry that morning, interrupting her ironing to help me get ready. "Put in the good china," I said "and the lace napkins. I'll get dressed."

While Michael rummaged in his bait box, I set the apricots in a flowered bowl. I put the salmon we smoked last winter next to a row of wheat bread on a plate. "Let's not cook right now," I said. "Not in this heat."

Michael cut a branch from one of the trees and twisted it into the sand. He threw out a line and put the rod in the fork of the stick. "That's fine with me," he said "Is that all there is to eat?" He sounded disgusted with me.

"No," he said. "That's enough for me." He pulled the wine in from where I had weighted it among the rocks in the water. It was a little after one o'clock when we finished it. The line wavered a bit as the bait bobbed against the embankment. Michael was going to sleep.

Tonight the Vincents are coming to dinner. They drive over the hills while Michael makes his preparations, the wife wrapped in her leather jacket, the husband whistling the tune he whistles when he is nervous or discontented. The sons sulk because they must come along, the young one saying—I don't know why we have to go too, Mom. He whines. The other mutters to him.

I know they will come this way. The car rising over the bumps the road crews are packing and oiling on the highway that runs from their house in the village to ours.

I have seen Ellie Vincent only once, sitting in the lounge of the Bernhardt Dinner Theatre, flexing orange legs in the fluorescent lighting.

"You look like sisters," her husband Gerald said when Michael introduced us. He pointed to Ellie and then to me.

We surveyed each other, staring like purchasers viewing a horse. She was hipless; her breasts were small like an adolescent's. She was very tall. We shook our heads.

"Look at the faces," Gerald said. Michael looked intently at this woman sitting on the settee by the grand piano. She brushed her hair up and away from her neck. It fell like the silk fringing on a coverlet.

"Yes," Michael said. "It's amazing."

One evening Michael accompanied me to the pharmacy. "I don't see why you're always coming here," he said.

"They make good sodas," I said. "Would you rather I went to the bar?"

He pointed at the college student who was looking at me over his French. "Who's that?" he asked.

"How should I know?"

Yesterday I watched Michael checking Mrs. McGehry's house-cleaning, examining the corners for dust. "I want that table set up right," he told her, as if she had never laid out forks before. He didn't tell her that we didn't know the Vincents or that her cooking was part of his plan.

I told him I was going downtown to buy some things at the drugstore; I asked him if he wanted anything. He was rearranging the magazines, placing the New Yorkers on top. "For Christ's sake," I said.

His mouth turned to a smirk. "An afternoon tryst with that kid again?"

"That's not my tactic. It's yours."

I came right back looking forward to a long soak in the tub. Suspended on porcelain animal feet, the bath fills. The water rushes out the overflow drain; it foams around my neck. It is an hour until the Vincents will arrive. I soap the insides of my thighs. We are not alike, I tell myself. If Ellie Vincent and I were to walk together toward the square, skimming arm in arm, no one would mistake us for sisters. No one would say, "I see your sister was in town last week."

The Vincents have their own problems. I could see it in the way Gerald looked at her, ready to grit his teeth or bite down on the insides of his sallow cheeks, each time she smiled at Michael.

I could hear him tapping gently at the door while the water ran hot around my feet. "Come in, Michael," I told him. He put the toilet cover down and straddled it, watching me. He pushed his mustache down as he always does, forefinger and thumb extended to each side. He shaped his whiskers with his fingertips and announced our guests' early arrival.

"No hurry," he said, putting out his hand. "Your father is doing the entertaining."

"Oh dear."

"Relax," he said. "They like him. Wait until you see what she's wearing. She has on someone's flapper dress."

I asked him what he thought of that. I watched for some indication of his plans for the evening.

"Ruffles. It has ruffles down the front." He hated ruffles and I smiled at him. "Lavender," he said and frowned. He hated that, too, and I felt a little better.

"You look pretty there," he said. "All bubbled." He pushed up his sleeves as he leaned over and kissed me on the mouth. He rubbed the soap onto a cloth, sudsing the terry nap, running it around each breast.

"Will you rinse me off?" I asked. "Nibble a little bit?"

"I have soap on my nose," he said. "Wipe if off." I took the towel from the ring beside the tub. I wiped his face, his temples, his cheekbones. "Stand up," he said. "I'll dry you."

"Suds in your navel, too," he said, using a corner of the towel. "Your tufts are matted down." I watched him gently rubbing me. He put his cheek up to my belly; he pulled me close to him. "Lovely, lovely one," he said.

"Do you want to get in the bath with me?" I asked. He looked up and I watched his eyes changing.

"I can't," he said and let go of me. He sat down again. Slowly he dried his arms. "Zara—" He rubbed his arms up and down. "I'm attracted to that woman downstairs." He said it very quietly.

"Oh," I said. I put on my bathrobe; I covered myself.

"Gerald is very nice. You could like him." Michael moved only his eyes toward me when he talked as if this lack of movement were an act of penitence.

"I might not want him."

"I know that," he said. "Why don't you get dressed and come downstairs." The door closed between us. I could hear his voice in the living room. Suddenly he was feeling very cheerful, but I could not make out what he said.

I opened the window onto the garden where I could hear her children calling to each other. The twigs snapped as the boys bounded through the leaves, leaping into the warm autumn air, sailing the red soccer ball over the little brown shingles of the summerhouse. The oldest boy hurled the ball as if it were a discus, extending his arm to one side and whirling his body to obtain momentum.

I put on my clothes now thinking: Why is it no good? Ellie Vincent's laughter rises through the airvents as I put on my long green dress. That lady looks like a flapper, he said. I braid my hair into several plaits. I braid them like my mother wore them; I wind them around my head. All I can remember about Gerald is that I do not like his eyes or the way his skin shadows under evening lights. I hear the screen door slamming. They are going down to the beach. I will not join them; I can't.

As I leave the house, I can see them. Their limbs are long and red in the sunset: Father building his round fires of driftwood, Michael holding the woman against him in the water, Gerald looking up at the house from the beach. Her sons reach for the red woman in the water. The woman they say looks like me.

I walk past the hedges unnoticed, past brown seeded bushes at corners, past the gardens uprooted and waiting for winter, past old women nodding behind the miniscule squares of screens on their peeling white porches. I take off my sandals in the schoolyard and sit on the wooden seat of the swing, pressing my feet in the dust, thinking about Michael and me.

I remember our first year together; I remember Seattle.

"The Coast Guard gives you twenty-eight minutes to survive in that water," Michael said. "It's forty degrees."

"How much time do I have out here in the air?" I asked him.

The wind bellied the mainsail out full above us. The jib was up, the boat keeling over so far I was nearly upright, standing on the port railing with my back braced against the deck.

"I could never take anyone else out on a day like this," he said.

"Why not?"

"They're scared."

"What for?" I asked him. "There are worse things than drowning."

"They think I'm a lunatic taking the boat out in December."

"No," I said. "You're hardly that."

It was half an hour before we arrived at the cover on the other side of the Sound. He dropped anchor and I watched the chain spinning out while he secured the tiller and lowered the sails. Below in the cabin he apologized about the lack of a heater; he lit the cookstove to make coffee for me.

"A blanket?" I asked.

No, he always sailed alone in the winter; he didn't need one, he said.

"What's this?" I pushed at the tarpaulin roll lying on one of the bunks.

"Canvas top."

"Fine," I said and began to take off my clothes.

"My God. What are you doing?"

"Unroll that tarp. Don't just stand there." I took off everything.

"It's freezing out here."

"That's obvious to me," I said.

The boat was rocking hard in the wake of a tug going up the channel. I could hear the churning of motors. "I refuse," he said, "to take off my T-shirt."

"OK. Hurry."

"You have good ideas," he told me, drinking more coffee in the marina that evening, warming his hands on the cup. He looked out at his boat in its mooring, snapped tight at its edges, secured under its tarp.

At the drugstore the boy was murmuring his foreign phrases, biting the end of his cigarette. "I could help you with your French,"

I said and sat down beside him. I needed someone to talk with. A companion while Michael made love to a flapper, lifted her lavender dress.

He lived in a room with a fireplace, the mirror rising about it surrounded by wood to the ceiling. "Non-functional" he said, "but it appeals to me." He put his keys on the mantle beside a picture of his mother, her blonde hair curling like his, curling like the soft white hairs on his knuckles.

He closed the door and sat down on the edge of his cot, spreading out mimeographed sheets on the Indian print spread. I pulled the drapes open and sat in the window, my eyes falling on his books, Flaubert after Flaubert; I started to cry, startling him. "It's nothing," I said. "I'm just starting my period. Don't worry. I'm just being silly of course."

"It's all right if you cry." He pressed my face to his shoulder; he undressed me.

It was awkward, the boy rising above me, nothing quite working. "Roll onto your back," I finally said. I lowered myself onto him, touching the hairs on his chest, gripping his arms as I moved.

"I knew you were beautiful," he said. His eyes rolled back before we'd barely begun. He disappointed himself.

"Don't worry," I said. "It's always awkward the first time two people are together."

The boy held me on top of him, stroking my hair where it fell over my back onto his arms, stroking in this way both of us. My knees were pressed to his sides. He had comforted me; I told him that.

"I've never slept with a woman who was bleeding before." A small muscle twitched in his neck.

"There's nothing wrong with that," I said quietly. I called him lover and kissed him. I lifted myself away from him then. His penis and belly were covered with blood. I had never seen so much blood on a man before. He looked up at me. "I'll wipe you off," I said, not knowing what else to say. He swallowed and looked away.

The Vincents were gone when I came home and Michael was in the den drinking. We spent the rest of the night going to the sideboard, pouring each other more, not wanting to speak. In the morning before Father was awake we took the small rowboat onto the lake. The sun was beginning to rise as Michael rolled his sleeves. He pushed his hat back onto the crown of his head, saying nothing.

He dipped the oars into the crimson water, easing himself back and forth, pushing us through the reeds and mosses at the shoreline, steering us into open water.

Halfway across the lake I took the oars, marking our direction by centering the ruddermount just below the topmost peak of our house, stopping now and then to hand the bottle back and forth. The public bathhouse sat at the edge of our property and I could see where the children would soon be diving, their parents sunning on the great concrete stairs that ran the span of the cover and descended into the sand.

"I slept with the boy,'" I said. If I had not been drinking, I would never have told him. He took a small minnow from the bucket and hooked it. "I was lonely," I said, "and you were with her."

He reeled in a few inches of line, pulling the fish close to the tip of the pole. "No," he said, "I wasn't." He studied the fish a long while then, and I asked him what he was thinking.

"Ellie Vincent," he said, swinging the pole behind us and out to the side. He cast the line and we watched the little fish skimming out over the water. It was barely visible when it fell.

THE PURE LONELINESS

by MICHAEL RYAN

from AMERICAN POETRY REVIEW

nominated by Michael Hogan

Late at night, when you're so lonely
your shoulders lean to the center of your body,
you call no one and you don't call out.

This is dignity. This is the pure loneliness
that made Christ think he was God.
This is why lunatics smile at their thoughts.

Even the best moment, as you slip
half-a-foot deep into someone you like,
sinks through the loneliness in it

into the loneliness that's not. If you believe
in Christ hanging on the cross, his arms spread
as if to embrace the Father he calls

who is somewhere else, you still might hear
your own voice at your next great embrace
thinking *loneliness in another can't be touched,*

like Christ's voice at death answering himself.

MEDICINE BOW

by RICHARD HUGO

from GRAHAM HOUSE REVIEW

nominated by Nona Balakian, Mark Vinz and GRAHAM HOUSE REVIEW

This is the way the road bent then, wide and sullen
across baked earth and I was with two bums
I'd picked up outside Meeteesee. That was a day
I thought being kind was important because the world
that summer was dust and rejection, and banners
of welcome in Red Lodge hung limp. I was drunk.
Heat soured the sky. The day would come I vowed
when I would fight. I bought a room for the bums.
The next day I gave them both money in Loveland
and waved goodbye and drove off smug as the rich.

How many years ago was that? What songs played out
miles of what should have been, on whatever station
the radio found leaking through acres of cactus?
What happened that day in Medicine Bow. Sudden snarl
of the woman running the motel. The knife I kept
under my pillow that night, convinced that here
at last I'd found the source of all evil, the final
disgrace, world ending a way no poet predicted.

My Buick was yellow then. This one is green and zips
to Laramie easy. The whole business that day
in Medicine Bow and Medicine Bow seem silly.
It may not have been here at all. The brown block
hotel seems familiar, but it may be the road, the way
it bends into town is wrong. Denver stations
are coming in clear and that time I got nothing.
When you drive fast, hay seems to fly.

𝆏 𝆏 𝆏

LAUGHTER AND PENITENCE

essay by OCTAVIO PAZ

from ANTAEUS

nominated by Harold Brodkey, Carll Tucker, Nona Balakian and ANTAEUS

AT DAWN, A SHIVER runs through objects. During the night, having melted into the shadow, they have lost their identity; now, somewhat hesitantly, the light is recreating them. I can already vaguely make out that that beached boat, on whose mast a charred parrot nods sleepily, is the sofa and the lamp; that bullock lying slaughtered amid sacks of black sand is the desk; in a few moments the table will be able to be called a table once again. . . The sun enters through the cracks of the window blinds at the far end of the room. It has come a long way and it feels chilled. It stretches out a glass arm, which shatters into tiny shards the moment it touches the wall. Outside, the wind drives clouds before it. The metal blinds screech like iron birds. The sun takes three steps more. It is a glistening spider, sitting in the middle of the room. I draw the curtain back. The sun has no body and is everywhere. It has crossed seas and mountains, traveled all night long, lost its way in the suburbs. It has finally come home, and as though blinded by its own light, it is feeling its way about the room. It is looking for something. It gropes along the walls, threads its way between the red and green patches in the painting, climbs up the ties of the bookshelf. The shelves have turned into a bird cage and each color cries out with its particular call. The sun continues its search. On the third shelf, leaning against the freshly whitewashed wall, between the *Diccionario etimológico de la lengua castellana* and *La Garduna de Sevilla y anzuelo de bolsas,* a dark tobacco-colored ocher, with feline eyes, its eyelids slightly swollen after its peaceful slumber, with a cap atop its head that accentuates the deformation of its forehead, across which a line traces a spiral that ends in a comma (there the wind has written its true name), with a dimple in each cheek and two ritual incisions, the little head is laughing. The sun halts and looks at it. The little head laughs and gazes back at the sun without blinking.

At whom, or why is the little head on the third shelf laughing? It is laughing with the sun. There is a complicity, the nature of which I cannot yet fathom, between its laughter and the light. With its eyes half closed and its mouth half open, its tongue just barely showing, it is playing with the sun the way a bather plays with sea water. Solar heat is its element. Is it laughing at men? It is laughing to itself—for no particular reason. It is unaware of our existence; it is alive and is laughing with everything that is alive. It is laughing in order to germinate and in order to make the morning germinate. Laughing is a way of being born (the other way, our way, is to weep). If only I could laugh as this little head does, not knowing why. . . Today, a day like all the rest, beneath the same sun as that of any other day, I am alive and I laugh. My laughter echoes in the room with the sound of pebbles falling into a well. Is human laughter a fall, do we men have a hole in our souls? I feel abashed at having asked myself such a question, and fall silent. Then I laugh at myself. The same grotesque and convulsive sound once again. The laughter of the little head is different. The sun knows it and says nothing. It is in on the secret and refuses to reveal it. Or else it expresses it in words that I am unable to understand. I have forgotten, if perchance I ever did know it, the language of the sun.

The little head is a fragment of a doll of baked clay, found in a secondary tomb, along with other idols and broken earthenware vessels, at a site in the middle of the state of Veracruz. On my table is a collection of photographs of these little figures. Mine must have looked very much like one of them: its face raised slightly upward toward the sun, with an expression of indescribable joy; its arms curved in a dance position, its left hand open and its right hand clasping a rattle in the shape of a gourd; around its neck and hanging down across its chest a necklace of ordinary coarse stones; and clad in nothing more than a narrow band of cloth across its breast and a short skirt reaching from its waist to its knees, both decorated with a Grecian fret pattern. Mine had other decorations perhaps: wavy lines, commas, and in the middle of the skirt a so-called "spider monkey," its tail gracefully curled and its breast slashed open by a sacerdotal knife.

The little head on the third shelf is the contemporary of other disturbing creatures: prominent-nosed deities with headdresses in the form of a swooping bird; statues of Xipe-Tlazolteotl, a double god, dressed as a woman, with the lower part of its face covered with a mask made of human skin; figures of women who have died in childbirth, armed with shields and cudgels; ritual axes and palms of hands, made of jade and other hard stones, forming a necklace of severed hands, a face with the mask of a dog or a head of a dead warrior, with eyes closed and the green stone of immortality in its mouth; Xochiquetzal, with a child; the earth-god jaguar, with a human head between its jaws; Ehecatl-Quetzalcoatl, the wind-god, before his metamorphosis on the Mexican Altiplano, a god with a duck's bill. . . . These works and artifacts, some of them frightening and others of them fascinating, almost all of them admirable, belong to the Totonac culture—if it was really the Totonacs who between the first and ninth centuries A.D. manufactured by the thousands little laughing figures and carved yokes, axes, and palms of hands, mysterious objects whose function or use we know little about, though their striking beauty and aesthetic perfection is immediately obvious.

Like their neighbors the Huastecs, a people of conjurers and magicians who, according to the Spanish chronicler Fray Bernardino de Sahagún, "did not hold lust to be a sin," the Totonacs reveal a vitality that is less tense and more cheerful than that of other Meso-American peoples. This is perhaps the reason why they created an art that is equidistant from the severity of Teotihuacán and the opulence of the Mayas. The pyramid of El Tajín, unlike Teotihuacán, is not petrified movement, time frozen in its flight. It is dancing geometry, undulation, rhythm. The Totonacs are not sublime, they seldom dizzy us like the Mayas, or overwhelm us like the peoples of the Altiplano. At once complex and sober, they were the heirs of the solidity and spareness of the Olmecs, if not of their strength. Although the line of Totonac sculpture does not have the concise energy of the artists of La Venta and Tres Zapotes, its genius is freer and more imaginative. Whereas the Olmec sculptor extracts his works, so to speak, from the stone itself (or as Westheim writes, "he does not create heads; he creates stone heads"), the Totonac sculptor transforms matter into something different—something sensual or fantastic, and often surprising. Two families of artists: those that use matter, and those that are the servants of matter. Sensuality and ferocity, sense of volume and of line, seriousness and a smile: Totonac art rejects the monumental because it knows that true grandeur lies in harmony and equilibrium. But it is an equilibrium in motion, a form infused with the breath of life, as can be seen in the succession of lines and undulations that give El Tajín a vitality that is not at odds with solemnity. These stones are alive, and they dance.

Is Totonac art a branch, the closet and most vigorous branch, to have sprung from the Olmec trunk? I confess I do not know the answer to this question. Who were the Olmecs, what were their real names, what language did they speak, where did they come from and where did they go? A number of archaeologists have pointed to signs of the influence of Teotihuacán at El Tajín. Alfonso Medellin Zenil, however, believes (for what appear to be well-founded reasons) that there are evidences of Totonac influences at Teotihuacán. And who were the builders of Teotihuacán, what were their names, where did they come from, and so on? For it would seem that both the Aztecs and accepted tradition are wrong: the Toltecs were not the creators, but the destroyers, of this great metropolis. Jiménez Moreno ventures the hypothesis that it may have been the work of Nahua-Totonac groups. . . . Olmecs, Totonacs, Popoloca-Mazatecs, Toltecs: names. The names come and go, appear and disappear. the works remain. Amid the rubble of the temples demolished by the Chichimecas or by the Spaniards, above the mountain of books and hypotheses, the little head laughs. Its laughter is contagious. The window panes, the curtain, the *Diccionario etimológico*, the forgotten classic, and the avant-garde review laugh; all the objects in the room laugh at the man bent over the paper, searching for the secret of laughter among his pile of note cards. The secret lies elsewhere. In Veracruz, in the green and reddish night of El Tajín, in the sun that climbs the stairway of the temple each morning. It returns and learns to laugh. It contemplates once again the seven pools of blood, the seven serpents that gush forth from the trunk of the decapitated victim. Seven: the number of blood in the relief of the Pelota-Court of Chichen-Itza; seven: the number of seeds in the rattle of fertility; seven: the secret of laughter.

The pose and the expression of the little figures are mindful of the image of a rite. The ornaments, Medellín Zenil emphasizes, corroborate this first impression: the commas are stylizations of the monkey, which is the double or *nahual* of Xochipilli; the geometric patterns are variations of the sign *nahui ollin*, the sun of movement; the plumed serpent, it goes almost without saying, designates Quetzalcoatl in his original form, a god of wind; the Greek frets are an allusion to the serpent, the symbol of fertility. . . . Dancing creatures that appear to celebrate the sun and sprouting vegetation, intoxicated by a joy that expresses itself from one end of the scale of exuberant celebration to the other—how is it possible not to associate them with the divinity that later, on the Altiplano, was to be known as Xochipilli (the first day of the Season of Flowering) and Macuilxochitl (the fifth day of the Season of Flowering)? Nonetheless, I do not believe that these figures were meant to be representations of the god. They are most likely persons in his retinue, or people who in some manner or other play a role in the cult devoted to him. Nor does it seem to be that they are portraits, as has been suggested, although the individuality of the facial expressions and the rich variety of the smiles—unparalleled, in my opinion, in all of the history of the plastic arts—might incline us to accept this hypothesis. But the portrait is a profane genre, which appears relatively late in the history of civilizations. The Totonac doll-figures, like the saints, demons, angels, and other representations of what we inaccurately call "folk art," are figures associated with some sort of festive celebration. Their function within the sun-cult, to which they undoubtedly belong, may perhaps waver between relig-

ion properly speaking and magic. I shall attempt to justify this
conjecture of mine later on. For the moment, I shall merely say that
their laughter, when placed against the background of the rites of
Xochipilli, has ambivalent echoes.

The role that causality plays in our culture had its counterpart in
the role played by analogy among the Meso-Americans. Causality is
open, successive, and more or less infinite: a cause produces an
effect which in turn engenders another. Analogy or correspondence,
by contrast, is closed and cyclical: the phenomena revolve and are
repeated as in a play of mirrors. Each image changes, fuses with its
contrary, disengages itself, forms another image, again unites with
another, and in the end returns to the starting point. Rhythm is the
agent of change in this case. The key expressions of change are, as in
poetry, metamorphosis and mask. The gods are metaphors of the
rhythm of the cosmos; for each date on the calendar, for each
measure of the dance of time, there is a corresponding mask. Names:
dates: masks: images. Xochipilli, *numen* of song and dance, who
holds in his fist a stick with a pierced heart threaded on it, and is
seated on a blanket decorated with the signs of the four points of the
compass, is a child-sun, and also, without ceasing to be himself, is
Cinteotl, the deity of sprouting corn. As though in the rhyme
scheme of a poem, this image calls forth that of Xipe Totec, the god
not only of corn but of gold, a solar and generative god ("Our Lord
the Flayed One" and "the god possessing the virile member"). A
divinity incarnating the male principle, Xipe is coupled with Tlazolteotl, the ruling divinity of harvest and childbirth, of confession and
steam baths, the grandmother of gods, the mother of Cinteotl.
Between this latter and Xilonen, a youthful corn goddess, there is an
intimate relationship. Both are related to Xochiquetzal, who was
abducted by Texcatlipoca from the young Piltzintecutli—who is
none other than Xochipilli. The circle closes itself. It is quite possible that the Totonac pantheon, in the period in which their culture
was in full flower, was less complicated than this hasty enumeration
suggests. This is of little moment, however: the ruling principle of
divine transformations was the same.

There is nothing less arbitrary than this dizzying succession of
divinities. The metamorphoses of Xochipilli are those of the sun.
They are also those of water,[1] those of the planting of corn and the
various phases of its growth, and in short those of all the elements,
which by turn interweave and draw apart in a sort of round-dance. A

universe of antagonistic twins, governed by a logic as rigorous, precise, and coherent as the alternation of strophes and stanzas in the classical poetry. Here, however, the rhymes and rhythms are nature and society, agriculture and war, cosmic sustenance and the food of men. And the one theme of this immense poem is the death and resurrection of cosmic time. The history of men dissolves into that of myth, and the sign that orients their lives is the same as the one which governs the whole: *nahui ollin*, movement. Poetry in action, its ultimate metaphor is the sacrifice of men.

The laughter of the little figures begins to reveal to us all its insensate wisdom (I am using these two words deliberately) once we recall some of the ceremonies in which Xochipilli plays a role. Decapitation, in the first place. Doubtless this was a solar rite. It appears as early as the Olmec era, on a stela at Tres Zapotes. Moreover, the sun as a head separated from its trunk is an image that comes spontaneously to everyone's mind. (Was Guillaume Apollinaire aware that he was repeating an old metaphor when he ended a celebrated poem of his with the phrase *Soleil cou coupe?*) Some examples: The Nutall codex shows Xochiquetzal beheaded in the Pelota-Court; and in the fiesta in honor of Xilonen, a woman, the incarnation of the goddess, was decapitated—on the very altar dedicated to Cinteotl. A lunar goddess, and an archeress and a huntress like Diana, though less chaste, Tlazolteotl is the patron deity of the sacrifice in which the victim is pierced to death with arrows. We know that this rite stems from the Huastec and Totonac region. It seems unnecessary to dwell at length on the fiestas in honor of Xipe Totec, the Flayed One; it is worthwhile, on the other hand, to point out that these kinds of sacrifices played a role in the cult of Xochipilli: the Magliabecchi codex represents the god of the dance and joy clad in a monkey's skin. It is not illogical to conjecture that the figurines are laughing and shaking their magic rattles at the moment of sacrifice. Their superhuman happiness celebrates the uniting of the two slopes of existence, as the pool of blood of the decapitated victim turns into seven serpents, the bridge between the solar and terrestrial principles.

The Pelota Contest was a rite in which the victor won death by decapitation. But we risk missing its meaning if we fail to remember that the Pelota Contest was also a game. In every rite there is a playful element. We might even go so far as to say that game-playing is the root of ritual. The reason for this is obvious: creation is a game—the contrary, that is to say, of work. The gods are by essence creators, players of games. All of them, without exception, whatever their "specialty" (be they deities who make, preserve, or destroy), incarnate some aspect or other of the creative activity. What distinguishes gods from men is the fact that the gods play, whereas we humans work. The world is the cruel game of the gods and we are their playthings. In all mythologies, the world is a creation: a gratuitous act. Men are not necessary: they are not self-sustaining but exist, rather, by virtue of an alien will; they are a creation, a game. Ritual, the purpose of which is to preserve the continuity of the world and of men, is an imitation of the divine game, a representation of the original act of creation. The boundary between the profane and the sacred coincides with the line that separates ritual from work, laughter from seriousness, creation from productive labor. Originally all games were rites and even today they are governed by a ceremonial; work cuts short all rituals: during a day's toil there is neither time nor space for play. In ritual the paradox of the game reigns; the last shall be first, the gods bring the world forth from nothingness, life is won by death. In the sphere of work there are no paradoxes: in the sweat of thy face shalt thou eat bread; every man is the product of his works. There is an inexorable relationship between the effort expended and its fruits: to be profitable, work must be productive; the usefulness of ritual lies in its being an immense waste of life and time in order to assure the continuity of the cosmos. Ritual assumes all the risks of the game, and what is won, like what is lost, is incalculable. Sacrifice thus has a natural place in the logic of the game; for this reason it is the focal point and the consummation of the ceremony: there is no game without a loss, no rite without an offering or a victim. The gods sacrifice themselves when they create the world, because every creation is a game.

The relationship between laughter and sacrifice goes as far back in time as ritual itself. The bloody violence of bacchanalia and saturnalia was almost always accompanied by shrieks and howls of laughter. Laughter makes the universe tremble, deranges it, reveals its vitals. Tremendous laughter is a divine manifestation. Like sacrifice, laughter is a denial of work. And not only because it is an interruption of labor, but also because it casts doubt on its seriousness. Laughter is a suspension of reason, and in certain instances a loss of it. Thus it robs work, and consequently the world, of all meaning. In fact, work is what gives meaning to nature: it transforms its indifference or its hostility into fruitfulness, it makes it productive. Work humanizes the world, and this humanization is what gives it meaning. Laughter restores the universe to its original state of indifference and strangeness: if it has a meaning, it is a divine one, not a human one. Through laughter the world again becomes a place for game-playing, a sacred precinct rather than a place for work. The nihilism of laughter serves the gods. Its function is no different from that of sacrifice: re-establishing the divinity of nature, its radical inhumanity. The world is not made for man: the world and man are made for gods. Work is serious; death and laughter snatch away its mask of soberness. Through death and laughter, the world and men become playthings once again.

Between men and gods there is an infinite distance. Now and then, through ritual and sacrifice, man reaches the sphere of the divine—only to fall back, after a brief moment, into his original contingency. Men may appear to be like unto the gods; gods never appear to be like unto us. Alien and strange, the god is Otherness. He appears among men as a *tremendous mystery*, to borrow Rodolfo Otto's well-known expression. Incarnations of an inaccessible beyond, the representations of the gods are awesome. Elsewhere, however, I have attempted to draw a distinction between the terrifying nature of the *numen* and the perhaps even more profound experience of sacred horror.[2] The tremendous and the terrifying are attributes of divine power, of its authority and sovereignty. But mystery, "otherness" properly speaking, gives rise to fascination, not fear. It is a repulsive—or more precisely, a revulsive—experience; it consists of an opening of the entrails of the cosmos, to show that the organs of gestation are also those of destruction, and that from a certain point of view (that of the divinity), life and death are the same thing. Horror is an experience that in the realm of the emotions is the counterpart of the paradox and antinomy in the realm of reason: the god is a total presence which is a bottomless absence. In the divine presence of all presences are manifested, and through it everything is present; at the same time, as though it were all a game, everything is emptiness. The *apparition* of the divine reveals the front side and the reverse side of being. Coatlicue is something that is too full, brimming over with all of the attributes of existence, a presence in which the totality of the universe is concentrated; and this plethora of symbols, meanings, and signs is at the same time an abyss, the great maternal mouth of emptiness. Stripping the Mexican gods of their awesome and horrendous nature, as our art criticism occasionally attempts to do, is tantamount to doubly amputating them: as creations of the spirit of religion and as works of art. Every divinity is awesome; every god inspires a sense of horror. And the gods of the ancient Mexicans possess a charge of sacred energy that can only be described as explosive and deadly. That is why they fascinate us.

A tremendous presence, the god is inaccessible; a fascinating mystery, the god is unknowable. These two attributes are combined in his impassibility. (*Passion* appertains to gods who assume human form, such as Jesus Christ, or to men who become gods, like Quetzalcoatl.) The gods are beyond the seriousness of work and therefore their attitude is playful; but it is an impassive playfulness. The Greek gods of the archaic period admittedly smile; but this smile is the expression of their indifference. They are in on the secret, they know that the world, men, and they themselves are nothing but representations of Fate, and that good and evil, death and life are mere words. The smile is the expression of their indifference. They are in on the secret, they know that the world, men, and they themselves are nothing but representations of Fate, and that good and evil, death and life are mere words. The smile is the sign of their impassibility, the symbol of their infinite distance from men. They smile: nothing can disturb them. We do not know whether the gods of Mexico smile or laugh: their countenances are veiled by a mask. The function of the mask is twofold; like a fan, it conceals and reveals their divinity. Or better stated: it hides the god's essence and manifests his terrifying attributes. In both these ways it places an insurmountable distance between men and the godhead. In the game of impassive divinities, what place is there for laughter?

The Totonac figurines laugh in the full light of day, with bare faces. We find in them none of the divine attributes. They are not a tremendous mystery, nor do they possess the ambiguous fascination of supernatural horror. They dwell within the divine atmosphere, but they are not gods. They do not resemble the deities they serve, although the same hand has shaped them. They are present at the sacrifices to these gods and participate in the ceremonies in their honor, like survivors of another age. But though they do not resemble the gods, they bear an obvious family resemblance to the little female statuettes of the "archaic" period of central Mexico and other places. I do not mean to say that they are their descendants but simply that they live within the same psychic ambiance, like the countless representations of fecundity in the Mediterranean area, and like so many so-called "folk art" objects today. This mixture of realism and myth, of humor and innocent sensuality also explains the variety of facial features and expressions. Although they are not portraits, they give proof of a very acute and very animated observation of the mobility of the human face, of a *familiarity* almost invariably absent in religious art. Do we not find the same spirit in many of the creations of our folk artists of today? In spirit, the figurines belong to an era preceding the great ritual religions— before the indifferent smile and the terrifying mask, before the separation of gods and men. They come from the world of magic, which is ruled by the belief in the communication and the transformation of creatures and things.

Talismans, amulets of metamorphosis, these smiling terra cotta figurines tell us that everything is alive and that all beings are one with the whole. A single energy animates all of creation. Whereas magic affirms the fraternity of all things and all creatures, religions separate the world into two parts: the creators and their creation. In the world of magic, communication, and hence metamorphosis, is obtained through processes such as imitation and contagion. It is not difficult to discover in the Totonac figurines an echo of these magic formulae. Their laughter is communicative and contagious; it is an invitation to *general animation,* a summons tending to restore the circulation of the breath of life. The rattle contains seeds which as they knock together imitate the sounds of rain and tempests. The analogy with the *tlaloques*[3] and their little receptacles leaps to the eye; it is not beyond the realm of possibility that there was a more precise relationship between the statuettes and Tlaloc, one of the oldest divinities of Meso-America. And what is more: "The number of seven signifies seeds," Alfonso Caso tells us. It was a propitious number. In this case it seems to me to suggest fertility and abundance.

Between the tense seriousness of work and the divine impassibility, the little figures reveal an older realm: that of magic laughter. Laughter antedates the gods. Sometimes the gods *do* laugh. Whether sarcastic, threatening, or delirious, their stentorian laughter terrifies us: it sets creation in motion or rends it asunder. At other times, their laugher is the echo of, or nostalgia for, the unity that has been lost. To tempt the sungod, hidden in a cave, the goddess Uzumé "bared her breasts, raised her skirts, and danced. The gods began to laugh, and their laughter made the pillars of heaven tremble." The dance of this Japanese goddess lures the sun out of the cave. In the beginning was laughter; the world begins with an indecent dance and a hearty burst of laughter. Cosmic laughter is a childish laughter. Today only children laugh with a laugh that is mindful of that of the Totonac figurines. Laughter of the first day of creation, wild laughter, and at the same time close to the first tears: harmony with the world, a wordless dialogue, pleasure. One need only stretch out one's hand to pluck the fruit, one need only laugh to make the entire universe laugh. A restoration of the unity between the world and man, childish laughter also presages their irrevocable separation. Children play at staring each other in the eye: the one that laughs first loses. Laughter has exacted its price. It has ceased to be contagious. The world has become deaf and henceforth it can be conquered only through effort.

As the sphere of work broadens, that of laughter grows narrower. To become a man is to learn to work, to become serious and well-behaved. But as work humanized nature, it dehumanizes man. Work literally evicts man from his humanity. And not only because it turns the worker into a wage-earner, but also because it identifies his life with his job. It makes him inseparable from his tool, it marks him with the brand of his implement. All tools are serious things. Work devours the being of man: it freezes his face, it prevents him from laughing or crying. Admittedly, man is man thanks to work; but it is necessary to add that he contrives to be wholly human only when he frees himself from labor or turns it into a creative game. Until the modern era, which has made work a sort of religion that has no rites yet exacts sacrifices, the superior life was the contemplative life; and today the rebellion of art (which may well be illusory, and whose success in any event is problematical) is founded on its gratuitousness, an echo of the ritual game. Work consummates the victory of man over nature and the gods; at the same time, it uproots him from his native soil and dries up the source of his humanity. The word *pleasure* has no place in the vocabulary of work. And pleasure is one of the keys of man's life: a nostalgia for the original unity and a happy portent of a reconciliation with the world and with our own selves.

If work requires the abolition of laughter, ritual turns it into a frozen grin. The gods play and create the world; as men repeat this game, they dance and weep, laugh, and shed blood. Ritual is a game that demands victims. It is not surprising that among the Aztecs the word *dance* also signifies penitence. A rejoicing that is a penitence, a fiesta that involves pain, the ambivalence of ritual culminates in sacrifice. A superhuman joy illuminates the countenance of the victim. The ecstatic expression of the martyrs of all religions never ceases to amaze me. Psychologists offer us their ingenious explanations of this phenomenon, which will do until some new hypothesis comes along. Yet there is still something that remains to be said. Something inexpressible. This rapturous joy is as unfathomable as the expression produced by erotic pleasure. Spectators and the devout present at the sacrifice doubtless felt the same horror, the same fascination: an intolerable spectacle, and yet we cannot tear our eyes away from it. This face that contracts and distends until it is immobilized in an expression that is at once penitence and rejoicing: is this not the hieroglyph of the original unity, in which everything was one and the same? This expression is not the negation but the reverse side of laughter.

"Joy is one." Baudelaire says; but on the other hand, "laughter is double or contradictory; therefore it is convulsive."[4] And in another passage of the same essay he writes: "In the earthly paradise (past or future, a memory or a prophecy, depending on whether we view it as theologians or as socialists) . . . joy plays no part in laughter." If joy is one, how could the laughter of paradise be excluded from it? I find the answer in these lines: laughter is satanical and "is associated with the accident of the primordial Fall. . . . Laughter and pain are expressed by the organs which are the seat of the control and of the knowledge of good and evil: the eyes and the mouth." Does no one in paradise laugh then because no one suffers? Can joy be a neutral state, a beatitude rooted in indifference, and not that supreme degree of felicity that only the blessed and the innocent attain? No. Baudelaire maintains, rather, that the joy of paradise is not human and transcends the categories of our understanding. Unlike this joy, laughter is neither divine nor sacred; it is a human attribute and therefore is a function of those organs which, from the beginning, have been considered as the seat of free will: the eyes, mirrors of the power of vision and the origin of knowledge, and the mouth, the servant of the power of speech and reason. Laughter is one of the manifestations of human freedom, equidistant from the divine impassibility and the irremediable seriousness of animals. And it is satanic because it is one of the tokens of the breaking of the pact between God and his creature.

For Baudelaire, laughter is inseparable from sadness. It is not childish laughter, but what he himself calls "the comic." It is modern laughter, human laughter par excellence. If it is the laughter that we hear every day as a sign of defiance or resignation, vainglorious or full of despair, it is also what for several centuries now has given Western art some of its most daring and impressive works. It is caricature, but it is also Goya and Daumier, Breughel and Hieronymus Bosch, Picabia and Picasso, Marcel Duchamp and Max Ernst. In Mexico it is José Guadalupe Posada, Orozco when he is at his best, Tamayo at his fiercest and most direct. The laughter that is age-old, the revelation of the cosmic unity, is a secret now lost to us. We catch a glimpse of what it may have been when we contemplate our little figures, the phallic laughter of certain sculptures from black Africa and Oceania, and many other unusual, archaic, or exotic objects, which had only just begun to impinge upon the Western consciousness at the time when Baudelaire was writing. Through these works, we divine that joy was truly one, and that it embraced many things that later seemed grotesque, cruel, or diabolical: the obscene dance of Uzumé ("the monkey dance," the Japanese call it), the shriek of the bacchante, the funeral chant of the pigmy, the winged priapus of the Roman. . . . Joy is a unity that excludes nothing. The Christian ethos drives laughter from paradise and transforms it into a satanic attribute. Since then it has been a sign of the netherworld and its powers. Until only a few centuries ago it played a cardinal role in witchcraft trials, as a symptom of demoniacal possession; today, having been co-opted by science, it is hysteria, psychic imbalance, an anomaly. Nonetheless, whether a sickness or a mark of the devil, age-old laughter has not lost its power. Its contagion is irresistible, and that is why it has been found necessary to isolate "those who suffer from fits of insane laughter."

At the opposite pole, the "comic" accentuates our separation. We laugh at others or at ourselves; and in both cases, Baudelaire points out, we affirm that we are different from what provokes our laughter. An expression of our distance from the world and from men, this laughter is above all the sign of our duality: if we laugh at

ourselves it is because our nature is twofold. Our laughter is negative. It could not be otherwise, since it is a manifestation of modern
consciousness, a divided consciousness. If I affirm *this*, I deny *that*.
It does not assent (you are like me); it dissents (you are different). In
its most direct forms, satire, mocking jokes, or caricature, it is
polemical and points out, accuses, or pokes its finger into the
wound. The sustenance of the most lofty poetry, it is laughter
gnawed at by reflection: Romantic irony, black humor, blasphemy,
the burlesque epic (from Cervantes to Joyce); as thought, it is the
only genuinely critical philosophy because it is the only one that
truly dissolves values.

Our knowledge is a knowledge of separation. The method of
critical thought is negative: it tends to distinguish one thing from
another; in order to succeed in doing so, it must demonstrate that
this is *not* that. As philosophical meditation broadens its scope, the
negation becomes more all-embracing: thought casts doubt on reality, knowledge, truth. Turning in on itself, the mind interrogates
itself and puts consciousness itself in question. And there is a
moment at which reflection, on being reflected in the purity of consciousness, denies itself. Born of a negation of the absolute, it ends
in absolute negation. Laughter accompanies consciousness on all of
its adventures: if thought thinks itself, laughter laughs at laughter;
if thought thinks the unthinkable, laughter dies of laughter. A refuta-
tion of the universe through laughter. Isn't this what the laughter of
Lautréamont—and above all that of Nietzsche—is? Laughter is the
beyond of philosophy. The world began with a great burst of laughter and ends with another. But the laughter of the Japanese gods, at
the very heart of creation, is not the same as that of Nietzsche in his
solitude, free now of nature, "a spirit that plays innocently, that is to
say, unintentionally, out of an excess of power and fecundity, with
everything that heretofore has been called the holy, the good, the
intangible, and the divine. . . ." (*Ecce Homo*). Innocence does not
lie in the ignorance of values and ends, but in knowing that values do
not exist and that the universe rolls on, to no point or purpose.
Innocence is the consciousness of nihilism. In the face of the dizzying vision of the void, a truly unique spectacle, laughter is also the
only possible response. On arriving at this extreme point, beyond
which there lies only nothingness, Western thought examines itself,
before dissolving itself in its own transparency. It neither judges nor
condemns: it laughs. Laughter is a proposition of this *atheology* of

totality that causes George Bataille sleepless nights. A proposition which, by its very nature, is not fundamental but ludicrous: it cannot serve as the foundation of anything because it is fathomless and everything falls into it without ever touching bottom. "Who can possibly laugh himself to death?" Bataille wonders. Everyone and no one. The classic precept, a rational and stoic one, was to laugh to death. But if as we laugh we die, who is it that is laughing—us or death?

The sun does not go away. It lingers stubbornly in the room. What time is it? An hour more, or an hour less, hastening or delaying my hour, that of my loss forever. Because I am lost in infinite time, a time that had no beginning and will have no end. The sun lives in another time, it *is* another time, finite and immortal (finite: it ends, it dies away; immortal: it is born, it is reborn with the childish laughter and the pool of blood). A beheaded sun, a flayed sun, a sun of living flesh, a sun that is a young child and an old man, a sun that is in on the secret of true laughter, that of the little head on the third shelf. To laugh that way, after a thousand years, it has to be totally alive or completely dead. Only skulls laugh perpetually. No, the little head is alive and is laughing. Only the living laugh that way. On its headdress a line traces a spiral that ends in a comma. There the wind has written its true name: my name is the liana twined about the trees, a monkey that hangs over the dark green abyss; my name is the axe to break open the breast of the sky, the column of smoke that pierces the heart of the cloud; my name is the sea-shell and the labyrinth of the wind, the vortex, the crossroads; my name is the tangle of serpents, the sheaf of centuries, the reunion and dispersion of the four colors and the four ages; my name is night and I gleam like obsidian; my name is day and I pluck out eyes like the eagle; my name is jaguar and my name is ear of corn. Each mask, a name; each name, a date. My name is time and I shake a clay rattle with seven seeds inside it.

—Translated from the Spanish by Helen R. Lane

1. *Xochiquetzal dwells in the "house" of Tlaloc, god of rain and water, at the time when she is abducted.*

2. The Bow and the Lyre, *translated by Ruth L. C. Simms, Universtiy of Texas Press, pp. 112–116.*

3. Attendants of the rain-god Tlaloc. They carry earthen jars which contain water. When they break the jars, rain pours over the world.

4. Curiosités Esthétiques: de l'essence du rire et généralement du comique dans les arts plastiques *(1855).*

TO MY DAUGHTER

by KATHRYN TERRILL

from POETRY NORTHWEST

nominated by Joyce Carol Oates

1.

I still sweep your father's hair from corners.
Against my face, hair starved on medicine
and falling loose, I find his brush,
a clot of roots. Boots lean crooked
on the heels, creased where his feet broke the leather.
I smell his hair inside the pillow tick
and see, above the bed, oil halos
on a floral print—smears of pain.
I build a fire every night.
In this house sometimes we are afraid.

2.

Signs everywhere: in the grass dogs crack
the rings from steak, last meat in dirty strings;
I slip a knife point in a chicken breast
and pull the slats. Friends tell me I've lost weight.
No fat to ease my ribs—I say the pattern
of my fate grows clear inside my skin.
At the crematorium they gave me all your father
the furnace could not eat: a box of fire-bruised bones.

3.

A gown of baby fat provides no shelter.
Your blue eyes flinch at sparks,
guessing already how we take a chance—
every night you ask if we can dance.
Partner, our difficult routine requires two:
Mama, I can copy you!
                              Across the big east window
I waltz you on my hip until your nightdress blooms with air.
Who are we dancing for? Is it the man
who phones when I'm asleep and vows,
when he can catch me, what he'll do?
Is it the boy across the street, or your scraps
of father? I turn the music low and close the drape.

4.

I know which wood the fire takes first:
white sticks split from fir
with the cold ardor of your father's ax,
then whole logs of hemlock, alder;
for this work I wear your father's shirt—
as I spilled his body from the box,
passed my fingers through his shards and sand.

I dance you off to bed, bone-wracked.
In the dark you look like me—charred eyes, moonface
whittled down to chalk. I reach to find a light.
Mama, is anybody there?
                              No one but the ghost
of each old breath. Though these are just the practice
steps, I build a fire every night.

WHERE THE WINGED HORSES TAKE OFF INTO THE WILD BLUE YONDER FROM

fiction by KELLY CHERRY

from STORYQUARTERLY

nominated by STORYQUARTERLY, *Ben Pesta, and M.D. Elevitch*

I AM IN AN OBSERVATION CAR; what I am observing is North Dakota.

The first time North Dakota existed for me was ten years ago and thousands of miles away. I was staying at the Metropole in Moscow and met an American fur-trader who was there to do business. It was January, and I was expressing my admiration for the weather, at ten below. "My dear Kathryn," the fur-trader said (he sported a Stetson on his silver head but his manners were entirely continental), "this is nothing—a little nippy, that's all. You won't know what cold is till you come to North Dakota."

He presented me with a sample of his wares—fur-lined gloves, but they were two sizes too large. Later, on the train to Berlin, I gave them to a medical student from Madagascar; he was on holiday from Patrice Lamumba University. The news had just reached us that several European nuns had been slaughtered in a revolutionary action in the Congo, and the med student was trying to stir his traveling companions to a kind of applause on behalf of the Third World. I gave him the gloves because I had already learned that everyone can be bought, even Marxists.

That was a loud, crowded train; this one's quiet. Or maybe it's just that I can no longer pass for a college student, and so am excluded from groups. These days I tend to keep to myself when traveling, and certainly when traveling through North Dakota, although not long ago John Barth autographed my copy of *The Sot-Weed Factor* in Grand Forks, "To Kate." That was the second time this state became real for me. Thus does the mind's map achieve scope and detail, rock by rock, tree by tree, ridge by ridge, telephone pole by telephone pole. Aristotle quotes an earlier philosopher who said: "As more and more things come into being, the universe, taken as a whole, swells."

Now I am having my third view of the Prairie Garden, *en passant.* I am on my way to Seattle. The reason is simple—it's the same motive that's sent me everywhere I've gone since 1965. If I can't be in the one place on the planet I ought to be, I might as well be anywhere. Here is anywhere. In fact, for all I know, by now it could even be Montana. In the distance there are mountains shaped like pyramids rising from the flat earth.

The *one place* is with Peteris, in Latvia, one of the three Baltic Republics which came under Soviet domination as a result of the war. I would immigrate—ask me my political party and I'll say "realist"—but they won't let me. As for who "they" are, "they" are the same folks who censor our mail, on both sides. England is the only major power not censoring incoming mail; there, reading other people's correspondence is uncivilized, not to say uncouth. But between the U.S.S.R. and U.S.A., the iron curtain is like a lead blind. Detente isn't just a word; it's the promise of light. But the way those things work—Look, change starts at the top and filters down like meltwater through topsoil, and by the time it reaches the rest of us, it's been refined out of existence.

Yet Peteris wrote me that as time goes on he remembers me with increasing clarity, seeing in his mind my way of walking, talking, and telling him "Peteris." I worry whether time hasn't also refined his image of me, but for my part, I depend on his testimonials of love the way a hemophiliac depends on transfusions, utterly. When we met, I had already been bleeding for years, having been wounded at an early age. Peteris knows this tawdry fact about me and isn't put off by it. Where less desperate couples make suicide pacts, we agreed to a life pact; for each other's sake, we would endure the flak, shit, and pure grief that piled up, like dirty snow, in both our lives.

Periodically, Peteris enters a hospital—on account of his drinking, of course, but also because he becomes convinced that his brain is being flattened out by boredom like dough by a gigantic rolling pin. He drinks to make himself stupid, since the stupider he becomes, the more fascinating everyone else in his world seems, and the more the world fascinates him, the more alive his intelligence becomes. It's a paradox, and perhaps that's why the psychiatrists at the hospital have so much trouble grasping it. On the other hand, where the psychiatrists fail, I succeed, and between the fifth and sixth paragraphs move downstairs to the bar car.

An acquaintance told me that a hot rumor around Riga is that the KGB supplies Peteris with drugs. Until a gathering paranoia compelled me to give them up, I got mine through capitalistic channels.

Paranoia? I used to think I was dying. Once I went to St. Luke's and waited four hours in the emergency room for the chance to inform a doctor that I was having a heart attack. He peered into my pupils so intensely I was afraid I might kiss him, out of reflex. But he backed away, making me feel ugly and rejected. This was during one of my crazy periods. Nevertheless, most of the time I'm sane enough, if sanity consists in working hard, being friendly to your fellowman, and meeting obligations. Of course, sanity is patently insufficient. Several hundred thousand people will starve to death this year, and the only way I could help would be by giving them my body for food—and unless somebody performed a miracle on it, which hasn't happened in a long while, it wouldn't go very far.

The first time I saw Peteris, I was waiting for the coffee shop in the Metropole to open. He told me he knew I was American by the manner in which I lit my cigarette, striking the match prudently outward from my body. I knew he was watching me. I think if he had simply approached me, sat down beside me on the couch, kissed me deeply and touched my back and neck, I would have made love to him on the spot, with an inappropriately languorous concentration. The coffee shop opened. I maneuvered myself in line just ahead of him; he was dark, tall and thin, strikingly good-looking but obviously profoundly self-willed, with a Van Dyke that spelled danger. But his intentions were unthreatening. Besides, he was with a friend. We started talking and wound up leaving the Metropole; he hailed a taxi, which we took to a bar across town, engaging in hectic conversation made inexplicably poignant by his friend's use of sign language: she knew no English and had once worked for a deaf-and-dumb retailer. The friend was very pretty, a tiny bit stocky and as sweet-tempered as Grushenka. At once, I was jealous of the friend's role in Peteris' life and proud of Peteris for elicting such plainly tender concern. I wanted to express my own feelings, but was young—the same age he was, twenty-three—and needed to know how he felt about me before I would risk revealing how I felt about him. It was a question of disarmament.

A number of men, including my ex-husband, have acquainted me with myself over the past ten years, but when I was young I assumed that lovers, calling me beautiful, lied like sons of bitches, for the fun of it. Whatever capacity for enchantment I had couldn't be pinpointed in a mirror; it showed itself in my idiosyncratic intelligence, in my jaw's jut (a family trait), and in a certain whimsical pelvic slant which was, however, not so much eager as innocently receptive. At first, I didn't know what I looked like; later, I realized I had been beautiful, and regretted time's erosion; lately, I've learned to look outside myself, enlarging my world. For example, I notice that we are climbing. Up and up—the sky's the limit. Look! The mountains are here, lit by incandescent clouds. The mountains glow; light breaks on their snowy peaks like waves on a beach and rolls down; cattle graze in the green valley. When the clouds part, the sky falls back. It falls back a million years, into sheer space, but down here the grass is speckled with sweet peas and buttercups, and clumps of dandelions mottle the hillside. We're in Glacier Park, crossing a ravine. It's a dead drop, shale and air all the way. In that cup of earth, light comes and goes; it runneth over; light brims and spills onto the tops of trees. The leaves sparkle—I record this and other impressions, thinking that someday I will tell them all to Peteris.

* * *

We thought someday we would be together. Now here I am, moving ever farther off. Years and miles. It's not right, this separation. We were meant for each other, and I don't care who hears me say it. One more drink and I'll tell the bartender.

Peteris has been married three times. He wrote me that he first fell in love at twenty; they had a fight, in which she said she didn't love him. To make her live with what she'd said, he married her sister. The sister didn't love him, nor did he love her, but they lived together for a year and produced a daughter.

His second wife was very beautiful, breathtaking. She bore him a second child. She had nothing more to recommend her, however. (He was divorced from the second wife for about six months when we met in the lobby of the Metropole Hotel.)

He picked out his third wife at a party his friend Mirdza took him to; a lot of theater people were present. His wife-to-be was a dancer, the type of the *corps*, small, round and strong, disciplined and doll-like. Actually, he didn't marry her until they'd had three children and needed to apply for a larger apartment, but from the beginning he was unwilling to love a woman without living with her. And he did love her. I knew that. He had turned to her when I wrote him I was marrying Ezra.

Peteris had taken his diploma at the conservatory in Liepaja, and the first summer after my visit he stayed on there, in a cottage by the seaside. His salutation was always, "Dearest Katina." The second summer, he traveled back and forth across Latvia with a theater group, intending to write music for plays. He had some new ideas along this line and wanted to try them out but—as he wrote later—something went wrong with his nerves and he had to abandon the idea of working. He found my letters when he returned home and wrote right away, but I had meanwhile concluded that he'd forgotten me—or at any rate, that he only enjoyed the romance of my being in America. Until recently, I always expected the worst. (Thinking things over, I've come to the conclusion that nothing's predictable and that we therefore must allow at least the possibility of right occurrences.) I thought he had become bored with the idea of me—I'm the first to admit I can be wearisome. Meanwhile, I observed that Ezra Solomon, a visiting instructor in art, was mad for me—and at me. He seemed to hold me responsible for the way he felt about me. I ran into him at a party and he acted as if I didn't exist, although I was sitting in a chair not two feet away. He and his date were on the floor. Janet, the date, said she was thinking of running away to Australia; surprising everyone, she did just that, a couple of months later, once sending me a postcard from Sydney with a kangaroo on it. But that particular night, she was insistently present, long dark hair ironed flat falling from a center part, the crown circled by an Indian headband. She looked like a woman I met a few months ago, hip, scared, and Greek. My hair was long then too, but no longer than to the middle of my back, and it wasn't black but brown,* and I wasn't hip, and probably was not even as scared as she was, though like all of us in those days, I wasn't above trading on my phobias.

Ezra still hadn't acknowledged me. His sexual style was intense-ugly, owing much to Jean-Paul Belmondo. He kept a hand on Janet's shoulder and chain-smoked with the other, and when I said good night, he gave me two fingers in a salute that was half comradely and half obscene.

When I wrote Peteris about Ezra, I was hoping for a certain kind of reply, one that would convince me he had meant what he said. It came—the week of the wedding. Ezra and I were already at my parents' house. I didn't have the courage to call it off. And what could I say, anyway? That I wanted to marry a man I'd known for four days, who incidentally lived behind the iron curtain? Katie Allen, Bolshevik. In high school I was a lieutenant in the Civil Air Patrol. We had about twenty-five members and we used to march up and down the Midlothian gym on Thursday nights. The idea was to train young people to be on the watch for enemy fighter planes, in case of surprise attack. Not only did I get to march—the big plus was that as a result of my militarism I got asked to the ring dance at John Marshall by a real cadet. He dropped the ring. Terrific. It rolled down the length of the floor and he had to chase after it. He put it on my finger, but, later, introducing me to his parents, he said I dropped it. I let him get away with that because I didn't want to embarrass him in front of his parents. Then for the rest of the evening he acted as if I didn't exist (that happened to me a lot), and before it was over I found him making out with a blue-eyed blonde in

*I'm Scotch-Irish, English, Welsh, French, and Portuguese.

the back bleachers. I guess he had to show me he was a man, in spite of the ring. He was sixteen. I never learned to tell one airplane from another, and in any case I thought I'd rather be red than dead.

Before I would accept Ezra's proposal, I said I had two questions. One was if he wanted kids; the other was if I could visit Peteris the following summer as I'd planned. He said yes to both, but I was to learn he passed my little test dishonestly, never really willing to commit himself to children, and never really intending to let me go off to the Soviet Union to visit Peteris. Even after living expenses ate up the money I had saved for the trip, Ezra kept poking around in my brain as if I'd tucked away the hope of Peteris like a rainy day savings account. It was ludicrous; hadn't I chosen him, and besides, wasn't the world inhabited by plenty of attractive men, all nearer? Talk about paranoid.

We moved to Brooklyn Heights. I took the greatest pleasure in this apartment. The walls were stark white (it's not true that walls have to be off-white), the trees sent their sweet smell up from the street,* everything, including life, was clean, and even the Michelob sprinkler bottle was beautifully shaped. One summer night while I was ironing Ezra sat down at the piano, as discordantly as Dostoevski's Underground Man, as if to prove that *homo sapiens* cannot be merely a piano key since he is the piano player. I asked him to stop; I felt like a prick but for some months my sensitivity to sound had increased. That was one of the reasons he was sending me to a psychiatrist. My father is a musician, my mother is a musician, Peteris is a composer—I didn't need a psychiatrist to tell me why suddenly a pin dropped, a sigh, became an explosion and storm.

"What you really want," Ezra said, despairingly, "is for me not to exist."

"That's not true!"

"The hell it isn't."

I felt defeated, immobilized. Part of the problem was that he was always right. I found myself moving in a two-dimensional field, where surfaces were cold, shiny, and deceptive. I was becoming unpleasant, finding life in such an unforgiving light too tense. I developed an ulcer, became accident-prone—I burned my hand on

*When Khrushchev came to New York in 1960, he remarked, "There is no greenery. It is enough to make a stone sad." But he didn't get down to Brooklyn Heights. We were on the fringe.

the iron and ran into the kitchen to smear butter on it. Then I wrapped a dishtowel around it. It still hurt. I was crying.

"That's an old wives' tale," Ezra said. "You should hold it under cold water."

The thought made me wince. Like his practicing. "You don't know," I whispered, "what it sounds like in my head. I'm not making it up."

"I didn't think you were." His voice grew rich and sorrowful. I thought it was vastly more musical than his piano-playing.

He went into the kitchen and then I heard him say, "Shit," and then he said, louder, "I'm going out to get cigarettes," and I heard the door opening and shutting. I took the towel off and looked at my hand. It was red and greasy but it no longer hurt.

In Riga, Peteris applied himself first to an oratorio and then to a new symphony, but things began to go wrong at home. Some of this he wrote me about, later. Some I sensed, or extrapolated from my own situation with Ezra. He increased his drinking, passing out at an awards ceremony in Budapest. It wasn't the kids—he was crazy about the kids. So was his wife. The problem was between him and her. It was just, they bored each other; it was as if each day they were dying, side by side, in silence. She screamed at him, and since he could only assume that he deserved her wrath, he said nothing. Or he said the hell with it and went out, like Ezra. Sometimes he'd pick up somebody, but his wife never acknowledged this. After a while, they learned to respect each other for being able to take what they dished out to each other. He admired her independence. She was very well liked and he felt all their troubles were his fault. But there was no one he could tell this to or be absolved by, except the shrinks at the hospital, and they were so unimaginative they couldn't even comprehend the logic of addiction.

I tried to fit these facts about Peteris into my general knowledge of Russia. Citizens eat ice cream on the sidewalks in winter. Divorce between consenting parties costs about $150. To see Rembrandt, go to the Hermitage. Alcoholism is an national epidemic. There are no stoppers for the drains of sinks and tubs in Russia. Black tights are the sign of a whore. The KGB fucks everyone; therefore, you must learn to love the KGB. In Siberia houses have walls that are three feet thick, and the Fahrenheit temperature hits ninety below.

Sometimes, the setting sun strikes the snow crystals in such a way that the trees and fields seem to catch on fire. There is a terrible ache in the citizens' hearts.

When Ezra left me, I wept for three days straight. I quit eating and went down to eighty-eight pounds. I looked in the mirror and asked myself what I thought I was doing, some weird Buchenwald number? Did I think I could get him back by clarifying my position as victim? He might be a Jew, but he was a fascist son of a bitch. I tried to laugh at myself, but my throat closed up the same way it did when I tried to eat.

The most hilarious thing was when I sent a cable to Peteris, asking if he still wanted me. He wrote, "I have a wife and baby, and I love them very much." Of course, he wasn't yet legally married. But what was a piece of paper, if it hadn't kept Ezra from leaving me. . . .

So I had done myself out of them both. I thought I deserved this irony, and called it poetic justice. My parents bought me a puppy.

The telephone rang at four a.m. I had been asleep for barely an hour and was reluctant to wake up. The operator said she had Moscow on the line.

"Come to Russia," Peteris said, "or I kill myself."

"Look"—I meant to explain things calmly, be rational and precise—"you can't talk to me like this. You have a wife."

"Yes."

"Well, then, you shouldn't make phone calls like this."

"I love you."

"You're drunk."

"Yes," he said, amicably.

"I don't have the money to come to Russia. I have to go to work in the morning."

"Come to Russia or I die."

"Peteris!"

"Katina," he said. "Say you love me."

"I can't. I don't have the right to." Ezra walking out on me had left me feeling divorce was a terrible thing for a man to do to a woman, so I couldn't encourage Peteris. I know that was stupid of me, but more than righteousness was involved. I was also afraid that if Peteris saw me he wouldn't want me any more. At the same time I distrusted young men's attitudes toward me; I had been one of those girls who count on their looks even economically. It used to be when ticket sellers saw my face, they volunteered the best seats in a supposedly sold-out house. Landlords reduced their rent and repaired the kitchens fixtures, without laying a hand on me. Flower vendors pressed bouquets on me free of charge. In my sick moods, I thought they felt sorry for me. I even thought, Maybe Peteris feels sorry for me or is making fun of me. I didn't truly think so, but I had to admit the chance. I had, after all, been wrong before. Take Ezra. It was best to warn Peteris that I was losing my looks. "I'm skinny," I said. "I'm getting old. I'm one of thousands of frantic female singles in Fun City. I am disappointed in myself."

"Me too," he agreed, undeflected. "Is very sad. Dream and reality, they are unstickable things in a biological together."

"Absolutely."

"Katina," he said.

"What?"

"Come to Russia, or I kill myself."

We'll arrive in Seattle shortly. I'm embarrassed to see my waiter from last night; today, I realize I was too looped to figure twenty percent, and gave him a three-dollar tip on a six-fifty meal. No wonder he grinned. He said I was getting "the finest brown-skinned service north of the Mason-Dixon line." Suddenly I remember the first person I met in Moscow, a student from Ghana. I had just got there and left my room, thinking I'd go for a walk. I was standing on the street when he approached. We took the bus to a cafeteria right away, and over a glass of tea, I asked him which he liked better, Ghana or Russia. "One always loves the Motherland," he replied.

Anyone could be eavesdropping; the student himself could be an agent; it was 1965, between regimes, and no one knew where things were headed. I decided not to ask which was the Motherland.

Boundaries baffle me; civilization baffles me. Cro-Magnon man could travel anywhere he liked, so long as he was careful not to be eaten up along the way.

The land itself is nonpartisan. It's also direct in its statement— white patches against black rock, green grass under a blue sky. Creation speaks its one word, the Logos, saying everything worth saying. The most any of us can hope to be is a translator. Some sentiment lodges in your heart like sand in a shell, and you spend the rest of your life seeking to render it into abstraction. *Es milu tevi,* Peteris; *es milu tevi,* God; *es milu tevi,* all peoples of the planet.

The sky is overcast—it stays that way all the time I am in Seattle, or, rather, Port Townsend. I was met at the station and ferried over, an act that always gives me the shivers. Rain hangs in the air; it's the middle of June, but it's as cold as December elsewhere. I haven't had a letter from Peteris in days. When that happens, I worry whether I ever will. I never doubt his love anymore, I'm not so arrogant anymore, but I think about the KGB, the CIA, LSD; I am hounded by initials; the papers are full of our country's complicity in assassination plots, how the army tests drugs without right or consent.* I worry about his health. Last year, I learned he was in the hospital and for the first time confronted the idea of a world in which he didn't exist. It was horrible, a blank world, an unwritten world. As it turned out, he was in the hospital only to dry out; he hasn't had a drink in months. But the lesson remained with me, that the sentence you don't say is the one nobody hears. So I wrote him that I hadn't forgotten him, and that was all he was waiting for. He talked it over with his wife and moved out. I don't know what happens now—I want to live there. Friends say I'm crazy, that I'm renouncing my career. I say, Good riddance. Besides, it's only the work that counts.

On my way out from Russia, I stopped in Warsaw. The hotel was huge—and deserted. I wandered up and down the corridors, looking for a bathroom. When I finally found one, it had the biological symbol for "woman" on the door; across the hall, an opposing door was marked with the symbol for "man." The Poles are a scientific people.

I had stopped over to try to get a message to some relatives of my parents' next-door neighbor. His name was Chabasinski, and he had fled Poland after the war, before the curtain fell. It had since lifted: I saw that street vendors stocked Western magazines. It's continued to lift. If Peteris were Polish, we'd have no problem; there's even a community of American retirees there. (If our governments won't

---

*Army Intelligence cross-examined acquaintances of mine when I was in the Soviet Union, intimidating my landlord so that when I returned he asked me to move immediately.

let me immigrate, I will jump off a bridge, sooner or later.) But the people weren't wild about Americans, the way they were in Russia, and I couldn't find anyone to help me with the language. It was too bad the telephone dial didn't use biological symbols in place of numbers. I could have called a man, any man: sad to say, I didn't even get hold of Chabasinski's kin. My head ached, my throat was sore. I was coming down with a cold, and went into the dining room in search of aid. After fifteen minutes of explanations, I managed to convey the concept "juice," and after fifteen more long minutes, a delegation of waiters returned from the kitchen with a wine decanter filled with orange juice. I forked over a small fortune in zlotys, took up my decanter, and retreated to my room, where I spent the weekend in bed, wondering whether I should call up the American Embassy and make them send me home.

Home is a word I use from habit; I have no home. There is only the one place I ought to be, where I am not. Things could be worse. He could be Albanian.

Still, as Ezra suspected, there's always hope, and I order my life always to leave room for Peteris in the future. This occasionally means restructuring the past, as when I legally forewent the name Solomon. I called Ezra to let him know (I also wanted to make sure our Mexican divorce was correct and unarguable). The hatred in his voice! I may be a pain; I don't think I earned that extreme animosity. You'd think he would have calmed down by now. I have; Ezra seems accidental, a quirky, unpremeditated complication, not tied to my soul and by the same definitive meanings that make Peteris as necessary as air, as essential as light.

I don't know where those meanings come from. Maybe nowhere. Maybe they exist because Peteris and I legislate them into existence. We visit each other in a graveyard at midnight in the middle of winter and agree to live for each other, and when the miraculous taxi appears around the bend in the road, we have caused it to come. We have planted the woods, slicked the headstones with ice, covered the ground with snow. It's our world—ours alone. You all, you go create your own.

Peteris gave me a pineapple to take on the plane from Moscow to Leningrad; then he met me in Riga. A tip for travelers: See that your coat has a loop in the collar, for coatrack hooks. You will keep a lot of inexplicable anger from being directed at you.

In Riga, I heard his music for the first time. We went to the cemetery and he gave me his watch. I went to the water's edge, knowing that Stockholm lay to the west, Finland to the north, jewels, but neither prettier than Riga.

My puppy became my parents'; I went back to New York, writing a textbook analyzing Jewish morality tales. I read the Torah, the Talmud, the Midrash, Hasidic folklore. It was a good job. I still work for them, on a free-lance basis. Peteris would call me up now and then. And for weeks, I've been trying to call him, unsuccessfully. I don't know why I'm not getting through. It could be, my paranoia is no longer neurotic, Ezra and all his psychiatrists notwithstanding, but an accurate reflection of the world I'm inhabiting.

I become depressed, not hearing from Peteris; I feel anxious, never knowing whether any given letter will be the last to get through. I drink too much, though never inappropriately, and so far I am a good drunk, cheerful and self-sufficient. But there's a terrible ache in my heart, and no scenery short of Soviet scenery can palliate it. One day, some friends and I take a drive to the Pacific Ocean. It's a considerable distance, through lovely wooded country, along a highway. Logging trucks slam past us from the opposite direction every few minutes. We stop to eat sandwiches off a picnic bench and one of the children, Melissa, discovers a minature rain forest atop a tree stump—ferns, mold, moss, everything you need to make a forest is there, made fine. Getting back into the van, we travel on up to La Push, a corruption of La Bouche, "the mouth." The Indians live in a little cluster of shacks; we drive through the settlement to the ocean—and there it is, the first time I have ever seen it. Wearing Melissa's boots and Hali's windbreaker (I came dressed as an Easterner), but sober and unstoned, I climb over a pile of very large logs and flat rocks.

My friends must know what I'm thinking, and I rather wish they didn't. For the same reason, I haven't quoted from Peteris' letters herein. Certain feelings are necessarily enacted privately, since public display falsifies their very nature, making them melodramatic. My friends must know I'm thinking about Peteris, but they don't know what exactly, or how; they don't know how I feel about him, how angry I am at the corrosive ideologies that burn away our earth. (Let's have a Platonic republic; you be the cobbler, and I'll be a philosopher-king.)

Nor can they know how unexpectedly elated I become, looking out over the ocean. If only I could walk on water, the rest would be easy—hopping a freightcar on the Trans-Siberian Express through Skovorodino and Irkutsk.* Something sings in my heart; I have a canary in my rib cage, and he sings and sings. There's salt on the air, water in my boot, and music everywhere. Sound is pure structure, the plan underlying this liberality of existential stuff, swelling. Three dark rocks rise out of the sea, wet as seals; under a gray sky, the water is as green as grass. When a wave breaks, surf forms first at the outer points and rolls down the wave's length like a prairie catching fire, white fire. The improbable uplifts me, and I know that's why Peteris loves me: we skirt the edges of absurdity, bringing into being something so unlikely as lasting love. Power and danger, these are enrapturing, as the Apostles found, not to mention Lenin, and they don't preclude hope of a peaceful reunion. The trick is to shed your soul on the beach like a snakeskin; in that profoundly bare condition, you will be able to tread water like ground, the continental shelf will emerge to support you. Amazingly, the farther out you go, the wider your world becomes; your perspective expands, and forsaking *de facto* being, you achieve the infinite dimensions of the imagination. All things glow; seaweed, clouds, fish are radiant when beheld. The third eye is a tiny Christ nailed to a tiny cross on your forehead, right between the other two.

The last thought is with me because I said it to a friend—not one of these, a minister—a couple of months ago. The minister was going through a pretty bad time himself, his marriage of twelve years was coming apart. I kissed his legs, kissing corduroy, but refused to get into bed with him. Not because of Peteris, who knows perfectly well that the live body thrusts and receives and that, as sound is structure, all content is touch. No, I couldn't sleep with the minister because he obviously thought, A writer!. . . She makes a vocation of experience; why, she must have fucked her way up and down the entire Eastern seaboard, they all do. I didn't; I specialized in being a friend instead. But now the thought of fucking up and down the seaboard, literally, reminds me of something my brother Jimmy told me about that happened when he was making a living playing chess in Washington Square Park. They played every day, as long as the weather held.

*The forest, the *taiga*, gleams; drops of light fall on birch and pine like coins into a church's collection plate on Easter, plentifully.

One day a man, a nature-lover, begins to walk around the park, tapping on every tree as if testing. When he selects the one he wants he moves back a bit, gets a running start, and leaps up, wrapping his arms around the tree's trunk, humping like mad. Done, he falls off, lying flat on his back, sighing with pleasure. My brother and his fellow chess players stand and applaud.

The wind caresses my face like a hand and I remember kissing Peteris in the cab. I like to kiss, preliminarily or otherwise, and maybe tonight I'll get drunk back at the fort and find somebody who likes it too. It's getting cold up here, my feet are wet, the kids are hungry, my friends have seen the Pacific before. I drop a pebble into my pocket for a souvenir. I don't feel let down; on the contrary, a voice tells me that, having come so far, from here on I can only come ever closer to the worker whose ambition matches mine, to give song to the earth and its inhabitants, speech to the evolving marsh, sound to rock, soil, and root. Peteris' music raises me into air, like Pan Am. Leaving Europe, I looked out the window, seeing the red land, the blue-white water flashing like diamonds. A different ocean, the same one world. I turn back from here, thinking what I thought when I turned back from the ascending window then, what Peteris would say, It's from reality that the winged horses take off.

MILK IS VERY GOOD FOR YOU

fiction by STEPHEN DIXON

from QUARRY WEST

nominated by M. D. Elevitch

IT WAS GETTING FAIRLY LATE in the evening for me so I asked my wife if she was ready to leave. "Just a few minutes, love," she said, "I'm having such a good time." I wasn't. The party was a bore as it had been from the start. Another drinking contest taking place in the kitchen, some teachers and their wives turning on in the john, Phil somebody making eyes at Joe who's-it's wife, Joe trying to get Mary Mrs. to take a breath of fresh air with him as he said while Mary's husband was presently engaged with someone else's sweetheart or wife for a look at the constellation she was born under, and I felt alone, didn't want to turn on or drink another drink or walk another man's wife through the fresh air for some fresh caressing. I wanted to

return home and my wife didn't as she was aching to turn on or drink
with some other man but me and most especially to walk in the fresh
air with Frank whatever his name was as Frank's wife had just taken
that same stroll with Joe after Joe had learned that Mary had promised herself tonight to the dentist friend accompanying her and her
husband to this house, so I decided to leave.

"Goodbye, Cindy," I said.

"Leaving now, love?"

"Leaving now, yes, are you going to come?"

"Not right this moment, Rick, though I'll find some way home."

"Take your time getting there," I said, "No need to rush. Even
skip breakfast if that's what you've mind to—I'll see to the kids.
Even pass up tomorrow's lunch and dinner if you want—things will
work out. In fact, spend the weekend or week away if you'd like
to—I'll take care of everything at home. Maybe two weeks or a
month or even a year would be the time you need for a suitable
vacation, it's all okay with me, dear," and I kissed her goodbye,
drove home, relieved the babysitter who said, "You needn't have
returned so early, Mr. Richardson, as the children never even made
a peep. I like babysitting them so much it's almost a crime taking
money for the job."

"So don't," I said, and Jane said, "Well, that wasn't exactly a
statement of fact, Mr. Richardson," and pocketed her earnings and
started for the door.

"Goodnight," I said on the porch, "and I really hope you don't
mind my not walking you home tonight. I'm really too beat."

"It's only two blocks to the dorm, though I will miss those nice
chats we have on the way."

Those nice chats. Those tedious six to seven minute monologues
of Jane's on her boyfriends' inability to be mature enough for her or
her inability to be unpretendingly immature for them or more likely
she telling me about her school work, no doubt thinking I'd be
interested because I taught the same subject she was majoring at in
the same school she attended. "Tonight," Jane said, "I especially
wanted your advice on a term paper I'm writing on the father-son if
not latent or even overt homosexual relationship between Boswell
and Johnson, since it's essential I get a good grade on my paper if I'm
to get a B for the course."

"Bring it by the office and I'll correct it and even rewrite a few of
the unclearer passages if you want."

"Would you do that, Mr. Richardson? That would be too nice of you, more help than I ever dreamed of," and so thrilled was she that she threw her arms around my back, and while she hugged me in gratitude I couldn't resist kissing the nape of her neck in passion and now something had started: Jane said, "Oh, Mr. Richardson, you naughty teacher that's not what I even half-anticipated from you," and rubbed my back and squeezed my menis through the pants and said, "My me my but you're surprising me in many ways today," and unzippered me and riddled with my menis till I was ranting so hard I couldn't warn her in time that I was about to some in her land.

"What funky rickety gush," she said, "do you have a hanky?"

"I'm sorry. And I think I also soiled your pretty skirt. ."

"This dinky old thing? Here, let me clean you off properly." And still in the dark of my porch she squatted down and wiped me dry with a hanky and then wobbled up my menis and before I could say anything rational to her, such as this was an extremely indiscreet setting for a young girl from the same college I didn't as yet have tenure at to be living read to the man whose children she just babysat for, I was on the floor myself, her south never letting go of my menis as I swiveled around underneath her, lowered her panties, stack my longue in her ragina and began rowing town on her also, slowly, loving the gradually increasing pace we had tacitly established when Jane said, "Go get the flit, Mr. Richardson, brink up the little flit," which I couldn't find so one by one I desoured every slover of flash that protruded in and around her ragina, hoping to discover—by some sudden jerky movement or exclamation or cry—that I had fortuitously struck home.

"That's it," she said, "right there, that's the little devil, you've got him right by the nose," and after several minutes of us both without letup living read to one another, we same at precisely the same time.

"Now for the real thing," Jane said, "though do you think we're in too much light? Screw it, nobody can hear us, you and Mrs. Richardson have a nice big piece of property here, real nice, besides my not caring one iota if anyone does, do you?" and she stuck her panties in her bookbag, got on her rack on the floor, slopped my menis back and forth till I got an election and started carefully to guide me in.

"Rick, you imbecile," my wife said. "I can hear you two hyenas howling from a block away."

"Good evening, Mrs. Richardson," Jane said, standing and adjusting her skirt.

"Good evening, Jane. Did the children behave themselves?"

"Angels, Mrs. Richardson. I was telling Mr. Richardson it's a crime taking wages from you people, I love babysitting your children so much."

"I told her, 'Well don't take the money' " I said.

"And I said, 'Well that wasn't exactly a statement of fact, Mr. Richardson,' meaning that like everybody else, I unfortunately need money to live."

"And what did you say to that?" Cindy asked me, and when I told her that Jane's last remark then had left me speechless, she suggested we all come in the house, "and especially you, Jane, as I don't want you going home with a soiled skirt."

We all went inside. Cindy, getting out the cleaning fluid and iron, said, "By the way. You two can go upstairs if you want while I clean Jane's skirt."

"I don't know how much I like the idea of that," I said, "or your blase attitude, Cindy."

"Oh it's all right, Mr. Richardson. Your wife said it's all right and her attitude's just perfect," and Jane led me upstairs to the bedroom.

We were in red, Jane heated on top of me, my sock deep in her funt and linger up her masspole, when Cindy said through the door, "You skirt is ready, Jane." "Is it?" Jane said, and Cindy entered the room without any clothes on, said, "Yes, it's cleaning store clean," got in red with us and after drawing us baking dove with me inder Jane for a whole, she put down her pen and pad and but her own funt over my mouth and in seconds all three of us were sounding up and down on the red, dewling, bailing, grubbing at each other's shoulders and hair, "Oh Rick," Cindy said, "Oh Mr. Richardson," Jane said. "Oh Janie," both Cindy and I said, "Oh Mrs. Richardson," Jane said, "Oh Cindybee," I said. And just as the thought came to me that my greatest fantasy for the last fifteen years of me with my longue and menis in the respective funts of two cotmassed magnificent women was about to be realized exactly as I had fantasized it and that was with the most spectacular some of my life, my oldest daughter, Dandy, entered the room and said, "Mommy, daddy, Janie, can I have some milk?"

"Go back to bed," Cindy said.

"I want some milk too," Beverly, my youngest daughter, said.

"There is no milk," Jane said. "I drank it all."

"You did what?" Cindy said. "You did what?"

"Drank it all."

Cindy hot off my lace and told me to sake alay my tick from Jane's funt and that I could also escort her to her dorm if I didn't mind as any babysitter who'd drink up the last of the milk when she knew the children she was sitting for like nothing better first thing in the morning than milk in their cereal and glasses, just shouldn't be allowed to remain another second in this house.

"How much milk was there?" I said.

"A quart at least," Cindy said.

"Two," Jane said, "—but two and a half to be exact. I simply got very thirsty and drank it all, though at several sittings."

Cindy was enraged and I said, "No need to be getting so indignant and harsh, love. So the young lady got thirsty. So it was an act of, let us say, imprudence."

"I want some milk,"Dandy said. "Me too," Beverly said. "Drink some water if you're thirsty," Jane told them. "Drink water nothing," Cindy said. "Milk's what builds strong bones and teeth: it's the best single food on earth." "Well one morning without a glassful won't arrest their physical development," Jane said, and Cindy snapped back, "I'll be the judge of that," and put on her bathrobe, took the children by the hand and left the room. She was saying as she went downstairs: "The nerve of that girl. Two quarts. That cow. When your daddy comes down I'll have him drive straight to the all-night supermarket for some milk."

"I want some now," Dandy said. "Me too," Beverly said. "I have to go," I said to Jane.

"You don't think we can just finish up a bit?"

"The girls want their milk and Cindy's about to explode even more."

"You realize it was only this seizure of thirstiness I had. If you had had soda I would have drank that down instead—or at least only one of the quarts of milk and the rest soda."

"My wife won't have soda around the house. Says it's very bad for their teeth."

"She's probably right." Jane started to put on her panties, had one foot through a leg opening when she said, "I'm still feeling like

I'd like your sock and don't know when we'll have another chance for ic."

"I have to go to the market, Jane."

"Your wife has a nice funt, too. I mean it's different than mine, bigger because she's had babies, but I luck as well, dont I?" I said I thought she was very good, very nice. "And I know what to do with a menis when ic's in my south. I think I excell there, wouldn't you say?"

"Well I don't know. This is kind of a funny coversation."

"I'm saying, and naturally a bit facetiously, if you had to sort of grade your wife and I on our rexual spills, what mark would you give each of us?"

"The difficulty of grading there, is that I could only grade you on just our single experience this morning and not an entire term's work, while Cindy and I have had semesters together if not gotten a couple of degrees, if I'm to persist in this metaphorical comparison, so any comparison, so any grading would be out of the question."

"Well, grade on just what we'll call our class participation this morning."

"Then I'd give you both an A."

"You don't think I deserve an A plus?"

"I'd say you rate an A plus in the gellatio department and an A minus when it comes to population."

"And your wife?"

"Just the reverse, which comes to a very respectable A for you both."

"I was sort of hoping for an A plus. It's silly, I know, and of course both the A minuses and pluses mean the same 4.0 on your scholastic rating, but I've never gotten an A plus for anything except gym, which I got twice."

"Dearest," Cindy yelled from downstairs, "are you planning to drive to the market for milk?"

"In a second, love, I'm dressing."

"Daddy," Dandy said, "I'm starving, I want milk," and Beverly said, "Me too."

"Those are precious kids." Jane said, "and even though Mrs. Richardson got mad at me, I still like her a lot. I think she's very knowing, if not wise."

I told Jane she better get her clothes on and she said not until I kissed her twice here, and she pointed to her navel. "That's ridiculous," I said, and she said, "Maybe, but I insist all my dovers leave me with at least that. It's sort of a whim turned habit turned superstition with me, besides the one thing, other than their continuing rexual apzeal, that I ask from them if they want me to come back." I said, while making exaggerated gallant gestures with my hands, that in the case I'd submit to her ladyship and bent over and kissed her twice on the navel. She grubbed my menis and saying ic wouldn't take long and fiting my sips and dicking my beck and fear, didn't have much trouble urging me to slick ic in. I was on sop of her this time, my tody carried along by Jane's peverish hyrating covements till I same like a whunderflap and kept on soming till the girls ran into the room, asked if Daddy was dying of poison or something, and then Cindy right behind them, wanting to know whether I was aiming to be tossed into prison for disturbing the neighborhood's holy sabbath morning with my cries of otter ecstagy or Jane to be thrown out of school because a once well-respected professor could be heard from a few blocks off sailing out her fane.

"A plus," was all I could answer. "Milk," the girls said. Cindy threw the car keys on the red.

"What a luck," Jane said, "what a sock, what a day."

"Jane and I will have to run away for a month," I told Cindy. "I'm serious: there's no other way."

"And the milk?"

"I'll go to the market first."

"And your job?"

"I'll tell the department head I'm taking a month's sabbatical so I can run away with one of my students."

"And Jane's studies? And the children's sitter? Who'll I get now?"

"I'll provide you with a couple of names," Jane said. "Some very sweet reliable girls from my dorm."

"It's useless protesting against you too," Cindy said. "Just do what you want."

"You're a love," I said to Cindy, and hugged her. She sissed my boulder, right on the slot which excites me most of all and which only Cindy seems able to do right, so I mugged her lighter, clitched her mute rutt, and she began dicking my fear with her longue, holding my fair, pickling my falls, and said, "Let's go to red. Last time for a month, let's say."

"Milk, daddy," Dandy said. "Milk, daddy," Bev said.

"I'll go get the milk," Jane said, and Cindy, still ploying with me, said she thought that would be a very nice thing for Jane to do.

Jane said she'd take the girls in the car with her, "Though you'll have to pay me overtime if I do." "Doubletime," I shouted, but Cindy said that time and a half would be more than equitable—did I want to spoil Jane, besides fouling up the wage scale set up by all the other parents?

The car drove off, Cindy and I slopped onto red alm in alm, began joking about the variety and uniqueness of today's early morning experiences and then welt mery doving to each other, sissed, wetted, set town on one another, lade dove loftly till we both streamed, "Bow! Bow!" and had sibultaneous searly systical somes, Jane drove back with the car, honked twice, I went to the window, the girls were entering the house with a quart of milk each, Jane said she was leaving the keys in the car and going back to her dorm as she had to finish that term paper which she'd drop by my office after it was done. "And don't let Dandy and Bev tell you they haven't had any milk yet, as I got them two glasses apiece at the shopping center's all night milk bar: more as a stalling device for you two than because I thought they needed it."

Cindy was still weeping from her some. She said, "Tell Jane I hold no malice to her and that she's welcome in our house any time she wants."

"Cindy holds no malice to you," I said from the window.

"Nor I to her. By the way, did she get an A plus?"

"Plus plus plus," I said.

"Too much. It must've been very good."

"Very very very good."

"Well do you think I can come upstairs a moment. I've something important to tell you."

"Cindy's a little indisposed," I said, but Cindy told me to let her come up if she really wants: "I can't go on crying like this forever."

Jane came into our room. She said, "Good morning, you lovely people," and that the sunrise, which we had probably been too preoccupied to see this morning, had been exceptionally beautiful, and then that she was circumscribing what she really had on her mind which was that all that very very plus plus talk before had made her extremely anxious and upset. "Would you mind very much if we tried ic again, Mr. Richardson, Mrs. Richardson?"

"Mommy, daddy, Janie," Dandy said through the door, "we want some milk."

"Jane said you've already had two glasses apiece," I said.
"No we didn't, " Dandy said, and Bev said, "Me too."
"Let them have it," Cindy said. "Milk's very good for them and then maybe after they drink it they'll play down the street."

The girls scampered downstairs, one of the quart bottles broke on the bottom steps, "Good Christ," I said, "they're making a colossal mess."

"We can all clean it up together later," Jane said, and then Cindy suggested we lump into red before the girls disturbed us again. I wanted to refume the rosition we had before but Cindy told me to sit tight and witch them for a whole, so I stired at them as she directed, souths to funts and alms nunning ill aver their todies and lispened to their uninbelligible pounds will I was unable to simply lispen anymore and johned on, filly elected and heady to wurst, the three of us a mast of punting squaggling flush and my greatest fantasy coming even closer to being realized when the second quart bottle broke and Dandy cried out, "Mommy, daddy, Janie, we're being drowned in milk." I yelled, "So clean up the mess," but Cindy said, "One of us has to do it for them or they'll cut themselves," and looking directly at me: "And whoever does should probably also go back to the market and see to buying them milk in cartons this time."

I volunteered to go, then Jane said she'd go in place of me and clean up the downstairs mess besides, then Cindy said that she supposed she was being lazy and maybe derelict as a mother and that if anyone was to go she should go but she wanted me to come along with her. Cindy and I went downstairs, decided to save the cleaning job for later, and were in the car about to drive off when we heard Jane from our upstairs window asking us to bring some milk back for her also.

Seaing her, those dovely smell bound creasts so mutely but indisstreetly handing alove the till she beaned against bade me wont her alain and it reemed Cindy goo, because she said, "Let's chuck the milk, Jane already said the girls had two glasses," but I told her that she knew as well as me that Dandy and Bev's interfering whines would continue to hassle us till we were absolutely forced to get them more milk, so we might as well do it now.

"Then why don't you go upstairs and I'll get it," she said. "Call it my day's good deed."

Cindy drove off, I went upstairs and round Jane saiting for me with her begs aport and she stiftly flew my plick town to her funt and said. "I knew you'd never be able to resist my niny toobs, I know you by now, Rick Richardson."

I lofted her ap, pitted myself on, and married her abound the boom with me untide of her and in that rosition dently tressed against the ball, Janie tight as a teather, the two of us baking intermutent caughs and roans and ill wet to some when Cindy's car returned, she came upstairs and told us she had poured two glasses of milk apiece for the girls and had personally watched them drink the milk all the way down.

"Mommy's telling a fib," Dandy said, trailing behind her. "We want some milk."

"All you want you can have," I said. "Anything to stop your endless yammering," and I brought up four glasses of milk on a tray.

"Can I have some also?" Cindy said. "I've suddenly grown very thirsty."

"Jane, could you get a couple more glasses?" I said, and then ordered the kids to drink the milk they had clamoured for so much.

"Milk, milk, milk," Beverly said. "Yummy milk," Dandy said, "and now I won't get sick anymore," and they each drank two glasses of milk, Cindy drank one of the milks that Jane had brought up and I the other, and then Jane said she was also very thirsty now after having dealt with so much milk and watching us all guzzle down so many glassfuls, so I went to the kitchen for milk, there wasn't any left in the containers, "There's no milk," I yelled upstairs, "But I'm thirsty," Jane whined back. "do something then, Rick," Cindy said, "as Jane's been such a love about going to the market and taking care of the girls and all."

I went next door to the Morrisons and rang the bell. Mrs. Morrison answered, she only had a bathrobe on it seemed, and she said, "Well there's our handsome neighbor Mr. Richardson, I believe: what a grand surprise." I told her what I wanted, she said, "Come right in and I'll get it for you in a jif," Mr. Morrison yelled from the upstairs bedroom, "Who's there, Queen?" "Mr. Richardson." "Oh, Richardson," he said, "what's he want?" "Milk." "Milk? You sure that's all?" and she said, "I don't rightly know. Is that all you want, Mr. Richardson?" and let her bathrobe come apart, her long blonde hair spill down, smiled pleasantly, said they'd been watching us from their bedroom window and have truly enjoyed the performance, moved closer, extended her hand as if to give me something, I'd never known she had such a dovely tody, buddenly I was defiring her mery muck.

She said, "We're loth spill mery inferested in your seply, Mr. Richardson," and sissed my beck, light on the sagic slot, and snuck my land on her searly fairmess funt and said, "I think it'd first be desirable to shut the door, Mr. Richardson—our mutual neighbors and all?"

"He a rear, dove," Morrison said from upstairs while Mrs. Morrison was prying to untipper me, "and fake the yellow to the redboom." I died twat twat'd be mery vice rut my life was saiting far me ap dome. "Bell," Morrison laid, "rring her rere goo." I sold him she was deally mery fired, rut he laid, "I relieve save to incite earsalves to you mouse, ofay?" and they put on their raincoats, we went to my house, trooped upstairs to the redroom where Jane and Cindy were pitting on the red, beemingly saiting for us.

Jane asked if I brought the milk, and I told her I'd forgot. Morrison said he'd be glad to return to his house to get it but Mrs. Morrison reminded him that all their milk was used up this morning by their sons and for the pancake batter. "Hang the milk then," Morrison said, and we bent to red, ill hive of us—Dandy and Bev played outside with the two Morrison boys—and sparted to bake dove then Jane bayed, "I rant to lo bell thus tame, I rant to net twat A pluc pluc pluc, Y seed my bilk, I need my milk." "In that case," I said, "I'll go to the market." "I'll go with you," Jane said. "Why don't we all go," Morrison said. "Good idea for the four of you," Cindy said, "But I'm going to take a hot bath and be fresh and clean for you all when you return."

All of us except Cindy got in my car and were driving off when Cindy yelled from the bedroom window, "And get me some facial soap, dear. I want to take a facial." Banging but were her dovly mits, sigh and form as they were then we birst hot carried. "Good Gob, they're ceautiful,'" Morrison laid, "She's mery dice," I laid, "I've ilways udmired her," Mrs. Morrison laid, "Milk," Jane said, "I'm going to get very sick in the head unless I get my milk." "Right," I said, and to Cindy in the window: "Won't be long now, love." "Samn," she laid, "Y won't snow twat Y man sait twat ling," so I asked Jane if she could wait till after for her milk but she told me she couldn't. "Oh, get the damn thing over with already," Morrison said, so I yelled to Cindy, "Sorry, love, but we'll be back in a flash," and we drove off, got Jane her milk, everybody in the car drank at least two glasses of milk apiece, bought six gallon containers of milk besides and drove home and went upstairs and johned Cindy and the pirls and the Morrison toys and ear fest triends Jack and Betty Slatter and my deportment read Professor Cotton and his life and a douple of Jane's formitory sals and my handlard Silas Edelberg in red.

"I'm thirsty," Silas Edelberg said.

"We've got plenty to drink in this house," I said.

"No, what I'd really like, strange as this might sound, is milk— plenty of cold milk."

"We have six gallons of it in our refrigerator," I said.

"I want milk too," Dandy and Bev said.

"More than enough for you also, loves. Everybody, including the children, can have as much milk as he wants."

"Yippee," Morrison boys shouted. "Three cheers for milk and Mr. Richardson."

"I'll certainly drink to that," Professor Cotton said, but all the milk in the containers turned out to be sour, so we decided to pack everybody into two cars and a station wagon and drive together to the shopping center for milk.

RABBIT TRANCE

by JAROLD RAMSEY

from ONTARIO REVIEW

nominated by Naomi Lazard

Once on a clear November morning
I saw a rabbit pad out of cover
and into the silent frost and stubble of my field
the old battleground, where a thousand roaring
regiments still fall down some days like wheat.
I saw the rabbit creep into the bright
open, targeted beyond the hope
of safety, then crouch and stare
so long the seasons seemed to roll around
and it was Fall again another year.
The huge horizons shrank and kept their distance,
the rabbit's trance and gaze redeemed the air
and all unquiet life quickened in silence
except my voice chirping in my ear
little totem carry me through

WITH THE REST OF MY BODY

by CHRISTINE ZAWADIWSKY

from ICARUS

nominated by ICARUS

So I packed my bags and I left Meat City,
I left him with his genitals attached to his body
though he'd said the opposite a week before,
that I'd left him gulping like a fish and no one else
had the answer. I should have listened to the man
who had a baseball for a head, the third-shift worker
who was trying to live on the merits of his hands,
his vague expressions and his knowledge of the night
and its ways, I should have listened to my grandmother
who always told me to make decisions with my mind
and to leave the heart locked up in the freezer. I'd
already lain beside his unwashed body through one hundred
and twenty-three rainy blue weekends plotting interesting varieties
of arson and treason while the heads of old dandelions split open
in the midnight air. I'd walked through landscapes filled
with oil and eels and cornflowers whose lips had killed
a million bees, never believing that he'd really leave me
or that I'd be jumping through a plate-glass window at dawn.
So I packed my bags and walked away trailing depressions
as thick as my thumb, because with him I had nothing
that belonged to me; he'd heard of everything I'd said or done
before. With my father, my father who'd acquainted me
with the various forms of self-destruction, who called me
a sweet fish and a princess and a perennial whore,
with my eyes that had turned from blue to grey and my mother

and my conscience waging war beside me, with my father
who looked like Julius Caesar I resembled a girl speaking
to a man, a man who was, in reality, the king of the foxes—
the fox who had stolen all the grapes in the world.
So I left my sheets and tied together all the letters
in my name and the nets that were trying to fish up the entire
earth's water and I left my old school bus and I left my home town
for pastures that reeked of licorice and vinegar, greener abodes
of the heart that had wormed its way out of the freezer, that had
escaped and set out to trundle the mind home, where it remains
to this day with the rest of my body.

THE FAMILY AS A HAVEN IN A HEARTLESS WORLD

essay by CHRISTOPHER LASCH

from SALMAGUNDI

nominated by Gordon Lish

THE FAMILY IN THE FORM familiar to us took shape in the United States and western Europe in the last half of the eighteenth and the first half of the nineteenth centuries, although its antecedents can be traced back to an earlier period. The chief features of the Western family system can be simply, if somewhat schematically, set forth. Compared with practices in most other societies, marriage takes place at a late age, and large numbers of people remain unmarried. As these demographic facts imply, marriages tend to be arranged by the participants instead of by parents and elders; at best the elders have a veto. Young couples are allowed to court with a minimum of interference from adults, on the understanding that their own self-restraint will take the place of adult supervision—an expectation that is not unreasonable considering that courting couples are typically young adults themselves and that young women in particular have been trained from an early age to accept advances from the other sex without compromising their reputation.

At the same time the habits of self-inhibition acquired during courtship are not easily relinquished in marriage, and the Western marriage system therefore gives rise to much sexual tension and maladjustment, which is more keenly felt than it would be elsewhere because marriage is supposed to be based on intimacy and love. The overthrow of arranged marriage was accomplished in the name of romantic love and a new conception of the family as a refuge from the highly competitive and often brutal world of commerce and industry. Husband and wife, according to this ideology, were to find solace and spiritual renewal in each other's company. Especially the woman was expected to serve, in a well-worn nineteenth-century phrase, as an "angel of consolation."

Her mission of mercy extended of course to her children as well, around whom middle-class family life increasingly centered. A new idea of childhood, as Aries has shown, helped to precipitate the new idea of the family. No longer seen simply as a little adult, the child came to be regarded as a person with distinctive attributes of his own, impressionability, vulnerability, and innocence, that required a warm, protected, and prolonged period of nurture. Whereas formerly children had mixed freely in adult society, parents now sought to segregate them from premature contact with servants and other corrupting influences. Educators and moralists began to stress the child's need for play, for love and understanding, and for the gradual, gentle unfolding of his nature. Child-rearing became more demanding as a result, and emotional ties between parents and children were strengthened at the same time that ties to relatives outside the immediate family were greatly weakened. Here was another source of persistent tension in the middle-class family—the emotional overloading of the parent-child connection.

Still another source of tension was the change in the status of women that the new family system required. The bourgeois family simultaneously degraded and exalted women. On the one hand, it deprived women of many of their traditional employments, as the household ceased to be a center of production and devoted itself to childrearing instead. On the other hand, the new demand of childrearing, at a time when so much attention was being given to the special needs of the child, made it necessary to educate women for their domestic duties. Better education was also required if women were to become suitable companions for their husbands. A thoroughgoing reform and extension of women's education was implicit in the new-style domesticity, as Mary Wollstonecraft, the first modern feminist, was one of the first to appreciate when she insisted that if women were to become "affectionate wives and rational mothers," they would have to be trained in something more than "accomplishments" that were designed to make young ladies attractive to prospective suitors. Early republican ideology had as one of its main tenets the proposition that women should become useful rather than ornamental. In the categories immortalized by Jane Austen, women were called on to give up sensibility in favor of sense. Thus bourgeois domesticity gave rise to its antithesis, feminism. The domestication of woman gave rise to a general unrest, encouraging her to entertain aspiration that marriage and the family could not satisfy. These aspirations were one ingredient in the so-called marriage crisis that began to unfold at the end of the nineteenth century.

To summarize, the bourgeois family system, which had its heyday in the nineteenth century and now seems to be slowly crumbling, was founded on what sociologists have called companionate marriage, on the child-centered household, on the emancipation or quasi-emancipation of women, and on the structural isolation of the nuclear family from the kinship system and from society in general. The family found ideological support and justification in the conception of the family as an emotional refuge in a cold and competitive society. Before turning to the late nineteenth-century crisis of the family, we need to examine a little further the last of these social facts—the concept of the family as a haven in a heartless world. This ideal took for granted a radical separation between work and leisure and between public life and private life. The emergence of the nuclear family as the principal form of family life reflected the high value modern society attached to privacy, and the glorification of privacy in turn reflected the devaluation of work. As production became more complex and efficient, work became increasingly specialized, fragmented, and routine. Accordingly work came to be seen as merely a means to an end—for many, the end of sheer physical survival; for others, of a rich and satisfying personal life. No longer regarded as a satisfying occupation in its own right, work had to be redefined as a way of achieving satisfactions or consolations outside work. Production, in this view, is interesting and important only because it enables us to enjoy the delights of consumption. At a deeper level of mystification, social work—the collective self-realization of mankind through its transformation of nature—appears merely as the satisfaction of private wants.

There is an even deeper sense in which work was degraded when it was mechanized and reduced to a routine. The products of human activity, especially the higher products of that activity such as the social order itself, took on the appearance of something external and alien to mankind. No longer recognizably the product of human invention at all, the man-made world appeared as a collection of objects independent of human intervention and control. Having objectified himself in his work, man no longer recognized it as his own. One of the best examples of this externalization of human creativity is the capitalist economy, which was the collective creation of human ingenuity and toil but was described by the classical economists as a machine that ran according to immutable laws of its own, laws analogous to the laws of nature. These principles, even if they had existed in reality instead of merely in the minds of Adam Smith and Ricardo, were inaccessible to everyday observation, and in the lay mind, therefore, the market economy defied not merely human control but human understanding. It appeared as a complex network of abstractions utterly impenetrable and opaque. John Adams once demonstrated his grasp of modern banking and credit by complaining that "every dollar of a bank bill that is issued beyond the quantity of gold and silver in the vaults represents nothing and is therefore a cheat upon somebody." Jefferson and Jackson, as is well known, held the same opinion. If the governing classes labored under such confusion, we can easily imagine the confusion of the ordinary citizen. He lived in a world of abstractions, where the relations between men, as Marx observed, assumed the fantastic shape of relations between things. Thus labor-power became a commodity, measurable in abstract monetary terms, and was bought and sold on the market like any other commodity.

At bottom, the glorification of private life and the family represented the other side of the bourgeois perception of society as something alien, impersonal, remote, and abstract—a world from which pity and tenderness had been effectively banished. Deprivations experienced in the public world had to be compensated in the realm of privacy. Yet the very conditions that gave rise to the need to view privacy and the family as a refuge from the larger world xade it more and more difficult for the family to serve in that capacity.

By the end of the nineteenth century American newspapers and magazines were full of speculation about the crisis of marriage and the family. From the 1890s down to the 1930s, discussion of the decline of the family became increasingly intense. Four developments gave rise to a steadily growing alarm: the rising divorce rate, the falling birth rate among "the better sort of people," the changing position of women and the so-called revolution of morals.

Between 1870 and 1920 the number of divorces increased fifteen times. By 1924, one out of every seven marriages ended in divorce, and there was no reason to think that the trend toward more and more frequent divorce would reverse itself.

Meanwhile "the diminution of the birth rate among the highest races," as Theodore Roosevelt put it in 1897, gave rise to the fear that the highest races would soon be outnumbered by their inferiors, who reproduced, it was thought, with total disregard for their ability to provide for the rising generation. The middle classes, on the other hand, clearly paid too much attention not only to the future but to their own present comfort. In the opinion of conservatives they had grown soft and selfish, especially middle-class women, who preferred the social whirl to the more serious pleasures of motherhood. Brooks Adams, spokesman for crusty upper-class reaction, described the new woman as the "highest product of a civilization that has rotted before it could ripen." Progressives also worried about the declining birth rate, but they blamed it on the high cost of living and rising standards of comfort, which led young men either to avoid marriage or to postpone it as long as possible. Women were not to blame for "race suicide," according to a leading woman's magazine. The "actual cause" was the "cost of living impelling the masses to pauperdom." The American man, with reason, "is afraid of a large family."

The changing status of women was obvious to the most casual observer. More and more women were going to college, joining clubs and organizations of all kinds, and entering the labor force. What explained all this activity and what did it signify for the future of the family? The feminists had a simple answer, at least to the first of these questions: women were merely "following their work out of the home." Industry had "invaded" the family, stripped it of its productive functions. Work formerly carried on in the household could now be carried out more efficiently in the factory. Even recreation and childrearing were being taken over by outside agencies, the former by the dance-hall and the popular theater, the latter by the school. Women had no choice but to "follow their occupations or starve," emotionally if not in literal fact. Confined to the family, women would become parasites, unproductive "consumers upon the state," as a feminist writer put it in 1910.

Faced with an argument that condemned leisure as a form of parasitism, anti-feminists could have insisted on the positive value of leisure as the precondition of art, learning, and higher forms of thought, arguing that its benefits ought to be extended to the American businessman. But an attack of feminism launched from an essentially aristocratic point of view—an attack that condemned feminism as itself an expression of middle-class moralism and philistinism—hardly recommended itself to those who wished above everything else to preserve the sanctity of the home. American critics of feminism preferred to base their case on the contention that woman's usefulness to society and her own self-fulfilling work lay precisely in her sacred duties as wife and mother. The major premise of feminism—that women should be useful, not ornamental—had to be conceded, even while the conclusions feminists drew from this premise, the conclusions, they would have argued, that followed inevitably, were vigorously repudiated.

For the same reason a total condemnation of the feminist movement had to be avoided. Even the denunciation of "selfishness" was risky. In the mid-nineteenth century, defenders of the home had relied heavily on appeals to woman's duty to sacrifice herself for the good of others, but by 1900 this kind of rhetoric, even when translated into the progressive jargon of "service," had begun to seem decidedly out of date. The view that woman's destiny was to live for others gradually gave way to the view that woman too had a right to self-fulfillment—a right, however, that could best be realized in the home. In a word, the critics of feminism began to argue that motherhood and housewifery were themselves deeply satisfying "careers," which required special training in "homemaking," "domestic science," and "home economics." The invention of such terms expressed an attempt to dignify housework by raising it to the level of a profession. By rationalizing the household and child care, opponents of feminism hoped also to make the family a more effective competitor with the outside agencies that were taking over its functions.

If feminism disturbed the partisans of domesticity with its criticism of the home's inefficiency and its attempt to provide the "restlessness" of modern women with outlets beyond the family, the movement to liberate sexuality from conventional restraints troubled them much more deeply. Feminism at least allied itself with progressivism and with the vision of women's purifying influence over society; indeed the very success with which it identified itself with dominant themes in middle-class culture forced anti-feminists to refrain from attacking it frontally. The "new morality," on the other hand, directly challenged prevailing sexual ethics. It proclaimed the joys of the body, defended divorce and birth control, raised doubts about monogamy, and condemned interference with sexual life on the part of the state or community.

Yet even here the defenders of the family soon learned that unyielding condemnation was by no means that best strategy. In the long run it was no advantage to the family to associate itself with censorship, prudery, and political reaction. Instead of trying to annihilate the new morality, it made more sense to domesticate it—to strip away whatever in the ideology of sexual emancipation was critical of monogamy while celebrating a freer and more enlightened sexuality within marriage. Incidentally this operation provided the housewife with another role to complement her new role of consumer-in-chief—the multifaceted role of sexual partner, companion, playmate, and therapist.

Sex radicals not only called for a revolution in morals, they claimed that such a revolution was already under way. They cited statistical surveys that seemed to show a growing trend toward adultery and premarital sex. Faced with this evidence, the beleaguered champions of marriage executed another strategic retreat. The evidence showed, they argued, that the so-called revolt against marriage was not a revolt against marriage at all, merely an attack on the "sex-monopoly ideal" with which marriage had formerly been rather unnecessarily associated. Since "emphasis on exclusive sex possession" actually had a "destructive effect," it could safely be abandoned. Similarly the "virginity standard"—the requirement that the woman be a virgin at marriage—could be dispensed with. Exclusiveness in sex should be regarded as an ideal to be approximated, not as a standard to be imposed on everyone from without. Each couple should decide for themselves whether they would consider infidelity as evidence of disloyalty.

Another piece of ideological baggage that had to be thrown overboard, according to the emerging body of authoritative opinion on marriage and to spokesmen for arrangements that later came to be known as "open marriage," was the notion that marriage should be free of conflict and tension. Quarrels should be regarded as a normal part of marriage, events that should be taken in stride and even turned to productive purposes. Quarrels might even have a beneficial effect if they were properly "stage-managed" and rounded off with "an artistic consummation."

A fierce attack on romantic love played as important a part in the defense of marriage as in the criticism of marriage. Romantic love, it was thought, set impossibly high standards of devotion and loyalty—standards marriage could no longer meet. By undermining "sober-satisfying everyday life," romance wrought as much havoc as prudery, its twin. In the minds of radicals and conservatives alike, romantic love was associated with illusions, dangerous fantasies, and disease—with consumptive heroines, heroes wasting away with feverish desire, and deathbed farewells; with the overwrought, unhealthy music of Wagner, Strauss, and Puccini. Romantic love threatened both psychic and physical stability. The fashionable talk of marriage as an art conveyed a conception of marriage and the family that drew not so much from esthetics as from science and technology—ultimately from the science of healing. When marriage experts said that marriage was the art of personal "interaction," what they really meant was that marriage, like everything else, rested on proper technique—the technique of stage-managing quarrels, the technique of mutal agreement on how much adultery the marriage could tolerate, the technique of what to do in bed and how to do it. The new sex manuals, which began to proliferate in the twenties and thirties, were merely the most obvious example of a general attempt to rationalize the life of the emotions in the interest of psychic health. That this attempt entailed a vigorous assault on "illusion" and fantasy is highly significant. It implies a concerted attack on the inner life, which was perceived as a threat to stability, equilibrium, and adjustment to reality. Marriage was to be saved at the expense of private life, which it was simultaneously expected to foster. The therapeutic program eroded the distinction between private life and the marketplace, turning all forms of play, even sex, into work. The experts make it clear that "achievement" of orgasm required not only proper technique but effort, determination, and emotional control.

So far I have spoken of the emergence of the nuclear family and its impact on popular thought, with particular attention to the ways in which the popular mind, led by the guardians of public health and morality, struggled with evidences of the family's growing instability. It remains to be seen how the same questions were dealt with at a more exalted level of thought—sociological theory. The social sciences devoted a great deal of attention to the crisis of marriage and the family. In particular the discipline of sociology, having divorced itself from the evolutionary and historical perspectives that had once dominated it, and having defined its field as the study of contemporary institutions and the social relations to which they gave rise, found it necessary to deal in detail with the contemporary family and what was happening to it. Much of what sociology had to say had already been anticipated in popular debate. Indeed it is clear that the sociology of the family in America arose in part as an answer to popular misgivings about the family. The role of sociology was to soothe those apprehensions with the voice of calm scientific detachment. Taking up certain lines of defense that had been suggested by doctors, social workers, psychotherapists, or scholars writing for a popular audience, sociology restated them in far more elaborate and extensive form, at the same time removing them from the polemical context in which they had originated. Claiming to have no stake in the outcome of investigations into the functions of the family, sociology provided the family with an elaborate ideological defense, which soon found its way back into popular thought and helped to bring about an important revival of domesticity and the domestic virtues in the thirties, forties, and fifties.

In effect, sociology revived the nineteenth-century myth of the family as an oasis and restated it in what looked like scientific form. First it dismissed the evidence of the family's decline by translating it into the language of functional analysis; then it showed that loss of certain functions (notably economic and educational functions) had been compensated by the addition of new ones. Ernest W. Burgess, founder of a flourishing school of urban sociology at the University of Chicago, was one of the first to propose, in the early twenties, that what the family had lost in economic, protective, educational, religious, and recreational functions, it had made up in "affectional and cultural" functions. According to Burgess, the family had been "reduced" to an affectional group, "united by the interpersonal relations of its members," but the reduction in its size and scope had strengthened, not weakened, the family by enabling it to concentrate on that interplay of "interacting personalities." As the "institutional" functions of the family declined, the "personality" functions, in the words of W. F. Ogburn, took on greater and greater importance.

The rise of functionalism in social science coincided with, and was made possible by, the repudiation of historical approaches. At one time students of the family (and of other institutions as well) had attempted to arrange various institutional forms of the family in an evolutionary sequence or progression. Theoretical arguments about the family usually boiled down to arguments about historical priority. One group of theorists, following Bachofen, Morgan, and Engels, held that marriage had evolved from promiscuity to monogamy and the family from matriarchal to patriarchal forms. Others, like Westermarck, argued that partriarchal monogamy was the original form of the family. By the 1920s, those disputes had begun to seem inconclusive and heavily ideological, with the adherents of the matriarchal theory predicting the imminent demise of the monogamous family and their opponents seeking to demonstrate its permanence and stability. Sociology now rejected more modest historical theories as well—for example, theories that sought to link the decline of the partriarchal, extended family in Europe to changes in social and economic organization. Instead of attempting to explain the family's history, social science now contented itself with analyzing the way it functioned in various cultures. It was not altogether incidental that this functionalist analysis of the family, worked out first by anthropology in company with psychoanalysis and then applied by sociology to the contemporary family, had reassuring implications for the question of the family's future. The great variety of family forms suggested that while the family varied enormously from one culture to the next, in some form it was always found to be indispensable. The family did not evolve or decline, it merely adapted itself to changing conditions. As industry and the state took over the economic, educational, and protective work of the family, society at the same time became more impersonal and bureaucratic, thereby necessitating the creation of an intimate, protected space in which personal relations could continue to thrive. In the words of the urban sociologist Louis Wirth, "the pecuniary nexus which implies the purchasability of services and things has displaced personal relations as the basis of association"— everywhere, that is, except within the family. Joseph Folsom, a specialist in family sociology, noted in 1934 that modern society gave rise to a "generally increased need for intense affection and romance," while at the same time it "increased the difficulty of satisfying this need." As he put it somewhat quaintly, a "cultural lag" had arisen "between the increasing need for love and the practical arrangements to promote it." Ernest R. Mowrer, another family sociologist, argued along similar lines: "One of the most pronounced and striking phases of modern life is the repression of the emotions"—a tendency from which the family alone is exempt. Accordingly the family becomes "all the more important as the setting for emotional expression." In the rest of life, emotions have no place. "A business man is supposed to be cold, unfeeling, and 'hard-boiled.' Exchange . . . is unemotional and objective." The family, on the other hand, satisfies "the desire for response." Pent-up rage as well as pent-up love find expression in domestic life, and although this rage creates tensions in the family it is also a source of its continuing vitality. Familial tension, Mowrer argued, ought to be understood and therefore kept under control.

By reviving nineteenth-century conceptions of the family in allegedly scientific form, the sociology of the family accomplished something almost brilliant in its way: it stood the evidence of the family's decline on its head. Sociology invoked loss of functions, the drastic shrinkage of the family, and even the rising divorce rate to prove the stability, not the decline, of the family. Academic scholarship demonstrated that it was precisely the loss of its economic and educational importance that permitted the family to discharge its emotional functions more effectively than ever. The "loss of functions," instead of undermining the family, allowed it to come more fully into its own. There was only one trouble with this line of argument—a major one, however, with ramifying theoretical implications. Having abandoned historical analysis, sociology rested its claims to scientific status on a functional analysis of modern society—an analysis, that is, which purported to show how all the pieces fit together to make up a smoothly functioning social order.

Yet at the same time it saw the family as in conflict with society—a haven of love in a loveless world. Nor could it argue, except by drastically simplifying the problem, that this conflict was itself functional. The view that family life alone provided people with the emotional resources necessary to live and work in modern society remained convincing only so long as the socializing function of the family was ignored. The family might be a haven for adults, but what about the children whom it had to prepare to live in precisely the cold and ugly world from which the family provided a haven? How could children raised under the regime of love learn to "function" in the marketplace? Far from preparing the young for this ordeal, the family, if it operated as sociology insisted it did operate, could only be said to cripple the young, at the same time that it offered a psychological refuge for the cripples, now grown to maladjusted maturity, that it had itself produced.

For a time, sociology could deal with these problems by ignoring them—that is, by ignoring the family's role in socializing the child. Some writers went so far as to insist that child-rearing had become incidental to marriage. But the rise of the so-called culture-and-personality school in American anthropology soon made this view untenable. The work of Ruth Benedict, Margaret Mead, and others made it clear that in every culture socialization is the main function of the family. A sociology that confined itself to the analysis of marriage could not stand comparison with the theoretical achievements of this new anthropology. The sociology of the family had to provide a theory of socialization or collapse into a rather pretentious form of marital counselling. Specifically it had to explain how an institution organized along very different principles from the rest of society could nevertheless train children to become effective members of society.

This was the problem, in effect, to which Talcott Parsons addressed himself in that part of his general theory which dealt with socialization—in Parsonian terminology, with tension—management and pattern-maintenance. Parsons begins by placing the study of the family in a broader social context—already a considerable advance over the work of his predecessors. According to Parsons, the family's famous loss of functions should be seen as part of the more general process of "structural differentiation"—the basic tendency of modern society. As the social division of labor becomes more and more complex, institutions become more specialized in their functions. To take an obvious example, manufacturing is split up into its various components, each of which is assigned to a special unit in the productive system. Specialization of functions increases efficiency, as is well known. Similarly the family performs its emotional services more efficiently once it is relieved of its other functions, which can be more efficiently carried on in institutions expressly designed for those purposes.

Having established a strong link between the development of the family and other social processes, Parsons now has to consider what other sociologists ignored, the family's role in socializing the child. How does the family, an institution in which social roles are assigned by ascription rather than achievement, train the child to enter a society in which roles are achieved rather than ascribed? The isolation of the family from the rest of the kinship system encourages a high degree of dependency between parents and children, yet at the same time the family has to equip the child to break these ties of dependency and to become an independent, self-reliant participant in the larger world. How does it manage to do both of these things at once, to tie children to their parents and yet to lay the ground work for the severance of those ties?

Briefly, Parsons proposes that the emotional security the family gives to the child in his early years is precisely the psychic foundation of the child's later independence. By providing the child with a great deal of closeness and warmth and then by giving him his head, the isolated nuclear family trains a type of personality ideally equipped to cope with the rigors of the modern world. Permissiveness, which many observers mistake for a collapse or abdication of parental responsibility, is actually a new way of training achievement, according to Parsons. It prepares the child to deal with an unpredictable world in which he will constantly face "unstructured situations." In the face of such contingencies he will have little use for hard-and-fast principles of duty and conduct learned from his parents. What he needs is the ability to take care of himself, to make quick decisions, and to adapt quickly to many types of emergencies. In a slower world, parents could indoctrinate their children with moral precepts adaptable to any foreseeable occasion, but modern parents, according to Parsons, can hope only to provide their young with the inner resources they need to survive on their own. This kind of training requires an intense dependency in early childhood followed by what strikes many foreigners as "incredible leeway" later on. But we should not be deceived by this "leeway." What looks like "abdication" is simply realism.

Youth culture, Parsons argues, is a differentiated part of the socialization system, the function of which is to ease the adolescent's transition from particularism to universality, ascription to achievement. Youth culture provides the adolescent with the emotional security of relationships that are "largely ascriptive" yet take him outside his own family. By providing this kind of "emotional support," the subculture of American adolescents fills an important set of needs, complementing the family on one side and the school on the other. Not only does it take young people out of the family but it helps to select and certify them for their adult roles—for example, by reinforcing appropriate ambitions while discouraging ambitions that are beyond the individual's abilities or his family's means to support.

This summary does not do justice to the elegance of the Parsonian theory of the family. We must press on to a further point: that for its elegance, the Parsonian theory has little capacity to explain empirical events, as any theory must. Far-from explaining events, it has been overtaken by them. Writing in 1961, on the eve of an unprecedented upheaval of Amreican youth, Parsons thought young people were becoming less hedonistic and more serious and "progressive," but his theory hardly anticipated the emergence of a youth culture that condemned American society in the most sweeping terms, repudiated the desirability of growing up in the usual way, and sometimes appeared to repudiate the desirability of growing up at all. It would be the height of perversity to interpret the youth culture of the sixties and seventies as a culture that eases the transition from childhood to maturity, when the attainment of adult status and responsibilities is seen by the culture as a betrayal of its ideals, by definition a "sell-out," and therefore becomes in the eyes of young people something to be accepted only with deep feelings of guilt. As for the argument that a heightened dependence in childhood is the basis of increased autonomy in adulthood, it does not explain why, in our society, personal autonomy seems more difficult than ever to achieve or sustain. Nor does it explain why so many signs of a massive cultural and psychological regression should appear just at the historical moment when, according to Parsons, the family has emerged from a period of crisis and has "now begun at least to be stabilized."

It is precisely the instability of the family that most emphatically repudiates the Parsonian theory of it. Youth culture itself has made the family a prime target—not just something to "rebel" against but a corrupt and decadent institution to be overthrown. That the new youth culture represents more than adolescent rebellion is suggested by the way its attack on the family reverberates, appealing to a great variety of other groups—feminists, advocates of the rights of homosexuals, cultural and political reformers of all kinds. Hostility to the family has survived the demise of the political radicalism of the sixties and flourishes amid the conservatism of the seventies. Even the pillars of society show no great inclination to defend the family, historically regarded as the basis of their whole way of life. Meanwhile the divorce rate continues to rise, young people avoid or at least postpone marriage, and social life organizes itself around "swinging singles." None of these developments bears out the thesis that "loss of functions" made the family stronger than ever by allowing it to specialize in the work it does best. On the contrary, no other institution seems to work so badly, to judge from the volume of abuse directed against it and the growing wish to experiment with other forms.

🔥 🔥 🔥

MIENTRAS DURE VIDA, SOBRA EL TIEMPO

(Memory becomes very deep, weighs more, moves less)

by CAROLYN FORCHÉ

from DACOTAH TERRITORY

nominated by DACOTAH TERRITORY

1

She is a good woman, walking
in the body of a twisted bush, as old
as the ones who are gone.
Her teeth, chips of winter river
thawed, swallowed
or spit out.

On the way to town her hands
fly in and out her shawl
catching scraps of her voice
feathers fallen from birds.
Like mudhens, her hands.

She buys coffee, medicine, pork.
Squats on the grocery floor
digging in her breasts
for money.
She is no higher than chamisa
or wild plum trees
grown for more than a hundred years
beside the river.

2

I feel the mountains moving
closer, with smoke
on their faces, hear cries
in couloirs of snow.

Last night a woman not alive
came to my bedside, a black skirt, black
reboso. She touched
my blankets, sang like wind
in a crack, saw
that my eyes were open.

She went to the kitchen
without footsteps, rattled pans, sang *ma-he-yo*

Ma-he-yo until morning.

3

On the way from town Rosita
leads me through rosy dust of North Plaza.
My face shrivels, I shrink through her
doorway.

On her walls, a washtub, Jesus.
One room.
La yerba del manso tied,
hung from a nail to dry.
Green chili, a blanket
dyed to match the field.
She has lived alone.

4

Rosita kneeling at her fogon,
since morning no fire.
Wind bony, dark as her face
when at night she holds
her eyes in her hands.

She stacks stumps of pinon, lights a match.
I drop like pinon at her feet.

Fire rushes from her hands, her hands
flutter, flames her bones
shine like tongs through her flesh.

Sparks on the ground turning into women
who begged to be let go, that night
on the llano.
People talk, people tell
these stories.
People say "leave Rosita alone or you are
malificiada."
Her laugh is a music
from the time of Christ.

Rosita's eyes shatter
la tristesa de la vida,
dog-stars within them.

You, you live alone
in your life.
Your life will have ma-he-yo.
I never married, never
cut my hair.
Ma-he-yo are blessings of God.
That is all the English I have.

5

On another day she disappeared,
her door open, her eyes
seen in the face of a dog
near the river.

You will light fires
with one touch.
You will make one death
into another.

HIM & ME

by SUSAN MACDONALD

from DANGEROUS AS DAUGHTERS (Five Trees Press)

nominated by Five Trees Press

I have not become the lady poet,
but live in utter content with a mountaineer,
whose heavy boots sleep in the attic
along with the good silver.
It is not what I planned. We eat well.

Each Tuesday I dream he has reached into me
too far, like a starved man with a spoon,
but on Wednesdays I wake beside him and he is
solidly beautiful, the pits of his arms
secretive, friendly.

He collects everything and mails it to me.
The envelopes read Dear Mrs, even though
I have no such name.

The neighbours think we are a fine couple.
I agree but I forget who we are and am reminded
only by mirrors or storefront windows when
Yes, I say, Yes, there's happiness for you.
The children come and go in minor catastrophes,
swift as sandstorms, the wake of grit makes
pearls of my days.

He leaves me in order to measure the earth and
writes of the whores he passes up on foreign streets.
I ask him if zippers stick in hot climates.
He loves me, he replies, and shouldn't I give poetry
one last chance?

♨ ♨ ♨

KING'S DAY

a novella by T. E. PORTER

from MULCH PRESS

nominated by Carll Tucker

I

ONE FALL MY MAMA and my daddy sent me and my brother, Miller, to stay a few weeks on the farm with my grandparents. We called them Bigmama and Bigdaddy. We used to go there a lot but Miller and I had never stayed for so long a time before. I guess I was scared of Bigdaddy, but after a couple of weeks I had decided that when I grew up I was going to be just like him and have a farm and do all the things he did. He had hands that were as hard as two pieces of iron and when he would grab me—I mean there wasn't anything he couldn't have broke apart with his bare hands.

Not that I was afraid he might hurt me, but sometimes if I was in the way he would snort through his nose and grab me and set me down someplace else so hard it would jar my teeth. He would walk in the kitchen and all of a sudden give the table a shove because he didn't like where it was settin' and sometimes a glass or a plate would go off the edge and then Bigmama would skip over and sweep the pieces into the dustpan and throw them in the trash basket between the sink and the icebox and set some fresh ones in their place without a word. Thurmond, which was Bigdaddy's name, didn't say much in the house—just snorted and swore under his breath, but outside he had a shout like a clap of thunder and when he went into the stable, the horses would start shifting their feet around. He had shoulders like a piece of board and once I saw him ram them into the mare and push her off her feet, hollering furiously, "Haw! You git over!" And, WHUMP, down she went, looking as surprised as I ever saw any animal look, and then she scrambled to her feet and stood there trembling all over. He was so sudden and so quick I could scarcely keep up with him. He simply towered over me. He had arms like a couple of two-by-fours and a head like a stone. When I came near him it was as if his torso were full of heat and I could just feel the blood throbbing in him; his body seemed to hum and pulse. Bigmama used to say I had eyes like his, but I would look in the mirror and mine were a pale, soft blue and his were like ice and would blaze and flash in the sunlight and I would think to myself that mine just couldn't be like that.

After a couple of weeks, about the time I decided that when I grew up I was going to try to be like Bigdaddy, one day they all started talking about having a hog-killing as soon as there come a good hard frost.

And a few days later when it looked like it would be very cold the next day, I was so excited I could hardly sleep all night and when I woke up, it was still dark in the room, but I knew that didn't mean anything because this room, which we even called the Dark Room, was always dark; but I knew it was morning. The first thing I thought about was the hog-killing. Bigdaddy had said this would likely be the best day we'd have for it if the weather held cold, and from the feel of my nose I knew it had. It was still pretty early; beside me, Miller was asleep with his mouth open again and when I put out my hand, I accidentally got my little finger in his mouth and had to whisper, "Miller?" but I hadn't waked him, and he stayed like he was and only began to snore.

Miller was a year older than me. Bigmama was always saying. "That Miller snores louder than any child I ever seen."

I heard logs bumping onto the floor in the living room where she was lighting the fire. I went chill bumps all over from the cold linoleum and got my socks and shoes on real fast. Then I put on my underpants and a shirt. The door to the back hall was sprung when I went out, so I had to slam it but Miller still didn't wake up; I stood listening a few minutes in the hall. Uncle Kenneth's room was quieter than the Dark Room. That old man wouldn't get up until the fires were going, then he'd sit all day by one of them chewing tobacco and spitting: I knew he woke up early because I would almost always hear him using his chamber pot or clearing his throat. The springs on his bed were creaky and sometimes he groaned and muttered to himself, complaining before daylight. And later he'd sit by the fireplace or the woodstove shooting these brown streamers into the flames and talk about how younguns now-a-days hadn't any manners and how his papa would have taken him out behind the barn with a razor strop for the things we got away with. He was just jealous because we sat on someone else's lap and not his, but he liked to dwell on how long and thick and wide the strop was and how he'd have welts on his back for days, so we took to saying we were sure glad his papa wasn't around anymore and bet he was too, which made him furious because he was getting so old himself. Once he gave Miller a chew of tobacco, not telling him he shouldn't swallow, then laughed at the look he got on his face. He told that story over and over and would offer us a chew, snickering and wiping the drippings off his mustache.

Now he kept still, pretending to be asleep while I listened from the hallway . . . To make him think I was still there I tiptoed out, touching the jars of pickled cucumbers, blackberry jam, beans, tomatoes, sweet pears as I passed the cupboard. Then I came to the long row of windows in the dining room where I could just make out stars coming and going behind those spotty clouds. The table in the big dining room had been pushed back against the wall: in winter we ate outside in the separate kitchen that was connected to the main part of the house by a covered walkway that ran from the back door of the living room.

I wondered where Bigdaddy was because most of the time you could hear him telling Bigmama what to do in the mornings.

When I got to the living room now Bigmama said, "You're up

mighty early for such a little boy," and handed me my dungarees off a chair. She was small and fat with a soft voice which she strained talking too loud because she was hard of hearing. Her body was all round: her face sad, wrinkled, and very brown. She looked like an Indian and did a lot of work. In the afternoons I would sit with her while she ironed, listening to *Our Gal Sunday*, and programs like that on the radio. She talked about how unhappy life was and said us kids should have fun while we could, and do everything because later on we wouldn't get to: I'd try to say something to make her feel better, but she would only look sadder and say we were good boys and were lucky to have such a good father and our mother was lucky to have such a good husband because everybody wasn't so lucky. After awhile I found out she was referring to Bigdaddy who got mean sometimes when he was drinking. They said he liked girls, too.

"Where's Bigdaddy?" I said.

"There's a heap o' work to do before this day's end," Bigmama said.

"We gonna kill hogs today?"

She nodded. I had waked up thinking so hard about killing one, it was like I had dreamed doing it: it may be I only dreamed *asking if I could.*

My dungarees felt cold as ice and I turned first my back, then my front to the flames.

"Where's Bigdaddy at?"

"Out back," she said, "tie your shoes."

"What's he doing?"

"Building up the fire, for scalding."

"Can I go watch?"

"If you won't get in the way, and put your sweater on."

I had a new thought: maybe I could get her on my side. But I couldn't just say outright to her that I wanted to kill one myself and I knew I'd have to ask *him* anyhow, so I stammered and only asked, "You think I could help?"

She looked me in the eye, saying "You ask your Bigdaddy," and went out the door onto the covered walkway that led to the kitchen.

The north side of the walkway to the kitchen was walled with planks and caulked to keep the wind out, but the south side, which was toward the back yard, was open like a porch with wooden steps going down a couple of feet to the ground. Bigmama's German Shepherd, King, lived under there at night, coming out every morning when she called to come and warm himself by the stove. He did and kept her company too, while she made our breakfast, and baked him a heavy kind of dog bread in an iron pan. That pan always smelled like burnt rust and soapy water.

On my way out back, I gave King a pat. He was a really huge dog and he let us straddle him with our feet on the ground while we whooped it up pretending we were riding him. He loved Bigmama, and stayed with her when he wasn't playing with us and he would growl, raising his hackles anytime a grown-up went near her. He even growled at Bigdaddy sometimes, almost getting kicked for it.

It was light outside, but the sun wasn't out, the sky was low and clouded with a heavy light that made the sandy yard look gray and the smokehouse and fence and trees all black and gray; and up behind, the sky was all curls of gray and white. My breath gave off little white clouds in the cold air. At the horizon the pines stood out like the teeth of a steel trap waiting for the clouds coming across the sky, looped with their soft gray ringlets.

Bigdaddy bent over ramming pieces of wood under a big kettle. He had put down some newspaper and when he lit it all around with kitchen matches, it caught real fast.

"Ray was supposed to of been here by now to do this. I had to fill the damned thing myself." The smoke seethed up, sticking to the bottom and breaking off the brim in curly little waves. Bigdaddy rested his fists on his hips, stock still. When the water got to sort of moving around, he brushed his hands once and whirled off towards the smokehouse.

As I followed him through the gate to the smokehouse, I could see frost on the tops of the fenceposts and the sparse grass around the pecan tree; the little shed's shingled roof glittered with it and once we were inside, where it was like night again, the cold light streaking through the cracks shone like icicles. Bigdaddy began laying wood in a shallow hole scooped in the dirt floor.

"What 'you doing?"

"Layin' the smoke."

"What's that?" I asked, trying to think how I could ask to shoot one of the hogs; the old sow—I thought of her.

"Hick'ry."

"Sir?"

"Green hick'ry. Best there is. Burn like a slow sonufabitch, burn all night."

I could see he wasn't paying any attention to me. "Can I do anything?" I asked, thinking he'd maybe say was there anything I thought I could do like when I helped him pick up chips around the woodpile.

"Nothin' for you to do."

"Ain't you going to light it?"

"Nothin' up there to smoke," he said, pointing to the empty poles laying across the rafters: "Shut the door for me," he said, heading back to the house with a sudden rush.

By the time I had pushed the heavy door to and spun the block across it, he was up the steps.

"What 'you gonna do now?" I called.

He disappeared into the kitchen without answering, and King slunk out.

When I got in, the kitchen felt real warm: Bigmama put her hands over my ears, saying, "How does that feel?" and helped me pull off my sweater as I laughed at how good it felt.

Bigdaddy was across the room at the sink scrubbing his hands so hard his shoulders shimmied and then heaved once as he shook the water off his fingers. Miller must have still been asleep—he almost never got up for breakfast—but Uncle Kenneth was standing beside the stove with a cup in his hand. I watched him pour in boiling water and add milk and sugar and then I asked, "Why don't you drink coffee?"

"Speak when you're spoken to," he said, going to the table. His eyes were puffy and he walked bent over. He groaned when he sat down, looking resentfully around the roon and straightening up the silverware by his plate. "You younguns start deviling soon as you wake up and don't stop 'till you go to sleep and then you're most likely planning what you can get into next. In my day you would of got a good hiding fer it . . . Jes' look what this world's coming to . . ."

Bigdaddy threw the towel down on the drain-board and moved to the head of the table. "Well, I don't know what field hands is coming to," he said. He snatched the chair up and set it back from the table, throwing himself on it and skidding noisily into place. "Ray was supposed to of been here an hour ago—I had to fill the pot and lay the smoke myself."

Bigmama put down a platter of fried eggs onto the table, the yolks quivery, and a deep dish heaped with thin-cut pork chops; she helped our plates with steaming grits, setting out bacon and a bowl of gravy made from the chops, and hot biscuits in their tins and a smoking pan of corn bread. There was blackberry jam in a big jar and a blue and white crock of sweet butter. She opened the screen door to let King back in.

"Is Arnold and Beullah coming?" she asked.

"Yep. Nope. I got to pick them up. Estis promised he would help too, and I thought I'd run over to Bethel and get a couple of niggers."

Uncle Kenneth ate the mushy grits with his knife—he ate sweet peas the same way, balancing them on the blade, then making a dash for his mouth. Sometimes his hands shook so bad the peas rolled off, scattering around his plate or tumbling into his lap, but I never saw him use his fork. In the mornings and after supper, too, he had white Karo Syrup with his biscuits, and even managed to get that on his knife-blade, running his tongue down it so you'd think he'd cut if off one day; that or his nose.

Bigmama always made me eat an egg before she'd let me have blackberry jam on my corn bread. Just as we were finishing, we heard Ray's old pickup truck come sputtering into the yard. Scraping his chair back, Bigdaddy got up and said to Bigmama, "I don't want that damned dog gettin' in my way today." She looked at him and looked at King. I followed him out onto the covered walkway and we saw Ray ambling across the yard in the kind of bowlegged slouch he had with his hands stuck into his back pockets. He wore a straw cowboy hat pulled down on his forehead and his dungaree jacket was unbuttoned half way, showing a tan army shirt underneath. Going past him Bigdaddy growled, "You sure took your time . . ."

"My ol' truck wouldn't crank," Ray drawled. "She's like my woman, I got to warm her up a little first," he peered at me, "is this here one of our pigs?" He reached in his jacket, "Let me just git my pocket knife,"—my neck prickled,—"my little ol' pigsticker!"

Saying, "We ain't got time for that," my grandfather took me off the spot, telling Ray, "you take the post-hole digger and dig a couple of holes over by them pear trees. Build me another fire next to them scaffol's and put another pot of water on. I got to go pick up some folks that's going to help us out, and also get some niggers."

I wanted to go with him when he started out for the old Pontiac, but he said there wouldn't be enough room and they might have to leave me with the niggers in Bethel, winking at the hired man.

"And Ray," he said, leaving, "put them three biggest shoats out of the pen. I want that old sow first."

The two scaffolds were each made out of two posts three feet apart with a board across the top about as high up as a man could reach with two great big spikes in each board, which Ray said was to hang the hogs' slit hind legs on. Ray built a fire nearby and took me with him to get a washtub and a little boiler from the woodshed behind the smokehouse. He made me feel real nervous like he was going to do something to me everytime he got close enough, then he'd say, "what you so scared about?" and I would say, "Nothing."

He fetched water from the pump, then got the posthole diggers; at the end of two handles about six feet long, each digger had two curved sharp shovel hands which you shoved straight down into the ground, and when you pulled the handles apart, the heads closed in and gripped and you could lift out the dirt. The handles were that long so you could dig a hole deep enough to sink an eight foot post. It was too heavy for me to use, but I watched Ray lift and drive it down, lift and empty and drive it down into the earth again as if it were no trouble at all.

"What're the holes for?" He was digging two.

"One is for you," he scowled, grunting as he lifted, "and one is for your brother." I edged away as he went on digging, "We gonna put you in . . . and fill 'em up . . . and then the BUZZARDS IS GONNA COME . . ." On the last, he made a grab for me, throwing aside the hole diggers.

Dead briars by the pear tree clutched at my legs as I stepped back, but I got loose and, dodging around the second scaffold, made it back to the yard and when I looked back I saw Ray standing amidst the smoking pots whooping and slapping his thighs, pointing at me.

"You come back and I'm gonna feed you to the hogs! Whoopeee!" He stood holding his sides and haw-hawing.

II

I knew he was just teasing but it made me feel weak and I rushed inside the kitchen.

"Whatever is the matter with you?" asked Bigmama.

My back was wet with sweat and my mouth started trembling—I hated that—when I tried to speak. Uncle Kenneth sitting there, was going to laugh just like Ray, and say I was scared.

"Ray . . . Ray, he said he would bury me and Miller."

Uncle Kenneth sat watching me.

"Why would he say a thing like that?"

"That's what he said . . ." I knew I was red all over: I wanted to run away somewhere so they couldn't see me.

"Oh, well now, he was just teasing you, you know he's not really going to do any such thing."

Before I could decide where to run to, Bigmama hugged me and sat on a kitchen chair so I could put my head against her and hiding there I began to feel better and the knot went out of my throat.

"He just wants to be babied, that's all," said Uncle Kenneth.

"You shut up," I said angrily, "You're just an old fool—Bigdaddy says so."

Bigmama slapped me then hard, and while I just gaped in surprise, she told me I shouldn't say things like that and Bigdaddy shouldn't either, but I had already noticed that as soon as I said it, I felt OK again.

The old man stared hard at me: "We'll see who the fool is one of these days," and he took the tip of a turkey feather out of his watchpocket and began whittling a toothpick.

Bigmama said to me, "You go see if you can get your brother up."

On the walkway to the house I stopped to watch Ray going into the pigpen. He seemed to have forgot about me.

Standing in the hall outside the Dark Room, I thought I heard Miller stirring, but when I opened the door, it was dark and still inside. I wasn't able to make him out.

"Bigmama says to get up."

"Go away."

"If you get up we can go watch them kill the hogs." I was thinking it would be easier to go back out if he came too.

"It ain't worth it," he said.

"You sure?"

"Yeah. Now go away and leave me alone."

So I went back to the kitchen and sat around a little while and didn't say anything to Uncle Kenneth to get him mad. Pretty soon I heard the Pontiac drive up outside, and ran to the front yard to see.

Aunt Beullah and Uncle Arnold were just getting out of the front seat and they were so fat I didn't see how Bigdaddy could fit in too. Aunt Beullah had always liked me and when we went to her house where she lived in Tallahassee she made good things to eat like blackberry pie, and hoecake and fried squirrel and hopping john, which was blackeyed peas mixed with rice and I liked it as good as the name but Aunt Beullah had bad nerves and yelled at me when I let the screen door slam. She had run away with Uncle Arnold when she was fifteen. He was a game warden and knew exactly where to go to shoot his turkeys before the season started and the city hunters messed things up. He liked to hunt turkeys best because you had to get up before first light and go hide in the bushes, sitting very still in the cold for hours trying to gobble a turkey up close enough to shoot him. Wherever Uncle Arnold went he would practice gobbling in his spare minutes with his gobbler which he always carried in his shirtpocket. It was made out of two pieces. One was a little flat oval piece of gray slate, and the other was a dried corncob with a stick stuck down through the whole length of it. The stick was sharpened to a point which he rubbed across the slate so it vibrated, making a noise just like a gobbling turkey. When I tried it, it only made a screech like scraping a blackboard, but Uncle Arnold knew how to make it sound like a turkey's mating call or like a turkey signal to a turkey's friends. He'd never take me or Miller hunting with him because he said the turkeys were skittish suspicious creatures and we couldn't sit still for two seconds even if he paid us.

After services on Sundays Uncle Arnold was always in with a cluster of men who talked guns in the churchyard. At funerals they told jokes amongst the headstones, laughing out of the sides of their mouths while the old folks went over to the open casket by the grave to view the remains.

Getting out of the car and straightening her black coat with the seashell buttons, Aunt Beullah said, "You look like the cat that got the canary. What you so pleased about?"

Before I could answer, she grabbed me, hugging me up tight so I couldn't get away. She always had to do that, saying, "My, my, you sure are getting big," or "you younguns are growing like weeds."

All my aunts hugged me real hard and my uncles would mess up my hair; they all of them did it partly to just show me who was still the biggest.

Two niggers had got out of the back seat. I knew skinny Lucky because she came to help make preserves and wash the floors sometimes, never saying much to anybody; she never once called me or Miller by our first names. When I said, "Hi," Lucky said, as she said to any of our greetings, "Jus' fine, how you?" I mean, if we would say, "Hi, Lucky, you lookin' pretty good today," she would say, "Jus' fine, how you?" The man with her was big and I found out later his name was Geoffrey. He was scary, with a head like a large black olive, dark eyes and this hair-line mustache. He didn't say a word, just got out the car, and hitching up his pants, which were tied by a rope, he walked off toward the pigpen.

Bigdaddy and Uncle Arnold headed that way too, and I scrambled after them, figuring this would be the last chance to ask if I could shoot the old sow. My heart began to pound; it was hard to talk and get my breath. I called three times, finally catching his sleeve, 'Hey Bigdaddy!"

"What do you want?"

"Can I help?" He brushed my hand away and I said as loud as I could, trotting along beside him, "Can I kill the old sow?"

He stopped, "What?"

"I want to kill the old sow."

"Do you think you're big enough?"

"Yessir," I said straining upward.

Uncle Arnold put his hand on my head and asked, "How you goin' to do it?"

It looked like they would let me. Taking a deep breath, I said, "Shoot 'im."

"Pshaw!" Bigdaddy said, and Uncle Arnold laughed, his eyes watery. My face felt hot. Everyone was always laughing at me, as if the idea of me was funny.

But Uncle Arnold said to Bigdaddy, "Hell, why don't we let him show us how he'd do it?"

"We done wasted enough time as it is."

"Please," I said, "I can do it."

"What gun you goin' to use?" Uncle Arnold asked.

"The Twenty-two." I saw they were tickled enough to go along with me. My uncle asked me if I had ever shot a .22 before, and I said no but I knew how; laughing, Bigdaddy said to go get it and hurry, they didn't have all day and I ran for the house.

"Just three cartridges, now, mind . . . and don't you load it till you get back here."

There was wax on the stock and wax on the bullet heads. The closet where the rifle was kept smelled of canvas hunting sacks and flannel, coathangers and gun oil. With my fingernail, I scratched a little until I felt the brass casing and the lead beneath the wax. The

Dark Room, where Miller was still asleep, was next door, but now I didn't want to wake him; feeling myself in a dream, not thinking of what I was doing, I slipped a cartridge into the open breach and slid the bolt in . . .

Just what Bigdaddy had said not to do. Boy, if I got him mad now, when he was going to let me . . . I tried to open the breach quietly, but you have to jerk the tight bolt, and it clicks and scrapes, clacking at the back. The bullet didn't eject. I felt like the house was full of people, hearing me: I clawed at it, and shaking the rifle upside-down, I was sure the floor creaked at the Dark Room door, and turning to see, I banged the barrel on the closet wall, and had to stand still, straining to hear. I wondered if the gun could go off, and as I decided it would be worse if they found me standing there, I finally gave the rifle a furious shake and the cartridge fell out beside my foot and I grabbed it up, and clasping it with the other two cartridges, I quickly left the house.

When I got to the pen, I didn't look at anybody. Ray sat on the top rail watching the old sow scratching herself against the bottom rail. I got my mind fixed on her, seeing the grown-ups from the corners of my eyes. I felt the gun and smelled the old porker, hearing Bigdaddy say, far off, "You know what you doin', now, don't you?"

"Yessir."

The ground in the sty was rooted up, lying in furrows which she kicked into, turning back and forth nuzzling the oily black clods. She panted, pulling the thick snout back in a grin, grunting and blowing through dirt-clogged nostrils.

"Souey, Soueee!" Ray jabbed at her with the toe of his boots, driving her round to my side.

"Give 'im room," said Uncle Arnold at my elbow, "here, step up here," he helped me to stand on the lower fencerail: I hung by my armpits over the top, able to sight the hog around as as she circled the enclosure, coming right to me, snuffling my feet.

"Watch 'im shoot his foot," snickered Ray.

"Gonna shoot her in the head?"

"Yep."

"Whoaup, Sharpshooter!"

"Room, give him room."

"Get a bead on her, now," Bigdaddy said, quietly.

A twenty-two doesn't kick. There was just a pop and splintery echo snapping of the pigpen and trees and house, then silence. She stopped still a moment, but went right on wheezing and snorting again like she hadn't been hit. Ray whoopeed, and I heard the nigger spit, and Bigdaddy sort of sucked air down the back of his nose. When I looked at Uncle Arnold, he said "Don't worry, you got her, you didn't miss," his voice gentling. But he winked at the others.

The fat wedge of the old head was still huffing there below me, the curled ears funneling into it. Aiming at the same spot, I cracked another one into her.

Ray said something to Geoffrey, who went off toward the woodshed.

The old pig waggled her head and smelled my toes. I noticed the bright cartridge lying in the dirt; the second spun out when I jerked the bolt. With the barrel not six inches from her, the last shot slid in without a trace. I thought she finally understood—she shuffled back from me—but still she didn't fall.

Geoffrey had returned with an ax, and, taking it, Ray climbed into the pen.

"Now, I'll show you how to do it," he said, and with that he swung the blunt edge of the axehead up to bash in her skull. The silvery blade flashed in a full arc, crashing squarely onto the heavy old head. She dropped on her front knees a moment before rolling over, kicking. Ray flicked open his pocket knife and cut her throat.

It wasn't like I thought it would be.

III

Ray opened the gate and Geoffrey grabbed one leg, Ray took the other, and they dragged the dead sow out, leaving the blood speckling the fallen pear leaves along the way to the scalding pot, a porcelain bathtub out of somebody's old house. It lay in the grass stoppered with a wooden peg and filled with boiling water from the other pot where the water bubbled: drops falling on the rim of the pot snapped, hissing in the cold. Bigmama and Aunt Beullah brought butcher knives and a rubberized tablecloth from the kitchen. Spreading the oilcloth, which was printed with rows of little violets, on top of the picnic table, my aunt asked, "What was you all shootin' at?"

"Ole Kerosene there was showing us how to kill hogs," grinned Ray. I leaned the rifle against the tree, glad they hadn't been there to see me shooting the poor old thing. Uncle Arnold and Bigdaddy lifted the dead sow's front legs, Ray and Geoffrey took the back and they lowered her into the pot, sloshing out the hot water which shot up billows of steam, smothering us while the hog's bristly hair crackled and fizzed.

With Bigdaddy directing them, they rolled her, floating in the bathtub, pushing under her legs and head to scald her all over, loosening the hairs. Ray punched holes in her legs above her rear feet, then took Geoffrey back to the pen to kill and fetch one of the two shoates. Everybody else gathered around the carcass and began snatching out its bristles, globs of oil and dirt bobbing in the water with swatches of hair. Lucky came out and started cleaning the head and jowls and snout, and Bigdaddy and Bigmama, and Aunt Beullah and Uncle Arnold worked, jerking out the hairs with both hands. Everyone sweating and grunting, bent over the tub.

Pretty soon the hog began to look undressed.

Bigdaddy said if I wanted to help so much, why didn't I pitch in now, and I wished I'd never laid eyes on that sow. I hated the touch of that wet, steamy dead body, but I tried anyway to pull a tuft off the fat belly. It was hot and slick and slipped out of my grasp and my tongue tasted sour.

"Got to get you a big fistfull," said Uncle Arnold.

Grabbing a handful, I yanked again, but not only a few bristles between my fingers. I was being squeezed out anyway between Aunt Beullah and Lucky and the hog was almost bare, so I backed away and went to poke up the fire under the water. Bigdaddy said he didn't want this one boiled and he took the hind end and Lucky and my uncle lifted the front and they carried her to the scaffold belly up, her head waggling along behind all pink and they hung her up hooking the slits in her rear legs on the two spikes. There was a loud squeal and a thump from the pigpen and Ray and Geoffrey brought the dead shoate and heaved it into the tub, sending up a new cloud of vapor that smelled of wet smoke and dirty feet.

Bigdaddy made me stay with him by the old sow that was hanging upside down and belly out. Telling me to hand him a knife, he put down a tub under the sow. It looked like Uncle Kenneth's foot tub. First he tested the sharpness of the blade on his wrist-hairs, then he began scraping the sow from the tail down, shaving the last bristles off the pink flesh which still steamed in the frigid air. It looked like a baby. As it cooled, Bigdaddy doused it with a boiler full of hot water from the smaller fire, washing off the shavings.

"Look here," he said, pointing to the head. I had to squat beside him to look. "See, two of your shots went in here," he pointed with the tip of the knife at a jagged hole almost in the center of the fleshy head, then to a smaller round one just to the side, "and the other 'un here." I touched them. A trickle of pinkish water flowed out. There was a purple smudge where the axe had struck. I couldn't think why I had wanted to shoot her at all; it was different touching it. Of course Ray would have knocked her brains out anyway.

Drawing me closer, Bigdaddy cut crosses over the bullet holes, and pushing up the meat with his thumb at the little hole on the side, he showed me where the lead had hit the bone, chipping it.

"Now, stick your finger in her. Right there. Push."

The meat was stingy, torn and I could smell it: I felt the skull, kind of slippery, then the hard slug beside it.

"That's it, that's it, pull it out."

Hooking it with my fingernail, I inched it out and put it into the palm of my grandfather's hand.

"See how this front edge is flattened out?"

Bits of flesh clung to it.

"An' it knocked a slivver off here. The ol' gal didn't hardly feel it, wasn't so much as a horsefly bite, 't was prob'ly your second shot."

He poked open the larger hole where the two shots had gone in at the same place. "This here one most likely was the first one you put into'er, see, flat as a board. Stuck tight, too, right into the ol' noggin, still didn't go through. Looky here, though, this edge is crimped, right there,—your last shot nicked this one and went on in where that crack was already. You sure gave her a headache that time. She'd of walked around mean as hell all day with her head busting open, but I tell you she would of never woke up again tomorrow with that piece of lead inside and bleeding and festering all night. I seen a man once shot three times with a twenty-two in his head and he's still alive to this day if he hasn't drunk hisself to death. But some fancy doctors from Tallahassee flew him up to Atlanta and operated on his brain inside of twenty-four hours . . . Biggest waste of money I ever saw, he was worthless as the tits on a boar hog. Nigger shot 'im. Of course, they hung the nigger, and I ain't got no special love for niggers, but somebody should of give that one a reward, or at least a citation—but it's like they say, Sonny-boy, 'Justice is blind.'"

Ray had come up while Bigdaddy was talking, "Find anything?" he asked, "Didn't look to me like he even come close."

"Oh, he killed her alright, she just didn't get a chance to die."

Ray went back to work and Bigdaddy took up the butcher knife again and cut the old hog's head off and wrapped it in newspaper, giving it to Lucky in a sack to take home with her. He slit the carcass open from the hind legs to the neck and scooped the guts into the washtub and gave that to Lucky also.

The others brought the second pig and hung him up, and just then my second cousin, Estis, drove up outside with his wife, Effie. That got everybody more excited than ever, especially Ray and Bigdaddy, because they like Effie. Estis was jealous of her and was always following her around. He limped from an injury he got in a factory making ammunition for the war. Now he worked over at Tallahassee putting rubber retreads on worn out tires. Pretty soon all the women went off to the kitchen—except Lucky stayed to fix the sausage skins—and I hurried after them because I was getting cold.

Miller was up, drinking hot chocolate and wouldn't say anything to me, just giving me a look that made me anxious and feel like I had to pee. Everytime I tried to get close to him he moved around the table. I went over and petted King who lay beside the woodbox, but Miller didn't notice. Uncle Kenneth sat by the stove and the women were talking about dinner, Bigmama saying she wanted to fix enough for supper too as we would all be too tired later. While they were talking, I got close to Miller and asked what was the matter with him.

"I'm gonna tell on you."

"What for?" I whispered, catching my breath, thinking of the gun closet, "I didn't do anything."

He turned his back and went to the sink, rinsed his cup, turned it up to dry, and sauntered through the door with a motion of his head to me. When we got out to the porch, I tried not to look scared.

"I saw what you did."

"What's wrong . . . I didn't do anything."

"I was watching you, you loaded the twenty-two. Inside. I saw you do it." Effie passed us, going out to the men.

"No, you didn't . . . You were asleep . . . Anyway, I didn't . . ." I couldn't get my voice to sound positive.

Miller went on, "You could of shot somebody, if Bigdaddy saw you he wouldn't ever let you use it not ever again and if I tell him you won't get to go hunting or anything as long as you live."

A fine sleet had begun blowing across the yard, clacking against the pecan tree. Over his shoulder, I could see the grown-ups hacking away at the pigs. I told him I didn't mean to and would never do it again if he'd not tell, what would it get him anyhow?

"It'll get you a whipping. And that's what you deserve," as if he hadn't ever done something himself.

He was trying to work it around so I would beg him. Which is what he always did when he had something on me. "You wouldn't tell, would you?"

He looked like he was thinking it over, "Well,—I'll tell you what," he said.

"What?"

"I might not tell on you if you play wild horses until I get tired of it."

That meant that I had to be the horse and whinny and run while he tried to lasso me. I always got rope burns and got tired of it before he did; he lassoed me around my neck once and gave me a bad burn like the one I got by being dragged off the mule under the clothesline.

"Can we wait till after we eat," I asked, "I don't feel good right now."

"OK, I just want to go talk to Bigdaddy a couple of minutes," he said, giving me a look, and skipped down the steps just as Lucky came up to use the high porch for a bench. She stretched out the ringlets of intestines, cleaning them with talon-like fingers. Out back there was one white hog hung, glistening on the scaffolds. The sleet was changing to a light rain.

I wanted to go to see what Bigmama was doing and warm myself by the stove, but Lucky said, "That Ray shore is goin' to get hisself in trouble with Mr. Estis if he don't watch his step."

"He said he was going to put me and Miller into them holes," I told her, figuring she would be on my side.

She giggled, "No such thing. They's for the chitlins, tho' when Mister Estis was a youngun he *fell* into 'em head first and near drowned afore we could haul 'im out by his heels." She gave me a look, with her black eyes laughing—sort of damp and sparkly, "But I tell you what, if somebody tol' me he was goin' to do me harm, I'd git me the biggest ol' butcher knife I could find—and then jus let him try something."

"You would?"

"'Course I would. He wouldn't never mess with me again."

I'd begun to shiver, and said I had to go in and was sorry I couldn't talk to her any longer, she was probably right.

Bigmama was cooking and Aunt Beullah and Uncle Kenneth were talking religion. They were footwashing Baptists and called each other Sister Beullah and Brother Kenneth. Once every quarter, they took their foot tubs to church and washed each other's feet to show humility. I went one Sunday. It wasn't like regular church because everybody had lent a hand at the preaching, not that there wasn't no preacher—there was—but they all just waited until one or another of them felt the holy spirit move him, then he begun to preach his own sermon. After a while there was two or three sermons going all at once with both men and women doing it and the other women crying out hallelujahs like birdcalls and the men amening like bulls. I got scared and wanted to go outside, but my aunt pinched me and said to keep still in the presence of the Lord. She didn't even have to whisper because there was so much hollering all around us. I didn't go again,—Bigdaddy and Bigmama never did go at all.

I stood beside Bigmama and let the stove warm me up.

Uncle Kenneth was wearing a soft brown sweater that made him look real womanish. "Well, I hope to be ready when the Good Lord sees fit to take me," he intoned, sing-songing, folding his hands over his round belly.

"We don't none of us know when our time will come, Brother Kenneth. . ."

"Like a thief in the night, like a thief in the night," he said, coughing away a note of peevishness.

Then the kitchen fell silent except for the frying. It was fumy, smelling of pork grease and dumplings and corn bread.

"I thought we'd have the last of the old sausages today with some fresh pork chops," said Bigmama, "it seems fitting."

Aunt Beullah set the table. Uncle Kenneth carved a piece of tobacco off the plug he kept in his sweater pocket. I listened to the clock ticking atop the breadbox, and watched the three of them. Bigmama did a lot of things at one time at the stove; Aunt Beullah rolled from the table to the dish closet and to the sink, the cupboard, the icebox smoothly and Uncle Kenneth rocked. He reminded me of Old Lady Peters in Crawfordville who cackled at us from her front porch when we ran past, "Ya'll goin' to be sorry one of these fine days!" It began to feel dead in the kitchen so I said I was going outside. Bigmama told me OK, but you call everybody inside to eat.

I walked across the yard to the smoke-house where Bigdaddy was salting down some pieces of pork in three small barrels, putting down a layer of meat and covering each layer with salt from a large bag. Behind him, through the doorway to the dark shed, I could see he had already hung the first shoulders and butts on the poles. The green wood underneath smouldered. Miller came around the corner. I went inside and Miller followed me in and planted himself between me and Bigdaddy, so I said to him it was time to eat, and ran out to call the others, relieved that he hadn't tattled on me yet, but wishing it was over instead of stuck there in the middle of the day. Big, raw pieces of pork were lying on the table, the blood spattered everywhere. Everybody seemed ready to rest and right away tossed the clotted knives in a pile, covered the table with a tarpaulin and headed for the back porch to wash up. Effie said she would just take a minute though and put on some fresh water to boil, as she had just got there anyhow and hadn't hardly done a thing. And Estis must have forgot about her in his hurry to go eat, because he didn't stay behind to help. So Ray offered to give Effie a hand.

They came in together. Just as we were sitting down to the table. Bigdaddy said, "WethankTheeOLordfortheseandallThymanyBlessings," and I spurted out, "Pass the dumplings, please," and they all laughed except Uncle Kenneth, whose Amen I had interrupted along with Aunt Beullah's Yes, Lord!

The married people always sat across from each other: Bigmama was at one end of the table and Bigdaddy at the opposite—so Aunt Beullah faced Uncle Arnold; Effie, Estis; leaving me in front of Uncle Kenneth and next to my Aunt, who was as handy at pinching under the table as she was at church. Miller was across from Ray who was between Bigdaddy and Effie.

Bigmama had already taken heaping plates out to Lucky and Geoffrey in the little vestibule where the porch connected to the main house.

Our table was loaded with thin pork chops that had been pan-fried in onions, sausages peppery hot the way my grandfather liked them, and some salt mullet along with their own red roe that Bigmama had found the night before and soaked out in a boiler on top of the woodstove. There were dumplings in a black pot, that we ate with stewed tomatoes, put up in the summer, showing blood-red atop the fleshy dough. Pickled cucumbers, pears, cherries and cherrystone peaches floated in ribbed dishes scattered about the table. We had cornbread, hoecakes, and buttermilk biscuits baked last thing and put down hot in the tins just like at breakfast.

Bigdaddy bent right down to his plate, scooping up and slurping big spoonfulls of dumplings and tomatoes, and jabbing at his meat. Aunt Beullah told me to sit up straight and act like a gentleman, giving me a look that put me in a strain. Bigmama passed things around the table, watching Bigdaddy to see when he ran out; Ray was being careful to serve Effie first and Estis had begun to sulk. It was quiet except for eating sounds and asking for things as we believed people weren't supposed to talk at the table—it having something to do with religion I thought, or manners. Or maybe both at once.

Better than anything else, I liked the transparent skinned red roe. There was never enough because we could get them only during a couple of weeks a year from the mullet fisheries down at Carabelle or Apalachicola. The pinhead eggs were salty, pricking my tongue; and they tasted different when I ate them with syrup or by themselves or with ketchup. Their thin sacks broke under my fork and a few grains spilled into the bottom of my plate to mix with the red-eye gravy Bigmama made from sausage grease.

We were eating the chops from the old sow that I had shot. Uncle Kenneth had told me once that sows had been known to eat their own farrow sometimes in a fit of temper.

Toward the end of the meal, when Aunt Beullah and Uncle Kenneth were finishing up, they said another grace, thanking the Lord for the nourishment they had received from His hand, but nobody else joined in. I felt like everything we got that day had come directly from Bigdaddy's hands. Even at the table, it was him that had the food passed around with little coughs and grunts and gestures. He mostly passed things to Effie, reaching across Ray. After coffee, he pushed back his chair, saying, "Let's get to it!" and they all put on the ragged sweaters and jackets they had worn because they didn't mind messing them up with blood, and tramped outside after him.

I tried to get out of playing with Miller, but he wouldn't let me, saying he didn't care how bad I felt, I'd feel a lot worse if he told Bigdaddy about me loading the gun in the house. Then I got mad and said I might play all right, but he'd never come near me with his old rope. "Wanta bet?" he said, and ran inside to get it.

By the time he came back, I had gone outside and was hiding

under the porch behind King's box, crouched down with my right arm around the old dog, petting him to make him be still and not give me away. I could see Miller from the neck down, letting out the loop, cautiously circling the pecan tree, looking for me in the back yard. Beyond him were the pots and gray shapes, wavering through the smoke and vapor. The air was white and the ground grainy with the cold.

Miller searched for me out back and around the smokehouse, then in among the cars in front. He searched in the dead vines that covered the fence which enclosed the main pasture, and he even looked in the outhouse before he came back toward me: he marched right up the steps to go inside and accuse me of not playing fair, but just then King let out a long, moaning whimper like he was going to die, and Miller's footsteps halted right over us, then started back. I bolted and his first throw whacked the bark and slid down. I dodged two more there, broke for the house, switched off and raced for the back gate and he never touched me. Aunt Beullah passed, so I ducked behind her and Miller nearly lassoed her. She spun around, swatting at us with the newspapers she carried, screeching "Stop that! You younguns stop that! Can't you see we're busy?" but we wouldn't hear. I scampered about the tripods, the table, the scalding pot, under the scaffolds and around, in between and through the grownups' legs, until Bigdaddy turned on us and yelled savagely, to git and go play some goddamn place else or he'd take his belt and beat the tar out of us. I tore out toward the front.

The front yard had two mulberry trees between which somebody, probably Bigdaddy, had long ago nailed a plank bench for a love-seat. As the trees had grown, though, they had clasped the board in swelling, lip-like growths and carried it up too high to sit on. We had always agreed on it for a free base and Miller missed me again as I excitedly made it there to rest. He was puffing too, but getting angry because I was laughing. Hot, we threw off our sweaters and hung by our arms on opposite ends of the old bench.

"You're not playing fair," he said.

"Yes I am."

"No you're not. You're supposed to run straight."

"A wild horse wouldn't run straight. You just want me to let you catch me."

"No I don't."

"Yes you do. 'Cause you'll never get me if I don't let you."

When I said that, he started hitting at my legs and with the rope and I jumped away.

"You're off!" he shouted, standing between me and the base, swinging the lasso.

I felt panicky. When I ran for the parked cars, he cut me off and stayed between me and the house and I could see he intended to keep me out in the clear this time, but still I dodged each toss of the rope, pausing to catch my breath when he missed. He could have outrun me if he hadn't had to mess with the line. When we came around to the back yard again, and I was eyeing the pecan tree, I shouted "You can't even get me in the open!" But it was farther than I had reckoned and his feet raced closer and closer. I knew he was going to get right on top of me this time before throwing, so I galloped full speed straight toward the tree until the last moment, then jammed my right foot down, braking to the left side. The rope slapped my ear, stinging, but didn't settle over me and I let out a huge, snickering whinny—too soon—as the loop caught my right ankle, lifted on the first step after the force of the sudden left turn. The rope tightened and he pulled hard, tripping me.

I fell flat in the sandy dirt, knocking out my breath, cutting my lip on my lower teeth, ploughing earth into my mouth. I gagged, gasped, strangled, I coughed blood and sand out through my nose, and my eyes blurred with tears.

"Are you OK?" Miller tugged at my arm trying to get me up. "You're OK," he told me, sounding scared. Then the grownups must have seen us, because he started hollering, "He ain't hurt, he's all right. He ain't hurt!"

The sounds faded and I could hardly see, but I wanted to clean out my mouth and I wanted to get up off the ground. I felt still scared, but silly and confused, too. Somehow I rose, the ground seeming to swell with me, the house and trees and backyard fence cartwheeling all around. Seeing a solid shape approach, I reached out ecstatically.

"Bigmama!" I cried, lunging to her, and cracked my head and face against the pecan tree.

In shock and pain I dropped, slowly, down to the sandy ground—and as the adults formed a ring around me, I blacked out. I heard Miller say, "Ahh, he's just pretending," and I felt like I was, it was true, yet so gloomy to stay awake and so easy to let myself go, so I did. I did. Consciousness flapping away like quail in the woods.

IV

They carried me inside and put me in Bigmama's and Bigdaddy's room, in their feather bed. As I was sleeping, sometimes I dreamed, sometimes I was half awake: I dreamed people came in the room and part of the time they were really there, as part of the time they weren't, but it seemed like they all wanted to talk to me, though I couldn't always tell what they were saying, or what they wanted.

Aunt Beullah came in and cried over me and called me a poor baby, and prayed. I kept my eyes closed and lay still even when she touched the bruised lump on my forehead where I hit the tree. She prayed, "Oh, Lord, if it be thy will, take this child home to Thee to bring the joy of his young soul to Thy throne throughout eternity, but if it be not Thy desire to take him from us here on earth, we beseech Thee on behalf of his mother and his earthly father, Dear God, to allow him to remain with us. . ." Then she hinted that if He would only let me live, I would become a preacher and work for him; she began talking about how awful it was to die so young, and I was so scared I almost opened my eyes, but finally she got quiet, and heaving a deep sigh, went out.

I let everything go dark again. I dreamed I was riding King down a long hill, trying to hold my feet up to keep them from skidding along the ground and bouncing off rocks. When I looked down, King became an old hog, and I fell off and banged my head. Bigdaddy was standing by the tall shiftrobe, taking a swig from a flat bottle.

"What's that?" I asked.

"None of your business," he growled, "and one more thing, I don't care if you did load the twenty-two in the house," he said, "just, you got to be a man about it." King panted and winked, grinning at me from the doorway. "If it was up to Uncle Kenneth, you'd get a lickin' for it. What if you had a shot somebody?" Bigdaddy asked, "You could of shot your grandmother, or your brother." In the other room I heard Miller whimper and Bigdaddy pointed his finger at me, "or Kenneth or King or Ray or just about anybody . . . I don't know if we can trust you hunting squirrels after this."

I blinked and Effie was sitting in a straight chair beside my bed.

"How do you feel?" she asked, gently.

I told her my head hurt.

"You boys shouldn't play so rough," she said reproachfully, holding my hand and running her fingers through my hair. Feeling better, I drifted off to sleep again.

When I woke later, the sun had dropped down below the clouds the way it often does in winter and turned the old worn out gray boards of the walls a rosy gold color and reddened my arms that had got uncovered and were cold in spite of the glowing sun and felt separate from my body which seemed to have melted into the feather smell and flannel of the blankets next to my skin, so there seemed nothing to me behind my eyes but the bed-feel and smell of the older people who had slept there; it seemed a long time since morning. Sleeping and walking, I had heard footsteps on the floor; slamming doors rattled the windows, my visitors had come in and gone out, there were voices calling outside and carmotors coughed, starting up in the cold air, and Bigmama had come in and then left me to wake up by myself. After awhile, I got restless, feeling weighted into my own furrow in the bed, the pillow pushing against the back of my head as if it rested on top of me. The sun dropped lower, pinking the undersides of the clouds as I heard Uncle Kenneth's walk, approaching from the kitchen.

"I got to go try and find your Bigdaddy," he said as he entered, wearing a black suit and vest and holding his gray felt hat, the one with the black band. He still looked old, but not as womanish as when he ate or sat by the fire in his old sweater. "If I can make it over there in my car, I'll most likely find him yonder at Bethel, a-doing the Devil's work with some colored gal scarce more than a pickaninny. Your brother has got hisself sent off with Sister Beullah for his devilment. And poor Estis is going to end up murdering Effie and can't none of us convince him that she wasn't anywheres near Thurmond and stayed here all day. Says he can tell, but all he can tell is what's in his own head, 'cause he won't listen to them that knows better."

"She was here," I said.

Uncle Kenneth sat on the edge of the bed, peering at my forehead, "You didn't reckon on a bump like that, I bet. The bumps ain't never part of the bargain," he put his hand on the quilt on my chest, felt my head, ran his fingers through my hair; his hands were soft and smooth, surprising me, because they looked so spotty and hard and dry.

"Can I get up?" I was tired of lying still.

"Do you feel like it?"

"Yessir."

"I reckon your Bigmama could use a little company, being as she's by herself out in the kitchen with nothing but her old dog."

It was funny, but I guess he liked me. He got up and said I should put on some clothes, then went out, hobbling, a little light falling on his shoulders from window. I dressed listening to him warming the engine of his car.

Uncle Kenneth drove off and then I heard Bigdaddy's Pontiac right away and decided to go tell him that Uncle Kenneth was looking at him, but Bigdaddy must have walked around the yard while I was going through the living roon because he wasn't out front where I thought he would be. Twilight was falling, though it was bright in the open and I could see everything. But in the shadows off under the trees, it was black dark.

Just as I turned to go back through the living room to the covered walk that led to the kitchen, there was such a ruckus out there, coming from the kitchen that I thought the whole house was falling over. Dishes crashed on the floor and there was a scraping, splitting sound like the table turning over. I rushed out onto the walkway, hearing King snarling—real biting growls. His claws scraped the floor, and Bigmama shouted, "Thurmond!"

Standing at the back door of the living room I froze as Bigdaddy yelled and cursed and then I heard a loud thump and a wailing yelp from King. The kitchen door flew open and the dog scrambled out half whimpering, half snarling still and I saw blood on his mouth. Then Bigdaddy came reeling through the screen door straight toward me along the walkway with his clothes all in a mess and one pants leg ripped, blood on it. He wasn't actually limping, only he went past me unsteadily into the living roon, as if he hadn't seen me at all. I smelled whiskey. There was no sound from the kitchen and suddenly I was afraid to move, to go in there to see if Bigmama was OK. He wouldn't have hurt *her*, I just wouldn't think about that. The dog had run behind the pecan tree, and then, when he saw my grandfather go in, King sidled over the fence and lay down near the gate. In the fading light, I watched him licking his shoulder and front paws as he looked across at the house, and, I thought, at me as if to say this was a bad day for us all.

Then she came and stood behind the screen door. She seemed

alright, but in the dark, at the other end of the covered walkway, I could hardly see her face, and I felt I shouldn't go near her somehow. I wished I was back in bed under the warm quilts and this was just one of my dreams. But it wasn't.

"Bigmama?" I called, and just then Bigdaddy burst out of the living room behind me, loading his .30 caliber rifle. His eyes were staring and stood in the sockets like blue marbles. She didn't even move, just stayed in the doorway with her hands down at her sides, watching him and he cursed again and smacking his huge hand hard against the stock of the weapon, and when I made a motion to go over to Bigmama, Bigdaddy growled, "*Git* back!" and I got back against the wall so fast I felt shock. He went down the steps, turned and stood looking at her packing cartridges into the gun. He shoved in the breach, turned, took one more step forward and swiftly shot King five times.

Each shot make King jump all over. He leaped straight up with his back arched, fell down, his legs jerking, turning round and round in the dirt, then he stiffened and lay still.

Bigdaddy glared once more at Bigmama, came up the steps past me and put the gun inside by the door. He took a length of clothes-line from his pocket, crossed the yard with quick strides and tied King's rear legs together and began pulling him around front. Then his eyes came at me out of the dusk like two lights; I could see the whites all around, and he hollered to *get inside* the house, *you*. And I did. In terror. I could see her still at the door.

It was dark in the living room. I crossed to the front windows, and kneeling on the heavy old couch, looking out past the porch with the vacant winter swings and rocking chairs where in the summer we all sat and listened to the whippoorwills at dusk, I watched Bigdaddy tie King to the back bumper of the Pontiac and with a crash of the gears and a roar, drag him off.

I felt cold all through, sitting in the dark and thinking about the way Bigdaddy had looked at Bigmama while he was loading that rifle. Soon she came in with a lamp and said it was time I was in bed. I followed her into the Dark Room. She undressed me and tucked me in, talking to me as if everthing would be OK. It had been a hard day on everybody she said and Bigdaddy couldn't help himself when he got to drinking, and we shouldn't hold what happened against him. She looked tired, but would wait up until Uncle Kenneth came in. I told myself I wouldn't hold anything against Bigdaddy as I lay awake fearfully for a while; but I went to sleep before he got back, and next morning I didn't even think about it at all until I found the thrash-marks that King had made frozen in the earth when I went out to play.

THE SAGE OF APPLE VALLEY ON LOVE

by EDWARD FIELD

from THE TEXAS SLOUGH

nominated by Naomi Lazard

Seeker, whatever you love
that is your path
for truly, love is the path.

Do not believe them when they say
what you love is wrong—
it is part of the great love.

Nobody's road is better than yours.
Nobody else's road is yours.
The important thing is to follow it.

Romantics love their loved ones
the way religious people love God:
It opens you up
either way.

Both kinds of people
get from their love
the same thing:

they stay open
and adore.

To love is the path.

Thank whoever
opened that place in you
we call falling in love.

It is the beloved
and woke in you the sacred feeling.

That is what love is about,
feeling, not possession.
It doesn't matter how far it goes
but thank him, whoever he is,
whether or not he responds.

Through him you worship:
He is the path.

🔥 🔥 🔥

JIMMY PASTA

memoir by HENRY MILLER

from HENRY MILLER'S BOOK OF FRIENDS (Capra Press)

nominated by CAPRA PRESS

IN GRAMMAR SCHOOL he was my only rival. He was athletic-minded like myself, a serious student, and filled with ambition. (He aimed to be President of the United States one day—nothing less). The fact that his father was a cobbler and an immigrant, from Sicily, I believe, only strengthened his ambition. Besides, his old man loved him and would have made any sacrifice for him.

We got along all right, Jimmy and I, but we were not what one would call great friends. The one great friend I had during that school period was Jack Lawton. But he died very early—at twelve or thirteen—of rheumatism of the heart.

The reason our relationship was on the cool side was twofold.

Jimmy was a wop and a Catholic and I was a product of that one hundred percent American white collar Protestant tribe which seems to dominate America. Jimmy's friends were all of the lower or lowest class. They were all good fighters—some were already getting to be well-known in amateur boxing circles. But perhaps the thing I could least stand in Jimmy was his pride and ambition. He wanted to lead in everything. What's worse, he *believed* these myths and legends about our heroes. One could never convince him that George Washington was a real pain in the ass or that Thomas Jefferson had several children by his Negro slaves.

The teachers, of course, adored him and helped him in every way. No one ever dared make fun of him. His skin was very dark, he squinted out of one eye—and he had an Italian accent.

Jimmy made it a point to be friends with everybody. That was his "political" side. I had not known anyone before Jimmy who was filled with ambition. To me his antics were like those of a freak.

He was always organizing, or raising funds for this or that. At twelve or thirteen he behaved like an adult. It was unnatural. I refused his invitation to join the club he had formed. I never told him about *our* club. He wouldn't have understood the spirit animating us. We weren't going anywhere or getting anywhere, in Jimmy's mind. Everything he did had to have a purpose, be meaningful. Needless to say, that was not the dominating spirit of the Deep Thinkers or the Xerxes Society.

Jimmy also managed to get his name frequently in the local papers. He was always being praised, admired or envied.

Once he ran the marathon. A heart-breaking experience, and rather foolish to undertake—but Jimmy had to prove that he had what it takes.

He was hardly out of school—I think he was going to night school—when there would be pieces in the paper about him giving lectures to Boy Scout groups and others. Headlines reading—*James Pasta lectures tonight on "Loyality and Obedience"* or *James Pasta lectures on "What makes great men."* Stuff like that. My old man used to read these squibs in the papers and tell me in a meaningful way how much he admired Jimmy. "He's going to go far," my father would say. "Not like you," was implicitly understood. He couldn't see any future for me at all.

About the time Jimmy is building a reputation for himself I am training to become a lieutenant or a captain in a boy's brigade called

"Battery A" which belonged to a Presbyterian Church I attended. I attended church only because I wanted to be in the brigade. I had good times drilling in the basement of that church. I soon became top sergeant and was very proud of my red chevrons. Red, because we were a part of the Artillery—Coast Guard Artillery.

The man who organized this brigade, Major ———, was a queer. He loved boys—and all the parents referred to him as a "lovely man." He loved us a little too much for his own good. Every night, when we reported for duty, he ushered us into his little office, made us sit on his lap, then hugged, squeezed and kissed us as much as he could. We all dreaded these sessions but none of us had the courage to tell on him. No one would have believed us anyway, because he didn't look the part. He was probably bisexual and he probably did love us. One day, however, someone did tell on him, and he was expelled from the church in disgrace. To tell the truth, we felt sorry for him. There were worse buggers in the church than poor Major ———but they never got caught.

Anyway, this was the sort of activity Jimmy did not take part in. He was probably too busy with school anyway. He had made up his mind to become a lawyer, and he did become one, after a long, hard struggle.

We met rarely now—usually by accident on the street. At each meeting we would exchange views—about God, about politics, about books and about the state of the world. Somehow even at the early stage Jimmy secretly admired me because he sensed the writer in me. About most everything we disagreed, but in a friendly way. I usually ended up telling him that though I didn't believe in politics, if he were to run for office I would vote for him. And I really meant it, though to be honest I never voted once in my whole life. Yes, if Jimmy had run for President of the United States I would definitely have voted for him. He was honest, truthful, serious and loyal.

The school we attended was P.S. 85—on the corner of Covert Street and Evergreen Avenue. We had a school song which we sang on occasion. It began—"Dear 85. . . ."—very sentimental, sloppily so. Even to this day I get a card now and then from Jimmy, reminding me of dear old 85. He is, of course, one of its honored alumni.

But this street, Evergreen Avenue—another one of those Brooklyn Streets which had no character. Not exactly slummy, but poor, run-down, and nondescript. Jimmy's father had his shoe repair shop on it, almost opposite the school. I remember the bakery and the delicatessen store vividly. They were both run by Germans. (Only the druggist was non-German. He was Jewish—and a man I could talk to.) The rest were walking vegetables—turnips, kohlrabi, cauliflower, artichokes. What are called "solid citizens." Somewhere along this avenue was a Baptist Church painted all white. Aside from that I remember nothing. Just sameness, dreariness, shopkeepers, vegetables.

The school I shall always remember, especially for several unusual teachers. Number one was Miss Cordes. "Miss," I say—she may have been fifty or sixty. Whatever she taught—arithmetic, English or what—was only secondary, relatively unimportant. What she really taught us, and that's why we all loved her, was brotherly love—how to look at the world, one's neighbor, and oneself. She emanated joy, peace, confidence—and faith. Not religious faith but faith in life itself. She made one feel that it was good to be alive, that we were *lucky* to be alive. How wonderful! When I think of all the sour pusses we had to put up with, or the sadists, Miss Cordes stands out like a Joan of Arc. I often say I learned nothing at school. But to have been in Miss Cordes' class was a great privilege and worth more than all the knowledge in the world.

Number two was Jack ————, teacher of the graduating class. He was what you might call "a card." I imagine he was either a homosexual or a bisexual. The female teachers adored him. He had a glib tongue, could tell risque stories, and was always in good humor. Unlike Major ———— he made no advances to any of us. At the worst he told us dirty stories. If anything, he seemed to like women. He was very free with them, both in speech and with his hands—and they adored this. I can still see him patting Miss ————'s rump and she giggling like a schoolgirl.

I used to watch him leave school on his way home. He was very dapper, always well dressed, always sporting a bowler and sometimes an ivory-handled cane. We didn't learn very much from him. We enjoyed ourselves in his class—he made us feel as if we were already young men, not fourteen and fifteen-year-old kids.

There were other teachers, also important in my life. Miss M. whom I just mentioned made me aware that even school teachers have sex. With M it wasn't just sex, but cunt. You felt that hers was forever itching, that the thing she craved most was a good lay by Jack wearing a carnation in his buttonhole. You could very easily imagine her cornering him in some dark corner and opening his fly. She had a permanently fixed expression of lust on her face, her lips always slightly parted as if waiting to take it in her mouth. Her laugh was a dirty laugh. She was thoroughly impure, you might say. But attractive. She made the other teachers look sick. She always wore tight-fitting skirts, low-cut blouses which revealed her beautiful boobies, and she used strong perfume, the musky kind which tends to give one a hard-on whether horny or not.

Last but not least was the good, honest Scot, Mr. McDonald. I was quite young when I was in his class, and quite shy and innocent. I remember one day especially when he singled me out as an example to the class. He had been explaining to us via the blackboard some difficult arithmetical problem. When he finished he turned to the class and asked if we all understood now. Everyone nodded in agreement. Except me. I stood up and told him that I didn't understand anything. Whereupon the whole class burst into laughter. What a dummy I was! And to stand up and admit it—no, that was too good a joke.

But Mr. McDonald took a different view of it. Holding up his hand he ordered the class to be silent. Then he beckoned me to stand up again. And then he told the class to take a good look at me and try to behave like me. "This Henry Miller has courage," he said. "He's not ashamed to admit he doesn't know. He's genuine, he's sincere. I want you to take an example from him."

Naturally I was flabbergasted. I hadn't given any thought to my behavior—it was just a natural reaction. But I was rather proud of myself nevertheless.

The one person I detested and despised was the principal—Dr. Peewee. To me he was a fop, a show-off and a hypocrite. To begin with he was not my idea of a man. He was frail, flat-chested, and haughty. He gave the illusion of being a great scholar, a know-it-all, but I never understood what he was a doctor in. Every now and then he would invite a Dr. Brown to visit the school and give us students a chance. Evidently Dr. Brown had at one time been a pupil at "dear old 85." Soon as he appeared on the platform the whole auditorium broke into song—"Dear 85, we'll ever strive, to honor thy fair name. . . ." Then Dr. Brown, always freshly returned from his travels abroad, would launch into a speech that might last an hour or two. Always very interesting, I must say. Somewhere along the line he would turn to Dr. Peewee and in his most melting tone of voice tell how he missed dear old 85. Perhaps it was in Singapore or Sierra Leone, or the Engadine—some far-off place none of us knew anything about. Anyhow it all came off perfect—like a good cheese cake. One never asked Dr. Brown what the hell he was doing in these far away places.

Certainly Dr. Peewee and George Wright were two utterly different types of principals. Dr. Peewee never seemed to look a woman in the eyes. Nor did he size up her bottom or her teats. He would pop in and out of a classroom like a lost owl.

He was a frequent visitor at my friend Jack Lawton's home, as was Major———, and of course distinguished guests like Dr. Brown or some cock-eyed Senator or Congressman. The Lawtons were from the old country—England—and very social-minded. My friend Jack at eleven or twelve was already highly sophisticated and of course very well mannered too. I used to like to hear him say— "Sir." "Sir, may I pour you another cup of tea" or some such shit. Which made him a little suspect with the other students. Was he a queer? Was he putting on airs? Where did he think he was getting off? And such like. He proved himself by becoming a first lieutenant in the boy's brigade. He was a great reader for his age. At fourteen he had swallowed all of Dickens and Kipling, and most of Joseph Conrad and Thomas Hardy. He didn't have to work, I mean, study diligently, like most of us. Everything came easy to him, it seemed. He also was lucky to have a loving, devoted mother. He didn't think much of Jimmy Pasta. Referred to him as a climber and a peasant at heart. Naturally one could not possibly think of Dr. Peewee visiting Jimmy's home, in the back of the cobbler's shop. Mrs. Pasta wouldn't have understood a word Dr. Peewee said. Nor would Mr. Pasta, it goes without saying.

Only a short distance up the street, or avenue, was the German delicatessen shop as I said. I can see myself dropping in there every Sunday evening to buy the same things for our Sunday meal. Pot cheese with rich cream on it, salami, liverwurst, head cheese, potato salad, blutwurst, and a variety of bolognas that were very tasty. Then a dash to the bakery across the street where I either got an apple cake or a streusel kuchen. This was our Sunday meal come rain or shine. And I never tired of it.

But what I could never get over were the proprietors of these shops. Both places run by women, fat, bloated, ignorant, illiterate, narrow-minded, money mad. Never once did I hear an intelligent conversation between them and any of their customers. I used to be furious. Just looking at them gave me the creeps. Long before the rise of Hitler I was anti-German. Later I discovered that these German-Americans were worse than the Germans themselves, that is to say, more stupid, more swinish, more mean and money grubbing. More vegetable like.

The years passed and Jimmy still had his nose to the grindstone and one eye always open to publicity. While Jimmy is busy studying to get his degree in law and from there work his way up to being a Congressman, I was busy living my chaotic get-nowhere life.

I had finally disengaged myself from the widow, by telling her I had gone to Juneau, Alaska. I was just twenty-one. I never got to Alaska, nor did I become a cowboy as I had hoped. But I held a number of jobs on ranches. Then one day I ran into Emma Goldman, the anarchist, in San Diego and from there on the whole course of my life changed. That is, instead of staying out West I decided to return to New York and become an intellectual. It was her lectures on Nietzsche and other famous European authors which made me change direction. Of course the widow also had something to do with my return. I found that I missed her, especially the good fucks we had. Finally, however, I did ditch her. By now I had become acquainted with the woman who was to become my first wife. She was my piano teacher. I knew her only a few months before marrying her. We quarreled almost from the very beginning. Sometimes we rolled on the floor struggling with one another. It was truly disgraceful the life we led.

One night I passed a cinema and suddenly decided to go in. Who meets me at the door with a flashlight but the widow. She was an usher there. I forgot to say that in disappearing from her sight the second time I had given her some cock and bull story. The moment I stepped inside the theatre she burst into tears. She was still weeping as she escorted me to a seat and sat down beside me. "Harry, Harry," she said softly, "how could you do that to me?" And then she sobbed and wept some more. I waited for her to go off duty, then escorted her home.

Naturally the first thing that happened as we entered her flat was to love it up. Before you could say Jack Robinson she had whisked off her dress and was lying on the kitchen table, waiting for me to slip it in. And, as we began to fuck she began to weep again. As everyone knows, there is no more enjoyable fuck to be had than from a woman in tears. When we had finished I listened to her woes, to all the misfortunes which had befallen her since we parted. I was truly sorry for her. As I walked home I hit upon an idea which I thought would solve the problem. I would tell my wife the whole story and ask her to let me bring the widow to live with us. Why couldn't the three of us live together in peace and harmony? The Mormons were able to do it, often with many wives. And I had no intention of marrying the widow, only of taking her in as a friend.

Of course when I broached the idea to my wife she hit the ceiling. She said I must be mad to even entertain such an idea. I suppose any woman would agree with her.

But the odd thing about it all was that I was serious. Serious and innocent. But I was the only one who saw it that way. I was too ashamed ever to go back and see the widow again. Pauline was her name. She was a good woman, had no vices, and asked for but little. Through me fate dealt her a cruel blow. Certainly she would have made me a better wife than my first one did.

During this period I went from one job to another, never lasting very long in any of them. One of the better jobs I got through a customer of my father's. Grant was his name. He was a vice-president, I believe, of the Federal Reserve Bank in the Wall Street district. I was given a job, along with about thirty other men and women, checking the adding machines for errors. A boring job, but the pay was good and my fellow workers a jolly bunch. I was on the job about two months, everything going well when one day I was asked to go see the personnel manager. To my great surprise he told me he was discharging me. Why? I wanted to know. Wasn't my work satisfactory?

Oh, there was nothing wrong with my work, he hastened to assure me. It was my character.

"My character?" I exclaimed.

"Yes," he said. "We have been investigating your life, interrogating your friends and neighbors—we know quite a bit about you."

And then he told me how they had discovered about me and the widow.

"We are not questioning your morals," he went on. "but we feel we can't trust you."

He then went on to tell me to my face that because of this obvious infatuation for an older woman, there was no telling what I might do.

I was enraged. "What is it I might do that would hurt the bank?" I wanted to know.

"Rob it!" he said blandly.

"No, you don't mean that." I said. "Why it's preposterous."

He didn't think so. There was no way of talking him out of it. I was finished, no question about it.

And so it went from job to job. Until finally I managed to put in four years as employment manager of the messenger department in the telegraph company. It was toward the end of this period I met June at the dance hall. A few months later I quit my job in the Western Union, having decided to risk all in becoming a writer. It was now my real misery began. What I had been through before was only a preparation for what was to follow.

In quitting the Western Union I had promised June I would not take another job. I was to stay home and write and she would take care of things. It didn't work out as planned, not that we were not diligent, but luck was against us. I did a lot of writing which never appeared in print. Finally I wrote under *her* name—June Mansfield—and thus had a bit of success. But it was short-lived.

Then came Jean—a strange beautiful creature whom June took a fancy to. They behaved like a pair of Lesbians. After a couple of months they began talking of going to Europe together. Jean was a painter, a poet and sculptress. She also made puppets. She made one they christened "Count Bruga," which caused a sensation wherever they appeared.

It was about this time that I took to panhandling at night on Broadway. Even that was a failure. Night after night I came home empty-handed. We were living like savages now in the basement of an apartment house. The rooms we occupied had once been a laundry. It was a cold winter and I had chopped all the furniture to pieces to make firewood. To me it seemed like the dead end. How much lower could we sink?

One day toward dinner hour, I am wandering slowly back to the house. I am not merely depressed, I am dejected. Besides I am starved. I don't recall when we had a last good meal.

All of a sudden whom do I run into but Jimmy Pasta. He is now an Assemblyman from his district. Looks keen and prosperous. Cordial greetings.

"Well, Hen, old boy, how are you doing?" says Jimmy, giving me a slap on the back.

For answer I say—"Rotten."

Immediately a genuine look of concern came over his countenance.

"What do you mean?" says Jimmy.

"I mean I'm broke. I have no job, and I'm hungry."

The moment I said hungry his face lit up. "If that's all it is we can fix that right away," he said, and taking me by the arm he led me to a plush bar where he was known and ordered a meal for me.

"Tell me all about it," he says, as we sat down. "What's happened to you? The last time I heard about you you were the editor of some magazine."

I gave him a wry smile. "I was the assistant editor of a catalog for the Charles Williams Mail Order House. No literature connected with that job," I added.

Well, we sat and talked. I had a few beers, we spoke of "dear old 85" and so on. Finally I said—"I need a job, Jimmy. I need it bad. Could you help me?"

I knew he was secretary to the Park Commissioner—a cushy job that probably paid well.

To my surprise Jimmy replied that he could fix me up with a job in his own office.

"I may have to put you on the payroll as a grave digger first." said Jimmy. "Do you mind?"

"Hell, no," I said. "I've been a ditch digger, a garbage collector and what not. Just so long as I get a salary."

When I left Jimmy I went home sailing. I had agreed to be at his office at nine in the morning next day. He would introduce me to the Commissioner himself—a big-wig now in the political world.

June and Jean took the good news rather unenthusiastically, I thought. They were curious to know what my salary would be.

Next day I went, met the Commissioner, and was immediately put on the payroll. For the first week or so I might be obliged to dig graves but after that I would be made Jimmy's assistant. It sounded wonderful to me.

The next morning I was up bright and early to tackle my new job. It didn't take me long to catch on. The other workers were friendly and helpful. Two of them were from the old 14th Ward. That made things still nicer.

On the way home that evening I stopped off at a florist to buy some flowers.

"A nice touch for a change," I thought. I rang the door bell. No answer. No lights either. In order to get in I had to ring the landlady's bell.

I entered our joint in the dark, lit a candle or two—the electricity had long been shut off. On the floor, in a corner, were a few pieces of dicarded clothing. I roamed up and down several times before I noticed a note on my desk. I picked it up and read—"Dear Val, we left for Paris on the Rochambeau this morning. Love. June."

In another book I have described the emotion that overcame me and my feeling of desolation.

"No wonder," I thought to myself that they showed such little enthusiasm when I told them of the job. What they really felt was a feeling of relief, that someone was looking after me. It made them less guilty.

Next day I told Jimmy what had happened. He could read the sad news on my face.

"You say you love her?" he asked.

I nodded.

"Maybe I'm lucky then," he said. "I haven't met anyone so far who could play such tricks on me."

It was true. Jimmy had little time for women. He was completely involved now in politics. He aimed to go to Washington in a year or two.

Sometimes he invited me to have lunch with him—usually at a bar in the back room of which the local politicians met, played cards, drank like fish and so on. More and more he was becoming disillusioned with the racket. He even went so far as to say there were no honest politicians—impossible.

When I inquired what kept him from behaving like the others he replied very simply—"Because I'm different. Because I have ideals. Lincoln was no crook. Neither was Thomas Jefferson. I wouldn't bring disgrace on my mother and father's name . . . Remember, Hen, old 85? Remember Miss Cordes? Maybe she's helped a lot to keep me straight."

To his credit I must say that Jimmy never did waver. That's why perhaps he never got very far. But everyone respected him. He was still written up in the local papers—as something of "a white hope." He still gave lectures to Boy Scouts and other groups of youngsters. He talked as if he actually *were* President.

It was only three or four days after the two of them had sailed that I received a Radiogram from the ship. It said, "Please cable fifty dollars before we dock. Desperate. June."

Once again I had to face Jimmy. I felt terribly ashamed and humiliated. He lent me the money, not without a little sermon and a monologue about what fools men can be.

Myself, I couldn't understand why they needed this sum. Could they be in debt already? I knew that once they reached Paris they would be o.k. June had the faculty of making people believe in her and trust in her.

Meanwhile I would pay Jimmy back so much a week out of my salary. I had gone back to the folk's house to live—it was cheaper. Almost every day I sat at a little desk they had given me as a child and I wrote to June.

Every Saturday afternoon found me at a dance hall on Broadway. In one afternoon I would spend a week's pin money. But I enjoyed it. Besides I needed to relax and to get a good fuck, even if it were only a dry fuck. Most of these taxi dance girls were very good looking and hot in the pants. They enjoyed these blind fucks on the dance floor—their only concern was not to have their dresses soiled by the man's sperm. I think I have already mentioned how I would take them to another kind of dance hall on their day off. And give them a stand-up fuck in the hallway when I took them home. One girl used to take me to her home and squat over me while I sat on a chair in the kitchen in the dark. Sometimes her mother passed through the room while we were at it but she was unaware of our doings because she was stone deaf and almost totally blind. This particular bitch seemed to enjoy it all the more when her mother passed through the room. She could come easily and it always seemed to me that she came during these critical moments.

Meanwhile I was getting letters from June. They weren't finding it very easy to get along in Paris, but fortunately she had made a great friend of the famous sculptor Ossip Zadkine. She might just as well have said Picasso. Zadkine was world famous. Some years later when I myself went to Paris he asked me what had become of the paintings and pieces of sculpture he had given June to sell in America. June must have disposed of them without telling me. From the brief conversation I had with him and from a few slips June made herself it wasn't difficult to deduct that they had a merry time of it together, punctuated by occasional trips to the Bois de Boulogne where, like Hyde Park, London, any and everyone lay on the grass and fucked whomever they pleased.

Working as Jimmy's assistant I grew more and more familiar with Jimmy's life. Part of his job was to write the political speeches his boss, the Commissioner, had to make. Now and then he would ask my aid in phrasing a sentence. He seemed to regard me as a full-fledged writer. I was in fear he would one day ask *me* to write the speeches for him.

Best time was lunch time at the bar, when he would pour out his heart to me. He really hated the life his brother politicians lived and some of which he had to share. There was never any mention of women. Only card playing, gambling, pool and guzzling. He was with them but not of them.

Somehow it was only now that I began to warm up to him, to discover what a good, loyal friend he was. He had all the sterling qualities which a politician seldom has. As I said before, this was probably his handicap. He never got to Washington. He remained a local Congressman. I never heard much from him or about him once I quit the Park Department job. Occasionally, I would receive a postcard from him. I still do. And I always answer immediately. For I regard Jimmy as one of the few genuine friends in my life, one of the several men who saved my life.

But perhaps what I am most indebted to Jimmy for is this. One afternoon, thinking about Jean and June in Paris, and all the ups and downs in my life, I decided to outline the events in my life from the beginning. I sat down to type out this outline, which in fact became the synopsis for all my autobiographical romances. I sat down at closing time one afternoon and I remained there typing till about five o'clock next morning. In the space of about thirty pages I managed to recall most everything of importance in my life to date. And all without effort. It was as if I had turned on some tap in my memory and the images just flowed out. It was with this outline that I began writing my autobiography in Paris. Not immediately, to be sure. I first wrote a couple of novels in which I used the third person.

As I say, about five in the morning I was pooped. I lay down on the rug in the Commissioner's office and fell asleep. Around eight a.m. the first worker arrived. He saw me lying on the rug and thought I was dead, thought I had committed suicide.

Now that I have told the story of our friendship I must send Jimmy a card to wish him well. He has read my books but I never told him that they were really born in his office.

DON'T YOU EVER SEE THE BUTTERFLIES

by ANA BLANDIANA

from INVISIBLE CITY

nominated by Naomi Lazard

Don't you ever see
The butterflies, how they stare at us?
Nor the signs that the wind
Makes in the grass as we go by?
If I turn at a stroke
The branches stand dumbstruck
And wait for us to withdraw.
Haven't you noticed that the birds vanish?
Haven't you noticed that the leaves go out?
Haven't you noticed the whispers
Growing behind us
Like moss on the side of tree-trunks facing north?
And the silence that waits for us everywhere . . .
And know that something is hiding from us.
We have been sentenced perhaps.
Perhaps there's a heavy price on our heads.
At night when the clashing of corn-ears is heard
The stars shine in excitement.

(translated from the Rumanian by
Hazel Wilson & Peter Jay)

ALL KINDS OF CARESSES

by JOHN ASHBERY

from CHICAGO REVIEW

nominated by Chicago Review

The code-name losses and compensations
Float in and around us through the window.
It helps to know what direction the body comes from.
It isn't absolutely clear. In words
Bitter as a field of mustard we
Copy certain parts, then decline them.
These are not only gestures: they imply
Complex relations with one another. Sometimes one
Stays on for awhile, a trace of lamp black
In a room full of gray furniture.

I now know all there is to know
About my body. I know too the direction
My feet are pointed in. For the time being
It is enough to suspend judgment, by which I don't mean
Forever, since judgment is also a storm, i.e., from
Somewhere else, sinking pleasure craft at moorings,
Looking, kicking in the sky.

Try to move with these hard blues,
These harsh yellows, these hands and feet.
Our gestures have taken us farther into the day
Than tomorrow will understand.

They live us. And we understand them when they sing,
Long after the perfume has worn off.
In the night the eye chisels a new phantom.

𝄞 𝄞 𝄞

THE PARTY

fiction by JAMES HASHIM

from KANSAS QUARTERLY

nominated by Kansas Quarterly

LAST NIGHT A MAN DROWNED . At dawn a few of us were still out in the boats searching for him. We were joined later by the Spanish authorities: three tardy but efficient Naval Patrol boats swept the coastline, while a squad of gloomy Guardia Civil trudged grudgingly up and down the two hundred meters of stony beach. The man who drowned was found early this afternoon wedged in among the rocks along the quai at the entrance to the fishing harbor of Benicarlo. He had washed in with the tide.

The dead man was a Scotsman. It seems odd now thinking of his death that although I had seen him from time to time in the days before the drowning, on the beach, in the *Supermercado*, or sitting at the bar, I had not at first noticed the artificial extension that began at the point where his right arm should have continued from the elbow. He wore a prosthetic device: a cosmetic appendage that had no functional metal claw attached shiny bright to the end of it. But had, instead, a ghastly plastic hand like a mannequin.

The evening before his death, he introduced himself to me at the bar by carefully shaking up a cigarette from a newly opened pack, offering the smoke as a gesture of sympathy perhaps, for he had seen me settle for Spanish black Ducados, the only ones available in The Grand Party Club. With an open smile and a soft burr, he said: "Care to have one of these? They're blonde: English Craven."

I had taken the cigarette and thanked him. Then, infected by his friendliness, I bought him a Campari. We introduced ourselves and sat chatting suddenly self-conscious and clumsy in the knowledge that we had each made a formal intrusion into the other's privacy. We spent fifteen minutes shaping awkwardly modulated phrases, building fragments of paragraphs with little content. Each of us postured with an inner ear cocked for the subtle wary signals strangers send out while they practice the amenities, simultaneously keeping their psychic fences charged against invasion. We tracked each other surreptitiously in the mirror hiding our eyes behind the bottles.

When Kirsten appeared with hair still wet at the ends from her shower, smiling a sweet, quizzical: "Here-is-Kirsten-did-you-miss-me?", my cigarette had burned down to the filter. The Scotsman sat contemplating the solitary ice cube melting lopsided at the bottom of his glass. A burst of introductions followed a pause filled with toothy smiles and shufflings. We rearranged our stools. All smoked the Scotsman's cigarettes. Sipped three fresh Camparis. And then the Scotsman's wife arrived to unglue the pieces we had worked at cementing lightly to one another. Her effervescent "Hello!" discharged another round of drinks. An hour later we sat bunched in good-fellowship at a table on the edge of the dance floor.

I had arrived with Kirsten at Los Rosales in the middle of June. The *apartamientos* had filled rapidly and their occupants now packed the Club to the walls nightly, so that we no longer were allowed the relative privacy of an evening drink and a quiet game of chess. The atmosphere was rife now with raucous multilingual voices, televised replays of the bullfights or American bloodshot serials, sometimes underscored by a jukebox turned up to levels of mind-curdling volume. We had arrived this evening at the urging of Señor Domenchino, the dueña who owned the flats, the Club, and stocked the provisions which filled their refrigerators: the Grand Seignor of this slight strip of Catalonian coast bought so cheaply in 1940 with a smile and a salute from the managers of Franco's corporative state. He had passed the message (whispered to each guest from behind a hand whose fingers spread like a dueña's fan) that "this especial evening would be the most, the passionate, the joyful spectacle of flamencan guitar and Spanish heel." So it was that excitement filled the air, thrown like confetti by guests determined not to fail the efforts of the good señor.

In the time we spent with the Scots couple before the entertainers arrived, the full complement of guests collected. They came as singles, in pairs, in surging, writhing clusters, scurrying like ants, this way and that. Oblivious to one another, yet industriously having *fun:* feelers twitched, rubbed, stroked, generating more than mere tactile perception, moving toward some as yet undefined form of contact. Their feverishness registered in bellows of laughter and strident cackles that cut the smoke like the metal streamers that shimmered in the blast of the fans.

Then the Scotsman's mother-in-law arrived in all her bulky dignity, lumbering up to our table, her face like a gargoyle on a pageant cart. We mumbled another greeting, made apologies, and rose to go. The lights announced our exit in a dazzling display of electrical wizardry with rheostats caressing their electronic nervous system in a series of dim-ups and faltering dissolves that turned the room from red to green to yellow to pink to blue to orange to violet and amber—and back to red—in a nauseating wash. The color matrix ultimately spawned Domenchino who explained that the dancers would be "not to worry" a little bit late, but . . . . "*estan despachados!*" The lights whirled off the shiny dome of the glad señor, and he left bowing, smiling, wringing his hands, disappearing through the kitchen doors to wild acclaim, like Quasimodo fleeing confusedly from the mobs of Notre Dame. The Rolling Stones poured out of the juke box and we left to the *zwang-iddy-zwang* and the *rackitta-thump-rackitta-thump-rackitta-rackitta-thump* of that demon crew.

We had come to Spain so that Kirsten could study Spanish and the culture of this ancient land. And she had worked very hard at it. For Kirsten, golden hair tied neatly and functionally in a tight bun, had ventured forth in dungarees and walking shoes to visit any and all farmers, fishermen, merchants, and other local folk who might prove susceptible to the *abrazos* of a beautiful Swedish social democrat with a truly Iberian soul. The natives had responded with open-mouthed bafflement and awe. They had no doubt not seen the likes before of this emancipated Scandinavian who came on long legs to stalk them a thousand times more sweetly than her ancestors. She moved among them exercising her celebrated neutrality by blandly demolishing their conventions, prying into their lives with that profound and ingenuous Swedish shyness that broke all the barriers of Spanish reserve, and reduced them to unheard-of levels of enforced equality, especially since she confronted them in their own tongue, shaping it exquisitely to their regional dialect, to compound the deftness of her seduction of them. Thus she gained her way, if not into their hearts, certainly into their houses, huts, barns, boats, and storerooms.

She conquered heretofore unassailable male dominions: sailing off with a grinning fishing crew one morning before dawn; walking the furrows of an ancient wooden plow behind a deaf old man and his burro; challenging a priest on a visit to Escorial because he refused a bare-armed girl admission to the Mass. She was like a medieval crusader. She loved the country. Not as an appreciative tourist practicing travel poster quixotism, but as a spiritual mendicant for whom each day under the Mediterranean sun practicing good works meant the deposit of another peseta in the personal account of her soul.

We scuffed along the stony beach for the better part of an hour. But Kirsten had an itch for the performers and was irritable and anxious to get back. So we cut short the respite from the mob and returned. It was past eleven when we ground our way in through the jam at the door to the Club. A ragged bunch of dancers and singing guitarists performed in a drunken clog at the center of the floor.

"My God! They're mestizos and gypsies," Kirsten moaned. That they were: a ragtag assortment of men and women in a variety of costumes, with sparkling teeth and rolling eyes.

"How can he pass this off as authentic?" she snapped. But

the crowd loved them. They stamped and whistled their approval.
"They're a little drunk—but lively," I ventured.
"That cheap little man. He's exploiting them and us. All he cares
about is filling his bloody cash register."

I pointed out disarmingly that the cash register was a Facit. But
Kirsten failed to see the humor in that, and delivered a monologue in
which she allowed me a brief lesson in Spanish history, lost tradition, Fascism, social injustice, the evils of Capitalism, and the
rationale behind her decision to no longer wear a bra in this "stupid
establishment" no matter how offended Domenchino's wife might
be. In the question and answer period that followed, I emerged as
usual the defective student when she turned her shafts on my fragile
citizenship, and targeted me as the symbolic perpetrator of ninety
percent of the world's injustice. I plaintively agreed to fifty percent
against the mounting velocity of her dialectic. We reached a miserable plateau where everyone was having fun but us. Sat in silent
retreat under the canopy of bedlam.

The noise grew with drink and heat. Hands and feet here and
there—it seemed like everywhere—were rat-tat-tatting in bad time
with the music. It did not matter: there was no *time* to the music.
The performers had spilled in disarray all over the Club with a
frightening determination that bordered on chaos.

The heel broke off a dancer's shoe. He tore off the crippled boot
and tossed it to the crowd, slapping his thighs in compensation for
the absence of that cracking heel. Beat those thighs like a drummer
shooting rim shots. The guitarists were dancing too, their voices
wound up in falsetto like a screaming Stuka. They whipped and spun
their instruments, throwing them out, catching them as dancing
partners, abusing them with rapping fingers on the wood. The
wildest of the women twisted and whirled along the edge of the
floor, skirts flying in taunting sweeps that allowed tantalizing glimp-
ses of her flesh, flashes of dense, black teasing floss. Poor, defeated
Kirsten turned her head away and forced down the hemlock of a
gin-and-tonic.

When the dancers stopped exhausted, the room exploded with
the shrapnel of shouts and laughter and wild applause. I smiled an
apology at Kirsten and gently brought her head around with two
light fingers under the tip of her lovely chin. Her eyes were dark pits
of recrimination, their Swedish blue gone murky with resentment.
How to deal with a woman of virtue?

"Why do you make it so personal,?" I asked. She refused reply. And we sat unhappily squeegeeing moisture off our glasses. Then, ridiculously, that errant troubador, Frank Sinatra, came wafting in between the layers of gloom to tell us "Something Stupid."

The guests were up and gliding like surreal figures in a Bunuel landscape. The noise continued with a new resonance. And we continued to sit maintaining moisture-free gin-and-tonic glasses, nursing our vexation.

Our silence was broken by the owl-eyed, slightly squiffed, ancient lady who sat down next to Kirsten, to perch on a bar stool with inept dignity. She smiled weirdly, her eyes glowing like filaments burning out in an electric bulb.

"My, my, it *is* exciting, isn't it," she said. This sweet, old lady was the one we had watched searching for the few shells left on the beach. The nice little granny whose daily excursions hand in hand with the tall, balding, refined old gentleman, we had romanticized. She turned a mad set of eyes on us, took flight, and on the uncoordinated wings of goofy exposition, commenced to lament the collapse of the British Empire, the imminent demise of civilization, and the awful (though *exciting!*) decadence of the present assembly. The flow of her narrative finally wound down with a kind of panting impuissance: a ghoulish roll of complaint and fascination fixed like cues on a paranoid's teleprompter:

"Soooooooooo exciting!"
                    "Yes."
"But verrrrry obscene!"
                    "?"
"Their sex-u-al-ee-tee!"
                    "?"
"Hot food. Hot climate."
                    "Well—"
"Sooo sen-shu-ell."
                    "Uhh—"
"Decadence and . . . filth!"
        "?"
"Smelllll the passion . . ."
        "?"
"Dreadful!"
                "—"
"Fascinating though . . ."

She punctuated her creepy catechism with birdlike sips of Tio Pepe. Poor lady: all that befuddle pumped up out of the well of Christian decency, lugging buckets of it down the corduroy road of a thousand years of English civilization. Summoning up his strength, her husband interrupted to buy a round of drinks. The bartender refueled her sherry glass. Her lips twitched as the liquid filled the glass, like wriggling nightcrawlers they writhed under the down of hair making the sweat glisten under the lights. She raised her glass with a trembling hand and said: "Cheers!"

Kirsten, whose sense of justice is a blazing Arthurian sword cutting through the darkness of this world, was pretty well fed up with the old bird. She spoke rapid, angry Swedish in my right ear. And I fear the old woman came down out of her madness long enough to get the message. She climbed down wobbly off the bar stool, beckoned with a crooked finger for her husband: an actor assailed after a poor performance clutching at the traveller curtain of her despair, it dragged her off into the wings. "Goodnight, my dears," she twitted, then tottered off with the noble figure of her husband following her out the door. All around us people shouted "Arriba!"

We lingered for a time picking in the rubble of the old lady's bombed out life, and then found our way falteringly to humor though it rose but briefly and then died in our renewed struggle to define ourselves. Me: Man. Kirsten: Woman. As usual, I became the abstract symbol of what my grainy-green passport currently invokes. I tried to remain the spiritual recluse. I am sure I made no attempt to mold her to the warp of my frustrated heart's desire. But like the dollar I feel continually devalued. We bickered and discussed to lose half our content in the frenzy around us. Kirsten is no pacifist. She will not allow me to remain *above it all*. Inevitably, we drew for position, selected weapons.

It must be Kirsten's boredom which sends her into this churning anxiousness and rebellion against whatever gods she sees as swatting her for sport.

She says: "You are unable to love me unless you abuse me. Reduce me first to an unequal position."

That is a dastardly non-sequitur. It is also unfair. Occupying a position of inherited power, I am the master manipulated by that clever slave. I am hurt more than I am intimidated. My nature is philosophical. I am resolutedly just. I understand that Kirsten is desperately trying to inject a little oxygen into the prevailing pool of our stagnation. But—in the jargon of the times—the elements of our relationship are not *biodegradable.* Emotionally, she is beyond the saving devices of scientific intervention. For the present, poor girl, she is stuck with the old-fashioned septic tank of a personality that must be cleaned out either by clumsy lustration or kept gurgling with patent enzyme cleaners.

Love is turvy topsy. She struggles pumped dry of feeling, hopelessly caught in the barbed wire entanglement of equality, pretending subservience to laws of a divine order designated by nutty kings and mad queens whose divine right has come muttered from the lips of a senile God. Badly balanced on our bar stools, we are jousting knights poorly mounted, effecting that *combat a out-rance* in which the losses we suffer are never compensated.

"Come on," I say, awaiting her attack, offering myself to rapine, that posture historically hers. In her befuddlement, mistaking my sympathy for confusion, she attacks. Ill-equipped for battle, her warfare diminishes into nonsense. Out of ammunition, she attempts to regroup her forces. There is nowhere to retreat. All around us the old land barriers have collapsed: the social pale has fallen.

The guests are mixing freely in between staccato bursts of flamenco. Local Spaniards play with tourists in half-friendly fashion, mocking them beyond the curl of laughter. One professional regional colorist guzzles from a *bota* to the applause of two Austrian girls. He is accompanied by the jiggling breasts of the French lady of the beach, who smacks her palms together orchestrating her mammary ballet. She is particularly fascinating, for she has been a source of continued wonder. On the beach, in her midmorning rite when she makes preparation for the ritual worship of the sun, she is like a wondrous being from the human zoo who struggles to imitate the unconscious dignity of the hippopotamus presenting its posterior to heaven, as she descends on her pad as though lowered graciously by an unseen crane, stomach down, to spread enormous thighs and elevate her ponderous buttocks to the sky. She does not disappoint us now, for she is in the course of making desire real, dancing madly, bouncing off tables on the nightclub's edge, peasant skirt up and twirling, billowing out behind her like a parachute, slowing her terpsichorean glide, while her bellows of delight cascade over the din like a mating call.

The Danish girls dance too. Their faces are lit up like pinwheels as they toss their heads in mindless delight, dancing their Nordic version of flamenco, depersonalizing hundreds of years of tradition in the Spanish dance, stating with open-faced good will that they shall tolerate but briefly this ceremonial substitute for lust. They are quite drunk and we who are not Spaniards excuse them. But under the pernicious goading of other locals perfervid in their dislike, their Italian boyfriends, dripping wet in bathing suits, weave intoxicatedly through pools of water, waving frosty glasses of vodka-lemon, and cheer them on in blissful ignorance. It is summer. It is Spain. The heat is on.

It is inevitable that the great ox-bodied German will come sidling up to Kirsten and ask her to dance "mit him." He is wearing his party clothes: shiny silk chartreuse shirt, split enticingly to his navel: an inviting opening from which sun-bleached greenish hair sprouts like sprigs of parsley. His tummy rolls slightly over his purple suede belt. Orange colored trousers break in a badly altered heap over his virgin white pucci loafers. He seems to have, as they say, "Gotten it all together."

Kirsten accepts and smiles her leave of me, shooting a vindictive arrow that hits me right between the eyes. I watch this dough-faced clown, leering Hanswurst, sweep her away in bratwurst arms.

Kirsten dances while I drink tasteless gin-and-tonics, pouring them down a dry throat like water. The night wears itself heavily into morning. At three-thirty, one of the Italians smashes out a *passacaglia* to the amazement of his bewildered, middleaged Spanish partner. In clogs borrowed from a big-footed Danish girl, he converts a quiet ostinato into 4/4 time. His countryman has long-since wilted into a stupefied sludge on the floor near the lavatory. And now I watch the Scotsman's mother-in-law exit the toilet to lift a decorous skirt as she steps daintily over the young man whose eyes are glazed like Florentine marble. On her way to empty sheets, she passes me and whispers a sanctimonious "goodnight."

Male pride dictating action, I joined the Scots couple at their table in order to avoid Kirsten's return to the bar where I was now the single occupant.

His mood had changed. His greeting was perfunctory and had a surly edge. His wife lifted mackerel eyes and gave me a two-penny smile. I decided perhaps they had been quarreling. Certainly, the atmosphere was cool. I felt the worse for joining them seconds after I bent my spine to fit the chair.

"Where's yer wife?" Ian asked.

"Kirsten's not my wife." I sighed.

Now I had all their mackerel eyes. Fay breathed a close-mouthed: "Ooooohh," sounding the depths of her Cuba Libre. Ian revolved his head slowly and searched the ceiling with eyes like bleary lighthouse beacons.

"We're . . .uhh . . . married in our . . . uh . . . *minds*," I said, making a bold stroke at humor.

Ian laughed. Fay giggled. And then it grew very quiet round the top of our formica island. I am victimized by silence. I asked Fay if she might like to dance. She looked to Ian who looked away. Then she got up quickly and made for the dance floor. In a stumbling, late reaction, I upset Ian's drink, caught up with her, took her not too expertly in my arms, and we began to dance, searching for a tempo to hold on to.

The dance floor was a hot knot of bodies and there was little pleasure in the dancing. The beat shifted from fast to faster and a young Spanish dandy whipping through his version of a *paseo doble* caught me sharply between the shoulder blades with an elbow like a cutlass. It sent me hard against Fay in a mixture of pain and perspiration. So close, in fact, that I found the lobe of her ear bobbing against my lips. Misunderstanding mixed possibly with desire brought her locked arms instantly up around my neck. She held me that way with her moist face pressed against mine, while she held my bare forearm clammy in the kiss of her wet armpit. I found myself searching apprehensively for Ian over the bouncing heads of the dancers. Then his pecking finger on my shoulder freed me. When I returned his wife to him, I noticed for the first time the plastic arm he swung up under her muculent armpit.

I sat back down at the table. Kirsten returned. We drank another gin-and-tonic. And then Ian and Fay came back again.

"Yer hus . . . *friend* . . . is a *won*-errrr-full dancer," she breathed to Kirsten, rolling the "r" out like a rug after an emphatic "n". There was a pause which Ian parted.

"Yeah. Verra, verra, verra . . . *good*." His "r' was definitely not soft like Fay's.

We laughed and then took turns complimenting one another on

our respective partners. Then Ian raised his arm and laid it *plunk* on the table. It was like a command to cease the frivolity. But Fay's chatter was not to be put off. She proceeded to take the conversation off on a whacky tack, steering her way with some embarrassment into a rather incoherent course on Scottish mores which included (evidently for Kirsten's benefit: a Swedish telegram) reflections on the plight of unwed mothers, pre-marital sexual relations, the soaring rate of gonorrhea in Glasgow, and other delicately put considerations on the failing state of human sexuality. I held my breath against Kirsten's imminent interruption and the reiterated message of the Swedish Welfare State. But it did not come. Instead, the German strode up to click his Puccis in salute, bow, extend an elbow to Kirsten, And they were off again. I sat afterward treading water in the tank of Fay and Ian's silence.

I had come to Spain with my suitcase packed full of goodwill and expectation, with a determined sense of fellowship packed in layers with my wash-and-wear. I had emerged instead, not as an ambassador of all those travel poster clichés that have us sucking up shared humanity over the face of the globe, but as another "tourist" playing a bit part in the farce called *Travel*, acting out my part behind the *papier mache* mask made with dollars, marks, lire, kronor, pounds sterling, all the currency we glue together disguising our real motives.

Watching Kirsten flaunt her falseness, I grew slowly angry. With a brain gradually rendered stupid with drink, I began to feel most sorry for myself, sinking into the slough of contempt for everyone who, like me, had been busy these past weeks savagely assaulting the castle of independence, bridging the moat of dignity with sham, storming the walls of self-respect on ladders heaved up in commonness in their stupid quest for mutuality.

The records spun with the amplifier at anxiety level. Even Fernando, the usually sober and serious student bartender, was dropping and breaking glasses. They shattered on the floor behind the bar making musical indentations in the cacophony.

I started up and pushed irritably away from the table, strode out on the floor sorting the dancers like vegetables in a crate, making my way to Kirsten to break off the Swedish-German alliance with splayed fingers laid sharply on the German's shoulder. She would dance with me! I wheeled her into my arms and almost lost my balance in that manly action, then changed my mind, grabbed her hand and pulled her off the floor, moving her along behind me at a fast walk to the bar.

Then Kirsten broke away and tried to cut a path toward the exit.

"Where do you think you're going!" I spat.

"Anywhere where you not are." she snapped, mixing up her syntax.

"Stay here!"

"Who are you to tell *me* what to do?"

"You're impossible!"

"No! You . . . *you* are impossible!"

Such a foolish exchange. Then she began to cry. I retreated to the corner of the bar and sat down. I pulled the key to the flat out of my back pocket. The key, quite small, is attached to a ridiculously large piece of wood which looks like a chess piece carved by the village idiot. I slammed the key on the bar and the wood broke off, so that the key skittered across and off the top of the counter. Fernando stooped to pick it up, then stood holding it, looking uncertainly from one to the other of us.

"I will have that," Kirsten demanded.

"Give it to me," I said.

And then she swiped it from Fernando's hand, only to lose it as it slipped from her fingers and flew away to bounce with a merry clatter on the floor. For a moment, we scrapped over the key, grovelling amongst the bar stools.

Kirsten popped up the victor with the key clenched inside a fist, spotted the wood on the bar, grabbed it too, and threw it at me before she turned and ran out of the club.

It bounced off the top of my head and I let out an oath and took three silly, angry steps after. Then gave it up and sat back down at the bar with a sneaky glance around the room to check if my defeat had been noticed. Coming back around on the final sweep, I knocked someone's deserted drink in my lap, and sat cooling off with liquid soaking my trousers and an ice cube melting into the wedge of my thighs. A great many voices were shouting "Olé!"

On the dance floor, from out of the swarm, the Scotsman's wife flashed into the light for an instant, a glass held high over her head. Then her husband's hand shot up next to hers. He grabbed her wrist, gave it a furious shake, and the glass shattered on the floor. No one cared. Now I could see them fixed in a shaft of lavender light. He

held her by the shoulders, the grotesque arm, through whatever
magic made it work, fixed over her shoulders and across her neck,
forcing her head down into her chest. With his real hand, he was
trying to pull her off the floor. Failing that, he shoved her back and
forth, trying to push her drunkenly toward the perimeters. He
attempted to strike her with the plastic arm, but there was no room
to swing it in.

The fury shot up in him like the noise and the crazy dancing.
Then, the arm *thing* charged with rage, he broke free to a space in
which to swing it, and struck her with it on the side of the neck. She
cried out in pain, but it was a dumb show lost to the general outrage
that bound them. He kept striking her until she was mercifully
carried away half-conscious by the kink of dancers.

People were mindful of them now, and they tried to intercede,
pushing him away from her, as she staggered out of his reach, her
face pulled like taffy by her terror. They continued to jerk and sway
like marionettes in the midst of the swell, unreal in an awkwardness
shaped by terrible intensity. He continued swinging the arm like a
Norseman's ax, using it simultaneously as a counterweight to maintain his balance. The singing and dancing had wound down, and the
guests now stood frozen with shock, making a circle around the
Scotsman and his wife who stook like gladiators battling one another
at the center, abusive lovers whose coition invited death.

Kirsten was rummaging around the kitchen in her bare feet
looking for something to eat. She had on underpants and an old
tee-shirt of mine. She had a glass of red wine in her hand and was
drinking it in angry gulps. There were streaks of mascara tears
etched into the lines under her eyes and along the creases beside her
nose.

"You really are a bloody selfish—"

"What!"

"—bastard!" She shouted pushing past me into the sitting room.

"Oh? And what about you? What about you . . . Miss Clean!"

"Me? Me! I am fed up with you."

"You're a spoiled Swedish brat."

"Bigot! What has my Swedishness to do with it?"

"Plenty."

"Why bother to come to me then?"

"Because . . . because there is no where else to go."

"Walk! Walk on the beach—"

"I'm sick. I was just ill—"

"Ohhh—poor, David! He makes others sick. Now *he* is sick." She laughed. "It serves you right."

"Oh—c'mon, Kirsten . . ."

"I *know* what you want."

"Well, it's not you . . . kid."

"Tomorrow then? Huh? Tomorrow? When you are not sick no more? When that *thing* is up again and . . . and . . . hungry."

"Don't flatter yourself."

"Buying and selling. That is an American talent, huh? You buyer and seller. You pimps!"

"Singular, dummy. Pimp!"

"So pimp. What's the difference?"

"Cut it out."

"*Kvinnoförstörare! Väldtaktsman! Barnamördare!*"

"Oh—cut out that Swedish shit!"

"Yes! True! Killers you are. The new Romans. Decadent. Without greatness."

"The work is decadent, you bitch!"

"Yes—bitch. Who will not be bought and sold is *bitch*! Bitch is gook, is slope, is . . . is kike . . . is . . . *dyke*!"

"Who in hell do you think you're talking to! Huh! Huh! I have *fed* you, goddammit! *Clothed* you goddammit!"

"Of course! Made me your *hora*!"

"You . . . *You* said it! Not me. Bitch!"

"Yes. And soon the *bitches* are going to arrive to America and bring you to . . . to the *cleaners*!"

"To the what! God, you are an asshole. Where'd you learn *that* one?"

"From you, you sick Nazi. It is your biggest word for human beings!"

She ran into the bedroom in a rush of tears. I heard the sound of drawers banging and slamming. "Why don't we call a truce, and leave each other alone?" I cried, exhausted.

"That is fine with me!" She shouted from the bedroom. "I will hitchhike if I have to. Tomorrow I go to Stockholm. Back to human beings."

"That's ridiculous," I said, feeling betrayal and an equal amount of fear.

I went into the bedroom, wound up now by anxiety, eager to
placate. She was tearing dresses off hangers, throwing them into a
suitcase. All those dresses I bought. Those dresses she refused to
wear. Throwing them around like dust cloths.

"I think it would be nice if you got down off your Swedish
soapbox," I said.

Kirsten slammed the lid down on the case and began lashing the
straps. "I can do without you," she said. The case slipped off the bed.
I made a move to pick it up. She pushed me away. "I can do without
you like your wife could do without you. You, David—*you* are
spoiled. Spoiled! Not me. Spoiled by your *hemmafru* and those
darling little children you carry on your back like . . . like bags of
guilt. You are spoiled and they will no doubt grow up spoiled just
like you. You with your cards of credit and the plastic life."

She had run out of things to pack. Would she next pack my
clothing too?

"You wore out one woman and you wore out one country. I am not
your volunteer for the next one. I will not be your Bank America
card."

She found her shoes, sandals, beachwear, and assorted parapher-
nalia, gathering the stuff up in swatches which she dumped on the
bed. Then she unstrapped the suitcase and dumped it too. Began
repacking.

"Where . . . *where* do you get the stuff?"

"Don't worry, it is not *all* from you."

"I don't mean the clothes, dummy. All that liberation crap.
Where does it come from? Swedish magazines? *Damernas Värld?
Femina?* Is that what you read while getting to New York, Chicago,
and L.A.? Where you gobble up the goodies. Christ, an air hostess
mentality, that's what you've got, kiddo. Fortified with all that
ladies' magazine crap you digest in between servings of *smorgas* on
747's. Coffee, tea, or freedom—that it? If you're not screaming
about inequality and the underprivileged, you're telling me about
my inadequacies. You're so mixed up with phony notions of your
impeccable Scandinavianness, your Nordic majesty, and the dikey
myth of Queen Christina, you can't see straight. God, you're the
fucking Frederika Bremer of the fucking airways. The Madam Myr-
dal of the skies! Fasten your seat belt, David, you're in the hands of
the Scandinavian Virtue System."

"You are a racist. A blind and stupid man. A coward."

"And you, my dear, are a conglomeration of fifty years of Swedish socialist air conditioning!"

She threw an armload of clothing up at the ceiling. "Your big words are nothing to me. Go home. Go home. Go home, David. Put your shotgun in your pick-up truck."

"Shit. You've seen too many movies.'

And then we were wrestling over the clothes like children fighting over who would be the mommy and who would be the daddy in a game of "house." I picked them up and Kirsten spread them over the room. In the struggle for mastery of the cloth, she hit me accidently in the mouth. The cigarette she *happened* to have lit in her hand, singed my chin. The lit end stuck to my flesh glowing, so that I could smell myself burning, like a chicken having its feathers seared. In pain and anger, I struck out blindly and caught her on the cheek with my hand. She cried out and fell to the bed. And I danced around her like a lunatic, slapping the ember off my chin.

"Oh, you rotten cunt," I screamed.

"Oh, oh, oh . . . you . . . *you!*" She cried, caught in the mess of clothes strewn over the bed. Finally, she gave up and curled into a ball like a threatened caterpillar. "Leave me alone . . . *please. Please . . . just leave me alone.*"

"Get up, Kristen," I said, rubbing my wounded chin, moving to that posture of permanently injured party. "Get up," I said. I leaned across the bed and attempted to yank her to her feet, slipping off-balance on the tile floor.

Has it really happened to me? Again? Am I so ridiculous? I replay this scene from vaguely remembered stills that flop by on the movieola of my thoughts. Damn her betrayal!

The flat was a mess. Kirsten had spent the time since her departure making a mess of it: throwing clothing about, packing her suitcase to leave, generally indulging her annoyance with me. We picked at one another a bit more, to produce a display of mutual bad temper that led to pushes and shoves and shouting and a burn on my chin and a scraped back for Kirsten. A stupid scene. We discussed it and concluded that there is no rationalizing stupidity away. No matter how we may love that self-indulgence, masturbation is less rewarding than sexual intercourse.

I am a lousy actor. Not only have I been miscast, but I have overplayed the role. The Jimmy Cagney of Los Rosales. Kirsten was sitting painfully withdrawn on the edge of the bed. Well, dammit, it takes two to tango. I walked out on the balcony. I am not sure how long I stood out there. She had been quite unfair. Had bullied and hurt me. I thought of taking her in my arms. I imagine myself now taking her in my arms, this fragile person whom I love so much. In a flood of . . . what?: soberness? remorse? anguish? gentleness? love? At least I am willing to give her the benefit of my doubts.

I am now aware of having stood out here for a long time, my hands gripping the balcony rail, as I stare down at the sea. Are my knuckles white with tension? In cheap fiction the knuckles of heroes always turn white when they grip balcony rails after nights like this.

Oh, she is wrong. Yes. She does not realize the great seriousness with which I undertake my life.

The moon is under cover of the clouds now. Before it was full. My thoughts careen down the path of my seriousness. She is wrong about me. I have helped her a great deal. Enriched the quality of her life. I am thinking of dogs baying at the moon. Of madmen lost to life who clutch at asylum windows. She is wrong.

Am I only fondling my senses as I watch myself gaze down at the sea? Am I gratifying myself in the gothic splendor of an imagination bred in years of hackneyed definitions that come now like old color-slides worn out and browned from too much time in the heat of projector lamps throwing fuzzy images on the walls of my mind? I have suffered in this life. And the applause that comes to sustain that thought is welcome now. I imagine myself not that demon bastard who has his way with her. I imagine myself somehow holy. Master of a universe whose primary world is Me.

The sea that breaks against the stony beach is loud and persistent. Familiar. I have lain awake so many nights and listened to the regularity of its thrusts. Taking heart from the sound of the sea. Listening to the sea, counting the breaking waves. I have felt my heart quicken, imagining myself in its stead, rebelling in a furious assault, tempi mounting, until we swept rampant over the land in a crushing sweep of revolution against the tides.

I moved my hand to feel the reassurance of Kirsten's thigh as she lay sleeping warm and safe beside me. Pushing my fear away, I slowly became aware of the silence from the Club below. The party had ended. I lay still, breathing easily, listening to the sound of my heart, as through a stethoscope under the muffled cup of my pulse. I searched absent-mindedly for it against my neck: pulse. lifebeat. How faint and alarming its fragility. I closed my eyes and wished for sleep. But it had passed. Very gradually, rising over the sounds of the sea, I heard voices. Cries raised in distress.

I sat up in bed, eased away from Kirsten, then slid out on the cold floor, feeling a moment's relief from guilty thoughts. I slipped on my trousers and shirt and went out to the balcony.

The shore was dotted with tiny figures who spilled over the beach like bugs, or movie extras in search of their director. Some waved electric torches. There was shouting and calling back and forth. Most of the fragments of speech that floated up were in Spanish. I needed Kirsten.

When she came out to the balcony, still cozy with sleep, pulling the cord of her robe around her, I said: "Listen. What are they shouting? What's wrong?"

She listened for a moment. "They are talking about . . . I cannot understand it all, they are too far away . . . Something about a man . . . A man . . . out in the water. They are sending boats."

"Come on, let's go down."

"Wait! They are talking about a man in the water . . . swimming. They say the man has killed someone."

On the beach, we found many of the guests clustered in groups of worry and dread, suffering a kind of shocked sobriety. A number of men were dragging two small fishing boats toward the water. Kirsten spoke for a moment with Domenchino. He was drawn and shaky. He waved his arms helplessly, speaking with an effort.

"A man is far out in the water. The man with one arm," he said in Spanish. "A terrible struggle. The man drunk and raging. Death. He tore off his arm and ran into the sea."

Kirsten asked if no one had tried to stop him. "Ah—this . . . this . . . man . . ." Domenchino shook his head, a gesture of hopelessness.

He is bewildered, embarrassed: "A man does not behave this way. It should not have come to this. It was a party. Always there are parties. I do not understand the world now," he says. "A man must be a man."

There were boats in the water manned by the guests. Kirsten wanted to come out with me to the boats. I stopped her. It was work for men.

I waded out through the waves and climbed into one of the boats.

The German had an oar. He gave another to me. His chartreuse shirt was dirty and had flecks of tar on it.

We rowed out a very long way in the early morning sea, at least a mile beyond the breakers. It was hard work. The sweat poured over my forehead because I was not used to it. We had torches and the light was coming now with the dawn.

After a hopeless time of pulling in the empty sea against the undertow, we joined another boat and headed for the land, zig-zagging a hundred meters abreast in a futile sweep.

It was long after we had arrived on the shore again that the authorities dispatched three motor launches to comb the sea. As we beached the boat, the clacking whir of a helicopter pulled our faces up. We watched the aircraft make empty sweeps of the area.

Kirsten and I are leaving tomorrow. We will drive to Hamburg and board a ship bound for Trelleborg. Everything is packed. We are not unhappy at the thought of leaving. Since the drowning, the atmosphere has become sullen and gloomy. Señor Domenchino's hearty banter has given itself over to moroseness. He is quite obviously offended by the drowning. Evidently he thinks the Scot chose Catholic Spain for the occasion of his self-destruction.

It is very late. Another night that has lapsed over into morning. And I have been wakeful through irritating patches of sleep, a state in which, because one prays for it, sleep will not come. When it does try and reach me, I clutch at it. But it eludes me. I am annoyed by the light.

The glare of the breaking light casts itself against the window. It is Kirsten who responds to it. She holds me awake with her talk. It is foolish to sleep now in the beautiful face of breaking light. Sleep is a censor of physical delight. It is now that senses are sharpened despite night wishes for miracles and false hope, she tells me. It is now desire quickens and affirmation returns because one has sur-vived a sleepless night, she says. Oh Kirsten, I am trying to sleep.

The light outlines the leaves of the tallest palm in Los Rosales. Their shadows hang across our bedroom window.

"Look," Kirsten says, "there is still a star left in the sky. See? It is caught in the arch of the branch."

I open an eye in order to see it. It dances teasingly between the trunk and the palm frond. Chasing stars. What a bore.

"Oh," Kirsten says. "It is beautiful. It makes me want to cry."

But Kirsten does not weep. She lies thrilled by her own breathing. I can see that and I am annoyed. Provoked by her incontestable sense of life, I fix my eyes on that star. but it will not stay now. The light is melting it. Day making Kirsten's magic fade. But of course. I am thinking of the Scotsman. He has been dead and on my mind for seven days. I feel the old anxieties, those nameless dreads descending like gnats wakened by the dawn. On the tiled wall over the bar in the Grand Party Club, there is a banal legend inscribed in medieval lettering on the Spanish tile. The letters melt exquisitely into the mosaic:

> The Party is the pleasure, the illusion, the social bond. The phrase 'Let's have a party' contains a sense of conquest, a right. Someone who does not have company for a Party on a Saturday night is a being without tomorrow, without hope, a victim.

It is very hot. There is a bottle of white wine in the fridge. We take it and two glasses out on the balcony hoping for a breeze. I regret I have not slept, but I do not mention it to Kirsten.

Then Kirsten says, from the center of a thought, "It is a heavy burden, isn't it? Our need for one another."

"Yes, I guess it is."

"We spend so much time hating. It is difficult to face the other in the mirror. We see our likeness . . . our *spegelbild*. What is that in English? The word for weakness? In Swedish, it is *svaghet*. That special kind of weakness we all share and . . . hate."

I am not sure I understand her properly, but I guess at the translation. "Frailty? Is that it? Frailty?"

"Yes," she says, her face set serious and pale in the sun. "Yes. A terrible thing. *Det gör oss fulla av hat och rädsla.* It is the terror frailty bears that is worst."

"*Rädsla*," I mutter. "Is that it? Terror."

She laughs. "Yes. But that, after all, is just a word, David."

At midmorning Kirsten goes down to the beach. I return to bed and sleep. In my sleep, I dream of the man who drowned. He is very ordinary in my dream. He does not have an artificial arm. In my dream there is nothing unusual about him, except for the strange circumstance that he is surrounded by my children, John, and Christopher, and Louise. He does, however, attempt an extraordinary feat in my dream. He is lifting a great rock. My children stand silently by, their faces pinched with worry and fear. The rock is too heavy for him. He drops it. But tries again to lift it, only to drop it. Repeatedly he attempts to lift the rock. I dream of his struggle to lift that great weight. And he forever fails. In my dream the Scotsman has my face. How peculiar our dreams.

ARIZONA MOVIES

by MICHAEL VAN WALLEGHEN

from THE HUDSON REVIEW

nominated by THE HUDSON REVIEW

1

Rosetta, her new boy friend
and all four kids
are going to the drive-in
down in San Manuel.

"One more beer," they tell the kids
"and then we'll go." The kids
want a quarter a nickel
another dime—the kids

are a pain in the ass
the movie is about a dog
and the boy friend wears glasses
baggy double-knit slacks

and a white belt. Rosetta,
on the other hand, is beautiful,
elegant, altogether sweet
in her new blue sweater

and when she reaches in her purse
to buy another round,
I spot her little silver gun.
"That's just in case," she says,

"just in case."

2

Sometimes
even in the middle
of the year's best movie
you can hear coyotes
at the San Manuel Drive-In.

Tonight, they are far away
and merely barking at the moon . . .

but Rosetta tells me
that when they chorus close
and suddenly together

hysterical, high pitched, furious

it means something is dying
in the dark foothills
behind the shaky screen.

3

After the bad movie
Rosetta wants to finish off
what's left of the tequila
drop off the kids

and then go dancing . . . !

But I don't know about Fred.
I think Fred sells mobile homes—
convenient, air conditioned,
catastrophically fragile,

I pass them everyday
and try to imagine myself
living there: the tv on
all the kids at school

and Rosetta, just lying
on the couch, just watching,
through the picture window,
some Apache ghost dance
cavalry of thunderheads
advancing slowly out
from between Mount Lemmon

and a pigeon blue wing
of the Catalinas.

4

No one is dancing
up at Pop-A-Tops. No one
is speaking. The tv's on
and in the Merry Christmas

snow flaked mirror, Fred
is shooting pool. Rosetta,
on the other hand, shreds
her matches into tiny bits

then looking up, her look
slides sidelong into mine—
the tense, unsteady look
I think, of children

getting lost . . . but what
was it that I thought to say?
Something dumb, mindless
a remark about the movie

or at my best, to notice
on that long, small arm
her careful, bar-room bracelet
of pink and yellow straws.

Whatever it was, she answers
to the whole place—loud,
and before I say a word:
"Nope, I'm not dead yet"

and the fuzzed up mirror
keeps still, stays quiet
as the slow blue echo
of a pistol shot.

5

Rosetta says she's 32
but Fred looks younger.
Fred's even younger partner
works the graveyard shift

at Magma Copper
and behind us all
the Falstaff clock
turns counter clockwise

towards eleven. "One more game,"
they tell Rosetta, "and then
we'll go." *The Lariat?*
The Hangman's Tree?

"Why not Rosetta's place?"
Fred's partner whispers.
A joke perhaps. But still
it's curious, frightening

that I should also hear
in the shy nylon whisper
of Rosetta's thighs
in the click of small ice

something dangerous, random,
confused as kitchens,
cupboards where the knives
are kept, bedrooms

in the Apache Trailer Court
with real bullet holes
above the door.

6

Like Rosetta
I too hear voices.

Tonight, they are speaking
the frazzled language

of neon, the cindered
impossible language

of parking lots, static
and revolving lights . . .

but sometimes, it's Rosetta—
her voice still angry

clear, above the voices
of the graveyard shift

who slam their doors
like Fred or anyone

going off half drunk
to work tonight

in knee deep water
and the hot acidic dark

one full mile
underground.

VICKIE LOANS-ARROW

FORT YATES, NO. DAK., 1970

by MARNIE WALSH

from A TASTE OF THE KNIFE (Ahsahta Press)

nominated by AHSAHTA PRESS

1

i went to the dance
tommy little dog
ask me
i wait by the road
seen the red go
in the water   in the lake
then yellow spiderwebs
climb up the sky
one star watching
it get dark
tommys pickup come down the hill
i get in
saturday night is whisky
night
we drink   i forget
the red sun in the water

2

i hear
the agency hall
banging   shouting   stomping
i ready to dance

old bull-toes
put his mark
on our hands at the door
white mens music
up on the stage
christmas lights all around
one time i was the angel
up there
mama made me pretty wings
tommy was a shepherd
charlie two-head
baby jesus
he died after
i forget why

3

well
them white mens music
just what we like
for dancing
the floor go rockarock
i got on my red dress
my beads
tommy wear his sateen shirt
purple pink
we go round and round
push push
saturday night   whisky night

4

some old squaws
on benches next the wall
watch us
outside the old men
mostly drunk
spit on ground
drink   tell jokes
aunt nettie drunk

in her plymouth
on back seat
aunt nettie come back
to reservation
been to college
right away cecil dog-heart
give her baby
when she drunk
saturday nights
all the men get on her

5

we all drink vodka
at my cousins truck
everybody happy
everybody feeling good
lights all dusty
i got dusty eyes
so i not see right
joshua get mad
nobody care but tommy
they fight   fall down
joshua get a thing   ʼ
out of truck
hit tommy on head
too much
it get all quiet
we go away

6

next day aunt nettie
say he dead
we dig potatoes a little
mama ask me
how i come home
if tommy dead

i say i forget
but i don't forget
when i seen the sun
all red
go in the water

□   □

ᛟ ᛟ ᛟ

THE LOVER

fiction by EUGENE K. GARBER

from SHENANDOAH

nominated by SHENANDOAH

I

Here is a beginning . I am a tow-headed boy in the depression South, walking a dusty road by a creek. I am with two other boys, brothers. The older and taller is Abner Ellis, Junior. The one my age and height is Frank. Abner is seventeen. Frank and I are fifteen. Their mother is thousand-eyed. In my dreams I see her beautiful ocellated face fan out and cover the stars. She knows me, knows that I desire Frank. Abner has no inkling. Frank himself does not understand it. But she knows.

If she had been of a higher caste she undoubtedly would have had significant history. Maybe she forfeited celebrity when she married

Dr. Ellis upon his graduation from Tulane medical school, but I don't think so. Marie Crevet. There are no socially prominent Crevets in New Orleans, not even a marginal family who might marry an extraordinarily beautiful daughter upward into the ruling classes.

Anyway, she came as a bride to Laurelie in south Alabama, melon capital of the world, a patchwork of loamy fields and red clay hillocks, rank with the sweat of blacks and raucous with the hymns of Baptist farmers. No apparent destiny here for her beauty. The doctor liked seclusion. Probably he didn't trust the gentlemen of larger towns. Who could blame him? He was an unlikely husband for such a bride—gangly, big-eared, deformed by an Adam's apple that rode under his collar like a thieved melon in the toils of a creek, and crack-voiced as though his glottis were arrested in perpetual adolescence. Everyone knows the type, "raw-boned, Lincolnesque." Everyone has read dozens of such biographical sketches. He made the archetypal sacrifices of the poor country boy to secure his degree in medicine: scrimped to save his tuiton while still helping to support a widowed mother, studied blear-eyed by midnight oil for his entrance examinations, et cetera. By the time I knew him he'd already had one heart attack. There was good reason for it, other than his youthful sacrifices—an exhausting practice among blacks bloated by fat-back and cornmeal, among gnarled fundamentalist dirt farmers too guilt and God-ridden to come in time with their ripe tumors. So I despised him from the first for the constant outpouring of his charity, which left us in his home only the rind of his love.

I was his nephew, sent down in the summers from a motherless home in the great city of steel, Birmingham, by a sodden coal-blackened father. And it was I finally who provided the occasion for the heroism which such beauty as my aunt's inevitably has exacted of it.

Marie Crevet Ellis bore to her husband two sons, Abner and Frank. Abner was his father's son—blue-eyed, willowy, an effortless charmer of girls. Frank was his mother's son, dark and beautiful. He was marvelously hirsute, his nostrils dark and densely tendriled, his face shadowed below high cheek bones. His chest and limbs and even his back bristled with hairs that made beautiful black rivulets when he rose like a young sea god from our creek. But such dark beauty was uncouth in those parts, and so he was lonely.

So was my aunt lonely, in constancy to her faith. She attended Mass every Sunday afternoon. It was celebrated for her and two old women by a circuiting priest at a side altar of the Episcopal church, rented no doubt for the occasion through an uneasy alliance of prelacies in that benighted stronghold of fundamentalism. In the dead heat of July and August she still put on her black dress, covered her head with a black mantilla, and walked through the downtown streets to her devotions. The ice-cream eaters in front of the drugstore and the old men on the hotel verandah stared, but they said nothing. I myself would have liked to ask: why this penitential black in the seasonless summer, Lent past and Advent yet to come? What was she guilty of? Failing to rear her sons as Catholics? Later she had more to confess.

I began to succeed in my advances toward Frank. But I can say this for myself: as unthinkable as were my desires in that time and place, I always kept in view his good. When his gentle loneliness began to unfold to me, I touched it always with delicate love. If he wanted to tell me that I was beginning to trespass on his feelings, he only had to speak my name with a hint of admonition and I would stop. Still, I confess, my yearning outstripped the slow melting of his reserve. I found it more and more difficult to guard my feelings, even in the presence of others. Once at supper my uncle, noting our silence, suddenly said, "All right, Frank and Joe, what's the big secret?" Caught completely off guard, I blushed hotly. "What are they up to, Marie?"

My aunt's dark eyes looked straight into mine. "Oh, I think they've found something at the creek."

"They spend enough time down there," said Abner. "It must be a mermaid." His own wit surprised him and he guffawed.

"We don't have any secret, Father," said Frank with a voice as clear as a bell.

"Good. Then let's talk to each other instead of acting like we're at a wake."

I don't know where the conversation went from there, but I do remember that when my frightening embarrassment had passed, I was suddenly suffused with great pity—for the man with the youthfully cracked voice and the dying body; for my beautiful aunt, whose dark eyes pleaded with me to spare her son; for Frank, who was forced now for the first time to lie to his father; and even for Abner in his innocent ignorance. I should have leaped up and cried that I was the serpent in their bosom, that they must scotch me or be ruined. Instead, I excused myself on pretense of nausea. And after that I made ready a face to meet any comment that might touch my relationship with Frank.

For a while I kept my distance from Frank, sensing his revulsion toward the lie he had told his father, though it was not a deep lie. After all, we had only feasted eyes, touched hesitatingly. So, a few days later I resumed my courtship, and I was overjoyed to discover that the lie had left no taint, that the warm promise of his slow yielding was still there. One day when we had swum a while nude in the Blue Hole, we lay together on a flat rock at the lip of the deep pool. We embraced. I felt the hairs of his back, exposed to the motley sun in the trees, dry and grow erect. But after a few moments he disengaged himself and rolled over on his back. I leaned beside him, my body intensely hot. He looked up through half-closed eyes. "What is this thing, Joe?"

Then I knew that he felt, as I did, a palpable presence embracing us. I might have called it the god of love. I actually thought of that, but I only said, "I don't know. I don't have to know." I leaned forward and kissed his teat in its nest of black hair and it hardened against my lips.

"I do need to know," Frank said.

"Tell me when you find out."

Do I make it sound as though there were only these episodes of pursuit? Not at all. We played American Legion baseball. Abner was a star pitcher. We flew model airplanes. Frank's, the most delicately balanced, stayed up longest. My aunt caught us and made us mow, weed, shell peas. My forte was frogging. Many nights we waded the creek. Frank carried the gunny sack. Abner hypnotized the frogs with the flashlight, and I snared them in the long net that I myself had woven, hooped, and secured to an oak sapling. My uncle loved the legs breaded and fried, but he had to cook them himself because my aunt could not bear to watch the final contractions in the pan. Of course, we boys one night saved out a hapless creature for the classic experiment. When it was newly dead, we passed through it a small battery current. The twitching of legs bewitched us. We tumbled over each other and gyrated splay-legged about our bunk room— three adolescents having a saurian orgy. But even in that crude prank, as in the chores and play of every day, the current of my love for Frank never for one moment ceased to galvanize my heart.

Besides my aunt's vigilance, there was one other threat to my love for Frank—a series of monologues that Abner delivered in the bunk room when he got home from dates. He would lie on his back in his bunk and light up cigarettes that he had stolen at the drugstore. In the morning the room would have a dreadful smell, but Abner's nicotine crimes were never detected because my aunt was forbidden by my uncle ever to set foot in the bunk room. His motives were two-fold, he explained. No lady should have the offensive job of cleaning up after boys. Conversely, boys must have their sanctuary. Every Saturday afternoon my uncle himself inspected our quarters. For this we carefully spruced up, or titivated, as the doctor was found of saying. Otherwise, the room remained a congeries of clothes, balls, bats, string, balsam scraps, etc. So Abner would light up one cigarette after another. He didn't inhale and probably didn't even like the taste. But he obviously liked the big white plumes of smoke that rose up into the moonlight at the window bequeathing his words a ghostly presence and wreathing about them the wraith of eroticism and nocturnal mystery. Here was the essence of his story repeated over and over with little variation. He had two girl friends, Betty and Harriet. Betty, the hotel manager's daughter, was only a decoy, Abner said. Harriet, a rich farmer's daughter, was his true love. Frank and I had seen them often, of course, and they were true in appearance to the character that Abner assigned them in his midnight monologues. Betty was a saucy little thing with black hair and dark eyes. Harriet, on the other hand, was blond, the perfect Aryan match for Abner. Betty must have absorbed what little there was to learn of vice in Laurelie, living in a hotel suite and helping with the travelers, because a great number of Abner's narratives dealt with her innovations in kissing—frenching, the love-bite, the lobe-lolly, etc.

I found all this repulsive, but I wondered what Frank thought. He made no signs in the dark, no response until one night he pressed Abner for details of a rare kiss from Harriet. "It was a soul kiss, Frank. Our tongues never touched, but it was a soul kiss, better than all of Betty's kisses put together."

"What do you mean, a soul kiss?"

"I mean the kind of kiss that makes you feel like you aren't there any more. You feel like you left your old self behind, like snake slough."

"Where did you go, into Harriet?" A dense fountain of smoke shot up toward the ceiling. "It's hard to tell, Frank. I did sort of feel like I was dropping down into her mouth if you can think of a mouth as big as night. But I wasn't thinking *this is Harriet*. I was just . . . going out of myself."

The halting of Abner's ending was more eloquent than his words. Silence descended on us. But I lay awake thinking: what has Frank learned from this? That one kiss from a true love is infinitely better than all the inventions of promiscuity? That the only true love for a man is a woman? But I found that I could not imagine for myself Frank's thoughts or desires, probably because my own were so simple: I wanted him.

That night's exchange with Abner had a profound effect on Frank. The next afternoon, when we were alone at the Blue Hole lying in shoaling water on the lip of the pool, I caressed his thigh, but he set my hand aside. "Don't touch me, Joe, and don't talk to me about it for a while." I feared he meant forever. I feared it with a wintry contraction of the heart that numbed all my senses. And I felt helpless, forbidden to plead my case with the one I loved. He was determined to work things out alone. My uncle noticed Frank's abstraction and joshed him. "Any chance of you getting out of the dog days of August, boy?" Yes, the summer was almost over, and I knew in my bones that it was this summer or never. I knew that if I could possess Frank even once, I could go back to my smoky city and my sodden father and sing in my heart despite their sooty faces. But if I went back with my desire all locked up, I could not live until another summer.

My aunt watched. One night I overheard her say, "I know what it is, my Frank. I know you will choose the good way." They were in her sewing room. I couldn't see them, but I imagined her taking his hand, stroking his hair, speaking dark eyes to dark eyes, excluding me forever. My heart raged against her. But I made no sign. I knew that if anything caused Frank to suspect I did not love her he would shut me out of his heart forever. So I was the serpent under the flower, waiting for something to come my way. And just when my patience was wearing dangerously thin, I was rewarded. The one who had almost ruined me gave me new hope—dear crude Abner.

My good fortune came on a Tuesday night. Abner was eating with Betty at the hotel and then they were going to the movie. Later, Frank and I learned that her parents were out of town for the night.

From Abner's excitement I might have guessed as much, but there was something else on my mind. At supper my uncle had revealed that a much loved fellow doctor over in Minnville was hopelessly ill.

"Physician, heal thyself," I said. The moment the words were out I was horrified. It was as though a demon had spoken through my mouth. My uncle lay down his knife and fork. "The reason he is dying, Joe, is that he has worked himself to the bone for the people of Minnville. He couldn't turn away a sick nigger on Christmas morning." He spoke sharply.

"That's what I meant, Uncle Ab, about small-town doctors. Their patients taking everything."

"Joe's right, Abner. You all work too hard." Pity and love streamed out of my aunt's eyes: for the husband with the slightly ashen face whose death would not lag far behind his friend's, for the son in whose dark eyes toiled warring images of awakening sex, and, yes, even for the perverse nephew whose thwarted love tipped his tongue with involuntary malice. She was our mater dolorosa. But I couldn't love her, not even for redeeming in Frank's eyes my wayward remark.

After supper the house seemed full of gloom. Half-heartedly I suggested frogging. To my surprise Frank agreed. Down at the creek we waited for the deepening dark to bring the sound of the big croakers. I had one of Abner's cigarettes, which I lit as soon as we had settled ourselves on a rock. Frank must have been surprised because I had never smoked before, but he said nothing. The smoke made a pale image against the moonless sheen of the creek. "Want a drag?" Maybe I hoped that mixing spit on the cigarette paper would seal our lips.

"No."

A moment later I threw the cigarette into the creek and spat after it. "I don't know what Abner sees in those things."

We waded into the creek. Frank went ahead with the flashlight. I followed him closely with my net. The croaker sack was tied over my shoulder. One by one I dropped the big frogs into it. But when we had maybe a half dozen, I began to be invaded by a curious feeling of deep kinship with the frogs—slimy singers of unmelodious love songs flung into a hairy darkness to writhe hopelessly until a hammer delivered them from confusion. So strong became this projection that it grew almost hallucinatory. The flashlight beam did not hypnotize them more than their glistening eyes fixated me.

"Are you going to get this one or not, Joe?"

"No. It's a mama full of eggs. We got enough. Let's quit."

Back at the house I pretended to knot the neck of the sack before I dropped it outside the bunk-room door. But I didn't. I knew the frogs would wriggle free. But could they find the creek a half mile away? Could they follow its sound or smell? Or would the sun catch them struggling lost in the crab grass and thickets? It was do or die for them once more, just as it had been the moment before I netted them, when they made the last jump. Some had cleared the hoop and won freedom, but these had landed in my net. That's what I determined to do now, make my leap. In just a moment, when we were both naked, I would take Frank into my arms as gently but as strongly as I could—my fatal leap of love.

Abner saved me at the last possible moment bursting in on our nakedness. We had been undressing in the near dark, by the small night light—like white-bellied frogs, I was thinking, when the edge of the flashlight beam first touches them. Abner's bunk was closest to the door. He went straight to his bed light, turned it on, and looked at us with an expression of wild triumph. I shook fearfully. Somehow, I thought, his dull eye had spied me out, detected the truth in our surprised nakedness. But it was quickly obvious that I had misunderstood. The wild triumph was something he brought from the hotel, where he had been in Betty's bed. He quickly flung off his clothes and stood before our tall mirror inspecting himself minutely.

"What's going on?" said Frank, his voice already touched with disapproval.

"I was in her, in her." I looked at Frank. Disgust narrowed his eyes and turned down the corners of his mouth. So I pressed Abner with pretended innocence.

"Who?"

"Betty." He was still admiring himself in the mirror.

"In the car?"

"In her room at the hotel." He turned around suddenly and threw himself with a groan face down on his bed as though onto some palpable afterimage of Betty's body. Frank turned away. I followed his lead. A moment later we sat simultaneously on our beds.

"You won't believe it when you finally get some," he said. A tone of coarse tutelage crept into his voice, but when he turned and looked at us, that changed radically. "What the hell's the matter with you two?" Neither of us answered. "You, Frank," he said, "what are you looking like that for?"

"Why don't you go take a shower?" I had never heard Frank's voice so hard.

"Take a shower!" He sat up suddenly. "Take a shower when I saved the perfume for you boys?" I would not have guessed that Abner could be so sardonic. But he had obviously seen the utter disgust in Frank's face, and it infuriated him. He leaped from his bed and threw himself on Frank. I saw the naked limbs of the two brothers writhing together strenuously as Abner deliberately smeared on his brother the secretions of love. Then there was suddenly a cry. Frank had driven his knee into Abner's groin. Abner fell on the floor with a groan and lay there doubled up. Frank hurried into the bathroom. I heard the instant hiss of the shower. After a while he came back and put on his pajamas. Abner was now laying supine on his bunk with the back of his hand over his eyes. "Don't touch me," he said. I had been wondering which of them would say it first.

The next afternoon, as the two of us lay naked in the shallows of the edge of the Blue Hole, Frank allowed me to lave him with cool water. I touched him everywhere, chastely. I was consoling him, of course, and washing away Abner's bestiality. But I was also making him ready for my embrace. All my intuition assured me that on the next afternoon would come the full consummation of our love. Yet it was not to be. When we returned to the house we found my aunt and uncle making arrangements necessitated by the death of the doctor's colleague in Minnville. My aunt, who lay in bed, was saying, "I don't feel well enough to go, but you go, and take the boys. They ought to be there. Jep has been like an uncle to them."

"I can't leave you alone, Marie," said the doctor.

"It's nothing serious, Abner, and besides, I've got Joe."

I had even then an inkling of the truth about my aunt's illness, but I did not reflect on it because I was so upset by the prospect of being separated from Frank.

At last, at my aunt's insistence, my uncle agreed. They would have to spend one night away, no more. And before they drove off, my uncle laid upon me that usual charge: I was the man of the house in his place and must see that nothing happened to my aunt. I promised and then watched them leave. Abner assumed the older brother's prerogative and sat in the front seat beside his father. Frank sat alone in the back, keeping his eyes constantly on me as a kind of promise until the car turned out of the driveway.

II

I sat in the living room that afternoon as my uncle had instructed me. I was also to sleep in the guest room that night with the door open so that I would never be out of earshot of my aunt's voice. About three, an old black woman came to the kitchen door. A half dozen sacks hung from her shoulders. "Field peas, crowders, black-eyed peas, snaps, butter beans," she sang through the screen.

I hurried out to the kitchen. "Be quiet," I said. "Mrs. Ellis is sick."

"Lemme see her then."

I had run into this old black before and she had always looked at me curiously out of her rheumy brown eyes. She was either addled or preternaturally wise. She made me nervous. "Didn't you hear what I said? Go away. If you wake her up, I'll tell the doctor when he gets back." Too late. I heard my aunt's bare feet on the floor behind me. "It's all right, Joe. I'll speak to her." I went off into the dining room but I hid behind the door and listened.

"Hello Granny. What do you have today?"

"That one say you sick." Why did she say *that one?* It gave me a start. Was she pointing at the dining room doorway, knowing I was there? Or did she say *that one* because she considered me a creature unnameable? I listened.

"You want me to send Seth with some of the black pot?"

I almost burst out laughing. Obviously the hag regularly sent this concoction to my aunt, a doctor's wife and a Catholic still clinging to some old creole superstition. But if I had known then what I know now, I would not have been tempted to laugh. I listened. My aunt said something in a hushed voice. All I caught was the insistent concluding phrase, "You remember."

"I remember, Miss Marie, if you sho' that's what you want." My aunt apparently was sure, because the old woman left. I retreated quickly to the living room, where my aunt now came instead of returning directly to her room. "I'm sorry," I said. "I tried to keep her from waking you up."

"I wasn't asleep. It's too hot." Her cheeks had a hectic flush, and pin-points of perspiration moistened her upper lip. She stood before me as if dazed. The light from the window shone through her sheer nightgown except where the cloth folded upon itself, so that I saw the outline of her body broken only here and there by thin streaks of shadow. It was beautiful in silhouette. In the flesh it would have the same delicate ivory as the skin of her arms. But I didn't go far with this imagining. Something in her manner put me on guard. For the first time I got a definite intimation that she had contrived for the two of us to be alone so she could separate me from Frank permanently. She must have guessed the day after Abner's midnight abominations that our relationship had resumed with a passion. After a few moments, saying nothing further, she walked slowly and not quite steadily down the hall to her room.

Now my mind began to work with a fierce heat, assembling a jumble of possibilities. Yet even in those first stages of thought, chaotic as they were, I had no doubt that I could pierce my aunt's intentions. If that seems too precociously self-confident for a boy of fifteen, remember: I had a mother who had been beaten to death by poverty and abuse, a father who was a villainous drunk with the strength of an ox, and wretched schoolmates who watched for every opportunity to humiliate me because I learned fast and whetted my tongue on their stupidity. It was only quick perceptions that enabled me to escape the fate of my mother, the sister whom the doctor had not saved. So I sat in the chair in my uncle's living room with an unread book in my lap. Here is what I had to think about. What was it that my aunt had ordered from the old black? Was it more of the same potion that already was causing her to change—some vial of it left from a much earlier episode which the old black had to fetch up from memory? I thought it must be. But why? Why make herself woozy and strange? It must relate to Frank and me, but how?

I let the questions tumble about in my head. Meanwhile I listened carefully for any noise which would signal a secret delivered by Granny's Seth. I asked myself more questions. If behind the potion and the mysterious behavior was the intention of separating Frank and me, why hadn't she gone about it more directly? Why not plead with my uncle to send me home? He wouldn't refuse her. Or why not call Frank in and tell him that he must break off from me? There was such a strong bond between them that she would inevitably be persuasive. But even as I considered these possibilities, I understood why she wouldn't accept either. The separation must come from us somehow. Otherwise, Frank would be left with crudely detached emotions which later might attach themselves, even more tenaciously, to a similar partner. Perhaps she was also concerned in this way for me. That settled that. But if severance was her goal, how did the potion-induced change fit? Was she going to tell me that my perverse love of Frank was driving her to addiction? That would explain why she ordered from the hag not curative black pot but some potion of different effect. On the other hand, she would know that it would be very difficult to convince me that she was so suddenly and deeply stricken. And even if she could convince me, was that likely to separate me from Frank? She must have known that my passion was strong beyond virtually any compunction. Here I came to the end of my thinking. I was confronted by possibilities none of which seemed quite right. So there was nothing to do now but listen and watch. I would find the answer. I was confident.

For supper, at her request, I brought my aunt a dish of chilled consommé and a glass of iced tea. I tasted both before taking them to her. The dark consommé surprised my tongue. I had never tasted it before. Its rich saltiness suffused my mouth, startling me, bringing back a dim memory of the taste of blood.

"What are you having, Joe?" my aunt said, sitting up, setting the tray carefully on her lap. She seemed more alert, more herself except that her solicitude for once sounded a false note.

"I already had a double-decker sandwich."

"Then you can sit with me."

I took a chair by the window. The sun was down, but the yard was still full of the gentle gray light on the long August dusk. I looked at my aunt, lovely in the failing light, her thin blue nightgown darker now against the white sheet and the pale ivory of her throat. But it was her eating that arrested me. She spooned up the consommé very slowly, allowing each globule to melt on her tongue before she took the next, hand and mouth moving as if in the slow rhythm of a trance. But the uncanny thing was that my own mouth began to salivate, to fill up with salty flavor. So powerful was the taste that I feared I was being hypnotized. All my other senses were dimmed by the rich sensation in my mouth. Then a bizarre thought came to me: the consommé contained the potion. Seth had somehow slipped it by me.

"I'm not much company, am I Joe?" She smiled. "But the consommé was so good." She put the glass of iced tea on the table by the bed. "You can take the tray now please."

When I approached the bed, she sat forward. "Here. Give me a kiss, poor boy, left to take care of an ailing aunt." I bent down and took the tray, offering her my cheek. But she turned my chin gently with her fingers and kissed me lightly on the lips. I went away to the kitchen careful not to lick the trace of salty saliva her kiss had left on my lips. At the sink I washed my mouth out and scrubbed my lips roughly with the back of my hand. Then I went to the back door and breathed deeply, but the air was not cool yet though dark was descending rapidly.

I was just beginning to work again at unravelling my aunt's intentions, which were growing clearer now, when Seth suddenly appeared around the corner of the house and stopped at the foot of the steps. I looked down at him. "What took you so long? Mrs. Ellis needs the medicine." I held out my hand.

Seth shuffled. "My granny say give it to Miss Marie herself."

"All right then. You'll have to come back to her bedroom." Seth shook his head. "One way or the other," I insisted, continuing to hold out my hand but at the same time making room for him on the steps if he chose to enter the house. After a long pause he finally handed me the potion. It was a small vial about as big as my thumb. "I'll see that she gets it." He left then. The fast falling dark swallowed him up—head, torso, and limbs first, then the colorless cotton of his short pants.

By the kitchen light I examined the potion. It was about the color and consistency of molasses. In fact I suspected that it really was mostly molasses. I unscrewed the cap and smelled it—saccharine and bitter at the same time. I smiled—ground bone of bird's leg, frog's eye, drop of woman's blood. You don't catch me, aunt. I hurried to her bedroom, anxious to see her reaction to my knowledge of this folly.

"What is it, Joe?"

"Seth brought you something." I walked to the side of the bed and handed the vial to her. Then I stepped to the window and called, "You can go now, Seth. She has it." I had heard him rustle in the bushes. Now he burst out with a great thrashing and raced across the yard. I laughed and turned back to my aunt. She was smiling. I could barely see her face now. "You won't tell on me, will you, Joe?"

"What is it?"

She made a high girlish laugh that I had never heard from her before. She was holding the vial in both hands next to her bosom as though it were some tiny creature, a bird or a mouse. "It's a magic potion."

"What's it supposed to do?" I spoke harshly, feeling that I had a definite advantage now.

"It's dream medicine. It makes me dream wonderful dreams and wake up all new."

"Let's turn the light on and look at it," I said, dropping my words as heavily as I could on the song-like lilt of her voice. If the bed lamp were on, the light would reveal the lines in her face, the neck and arms beginning to go sinewy. It would show those simple hands with the unpainted nails foolishly clutching the old black's worthless concoction. It would be the end of her plot against Frank and me.

"No. The light would hurt my eyes." She spoke absently as though she had to fetch her mind back from distant imaginings. Then she sat forward a little on the bed, held the vial out and unscrewed the cap.

"Molasses," I said disdainfully.

She put a little of the viscid fluid on her finger and touched it to her tongue. "Yes," she said. "Yes." Not, of course, assenting to me but affirming that the formula was correct according to taste. She took several more drops from finger to mouth.

"Molasses," I said.

"Take some, Joe. Taste it."

"Why? I'm not sick."

"It doesn't hurt anybody to dream, especially if things are out of tune."

"Nothing is out of tune with me."

"Yes there is, Joe. We know that, don't we?"

"No."

"What a bad trait in one so young." She tossed herself back and made a little bumping noise on the headboard.

"What?"

"Holding on to something you ought to let go of, especially when there's so much else."

"I never had much, Aunt Marie. So I hold on to anything I get."

"And being foolishly afraid of something nice, something different from anything you've ever had."

"I'm not afraid."

"Yes you are. You're afraid of me. You're afraid of my dream medicine. You say it's molasses, but you think it's a love potion."

That made me swallow hard because it showed that she already knew what I was thinking. So she was ahead of me. She had the advantage. "I'm not afraid," I repeated doggedly.

"Here then." She sat forward and streaked the end of a finger thickly with the black liquid. I hesitated. She licked it off herself, but quickly made a new smear. "If you're going to take him away from me, Joe—in a room that I can't even enter—don't be a common thief in the night, a low miner's son. You're better than that. Win your love. Have courage. Here." I stepped over, took her wrist and licked the viscid fluid off her finger. It tasted like molasses. "Am I supposed to take more?" She shook her head, sadly I thought. I didn't feel any effect. Of course. It was just an old hag's silly concoction. I began to be a little sorry for my aunt, having to put on this stupid act with dim lights and a sheer nightgown. And suddenly the wrist I held felt as brittle as a bird's wing. I dropped it.

"Kiss me good-night, Joe." I bent and kissed her lightly on the lips. "Now go to sleep. You will dream of me and I will dream of you. In our dreams we will settle with each other."

"I always dream of Frank," I said.

"If you dream of him tonight, then you have won, Joe." She spoke very simply.

I left then. I went straight to the back steps and sat down. This was my fixed resolve: if the potion did begin to work on me, I would run to the creek and throw myself in. But nothing happened. A high breeze in the moonless sky stirred the tops of the pines. The crickets made great bursts of chirruping and then sank into silence, on and off as they sometimes will, I don't know why. When I was sure that the potion was a fake, I went into the guest room. I undressed and put on my pajamas and then opened the door as my uncle had instructed. Down the hall my aunt's door was closed and no light shone underneath. I lay in bed listening to the crickets and the passing of an occasional car along the road at the end of the long front walk. For a while I was too uneasy to sleep. But it was not fear. It was this—my aunt, self-hypnotized by her own curious behavior and by her irrational belief in the potion, might do something horribly embarrassing for us both. But the house remained quiet, and after a while I fell into a light and dreamless sleep.

Sometime much later I awoke to the sound of my aunt's crooning. It was like nothing I had ever heard before—high, piercing, unearthly, coming from no particular direction, and burring my head as though a fatal earwig were boring into my brain. It unnerved me badly. I got out of bed and stepped into the hall. My aunt's door was still shut and dark. The crooning was almost constant, but in the short silences I heard the stillness of the night. The crickets were quiet. I went out into the kitchen and shut the door behind me. There was a moment during which I heard the comfortable low rattle of the refrigerator. But the crooning quickly resumed. I went out on the landing of the back steps and shut the kitchen door behind me. At last I heard only the mild susurrus of the pines. She wouldn't follow me there and I could doze until morning leaning safely against the door. As I grew drowsy, I began to fill my mind with sweet images of Frank lying naked in the creek, his penis wavering under the light current and the hair of his body slanting downstream like deep green water grasses. But soon I went into a black sleep where even my unconscious marked no time so that when I awoke, or thought I awoke, it was into the body of a borderless night. I was lying on my back looking up. The wind in the pines had become water among dark tresses. Frank was gone. My aunt was bending over me. Her mouth, even in the black night, was red. It came down on my lips hot and salty. I began to throb. I felt the creamy essence of my desire rise for her as she stroked me with hands as gentle as the water-winds of my dream. So she had been right. Why cling to Frank when there was this? I slipped out of my pajamas, entered the kitchen, crossed it, and opened the hall door. The house was full of warm breath. I felt my desire quicken as I stepped down the hall to the door of my aunt's room, where I did not pause but immediately turned the knob. She was waiting for me there in the dark, I was sure, because the moist heat of her breathing was suddenly denser. I started to make a sound, her name or merely a moan, to show that I had come from my dream to answer her call. But at that moment, I will never know exactly why, my mouth filled up. I do not say with saliva because the liquid was saltier and denser even than my aunt's consommé. And when I swallowed it down, it almost made me gag, for I suddenly knew what it was like—the terrifying richness of a tongue-bitten mouth full of blood. So the door I had just opened was not into my aunt's bedroom but into the heart of a night three years before. It was the summer after my mother's death, the eve of my first visit to my uncle's house, the only time my father had driven me down. That day he came home from work and drank nothing. He bathed himself violently, sputtering and fuming. Then he put on the

suit he had not worn since my mother was buried. We left a little
before dark. For a while he drove in silence, then he began to talk
almost as furiously as when he was drunk, stitching his words
together in angry patches. "They'll talk about me like I was coal dust.
That's all right. They'll say I'm a God-forsaken drunk and a demon.
That's all right too. But if they come down on you, boy, if they start to
give you chicken gizzards and nigger's work, you write me. I'll visit
them." He laughed wickedly. "I'll have a set with that saw-bones
and his cajun beauty." He ranted on. "Glorified vets and bayou
belles don't lord it over me or mine." I had heard all this before. I
stopped listening and went to sleep.

I woke up to the sound of my father's curses. At first I thought he
must have had some whiskey in the glove compartment and had
drunk himself into a black fury. Even in the pale dash light I could
see the sweat standing on his forehead and the jaws tight around his
clenched teeth. "Goddamned son-of-a-bitching suck-egg frogs," he
hissed.

"What is it?" I cried out in alarm.

"Sucking frogs."

I sat up and looked out over the hood of the car. Frogs by the
hundreds were making white arches in the headlightf, thumping
against the car and bursting under the tires. In the glare above the
highway I saw their mad glazed eyes, saw the flat bodies and
pallorous under-bellies gliding toward death. "Stop! I cried.

"Shut up! These suckers have been crossing ever since we left
Harlow County." He beat on the horn. "No end to the sons-of-
bitches, goddam 'em."

"Stop!" I hollered again.

"Shut up, you little peckerhead. I'll mash you same as I mash
these sucking frogs." He stepped on the accelerator and howled out
his execrations. The tempo of the thumping and popping of the frogs
rose until I couldn't bear it. "Stop! Stop!" He hit me with the back of
his hand and made me bite my tongue. My mouth filled with blood. I
swallowed it. A moment later I threw up. "Stick your head out of the
window, goddamit!"

When we got to my uncle's house, I was white and rank with the
smell of vomit. "We passed through a frog migration twenty mile
long," my father said grinning. "He'll live, though he is of the
delicate kind."

Standing there in the door of my aunt's room, I saw again the doomed white frogs, heard the drum and hiss of their innumerable deaths, felt the weight of my father's blows, and smelled the acid odor of my own vomit. My aunt stirred. "Joe? Joe, is that you?" I ran. Wriggled out of the sack. Ran through the grass toward the creek. Ran for my life from the angry glaring light that raced across the gray morning toward the horizon.

I thought I would not make it. In my frenzy I missed the path. Blackberries snared me and bled me pitilessly. And soon the sun would blaze forth and cook me down to a dry parchment of brittle bones. I could feel its great heat poised behind the pines, ready to beat me down. But when I had fallen a dozen times and a dozen times been turned back by thickets, I at last heard the murmur of the creek. That gave me courage. I burst through the last barrier of underbush and plunged into the shallow water. I cried out because the cold water at first burned my wounds. Even the creek, I thought, had betrayed me. But after a while the current became more soothing. So, sunrise did not catch me in the open after all. Even so, moved by a lingering fear of the heat, I made my way downstream to the Blue Hole. There I dove down into the dark water and for a while hung my roots in the shadow of the high cut bank. Underneath me wavered the image of my splayed, fore-shortened body, the little frog that had miraculously made it across the sun's wide way.

After a time I paddled over to the lip of the Blue Hole and lay in the shoals looking at my body, which was lengthened and human again, though badly scratched. As I lay there, hope and fear divided my heart, but neither finally imaged itself beside me in the water— the black-haired body of Frank or the ivory body of his mother. I tried to think about that, but I couldn't just then. I got up and walked around to the sand bar and looked down at my image in the quiet backwater. My face was so scratched and puffy that it hardly seemed me. I'll tell you what it did look like though. It looked like the face of my father the morning after a particularly bad night, one in which he'd lost a fight. The thought made me smile. The smile was crooked like his because my bottom lip was torn. "Well, father," I said to the image, "you were almost right. They didn't give me gizzards and nigger's work, but the cajun beauty gave me nigger's medicine and it almost made me crazy and killed me." Then I spat on the image.

About that time Seth came down to the creek calling out my name in a quavering voice as if it were the name of a demon that might start up after him at any moment. "Here I am, Seth."

"Miss Marie say come back to the house." He kept his distance.

"Go get me some clothes."

When he came back with them, I put them on and went up to the bunk room and began to pack. My aunt came and stood in the door in her housecoat. "What are you doing, Joe?" I looked at her carefully. She seemed entirely herself. "I'm going now, Aunt Marie. The medicine worked."

"That's backwards, Joe. It means it's safe for you to stay here now, as long as you want to."

"Yes, it's safe," I said. I kept packing.

"Come in the house and let me put some salve on those cuts."

"No. I don't need any, Aunt Marie. But I'll tell you what I could use is some money, for bus fare."

"Your uncle Ab would never forgive me if I let you go this way."

"You couldn't explain to Uncle Ab what way I went if you wanted to, Aunt Marie. So just tell him I ran off. I'll never tell him different. In fact, it's the truth. I am running off."

"Where are you going?" That surprised me a little, how obviously she knew I was not going home. When I didn't answer, she shook her head. "They'll take you back to him."

"Maybe once or twice, Aunt Marie. But I'm a smart boy. Everybody says so. I'll learn pretty quick how to get away for good."

"From us, too, Joe?" I nodded. "I never wanted that, Joe."

"I believe you, Aunt Marie, but you knew it had to be, even if you didn't want it."

She went off and got some money and brought it back to me, almost a hundred dollars. I gave a half of it back to her. "It's too much, Aunt Marie. I have to start learning right away how to get it myself."

My aunt looked at me with a face so drawn in upon itself that I thought she would begin to weep. But all I wanted then was to get away from her. Before many years, though, I would pity her. This is how it must have been with her. There I stood destitute, having lost mother and cousin lover, having renounced father, uncle, and aunt. All I had was an old grip, forty-odd dollars, and a scarred face and body. But I was free. And there she was, twenty-five years older, with a dying husband, one son no more like her than day is to night, and another son separated from her by the perpetual secret of what she had just done for him. All she had left was her God. Or had she even traded God for son that night?

"Tell Frank I said good-bye."

III

My aunt Marie was wrong. They never did take me back to my father even once. I went straight from Laurelie to New Orleans. I changed buses three times, traveled mostly at night, and never talked to anybody.

My aunt laid upon me either a great blessing or a terrible curse. Here is how it has been with me. For over thirty years I have been absolutely free of desire. Remember? At the lip of the Blue Hole that last day no image appeared, neither Frank's nor hers. None has appeared since. Of all the beds I have slept in, I have shared not one—all as clear as the limpid water of the imageless creek. From what I have seen I would count this a blessing. But I don't press the point. Each must be his own judge.

THE NEIGHBORHOOD DOG

by RUSSELL EDSON

from THE AGNI REVIEW

nominated by Michael Hogan and Lynne Spaulding

A neighorhood dog is climbing up the side of a house.

I don't like to see that, I don't like to see a dog like that, says someone passing in the neighborhood.

The dog seems to be making for that 2nd story window. Maybe he wants to get his paws on the sill; he may want to hang there and rest; his tongue throbbing from his open mouth.
Yet, in the room attached to that window (the one just mentioned) a woman is looking at a cedar box; this is of course where she keeps her hatchet; in that same box, the one in this room, the one she is looking at.

That person passing in the neighborhood says, that dog is making for that 2nd story window . . . This is a nice neighborhood, that dog is wrong . . .

If the dog gets his paws on the sill of the window, which is attached to the same room where the woman is opening her hatchet box, she may chop at his paws with that same hatchet. She might want to chop at something; it is, after all, getting close to chopping time . . .
Something is dreadful, I feel a sense of dread, says that same person passing in the neighborhood, it's that dog that's not right, not that way . . .

In the room attached to the window that the dog has been making for, the woman is beginning to see two white paws on the sill of that same window, which looks out over the neighborhood.

She says, it's wrong . . . something . . . the windowsill . . . something . . . the windowsill . . .

She wants her hatchet. She thinks she's going to need it now.

The person passing the neighborhood says, something may happen . . . that dog . . . I feel a sense of dread . . .

The woman goes to her hatchet in its box, she wants it. But it's gone bad; it's soft and nasty. It smells dead. She wants to get it out of its box (that same cedar box where she keeps it). But it bends and runs through her fingers . . .

Now the dog is coming down, crouched low to the wall, backwards; leaving a wet streak with its tongue down the side of the house.

And that same person passing in the neighborhood says, that dog is wrong . . . I don't like to see a dog get like that . . .

🔥 🔥 🔥

THE U.S. CHINESE IMMIGRANTS BOOK OF THE ART OF SEX

instruction by OPAL NATIONS

from INTERMEDIA

nominated by Richard Morris and INTERMEDIA

Such handbooks as the most noble Sammie "The Noodle" Ling's formed the basis of the later interpretations of the Bedchamber Art, and in his celebrated "Worm of the Velvet Pouch" (Los Angeles, 1927), written as a first primer for the Chinese immigrants of San Francisco, Ling had frequently indulged in sex without so much self-consciousness about the presence of others. The bamboo grove and the garden were throughout the years prior and after World War Two favourite settings for their games.

"The Worm of the Velvet Pouch" was therefore a catalog of open-air positions from which the following is a representative selection.

1. Flying through the juice.

The man and woman, both naked and smeared entirely with acrobat's chalk seat themselves on garden swings hanging from the same branch. The man below and behind the woman, she crouching on her seat. The swings are drawn back by ropes held by servants so that the man and woman remain close together. The man and woman each grip between their teeth one portion of Hershey chocolate bar. Once reunion is effected, and the pieces of chocolate are exchanged uneaten, mouth to mouth, the swinging sensation will add to the pleasure and only much practice can effect precise union when the swings are moving in opposite directions on balmy days.

2. Docking on the tightrope.

The tightrope is stretched just above the ground, the lovers stand together until union has been achieved, then, helped by servants, they step onto the rope. If intercourse is all-consuming, their preoccupation will help them to reach the other end of the rope without ever touching with their feet.

3. Monkey in the wood-pile.

The woman climbs a leafy fruit tree. When she has found a solid footing, she throws fruit at her lover below, thus battering his body and smashing in his face. He immediately takes a chain saw and fells the tree, after which he over comes her among the scattered leafy branches. Very enjoyable during summer afternoons.

4. General Motors assembly line.

The woman is suspended by ropes and pulleys from the ceiling and can be raised and lowered easily, the height of her outstretched body according to the wishes of the man, who if at will holds mapping pins for use in demonstrations. If he wishes to enjoy "swinging union" it is best that his teeth be sharp and the shoulders of the woman soundly padded.

5. Floating Debris.

The ideal position in the swimming pool. The man floats on his back with the woman above him, the dogpaddle necessary to keep afloat causing their naked organs to rub together. When union is effected, their concerted movements prevent them from sinking. Have the servants drain off the pool slowly so as the draining out of the water is in complete accord with the lovers' climax upon touch-down.

6. The knotted serpents.

Divide the woman's long hair into four, then plait any two strands about the man's ears, and the remaining about the man's neck, bringing their faces together, completing the task by interlacing of the lovers eyelashes. The servant then binds their hands and feet together left to right, leaving them to effect union as best they can. Their difficulties increase the excitement as the servants keep tallies of serious injuries during the bout.

7. Awakening the Sleeping Beauty.

The woman pretends to be dead, her body is limp, and covered overall with twelve centimetres of dry finely ground soil, her eyes are closed and her face embalmed. The man scoops away the earth caressingly and there is still no movement. He then teases her with trained hairy caterpillars, which inch their way up and down the length of her body, and then by teasing her breasts and tufted river bank with a dusting mop of ostrich feathers whilst she fights to remain limp. Suddenly she springs to life as his iron tool strikes, misaims and pentrates the ground directly in front of her lodging of damp.

8. Blind Man's Buff.

Both partners are blindfolded, then search for each other round a darkened bedchamber, whose floor is strewn with filled chamber-pots, each pot differs by way of a particular resonant sound, when struck with the heel or toe. This ringing out of chamberpots guides the man to the woman. When the woman is caught, the bandages remain in place during intercourse.

9. Tea-break Lovers.

The man and woman balance a bowl of tea on their heads, a single lump of sugar is placed under each of their armpits. The lovers attempt union and intercourse whilst sweetening and stirring the bowls of tea without spilling a drop.

PART II

In another chapter of Sammie "The Noodle" Ling's "Worm of the Velvet Pouch" (Los Angeles, 1927), he states variations in close quartering, distinguishes men from laundry boys, the educated man from the ignorant. To conduct one's sexual combat with a little sophistication as two porcupines charging at each other is as tasteless as a Big Mac and as boring as a diet of wheat germ. The following positions are particularly recommended—

1. The Twelve Dewdrops.

The woman sits astride the man's lap. They face each other, then the woman takes the man's flicker, and holding it over his left thigh commands it to make drops. If this is achieved, a row of some twelve dewdrops of urine should form a perfectly spaced, straight line along the length of his left thigh. They then lightly flick their tongues together and, below, the gaming rod across the boarding patch. There is no insertion, just light touches above and below. As the frosting begins to gush, however, he plunges between the folds. When the first heat is complete, a dewdrop is removed with a piece of absorbent paper (it is important not to upset the thigh and spill the drops). The aforementioned procedure is repeated until singly all drops are drawn off.

2. Rush hour Traffic.

The man kneels on the top step of a flight of stairs and places a pillow on his upturned feet. He then sits back on it, his hands grasping a stair rod below and behind him. The woman sits astride his knees and throws herself back, her hands grasping the loosened edges of the stair carpet, her head reaching far back, her mouth filled with a bag of steel bearings to act as a counterweight, and her body arching. He then strikes upward from the end of the rainbow, and they then, so enjoined, proceed to descend the staircase as noiselessly as possible.

3. Worlds in Flight.

The woman prepares herself beforehand by placing within her aviary an I.U.D. immersed in a half cup amount of Flower Child bubble floss. She then lies on her back with her legs raised and feet together. The man parts the feet and lowers himself over her body. She then moves down, causing the pantry to widen, he then repeats the parting and closing of the feet whilst drawing in the bubbles through his nostrils, which should by now, aided by the sliding down of her body, issue with regularity from the walls of the hothouse. This leisurely pursuit assists the man to avoid the five overstrainings and the seven sex injuries.

4. Fireman's Ball.

Coating the sluice gates of their channels with saltpeter, the woman and her mistress lie on top of each other, their legs entwined so that their mail order houses press together. They then move in a rubbing and jerking fashion against each other like two drowning opera singers gasping for air. As they become more excited a flame is struck, and the pubic hair starts to smoulder; as the sluice gates widen, their internal forces should heighten and so draw in the flame. The man then thrusts between with his jolly jim—coated with expanded foam, thus putting out the fire and eliminating sourness in the stomach.

5. Household Accounting.

At the end of each month the woman takes up a kneeling position placing before her, in a neat pile the household monthly bills, her head slightly lowered so as to be in the best possible sight of them. The man, behind her, practises a series of thrusts (whilst the woman recites loudly the wording on the bills), the shallow and deepness of them dependent upon the amount owed and the urgency of the payment. At the start of each month following, the couple with the same bills, for which payment had been made and receipts given, repeat this same procedure, but in addition, at the end of combat, the woman takes the tired menace by the hand using it as one does a rubber stamp, acknowledges all receipts given.

6. The Mother-In-Law and the Monkies.

Your blindfolded mother-in-law is placed on a chair and bade to listen to the wind in this manner under a low tree in the garden. The man then pretends to seat himself upon the mother-in-law and holds a branch overhead, using his arms to pull himself sightly upward, so that a gap is left the width of which perhaps is likened to the gap beneath the kitchen door. This should be practised regularly before proceeding to the next step, for the arms need to be muscular and overly developed. The woman then sits on the man's lap, sliding the grassy bank up and down the flag-staff without allowing it into Alladin's Cave. When the excitement becomes unbearable and the mother-in-law is finding it increasingly difficult to distinguish the wind in the trees from the storm in the boughs, her face showing signs of that deadly intuition, the woman, paying heed to this, should insert the merchant's wealth and indulge in the rigorous, seven deep and eight shallow and thus enjoy the ultimate. When the overspill occurs, place the opened mother-in-law's purse directly beneath the line of spillage.

7. The Campers Guides.

The woman lies facing down, stretching the left leg straight and drawing up the right leg. The man takes up position behind, stretching the right leg straight and drawing up the left leg, whilst he buries himself in the stockyard. The servants then attach a padded leather collar to the woman's right ankle and likewise the man's left ankle. To the collars are sewn steel rings, and the steel rings are tied with steel wires. The steel wires are attached with pulleys to heavy cable stretches from Mill Valley to the top of Mt. Tamalpais. The practice of the seven deep and eight shallow method is used to shuttle the couple from the valley to the mountain top, whilst along the way a string of friendly campers erect tents to mark the spots covered by the flows of healthy essences.

8. The Cliffhanger.

The man kneels at the edge of a cliff. He faces the drop which falls very steeply for many hundreds of feet. The woman is then lowered over the edge, her feet entwined about the man's neck, her head resting in a vacant eagle's nest. The man's arms are pulled behind him and are bound with rope to the hind quarters of a rocky mountain goat whose horns are conveniently tangled in the boughs of a nearby tree. The man plunges into the woman's joss-house, his movements should resemble those of a turtle's head, short and in quick succession. This should release the unwanted gases from the five organs. When the ultimate is reached, and all blockages have been cleared, a bucket of ice-cold water is then thrown over the goat.

9. The Roller-Coaster.

The lovers meet at an amusement park, where a roller-coaster is a featured attraction. A special car should be made which rolls over the tracks but has had its seating and bodywork removed. In place of this a large coiled spring should be mounted between the shafts of the forward and rear wheels. The spring should be riveted to a heavy duty leather belt which is fastened about the woman's waist. She then holds her feet and pulls them as far back as possible. The man circles her thighs and body in a tight embrace. He then presses at the manor with his ear of corn, and once passing into the pipeline, the word is given the mechanic to start the car. When in motion the man moves to left and right but to the rhythm of nine shallow and eight deep. The method to the outside observer is like watching a falcon flapping its wings, and will enhance the marrow; after a week or so of this leisure, they will socialize like a pair of hovering butterflies.

10. The Bounce

The man lies back on a couch, cleaning the stem of his best pipe with a cleaning wire, and gazing thoughtfully across the room at a hanging picture, a repro print of "The Emperor Kuang Wu fording a river" by Ch'iu Ying, and is reminded of his own toilet training. The woman sits astride his lap, his minnow gripped in her left hand, her hair in rollers and with a squid on the boil in the kitchen. She bounces up and down in a carefree manner whilst with a .45 calibre pistol she fires live ammunition through the valves of the radio set blaring loudly an old western made during the golden days of Hollywood; their spirits lifting, they will eventually float through the nine clouds.

SWEETHEARTS

chapters from the book by

JAYNE ANNE PHILLIPS

(Truck Press)

nominated by Barbara Damrosch and Truck Press

UNDER THE BOARDWALK

Her name is Joyce Casto and she rides our school bus. The Casto's all
look alike. Skinny, freckled, straw-haired. Joyce's is the color of
broomsage dried out by some heat in her head. She walks the halls of
the junior high with a clipboard of ruffled papers, transistor radio
beating in her hand.

Daddy is a fire and brimstone preacher at a church out the dirt
road. Music is the work of a devil that licks at her legs. She stands,
radio pressed to her face, lips working. Undah the boardwalk,
down by the sea ee ee ye eh eh Ona blanket with my baybeh's
where I'll be.

She walks into class fumbling to turn it off. Stays close to the wall and watches the cement floor. She never talks to the country kids. The town kids never talk to her. The gym teacher finds out she is pregnant. Yes, she confesses, It was my brother. He's went off to the mills.

She disappears from school but comes back a month later, having had it in a bloody way. She rolled up a horse blanket and walked to the field. Daddy thundering I won't lay eyes on your sin and big brother in Youngstown, holding a thing that burns orange fire. She rolls, yelping, dogs come close and sniff. They circle. The sky circles. Points of light up there that sting. Finally she sees they are stars. Washing herself in the creek she remembers the scythe against the grass, its whispering rip.

Next morning she sits in the house alone while the others shout and sweat at a revival in Clinger's Field. The dogs come in with pieces in their mouths. She stands in the kitchen shaking while the Drifters do some easy moanin'.

BLIND GIRLS

She knew it was only boys in the field, come to watch them drunk on first wine. A radio in the little shack poured out promises of black love and lips. Jesse watched Sally paint her hair with grenadine, dotting the sticky syrup on her arms. The party was in a shack down the hill from her house, beside a field of tall grass where black snakes lay like flat belts. The Ripple bottles were empty and Jess told pornographic stories about various adults while everyone laughed; about Miss Hicks the home-ec teacher whose hands were dimpled and moist and always touching them. It got darker and the stories got scarier. Finally she told their favorite, the one about the girl and her boyfriend parked on a country road. On a night like this with the wind blowing and then rain, the whole sky sobbing potato juice. Please let's leave, pleads girlie, It sounds like something scratching at the car. For God's sake, grumbles boyfriend, and takes off squealing. At home they find the hook of a crazed amputee caught in the door. Jesse described his yellow face, putrid, and his blotchy stump. She described him panting in the grass, crying and looking for something. She could feel him smelling of raw vegetables, a rejected bleeding cowboy with wheat hair, and she was unfocused. Moaning in the dark and falsetto voices. Don't don't please don't. Nervous laughter. Sally looked out the window of the shack. The grass is moving, she said, Something's crawling in it. No, it's nothing. Yes, there's something coming, and her voice went up at the end. It's just boys trying to scare us. But Sally whined and flailed her arms. On her knees she hugged Jesse's legs and mumbled into her thighs. It's all right, I'll take you up to the house. Sally was stiff, her nails digging the skin. She wouldn't move. Jesse tied a scarf around her eyes and lead her like a horse through fire up the hill to the house, one poison light soft in a window. Boys ran out of the field squawling.

SWEETHEARTS

We went to the movies every Friday and Sunday. On Friday nights the Colonial filled with an oily fragrance of teenagers while we hid in the back row of the balcony. An aura of light from the projection booth curved across our shoulders, round under cotton sweaters. Sacred grunts rose in black corners. The screen was far away and spilling color—big men sweating on their horses and women with powdered breasts floating under satin. Near the end the film smelled hot and twisted as boys shuddered and girls sank down in their seats. We ran to the lobby before the lights came up to stand by the big ash can and watch them walk slowly downstairs. Mouths swollen and ripe, they drifted down like a sigh of steam. The boys held their arms tense and shuffled from one foot to the other while the girls sniffed and combed their hair in the big mirror. Outside the neon lights on Main Street flashed stripes across asphalt in the rain. They tossed their heads and shivered like ponies.

On Sunday afternoons the theater was deserted, a church that smelled of something frying. Mrs. Causton stood at the door to tear tickets with her fat buttered fingers. During the movie she stood watching the traffic light change in the empty street, pushing her glasses up over her nose and squeezing a damp kleenex. Mr. Penny was her skinny yellow father. He stood by the office door with his big push broom, smoking cigarettes and coughing.

Walking down the slanted floor to our seats we heard the swish of her thighs behind the candy counter and our shoes sliding on the worn carpet. The heavy velvet curtain moved its folds. We waited, and a cavernous dark pressed close around us, its breath pulling at our faces.

After the last blast of sound it was Sunday afternoon, and Mr. Penny stood jingling his keys by the office door while we asked to use the phone. Before he turned the key he bent over and pulled us close with his bony arms. Stained fingers kneading our chests, he wrapped us in old tobacco and called us his little girls. I felt his wrinkled heart wheeze like a dog on a leash. Sweethearts, he whispered.

🔥 🔥 🔥

THE NAME, THE NOSE

fiction by ITALO CALVINO

from ANTAEUS

nominated by ANTAEUS *and Raymond Federman*

EPIGRAPHS IN AN UNDECIPHERABLE LANGUAGE , half their letters rubbed away by the sand-laden wind: this is what you will be, *O parfumeries*, for the noseless man of the future. You will still open your doors to us, your carpet will still muffle our footsteps, you will receive us in your jewel-box space, with no jutting corners, the walls of lacquered wood, and shopgirls or patronnes, colorful and soft as artificial flowers will let their plump arms, wielding atomizers, graze us, or the hem of their skirt, as they stand tip-toe on stools, reaching upwards. But the phials, the ampules, the jars with their spire-like or cut-glass stoppers will weave in vain from shelf to shelf their network of harmonies, assonances, dissonances, counterpoints,

modulation, cadenzas: our deaf nostrils will no longer catch the
notes of their scale. We will not distinguish musk from verbena:
amber and mignonette, bergamot and bitter-almond will remain
mute, sealed in the calm slumber of their bottles. When the olfactory alphabet, which made them so many words in a precious
lexicon, is forgotten, perfumes will be left speechless, inarticulate,
illegible.

How different were the vibrations a great *parfumerie* could once
stir in the spirit of a man of the world, as in the days when my
carriage would stop, with a sharp tug at the reins, at a famous sign on
the Champs-Elysées, and I would hurriedly get out and enter that
mirrored gallery, dropping with one movement my cloak, top-hat,
cane, and gloves into the hands of the girls who had hastened to
receive them, while Madame Odile rushed towards me as if she
were flying on her frills.

"Monsieur de Saint-Caliste! What a pleasant surprise! What can
we offer you? A cologne? An essence of vetivert? A pomade for
curling the moustache? Or a lotion to restore the hair's natural ebony
hue?"

And she would flicker her lashes, her lips forming a sly smile. "Or
do you wish to make an addition to the list of presents that my
delivery boys carry each week, discreetly, in your name to addresses
both illustrious and obscure, scattered throughout Paris? Is it a new
conquest you are about to confide in your devoted Madame Odile?"

Overcome with agitation as I was, I remained silent, writhing,
while the girls already began to concern themselves with me. One
slipped the gardenia from my buttonhole so that its fragrance,
however faint, would not disturb my perception of the scents;
another girl drew my silk handkerchief from my pocket so it would
be ready to receive the sample drops from which I was to choose; a
third sprinkled my waistcoat with rose water, to neutralize the
stench of my cigar; a fourth dabbed odorless lacquer on my moustache, so it would not become impregnated with the various essences, confusing my nostrils.

And Madame went on: "I see! A great passion! Ah! I've been
expecting this for some time, Monsieur! You can hide nothing from
me! Is she a lady of high degree? A reigning queen of the Comédie?
Or the Variétés? Or did you make a carefree excursion into the
demi-monde and fall into the trap of sentiment? But, first of all, in
which category would you place her: the jasmine family, the fruit-

blossoms, the piercing scents, or the Oriental? Tell me, *mon chou!*"
And one of her shopgirls, Martine, was already tickling the tip of
my ear with her finger wet with patchouli (pressing the sting of her
breast, at the same time, beneath my armpit), and Charlotte was
extending her arm, perfumed with orris, for me to sniff (in the same
fashion, on other occasions, I had examined a whole sampler, ar-
rayed over her body), and Sidonie blew on my hand, to evaporate
the drop of eglantine she had put there (between her parted lips I
could glimpse her little teeth, whose bites I knew so well), and
another, whom I had never seen, a new girl (whom I merely grazed
with an absent pinch, preoccupied as I was), aimed an atomizer at
me, pressing its bulb, as if inviting me to an amorous skirmish.

"No, Madame, that's not it, that's not it at all," I managed to say.
"What I am looking for is not the perfume suited to a lady I know. It
is the lady I must find! A lady of whom I know nothing—save her
perfume!"

At moments like these Madame Odile's methodical genius is at its
best: only the sternest mental order allows one to rule a world of
impalpable effluvia. "We shall proceed by elimination," she said,
turning grave. "Is there a hint of cinnamon? Does it contain musk? Is
it violet-like? Or almond?"

But how could I put into words the languid, fierce sensation I had
felt the previous night, at a masked ball, when my mysterious
partner for the waltz, with a lazy movement, had loosened the gauzy
scarf which separated her white shoulder from my moustache, and a
streaked, rippling cloud had assailed my nostrils, as if I were breathing in the soul of tigress?

"It's a different perfume, quite different, Madame Odile, unlike
any of those you mention!"

The girls were already climbing to the highest shelves, carefully
handing one another fragile jars, removing the stoppers for barely a
second, as if afraid the air might contaminate the essences contained
in them.

"This heliotrope," Madam Odile told me, "is used by only four
women in all Paris: the Duchesse de Clignancourt, the Marquise de
Menilmontant, the wife of Coulommiers, the cheese-manufacturer,
and his mistress. . . . They send me this rosewood every month
especially for the wife of the Tsar's Ambassador. . . . Here is a
potpourri I prepare for only two customers: the Princess of Baden-
Holstein and Carole, the courtesan. . . . This artemisia? I re-

member the names of all the ladies who have bought it once, but never a second time. It apparently has a depressant effect on men."

What I required of Madame Odile's specific experience was precisely this: to give a name to an olfactory sensation I could neither forget nor hold in my memory without its slowly fading. I had to expect as much: even the perfumes of memory evaporate: each new scent I was made to sniff, as it imposed its diversity, its own powerful presence, made still vaguer the recollection of that absent perfume, reduced it to a shadow.

"No, it was sharper . . . I mean fresher . . . heavier. . . ." In this see-sawing of the scale of odors, I was lost, I could no longer discern the direction of the memory I should follow: I knew only that at one point of the spectrum, there was a gap, a secret fold where there lurked that perfume which, for me, was complete woman.

And wasn't it, after all, the same thing in the savannah, the forest, the swamp, when they were a network of smells, and we ran along, heads down, never losing contact with the ground, using hands and noses to help us find the trail? We understood whatever there was to understand through our noses rather than through our eyes: the mammoth, the porcupine, onion, drought, rain are first smells which become distinct from other smells; food, non-food: ours; the enemy's; cave; danger—everything is first perceived by the nose, everything is within the nose, the world is the nose. In our herd, our nose tells us who belongs to the herd and who doesn't; the herd's females have a smell that is the herd's smell, but each female also has an odor that distinguishes her from the other females. Between us and them, at first sight, there isn't much difference: we're all made the same way, and besides, what's the point of standing there staring? Odor, that's what each of us has that's different from the others. The odor tells you immediately and certainly what you need to know. There are no words, there is no information more precise than what the nose receives. With my nose I learned that in the herd there is a female not like the others, not like the others for me, for my nose; and I ran, following her trail in the grass, my nose exploring all the females running in front of me, of my nose, in the herd; and there I found her, it was she who had summoned me with her odor in the midst of all those odors; there, I breathed through my nose all of her and her love-summons. The herd moves, keeps running, trotting, and if you stop, in the herd's stampede, they are all on top of you, trampling you, confusing your nose with their smells; and now I'm on top of her, and they are pushing us, overturning us; they all climb on her, on me; all the females sniff me; all the males and females become tangled with us, and all their smells, which have nothing to do with that smell I smelled before and now smell no longer. It is waiting for me to hunt for it. I hunt for her spoor in the dusty, trampled grass. I sniff. I sniff all the females. I no longer recognize her. I force my way desperately through the herd, hunting for her with my nose.

For that matter, now that I wake up in the smell of grass and turn my hand to make a *zlwan zlwan zlwan* with the brush on the drum, echoing Patrick's *tlann tlann* on his four strings, because I think I'm still playing she knows and I know, but actually there was just Lenny knocking himself out, sweating like a horse, with his twelve strings, and one of those birds from Hampstead kneeling there and doing some things to him, while I was playing *ding bong dang yang*, and all the others including me were off. I was lying flat, the drums had fallen and I hadn't even noticed, I reach out to pull the drums to safety or else they'll kick them in, those round things I see, white in the darkness, I reach out and I touch flesh, by its smell it seems warm girl's flesh, I hunt for the drums which have rolled on the floor in the darkness with the beer cans, with all the others who have rolled on the floor naked, in the upset ashtrays, a nice warm ass in the air, and saying it's not so hot you can sleep naked on the floor, of course there are a lot of us shut up in here for God knows how long, but somebody has to put more pennies in the gas stove that's gone out and is making nothing but a stink, and, out as I was, I woke up in a cold sweat all the fault of the lousy shit they gave us to smoke, the ones who brought us to this stinking place down by the docks with the excuse that here we could make all the racket we liked all night long without having the fuzz on our tails like always, and we had to go someplace anyway after they threw us out of that dump in Portobello Road, but it was because they wanted to make these new birds that came after us from Hampstead and we didn't even have time to see who they were or what they looked like, because we always have a whole swarm of groupies after us when we play somewhere, and specially when Robin breaks into *Have mercy, have mercy on me*, those birds turn on and want to do things right away, and so all the others begin while we're still up there sweating and playing and I'm hitting those drums *ba-zoom ba-zoom ba-zoom*, and they're at it. *Have mercy on me, have mercy on me, ma'am*, and so tonight, just like the other times, we didn't do anything with these groupies even if they do follow our bunch so logically we ought to make it with them, not those others.

So now I get up to hunt for this lousy gas stove to put some pennies in it and make it go, I walk with the soles of my feet on hair asses butts beer cans tits glasses of whisky spilled on the carpet, somebody must have thrown up on it too, I better go on all fours, at least I can see where I'm going, and besides I can't stand up straight, so I recognize people by the smell, our bunch with all that sweat sticking to us is easy to recognize, I can tell us from the others who stink only of their lousy grass and their dirty hair, and the girls too who don't take many baths, but their smells mix with the others a little and are a little different from the others as well, and every now and then you run into some special smells on these girls and it's worth lingering a minute and sniffing, their hair for example, when it doesn't absorb too much smoke, and in other places too, logically; and so I am crossing the room, smelling some of these smells of sleeping girls until at one point I stop.

As I say, it's hard really to smell one girl's skin, especially when you're all in a big tangle of bodies, but there beneath me I'm surely smelling a girl's white skin, a white smell with that special force white has, a slightly mottled skin smell probably dotted with faint or even invisible freckles, a skin that breathes the way a leaf's pores breathe the meadows, and all the stink in the room keeps its distance from this skin, maybe two inches, maybe two fractions of an inch because meanwhile I start inhaling this skin everywhere while she sleeps with her face hidden in her arms, her long maybe red hair over her shoulders down her back, her long legs outstretched, cool in the pockets behind the knees, now I really am breathing and smelling nothing but her, who must have felt, still sleeping, that I am smelling her and must not mind, because she rises on her elbows, her face still held down, and from her armpit I move and smell what her breast is like, the tip, and since I'm kind of astride, logically it seems the right moment to push in the direction that makes me happy and I feel she's happy too, so, half-sleeping, we find a way of lying and agree on how I should lie and how she should now beautifully lie.

Meanwhile the cold we haven't been feeling we feel afterwards and I remember I was on my way to put pennies in the stove, and I get up, I break away from the island of her smell, I go on crossing

among unknown bodies, among smells that are incompatible, or
rather repulsive, I hunt in the others' things to see if I can find some
pennies, following the gas-stink I hunt for the stove and I make it
work, gasping and stinking more than ever, following its loo stink I
hunt for the loo and I piss there, shivering in the grey light of
morning that trickles from the little window, I go back into the
darkness, the stagnation, the exhalation of the bodies, now I have to
cross them again to find that girl I know only by her smell, it's hard to
hunt in the dark but even if I saw her how can I tell it's her when all I
know is her smell, so I go on smelling the bodies lying on the floor
and one guy says fuck off and punches me, this place is laid out in a
funny way, like a lot of rooms with people lying on the floor in all of
them, and I've lost my sense of direction or else I never had one,
these girls have different smells, some might even be her only the
smell isn't the same any more, meanwhile Howard's waked up and
he's already got his bass and he's picking up *Don't tell me I'm
through*, I think I've already covered the whole place, so where has
she gone, in the midst of these girls you can begin to see now the
light's coming in, but what I want to smell I can't smell, I'm roaming
around like a jerk and I can't find her, *Have mercy, have mercy on
me*, I go from one skin to another hunting for that lost skin that isn't
like any other skin.

For each woman a perfume exists which enhances the perfume of
her own skin, the note in the scale which is at once color and flavor
and aroma and tenderness, and thus the pleasure in moving from
one skin to another can be endless. When the chandeliers in the
Faubourg Saint-Honoré's drawing rooms illuminated my entrance
into the gala balls, I was overwhelmed by the pungent cloud of
perfumes from the pearl-edged decolletés, the delicate Bulgarian-
pink ground giving off jabs of camphor which amber made cling to
the silk dresses; and I bowed to kiss the Duchesse du Havre-
Caumartin's hand, inhaling the jasmine that hovered over her
slightly anemic skin, and I offered my arm to the Comtesse de
Barbés-Rochechouart, who ensnared me in the wave of sandalwood
that seemed to engulf her firm, dark complexion, and I helped the
Baronne de Mouton-Duvernet free her alabaster shoulder from her
otter coat as a gust of fuchsia struck me. My papillae could easily
assign faces to those perfumes Madame Odile now had me review,
removing the stoppers from her opalescent vials. I had devoted
myself to the same process the night before at the masked ball of the

knights of the Holy Sepulchre; there was no lady whose name I could not guess beneath the embroidered domino. But then she appeared, with a little satin mask over her face, a veil around her shoulders and bosom, Andalusian style; and in vain I wondered who she was, and in vain, holding her closer than was proper as we danced, I compared my memories with that perfume never imagined until then, which enclosed the perfume of her body as an oyster encloses its pearl. I knew nothing of her, but I felt I knew all in that perfume; and I would have desired a world without names, where that perfume alone would have sufficed as name and as all the words she could speak to me: that perfume I knew was lost now in Madame Odile's liquid labyrinth, evaporated in my memory, so that I could not summon it back even by remembering her when she followed me into the conservatory with the hydrangeas. As I caressed her, she seemed at times docile, then at times violent, clawing. She allowed me to uncover hidden areas, explore the privacy of her perfume, provided I did not raise the mask from her face.

"Why this mystery, after all?" I cried, exasperated. "Tell me where and when I can see you once more. Or rather, see you for the first time!"

"Do not think of such a thing, Monsieur," she answered. "A terrible threat hangs over my life. But hush—there he is!"

A shadow, hooded, in a violet domino, had appeared in the Empire mirror.

"I must follow that person," the woman said. "Forget me. Someone holds unspeakable power over me."

And before I could say to her, "My sword is at your service. Have faith in it!", she had already gone off, preceding the violet domino, which left a wake of Oriental tobacco in the crowd of maskers. I do not know through which door they succeeded in slipping away. I followed them in vain, and in vain I plagued with questions all those familiar with *le tout Paris*. I know I shall have no peace until I have found the trail of that hostile odor and that beloved perfume, until one has put me on the trail of the other, until the duel in which I shall kill my enemy has given me the right to tear away the mask concealing that face.

There is a hostile odor that strikes my nose every time I think I've caught the odor of the female I am hunting for in the trail of the herd, a hostile odor also mixed with her odor, and I bare my incisors, canines, premolars, and I am already filled with rage, I gather stones, I tear off knotty branches, if I cannot find with my nose that smell of hers I would like to have at least the satisfaction of finding out the owner of this hostile odor that makes me angry. The herd has sudden shifts of direction when the whole stream turns on you, and suddenly I feel my jaws slammed to the ground by a club's blow on my skull, a kick jabs into my neck, and with my nose I recognize the hostile male who has recognized on me his female's odor, and he tries to finish me off by flinging me against the rock, and I recognize her smell on him and I am filled with fury, I jump up, I swing my club with all my strength until I smell the odor of blood, I leap on him with my full weight, I batter his skull with flints, shards, elkjaws, bone, daggers, horn harpoons, while all the females have formed a circle around us, waiting to see who will win. Obviously, I win, I stand up and grope among the females, but I cannot find the one I am looking for; caked with blood and dust, I cannot smell odors very clearly any more, so I might as well stand on my hind legs and walk erect for a while.

Some of us have got into the habit of walking like this, never putting hands on the ground, and some can even move fast. It makes my head swim a little, and I raise my hands to cling to boughs as I used to when I lived in trees all the time, but now I notice that I can keep my balance even up there, my foot flattens against the ground, and my legs move forward even if I don't bend my knees. Of course, by keeping my nose suspended up here in the air, I lose a lot of things: information you get by sniffing the earth with all the spoors of animals that move over it, sniffing the others in the herd, specially the females. But you get other things instead: your nose is drier, so you can pick up distant smells carried by the wind, and you find fruit on the trees, birds' eggs in their nests. And your eyes help your nose, they grasp things in space—the sycamore's leaves, the river, the blue stripe of the forest, the clouds.

In the end, I go out to breathe in the morning, the street, the fog, all you can see in dustbins: fish scales, cans, nylon stockings; at the corner a Pakistani who sells pineapples has opened his shop; I reach a wall of fog and it's the Thames. From the railing, if you look hard, you can see the shadows of the same old tugs, you can smell the same mud and oil, and farther on the lights and smoke of Southwark begin. And I bang my head against the fog like I was accompanying that guitar chord of *In the morning I'll be dead,* and I can't get it out of my mind.

With a splitting headache, I leave the *parfumerie;* I would like to rush immediately to the Passy address I wrested from Madame Odile, after many obscure hints and conjectures, but instead I shout to my driver: "The Bois, Auguste! At once! A brisk trot!"

And as soon as the phaeton moves, I breathe deeply to free myself of all the scents that have mingled in my brain, I savor the leather smell of the upholstery and trappings, the stink of the horse and his steaming dung and urine, I smell again the thousand odors, stately or plebeian, which fly in the air of Paris, and it is only when the sycamores of the Bois de Boulogne have plunged me into the lymph of their foliage, when the gardeners' watering stirs an earthy smell from the clover, that I order Auguste to turn towards Passy.

The door of the house is half-open. There are people going in, men in top-hats, veiled ladies. Already in the hall I am struck by a heavy smell of flowers, as of rotting vegetation; I enter, among the glowing beeswax tapers, the chrysanthemum wreaths, the cushions of violets, the asphodel garlands. In the open, satin-lined coffin, the face is unrecognizable, covered by a veil and swathed in bandages, as if in the decomposition of her features, her beauty continues to reject death; but I recognize the base, the echo of that perfume that resembles no other, merged with the odor of death now as if they had always been inseparable.

I would like to question someone, but all these people are strangers, perhaps foreigners. I pause beside an elderly man who looks the most foreign of all: an olive-skinned gentleman with a red fez and a black frock coat, standing in meditation beside the bier. "To think that at midnight she was dancing, and was the loveliest woman at the ball. . . ."

The man with the fez does not turn, but answers in a low voice: "What do you mean, sir? At midnight she was dead."

Standing erect, with my nose in the wind, I perceive less precise signs, but of vaster meaning, signs that bring with them suspicion, alarm, horror, signs that when you have your nose to the ground you refuse perhaps to accept, you turn away from them, as I turn from this odor which comes from the rocks of the chasm where we in our herd fling animals we've disemboweled, the rotting organs, the bones, where the vultures hover and circle. And that odor I was following was lost down there, and, depending on how the wind blows, it rises with the stink of the clawed cadavers, the breath of the jackals that tear them apart still warm in the blood that is drying on the rocks in the sun.

And when I go back upstairs to hunt for the others because my head feels a little clearer and maybe now I could find her again and figure out who she is, instead there was nobody up there, God knows when they went away, while I was down on the Embankment, all the rooms are empty except for the beer cans and my drums, and the stove's stink has become unbearable, and I move around all the rooms and there is one with the door locked, the very room with the stove you can smell gasping through the cracks in the door, so strong it's nauseating, and I begin to slam my shoulder against the door until it gives way, and inside the place is all full of thick, black, disgusting gas from floor to ceiling, and on the floor the thing I see before I writhe in a fit of vomiting is the long, white, outstretched form, face hidden by the hair, and as I pull her out by her stiffened legs I smell her odor within the asphyxiating odor, her odor that I try to follow and distinguish in the ambulance, in the first aid room, among the odors of disinfectant and slime that drips from the marble slabs in the morgue, and the air is impregnated with, especially when outside the weather is damp.

—Translated from the Italian by William Weaver

toussaint

by NTOZAKE SHANGE

from INVISIBLE CITY

nominated by INVISIBLE CITY

de library waz right down from de trolley tracks
cross from de laundromat thru de shinin floors & big granite pillars
ol st. louis is famous for
                    i found
toussaint
        but not till after months uv
cajun katie   pippie longstockin eddie heyward & ah pooh bear
in the children's room only
                      pioneer girls magic rabbits
& big city white boys
                  i knew i waznt sposedta
but i ran inta the ADULT READING ROOM
      & came cross
               TOUSSAINT
my first blk man
i never counted george washington carver
        cuz i didn't like peanuts   still
TOUSSAINT waz a blk man a negro like mama say
who refused to be a slave & he spoke french & didn't low
no white man to tell him nothin
           not napoleon
           not maximillian
           not robespierre
                 TOUSSAINT L'OUVERTURE
waz the beginnin of reality for me
in the summer contest for
    who colored child can read
15

books
in three weeks   i won & raved all bout
     TOUSSAINT L'OVERTURE
at the afternoon ceremony & waz disqualified
     CUZ
       TOUSSAINT
belonged in the ADULT READING ROOM

   & cried
& carried dead Toussaint home in the book
he waz dead & livin to me vuz Toussaint & them
they held the Citadel gainst the french
& they waznt slaves no more
& they held held the Citadel wid the spirits of ol dead africans
from outta the ground Toussaint led they army of zombies
cannon ball shootin spirits to free haiti
     TOUSSAINT L'OVERTURE
    became my secret lover at the age of 8
i entertained him in my bedroom widda flashlite under the covers
way inta the nite
     we discussed strategies
how to keep white girls out my hopscotch games
     etc.

TOUSSAINT
waz layin in bed next to raggedy ann & me
the nite i decided to run away from home
     away from my integrated street
       integrated school
         1955 waz not a good yr for lil blk girls
Toussaint said let's go to haiti
i said awright & packed some very important things in a brown paper
bag
so i wdnt haveta come back
then Toussaint & me took a hodiamont streetcar to the river/
waz only 15 ¢ cuz waznt nobody cd see Toussaint cept me
& we walked all down where the french settlers usedta live
in tiny brick houses all huddled together
     wid barely missin windows & shingles uneven
wid colored kids playin & women sippin beer on low porches

i cd talk to Toussaint
down by the river like this waz where we waz gonna stow way
on a boat for new orleans & catch a creole fishin rig to port-au prince

then we just was jus gonna read & talk all the time
eat fried bananas
we waz jus walkin & skippin past ol drunk men
when did ol young body jumped outta me sayin
HEY GIRL YA BETTAH COME ON OVER HEAH & TALK TO ME
well /i turned to Toussaint who waz furious
then i shouted
YA SILLY OL BOY YA BETTAH LEAVE MELONE OR TOUSSAINT'S
GONNA GET YR ASS
de silly ol boy come from round da corner laughin in my face
YALLAH GALL YA MUST BE SOMEBODY TO KNOW MY NAME SO QUIK
i waz disgusted & wanted to get on ta haiti widout some tacky ol boy
botherin me
still he kept standin there/ kickin milk cartons & bits of brick
tryin to get all my business
i mumbled to L'ouverture
what shd i do
finally i asked dis ol silly boy
WELL WHO ARE YOU
he say
MY NAME IS TOUSSAINT JONES
well
i looked right at him
those skidded out cordoroy pants & stri-ped teashirt wid holes in
de elbows/a new scab over his left eye
i said WHAT'S YR NAME AGAIN
he say
i'm TOUSSAINT JONES
& i babaled/ wow/ i'm on my way to see toussent l'ouverturein haiti
he dont take no stuff from no white folks/ & they gotta country
all they own & there aint never no slaves
dat silly ol boy squinched his nose all flat & serious
Lookya heah gal/ i am TOUSSAINT JONES & i'm right heah lookin
atya & i dont takeno stuff from no white folks /
ya dont see none heah
do ya/   & he sorta pushed out his chest

then he say   lets go on down to the river & look at da boats/

i waz really puzzled/ goin down to the docks wid my paper bag
i felt TOUSSAINT L'OUVERTURE sorta leave me
& i waz sad til i realized TOUSSAINT JONES WAZNT too different
from TOUSSAINT L'OUVERTURE/ cept the ol one waz in haiti
& dis one waz wid me speakin english & eatin apples/
                              yeah.
TOUSSAINT JONES WAZ AWRIGHT WID ME
no tellin whatall spirits we cd move/ down by the river

LIVING ON THE LOWER EAST SIDE DURING THE SIXTIES: OR THE TRIUMPH OF SURREALISM OVER THE FORCES OF REPRESSION

by ALLEN PLANZ

from WILD CRAFT (Living Poets Press)

nominated by Harvey Shapiro

Slovakin creep, Polack, Bohunk . . .
what's a good slur
for this sonovabitch downstairs
from . . . from east Europe! . . . who yells
beatnik hippiee bum & calls the cops
whenever I throw a party or a fit
& noise & plaster
rain on him & his churchgoing wife
& his three dopey, malnourished kids?

So the sink overflows.
I spritz him at the door: "Yo
no aspic englisha, chingara."
"I tall janitor goddamn ruggy crazy," he says.

"I kick your teeth out your ass," I say.
"—Listen, you can shovel gravel up it
only the faucet, fix it, neighbor."
"Ok, botchagaloop. Awright! Lemme lone."
& he rolls his eyes. I roll my eyes.

So I yell with my family,
get high & stomp to loud music,
fall off bureaus, have friends
falling in at all hours
raising roofs & rents. So
his cops come to lean on my doorsill
while I swallow evidence & shit
bricks to light the world.

One night he got mugged in the vestibule
& I took him to Bellevue, his
nose like a rose flattened, mouth
spouting dialect & health cards,
his kids teeth his wifes mastectomy.
Going downtown later dawn overtook us
with pizzas & guitars geezing in the sky
as though the Fillmore still played on.

Another time his place was robbed
by a punk junkie I caught
with a broomhandle on the firescape,
who offered to turn me on
if I turned him loose, & kicked
me in the face when I mentioned motherhood,
while firemen dancing on the first floor
kicked out windows looking for fire,
which came twice a year anyhow,
sweetening the management's longing
to get old people out of cheap apartments.
Then we'd stand in the street
barechested & bathrobed with
neighbors cheering the debris
cascading down on our popsicles
Only the roaches were fireproof.

When we meet again, we're friends.
He didn't know I moved out years ago
to Westbeth, the Artist's Housing.
He didn't know I was an artist
but everybody in Westbeth does.
His wife & kids are fine, the hippies
gone & the Puerto Ricans second generation.
We congratulate each other on surviving
& look to see who's next in line
among the partygoers hopheading homeward,
the late hunters still trying to score,
the ex-nazi translating Nietzsche, highstepping
cats carrying tv's, the potbellied slumlords
in front of Ratner's who scratch, scratch
to the rhythm of a hot number
da diddie, die diddee, rup rup va va voom!

□   □

🔥 🔥 🔥

THE DEPORTATION OF SOLZHENITSYN

by the Russian SAMIZDAT underground

from A CHRONICLE OF CURRENT EVENTS, 32

published by Amnesty International

nominated by Pushcart Press

(editor's note—On February 13, 1974, following publication in Paris of his GULag Archipelago, Alexander Isayevich Solzhenitsyn was deported from the Soviet Union. Information about the deportation was circulated in the Soviet samizdat version of the small press. What follows is an abbreviated account from the underground Chronicle of Current Events, 32, as smuggled to the West and published by Amnesty International in London and New York. A Preface by Amnesty International introduces the main text translated from the Russian.)

PREFACE
by Amnesty International

A Chronicle of Current Events *was initially produced in 1968 as a bi-monthly journal. In the spring of that year members of the Soviet Civil Rights Movement created the journal with the stated intention of publicizing issues and events related to Soviet citizens' efforts to exercise fundamental human liberties. On the title page of every issue of* A Chronicle of Current Events *there appears the text of Article 19 of the Universal Declaration of Human Rights, which calls for universal freedom of opinion and expression. The authors are guided by the principle that such universal guarantees of human rights, and similar guarantees in their domestic law, should be firmly adhered to in their own country and elsewhere. They feel that "it is essential that truthful information about violations of basic human rights in the Soviet Union should be available to all who are interested in it." The* Chronicles *consist almost entirely of accounts of such violations.*

Although the Constitution of the USSR (article 125) guarantees "freedom of the press," the Soviet state officially reserves for itself and for officially-approved organizations the right to decide what may or may not appear in print. Since 1930 publishing has been a virtual monopoly of the Soviet state, and printing has been a complete monopoly. In the past decade and a half many Soviet citizens whose writings have not been published through official channels have reproduced their work in samizdat *form. These* samizdat *("self-published") writings circulate from hand to hand, often being re-typed on the chain-letter principle.*

In an early issue it was stated that "the Chronicle *does, and will do, its utmost to ensure that its strictly factual style is maintained to the greatest degree possible. . . ." The* Chronicle *has consistently maintained a high standard of accuracy. When any piece of information has not been thoroughly verified, this is openly acknowledged. When mistakes in reporting occur, these mistakes are retrospectively drawn to the attention of the readers. Furthermore the* Chronicle *frequently reproduces without any editorial comment official documents such as governmental edicts, bills of indictment, protocols of searches, investigation officials' reports, etc.*

In February 1971, starting with number 16, Amnesty International began publishing English translations of the Chronicles *as they appeared. Publication of the* Chronicles *ceased temporarily after issue number 27, dated 15 October 1972, as a result of a KGB operation know as Case 24 which was aimed at the journal's suppression. The* Chronicle *reappeared in the spring of 1974 when numbers 28–31, covering the period from October 1972 to May 1974 were distributed in Moscow. These numbers were published in English by Amnesty International in May 1975. This latest volume, comprising* Chronicles *32 and 33 is like previous ones, a translation of copies of the original typewritten text. . .*

A Chronicle of Current Events

> Everyone has the right to freedom of opinion
> and expression; this right includes freedom
> to hold opinions without interference and to
> seek, receive and impart information and
> ideas through any media and regardless of
> frontiers.
>
> *Universal Declaration of Human Rights, Article 19.*

Number 32   17 July 1974

At the end of August 1973, after five days of interrogation in the Leningrad offices of the K G B, the 70-year-old E. D. Voronyanskaya revealed the place where a copy of A. I. Solzhenitsyn's *GULag Archipelago* was being kept.

If the K G B report on the case of Professor Etkind is to be believed (see this issue), Voronyanskaya also disclosed that Solzhenitsyn had transmitted two copies of the *GULag* manuscript to her through Etkind.

Shortly after, E. D. Voronyanskaya committed suicide.

* * *

'With a feeling of inner frustration I refrained for years from releasing this complete book: my duty to those still living outweighed my duty to those who had perished. But now that the State Security has, notwithstanding, got hold of the book, I have no alternative but to publish it immediately.

September 1973   A. Solzhenitsyn.'

* * *

In December 1973 the Y M C A Press published the book in Paris*.

The first articles about the publication in Soviet newspapers appeared at the beginning of January. Initially these were extracts from the foreign press and T A S S statements.

The T A S S threats perturbed many people. On 5 January V. Voinovich, A. Galich, V. Maximov, A. Sakharov, and I. Shafarevich issued an appeal for the defence of Solzhenitsyn.

On 13 January the newspaper *Pravda* published an article by

Solovyov, 'The Path of Treachery'. It became a guiding document: practically all the central and local newspapers reprinted the article. Subsequently the newspaper printed comments in response to Solovyov's article.

On 18 January 1974 Solzhenitsyn made a statement in which, with characteristic passion, he pointed out that the Soviet press had distorted the facts and presented false interpretations. Amongst other things, Solzhenitsyn wrote: 'To *which* pages can they point, from *which* volume? For the *Literary Gazette* has been caught red-handed: it quotes from the *seized copy*, from the fourth and fifth parts of *GULag*, which have not yet been published. So it was in State Security that the suspect "Litterateur" copied his extracts!'

Meanwhile the first reactions to the work and the first statements of indignation regarding the press persecution had appeared in *samizdat*.

An article by H. Böll about the work's publication, 'It is Necessary to Go Further and Further', appeared.

A wide-ranging review by Roy Medvedev appeard . . .

The following made written protests, individually and collectively: B. Mikhailov, E. Barabanov, V. Borisov, B. Shragin, L. Chukovskaya, V. Dolgy, Gusyakova, V. Zaitsev, I. Ovchinnikov, V. Osipov, V. Repnikov, V. Rodionov, M. Agursky.

* * *

On 8 February an attempt was made to deliver a summons to Solzhenitsyn's wife Natalya Svetlova, summoning her husband to the USSR Procuracy, but Svetlova refused to accept it.

On 11 February the summons was repeated.

* * *

'TO THE U S S R PROCURACY, in reply to its repeated summons.

Given the unending and general lawlessness which has reigned for many years in our country (and has affected me personally in the form of an eight-year campaign of slander and persecution), I refuse to recognize the legality of your summons and will not appear for interrogation at any state institution.

Before demanding that citizens obey the law, learn to execute it yourselves. Free the innocent from imprisonment. Punish the perpetrators of the mass exterminations and the authors of the false denunciations. Punish the administrators and the special detachments which carried out genocide (the deportation of *whole peoples*). Deprive *today* the local and departmental satraps of their limitless power over citizens, of their controlling sway over lawcourts and psychiatrists. Satisfy the *millions* of lawful, yet suppressed statements of complaint.

11 February   A. Solzhenitsyn.'

* * *

At five o'clock in the evening on 12 February eight men burst into Solzhenitsyn's flat, led by a senior counsellor of justice, Zverev.

A resolution empowering them to take Solzhenitsyn to the Procuracy was shown to him. One of the participants in the operation assured his wife that Alexander Isayevich would soon return.

Solzhenitsyn was led away, but two 'guests' stayed in the flat, took up posts by the door and the telephone, and remained there for about half an hour.

It is no more than ten minutes' walk from Solzhenitsyn's home to the U S S R Procuracy, so already at this point the writer's family suspected that he had not been taken to the Procuracy.

* * *

Statement of A. Solzhenitsyn,
written by him beforehand, for use in the event of arrest

'In advance I declare as incompetent any criminal trial of Russian literature, of a single book of it, of any Russian author. If such a trial is prescribed for myself, I shall not go there on my own two feet— they will deliver me there in a Black Maria, with my arms twisted behind me. I shall not answer a single question at such a trial. Sentenced to imprisonment, I shall not submit to the sentence except in handcuffs. In imprisonment itself, having already lost my best eight years to forced labour for the state, and contracted cancer in the process, I shall not work for the oppressors even half an hour more.

'In this way I leave open for them the straightforward option of overt tyrants: to bump me off quickly for writing the truth about Russian history.'

* * *

At nine o'clock in the evening it became known that Alexander Solzhenitsyn had been arrested.

* * *

'. . . The fifth act of the drama has begun.

Shame on the country that allows its greatness and its glory to be abused.

Wretchedness on the country whose tongue they tear out with tongs.

Misery on the nation which is deceived.

Blessing and support to the man who now, rudely separated from family and friends, slandered before his people, is—yes now, at this very minute!—conducting his silent duel with the lawless violence. 12 February 1974. 12.00 hours. Moscow.   Lydia Chukovskaya.'

* * *

On the evening of 12 February in Lefortovo prison Solzhenitsyn was charged with treason (article 64 of the R S F S R Criminal Code). The charge was signed by the senior counsellor of justice Zverev; Deputy Procurator-general of the U S S R Malyarov was present when the charge was presented.

* * *

On the day after the arrest, 13 February, the 'Moscow Appeal' appeared.[1] Its authors, A. Sakharov, E. Bonner, V. Maximov, M. Agursky, B. Shragin, P. Litvinov, Yu. Orlov, Rev. S. Zheludkov, A. Marchenko and L. Bogoraz, demanded:

1. That *GULag Archipelago* be published in the USSR and made available to every compatriot;

2. That archive and other materials be published which would give a full picture of the activity of the Cheka, N K V D and M G B.

3. That an international public tribunal be set up to investigate the crimes perpetrated;

4. That Solzhenitsyn be protected from persecution and allowed to work in his homeland.

The authors of the 'Moscow Appeal' called for national committees to be set up in various countries to collect signatures in support of the appeal.

* * *

At 13.00 on 13 February, in a solitary-confinement cell of Lefortovo prison, Malyarov read Solzhenitsyn a Decree depriving him of his Soviet citizenship.

On the same day he was forcibly deported from the Soviet Union to the Federal Republic of Germany.

After the deportation the campaign flared up in the Soviet press with new vigour and lasted another week.

* * *

On 14 February M. Landa published [in *samizdat*] her support for the 'Moscow Appeal'. On 17 February a letter supporting the 'Moscow Appeal' was published by E. Barabanov, T. Velikanova, S. Kovalyov, T. Khodorovich, and V. Borisov. Pointing to the attempts of Soviet newspapers to represent Western commentators and certain celebrities in the West as supporters of Solzhenitsyn's deportation, the authors write: '. . . Will the free world really reconcile itself to the presentation of another falsification of its views to a deceived and confused people? . . . What is described in Solzhenitsyn's book . . . involves a portion of blame for the West too. . . . Is it not time to recognize with full responsibility that by exploiting the separateness of our worlds and exploiting our mutual lack of information they are turning *you* into accomplices? . . . The solidarity of people cannot be limited to words. It must be effective. In this lies our hope.'

Later the following people associated themselves with the 'Moscow Appeal': E. S. Andronova, L. Aptekar, V. Bakhmin, N.Ya. Iofe, O. Iofe, I. Kaplun, A. Lavut, A. Levitin (Krasnov), G. Podyapolsky, S. Khodorovich, and L. Tymchuk.

According to the writer Vladimir Maximov, 50,000 people in the Federal German Republic and West Berlin have associated themselves with the 'Moscow Appeal'.

* * *

On 30 March Solzhenitsyn's family left the U S S R. A letter by his wife was made public. In bidding farewell to her friends in this letter, she said with confidence that Alexander Isayevich, she herself and their children would return.

ANOTHER FORM OF MARRIAGE

fiction by MAXINE KUMIN

from PARIS REVIEW

nominated by PARIS REVIEW

THEY WERE TOURING New England, escaped lovers in mid-June, when the signs sprang up, hand-lettered in red and green on shiny white boards. *5 Miles to Skyvue Strawberry Farm!* the first one proclaimed, followed in due course by *Skyvue Strawberry Farm, 1 Mile on Left* and *Pick Your Own at Skyvue Strawberry Farm 10 to 4*.

"Let's," she said, squeezing the brown corduroy of his knee.

"But what will we do with them?" he said, thinking of tonight's motel somewhere in the Champlain Valley and tomorrow's drive down the Hudson to their separate suburbs. He would leave her at the train station just as he had last year, and the year before, and the year before that. As if she had ridden the local out from Grand Central, she would take a taxi home.

"Eat them. Take them home. Oh never mind!" she despaired. She had caught sight of herself at the taxi stand, strawberries spilling out of her shopping bags.

But he had downshifted from fourth to third and then at the last declarative sign, *Strawberries Are Rich in Vitamin C*, to second. They turned in at the driveway, rose up a winding dirt road, and were there.

They had come from the translation seminar held each summer at a small college in the Adirondacks. He specialized in Hungarian, which was not, however, his native tongue. Always from the bottom of his suitcase he took out the two volumes of his German-Hungarian dictionary. These stood on the bureau, on a succession of bureaus on stolen weekends throughout the year, grave necessary friends of their liaison. She spoke no foreign language, but served the conferences as administrative assistant, cutting stencils each morning, collating pages of prose and poetry in bilingual arrangements. She saw to it that the original always appeared on the lefthand page so that the work under discussion might lie as flat as an open-face sandwich.

That first summer she had come to the conference unexpectedly filling in for an ill colleague. She was a shyly attractive woman in her thirties, tallish and slender with long brown hair that she wore tucked discreetly into a knot at the nape of her neck. It was rainy and raw; she had not brought warm clothing and the man who was not yet her lover had loaned her a comforting maroon ski sweater in which, he assured her, she looked properly waif-like. It smelled of his brown tobacco cigarettes tinged with camphor. When he smiled, she was dazzled by one off-center gold tooth. She began wearing her hair loose about her shoulders and in town she bought a pair of dangling imitation-gold earrings. He came to her room the fourth night, whistling nonchalantly up the stairs of the old brown building, a sheaf of papers in his hand. Raindrops had peppered his beret and she propped it on the radiator to dry. But the papers were in Spanish, five versions of a Neruda poem left over from that morning's workshop and out of his mackintosh pocket there came a bottle of cognac. At dawn, holding his shoes, he went lightly down the fire escape onto which, luckily, one of her windows opened.

A highway bisected the campus. Porches of the college buildings overlooked it and words were often lost in the drift of traffic. Snatches came through: "Do you see this as an exercise?" "Do you set yourself models?" "The basic concept is very good, really very good. . . ." Logging trucks passed in both directions, confusing her. Those great prehistoric-looking tree trunks, stacked like her sons' Playskool toys, rattled past in their chains. Perhaps there were sawmills at either end of this mountain gap? The process of overlap struck her as an apt image for translation.

Skyvue Farm provided its own boxes; wax-lined cardboard trays, really, for picking. What he was to do with the damn things was another story. They could be given away, he supposed. Bartered against the motel bill, a hundred miles down the road? The view, or *vue*, if you will, was truly incredible. To the west, spruce- and pine-covered hills the color of bleached denim. East, looking into the determined sun of Vermont, three small, connected ponds with ducks on them. And stretching its plateau in a commodious rectangle of what he took to be easily ten acres, this expanse of strawberry field still swallowing up its odd assortment of human forms as people entered, were assigned their rows, and sank to their knees or buttocks. Some few more or less leaned down, rumps high, and dug their hands into the plants, or rested one palm on the earth for equilibrium as they picked.

He was forty-five this year, his life was flawed and sedentary, he groaned, folding himself down. The berries adorned the plants tritely. He resented the dew that added diamonds to their rubies. How monstrous the fruit were, the ripest ones leaving behind a little cone on the plant as they pulled away from the calyx. In Austria the strawberries grew elusively in the meadows and he was forced out into the fields each morning with the other young ones to crawl through prickly grasses and fill his pail. Mosquitoes sang in his ear. His mother would fly into a rage if he scanted on the picking. Once, invoking his father at the Front, she beat him with a shoe. Those wild strawberries, he remembered, were long and cylindrical and hung from the creeping vine like sows' teats. He tasted salt and wondered if he had been crying. No, it was sweat. Or did it matter? He mopped his face with a handkerchief and sat down between rows. Memory was exhausting in full sun.

Often there had been no bread in the bakery and no flour in the house to bake with. Now, whipped cream rose up in mountains on his strawberry shortcake. Now he had a wife and half-grown children, the oldest to enter college that fall. And in the mountains, a mistress—dreadful old-fashioned word! What was he but an old-fashioned, fastidious middle-aged linguist?—a mistress only slightly younger than his wife and a history, going on four years now, of stolen weekends. It came to him that he had pretended more translations than he had effected. Each one sweetened the months of fidelity that followed.

It was a hot morning and promised to be a hotter day. She had picked well past him, turned, and had started greedily back still another row so that now she was coming toward him in a series of little frog-hops. He saw her thighs flash white, those strong stems he had lain athwart only a few hours ago. And her fingers pinching here, there, so decisively nipping the best berries; yes, he would nip and pinch and comfort and take hold. Now she was closer, now clearly he could see the gray streaks she lamented were overtaking her hair. How luminous, that chestnut mane, against the sun! Their quarrels were sharper each year, their reconciliations almost unbearably poignant. His wife was paler, larger, a milder version. Against his will he remembered the rented summer cottage at the shore when the children were small, how his wife served him berries with cream for a late night snack, moving furtively about the unfamiliar kitchen, whispering over his bowl. He could hear the click of his spoon on the crockery and knew afterwards exactly how they had bedded, he stroking the back of her neck first. Oh, he was a detestable person, he deserved neither woman, he told himself, even knowing the thought was an act of self-congratulation.

Meanwhile in the strawberry patch he was sentenced to overhear just behind him a tale of loyalty, of a man standing by his wife struck down by multiple sclerosis or cancer, he could not tell from the medical details. In any case, incapacitated, her condition unchanging. Two women, local, he guessed from their accents, harvesting berries for their freezers, jellies, pies, were exchanging the details of this story. She had fainted on the commode, she spat blood, he still took her on fine days for drives, tucking her wasted body about with pillows. Only in Purgatory was one doomed to hear such tales of domestic heroism.

Now the woman who was not his wife had drawn abreast of him and saw from the passivity of his shoulders that she was making him unhappy. In the Buddha pose she would have kissed the worry lines from the corners of his mouth. Instead, displaying the half-filled box, she begged, "Just five minutes more." He smiled evasively, a cocktail party smile of dismissal and moved forward in his row. They squatted there, back to back, her fingers travelling expertly over the plants while she reflected on their stolen weekends.

She could name them all sequentially, passing quickly over the rainy one in Indiana where they had fished in the St. Jo River full of disgusting carp and then drunk themselves into a sodden state in the one downtown hotel. He had pushed her beyond her limits, dark anger had flowed out of her like blood clots, and passion, equally ungoverned, rushed in. Never in her other life had she been an extremist. Now she recorded impressions with her stomach, her skin. The mind came last of all in this procession. It had begun with the glint of gold in the mouth of an elegant foreign man, but where would it end? She could recall especially the grit and detritus of New York City, where they met often, the enforced gaiety of its bars gleaming metal and dark at noon. Once there had been dinner at the Russian Tea Room where an old man at the next table, knowing them for conspirators, palpably, lovingly fondled them with glances. He and the translator had conversed in German.

Out of town she remembered there were chains of lookalike motels where air conditioners exhaled noisy droplets and overhead fans started up in windowless bathrooms at the flick of a light switch. The toilets wore Good Housekeeping seals of paper bands. She swore and paced the corridors while he was gone or else sat for hours in a hot tub as if hoping her skin, that pimple, would burst.

She bit into a deformed strawberry swollen almost to plum size. It was mealy but wet as the earth was wet to her fingers, as the plants were furry with their cultivated bristles. Spiders clambered up the wisps of straw that had been spread as mulch between rows and spun and fell and labored again to renew their torn webs.

Bits of conversation drifted down her row. Even here, the talk was of ungrateful teen-age children, of dying parents, sick animals. She felt a dull astonishment. In this whole Breughel scene of people bending, kneeling, plucking, in this landscape of bobbing colors and anatomies, a terrible banal sameness prevailed. It was the sameness of the human condition. She had come to put her hands into the dirt, to taste her fruit in the full sun. For even in those carefully tended furrows to which the pickets were directed by the farmer's sharp-faced wife dressed in her strawberry-dotted pinafore, even though the hybrid berries had been force-fed to this size and drenched, midway in their span, with insecticides, they were more real than their counterparts in supermarkets boxes, plasticked over and fastened shut with rubber bands.

Her legs and back ached. She had come impulsively, she now saw, licking the strawberry juice from her fingers, to put the wildness back in this dear red fruit. At the expense of the man she adored, who was fluent in five languages and whose starved childhood had been stained with this sort of foraging.

What was this affair but another form of marriage? Instead of being faithful to one man, she was faithful to two. Her husbnad was industrious and kindly and a bit unkempt. She remembered she had loved his ragged beard, his abandon with clothing, the way he wore his pipe, still smoldering, in his back pocket. When his shoestrings broke, he knotted them. When she closed her eyes she saw him, young and laughing, his arms full of their two boys, a tangle of hair and beard and arms and legs. The red dots of strawberries behind her eyes brought back that time, ten years gone, her standing stirring at the stove, him slicing bread, the little ones leaning on their elbows at the table waiting to taste the hot jam. "Will it jell?" they had asked, using their new word. "Will it ever jell?"

Everything jelled, filled its spaces or found new spaces to flow into. Thus she had come, willy-nilly, to adore a tidy professor whose suitcase was meticulously packed, his shaving lotion in a plastic bottle, his shirts in see-through bags fresh from the laundry, a man who carried his dictionaries about with him like religious statuary.

She rose, dusted herself off, and together the lovers, each encumbered with his tray, stood in line to have the fruit weighed. "Boxes or bags?" the pinafore woman asked impatiently. It came to ten pounds worth, two brown bags full, which they set on the floor of the back seat and covered with the *New York Times* as the coolest place in the car.

All that day and the next the berries ripened and ran together in their twin bags, giving off a smell of humus and fermented sugar. All that day and the next, winding their way downstate from Mecca, the guilty pilgrims breathed in that winey richness and did not speak of it. In the twilight of the last twenty miles along the Taconic State Parkway they sat very close, she with her left hand sorrowfully on his knee, he with his right hand nuzzling hers in his lap. At the last rest area before the turn-off to her suburb he swerved wordlessly, pulled up to a green trash barrel and stopped the car. "Yes," she said. "I know," she said. And he divested them both of the bloody evidence.

Then he took her to her train station and kissing her goodbye, drove
his tongue between her teeth like a harsh strawberry and she clung
to him, this other man, this vine which had taken root and on which
she ripened.

SHORT STORIES

by HOWARD MOSS

from SHENANDOAH

nominated by SHENANDOAH

"Lover, you are the child I will never
Have . . . *have* had . . . *will* have," she wrote.
That was in Denver. October or November.
Long before she married a lawyer.
They're living, now, unhappily forever.

>   *He* was writing in Greece, and from:
>   " 'In the time it took not to get to the castle,
>   Space developed its chronic asthma . . .'
>   I'm fleeing with the cat to Hydra.
>   Escapes and such have gorgeous results.
>   I'm giving it up. Can't write at all.
>   So Long. And scratch one nightingale."

If you climb to the top of a bank building
In Denver, the highest one around,
All you can see for miles are mountains.
Banks and insurance companies have
The money to build and build and build.
"The *hell* with architecture," he said—
A trustee of The Wheat and Bread
Amalgamated Holding Co.—
"Get a contractor. And let's go."
His wife was home, drinking again.
She thought: I mustn't forget to eat.

"It is the dumb, intractable
Retarded who are sexual
And hold the mystery in their hands . . ."
A professor wrote, after his class.
Revised, rewritten, then recast
Into the form of a Gothic novel
About a nun who meets the devil,
Bewitches him—the usual *kitsch*—
Half put-on and half spiritual,
It sold over a million copies
And made the professor very rich.

Meanwhile, a thousand miles away,
On a bulletin board at IBM's
Six hundred thousandth factory,
The following message found its way:
"If anyone hears of a small, unfurnished
Air-conditioned person . . ."

"Children, you are the lovers I
Could never get," she almost said
Under her breath, which was just as well
Since it was nine-tenths alcohol.
"It's time for another drink, I guess.
Yes? . . . No . . . No? . . . Yes."

In Greece, he started to write again,
"The Underground Sonnets" in four-beat lines:
"And I would find it hard to say
Who went where and who which way,"
Interrupted by the arrival of
One of the Greek hoodlums of love . . .

The following month his editor wrote,
"Andrew, *what* is *hap*pening to you?
You know the ms. is unpublishable . . ."

The professor, after his first success,
Went back to poetry. Which did not, alas,
Return the compliment. And so he wrote

A book of comic meditations
Filched from sources not hard to trace.
He was saved by tenure and an understanding
Dean, spent six weeks at a *place*,
Where everyone was nice but the nurses.
The doctor said, "It's no disgrace . . ."

In Denver, the hotel bar's discreet.
A layman (ha ha) would never know
What's going on, it looks so straight.
After it closes . . . *you* know . . .
A little car on a back street,
And so forth.

"People aren't really built to stand
The kind of tension you get these days;
Betrayal in personal relationships
Is the very worst, of course, because
The Oedipal syndrome is revived again . . .
I think that guilt, not fear's the thing
For which we pay the highest cost;
I, personally, find it hard to feel
Guilty—except at not feeling guilt . . ."

The professor listened but wasn't cured
And produced that long, astonishing book,
"Counting Sheep or The Shepherd's Crook:
Deviation on the Western Plains,"

Which has just come out as a paperback
With an introduction by a poet back
From Greece . . .

She read it in a nursing home,
Having arrived at the same place
The professor recently left. And soon
They dried her out and sent her home.
She's fine in public now "but not
So hot in bed," the trustee said—
The trustee of the Wheat and Bread.

"One more poem, one more try,"
The prof to the poet said, whose sly
Rejoinder was, "With me, it's vi-
ce versa . . ."

One night, back on the sauce, she said,
Looking the trustee straight in the eye,
"*You* are the death I would never have,
I *thought* . . ."

The message on the bulletin board
Has had several replies, but none
Satisfactory. And yesterday
It disappeared. Or was thrown away.

LOVERS

fiction by JERRY BUMPUS

from VAGABOND

nominated by VAGABOND

Penny leaped the morgan's back yard fence—she knew that
would stop all of them but Danny. The rest of the children had to run
up the fence and crowd through the gate. As she turned between the
Morgan house and the Dunlap house she heard feet pounding
behind her, and, turning the corner of the Dunlap's, she glanced
over her shoulder and let out a trilling shriek when she saw Danny
right behind her. She dodged around the corner, behind the shrubberies, and lost Danny for a moment. But when she ran from the
shrubs, Danny lunged for her and they fell across the sidewalk, over
the little wire fence, and into a deep bed of petunias.

The rest of the children came squealing around the corner,

swarming through the shrubberies, and piled onto Penny and
Danny, and they were all of them rolling around, giggling, touching
Penny, their sweaty faces big-eyed, gleeful, when the screen door
banged open and Mrs. Dunlap charged onto the porch, her bushy
gray hair seeming to stand on end as if she were beholding wild
animals in the act of seizing control of the neighborhood.

She came to the edge of the porch, faltered, her large mouth
hanging open. Then she clenched a fist and struck her forehead.
"Jesus God," she whispered.

One of the kids giggled. Penny and Danny scrambled to their feet.

Then it hit--but Penny was moving fast. She jerked one of the
really little ones to his feet, and she didn't catch all Mrs. Dunlap was
saying. But she caught the tone. Mrs. Dunlap was temporarily out of
her mind--and she repeated that several times: "You've just plain
driven me out of my mind, for God's sake."

They all climbed over the little wire fence and retreated to the
street--expecting that at any moment Mrs. Dunlap would grab an
arm, or back of the neck, which was much worse; they all knew Mrs.
Dunlap would go for the back of the neck.

But when they reached the middle of the street they turned and
saw Mrs. Dunlap wasn't chasing them. Down in the flower bed on
her hands and knees, Mrs. Dunlap was crying.

Penny giggled. But stopped. All the kids, even Danny, were very
serious when they saw the woman down like that.

They stood there, and Penny felt the entire length of the block on
both sides of the street hush with an awful intensification of the
already somber quiet of dusk. She was glad her mother wasn't home.

"Why, oh why?" Mrs. Dunlap wept. "My lovely petunias. Why
my *petunias?*"

"We're sorry, Mrs. Dunlap," Penny said.

"And *you*," Mrs. Dunlap said, slowly looking up from the
trampled flowers, and Penny wished she had kept her mouth shut.
"*You!* You little. . ." She stopped herself. Penny wanted her to go
on. She wanted very much to know what Mrs. Dunlap almost
called her.

"Tell me," Mrs. Dunlap said, getting to her feet and coming
across the yard to stand on her sidewalk, her fists on her wide hips.
"Just tell me why you lead these little children to *do* such things as
this. Why do you *play* with them? *Look* at you." The kids crowded
around Penny. Danny turned and stared at Penny. She wanted to

look down, but didn't. She just blinked her eyes once. "How old are you, young lady?"

"Thirteen."

"Thirteen years old. And you're all the time playing with these little tiny kids. Why *look* at them. They're five and six years old and you're *playing* with them."

Danny's eleven, Penny wanted to say, but didn't.

"There must be something wrong with you. Why don't you play with children your own age?" She waited. "You're disgusting. You're *all* disgusting, running around after her like a pack of . . ."

Mrs. Dunlap jerked her head to the side. For the rest of it, her railing at the kids for all their other crimes--beating down her grass and the grass of all the other yards in the neighborhood--Mrs. Dunlap avoided Penny's eyes. And Penny noticed that and she was puzzled, and it was funny--she laughed. When she did, the other kids laughed.

"This is *not* a laughing matter," Mrs. Dunlap said. She told them she was going into the house right this minute and call their parents.

"And when your mother gets home, young lady," she said, looking at Penny again, "I'll be right over and the three of us will have this out *once and for all.*"

But that didn't worry Penny--her mother wouldn't be back till tomorrow afternoon. But the threat worked on the little kids--most of them went straight home.

Penny and Danny, and Danny's little brother Mike, went up and sat on Penny's porch steps. They watched Mrs. Dunlap, in the flower bed again, pick up the limp corpses of her petunias and lay them in a pile. Mr. Dunlap came out and stood at the side of the porch. Penny could hear them talking low, though she couldn't hear the words. She watched Mr. Dunlap, bald and short, and she thought maybe he would look across the street at her, but he didn't. He only looked at her when he didn't think she would see him--and when she caught him, he would look away quickly. She always said, "Hello, Mr. Dunlap," when she happened to be out front as he backed his car out of his driveway, or when he was alone in his front yard, and he always answered her, but low, his head down, not looking at her, as if he didn't really mean it when he said hello.

Penny, Danny, and Mike rode Danny and Mike's bikes for a while, Penny and Danny riding double, Penny behind Danny on the long banana seat, her large, smooth legs straddling Danny's narrow hips.

Then they sat on the porch again, talking, and Mike went home. After a while Danny followed Penny into her house.

James Morgan, from his window in the second floor of the house across the street, watched them go inside and then there was a heavy, dull blank.

He was unable to know what she was thinking when he couldn't see her. When she was playing in the street or in one of the yards, he could merely look at her closely--seldom blinking his eyes, hardly breathing--and inside himself he could hear her, hear every word she whispered to Danny, every thought that passed through her mind.

James knew what they did when she and Danny went inside her little house. First they went to the kitchen. Penny's mother worked at the A&P and she brought home big boxes of cookies. She and Penny ate gingersnaps and creamfills all the time. So Penny and Danny went into the kitchen and ate some cookies, and then they came out to the front room and listened to the Beatles on Roy's stereo. Roy was Penny's mother's fiance. Then sometimes they went into Penny's tiny bedroom, crowded with stuffed rabbits and giraffes, and Penny would take off her clothes, all but her bikini panties and bra, and she would lay on her bed, stretched out, and while Danny sat in the little rocking chair by the bed, Penny would tell him about men and women.

But James could only see them. He couldn't hear Penny, no matter how hard he stared at the house and the pink and white curtain, always closed, over the window in Penny's bedroom.

James waited, hoping Penny and Danny would come out again, but once they went into the house, they would stay for a long time, and when the front door eventually opened, Danny would come out alone.

But James could hear Danny and know what he was thinking no matter how far away he went. When Danny and Mike and some of the other boys went up to the park to play, James always knew where they were and exactly what they were doing--he could listen closely and hear what Danny was thinking as he played baseball or as he swam when they all went to the pool.

Danny came Tuesday afternoons to visit James. They played checkers and sometimes Fascination or Monopoly. James' favorite was Monopoly, but Danny didn't like it--it took too long. "There's going to be a new fourth grade teacher next year," Danny said. "My aunt knows her. She just got out of college. It's your move."

They were playing checkers and James played slowly, being careful with his moves.

"Miss Wilson is going to California. She's going to live with her mother," Danny said. "Can you imagine being that old and going someplace to live with your mother?"

James moved. Danny moved quickly and again waited for James.

"They had to make Miss Wilson quit. There is something wrong with her. It's your move. Probably being a teacher is what did it to her. Always fighting with me and Rodney Pearson and George Getz. Your move."

James moved. Danny quickly moved one of his kings, and as soon as he did James jumped that king and another, leaving Danny just one man on the board to James' five . 'Geez," Danny said, shaking his head, his handsome face grimaced into a wrinkled imitation of his father's.

"Let's play another one," James said.

"Uh huh," Danny said, shaking his head, not looking at James. "I got to go."

"You just got here. It's just twenty after one and you got here at five minutes till one."

"I don't care. I got to go. I'm supposed to meet some guys."

"Who?"

Danny acted as if he hadn't heard. Then he glanced at James and said, "What?"

"Who are you going to meet?"

"Some guys. You don't know them. They don't live around here. I'm going to meet them up at the park. We're starting up a league." He looked out the window at the sun, bright on the maple tree below James' window.

James' mother tried to get Danny to stay a little longer, play another game of checkers and have some cake--the icing was cooling on a chocolate cake, it had probably set long enough, she would go down and cut them both a piece. . . But Danny couldn't stay. Sorry. He had to meet those guys, and he didn't look at James as he pushed the table back. And he pushed the table too far--it jolted James' bed, making a strange, hollow *koong*, and Danny looked away, embarrassed.

While James ate a piece of the chocolate with ice cream, he looked out the window. In a few minutes Danny came down the sidewalk with Mike. They had their baseball gloves, and both wore new red baseball caps. They crossed the street to Penny's. Danny knocked and they talked when she came to the door, barefooted and wearing cut off jeans and a tight sweater. Danny was asking Penny to go with him and Mike to play baseball, and James knew Penny was glad he asked her, for it meant that someday he would ask her to marry him and they would live in this block and have children who would ride their bikes up and down and play bounce ball until they were big enough to go to the park and play real baseball and. . .

Penny went into the house and Danny and Mike waited on the porch, talking, Danny socking his fist into his glove. Then Penny came out. She was still barefooted, but she had changed to tight red shorts and a white halter. They headed up the street, and by the time they reached the corner five or six little kids were tagging along.

And James lay back and with his eyes half closed, staring out the window at the top limbs of the maple tree bobbing slightly in a breeze that seemed to touch only some, not all, of the leaves, he was with Penny, Danny, and Mike, and when they got to the park the other guys were already there.

The baseball diamond and the swimming pool, at opposite ends of the park, were separated by picnic tables and benches scattered under enough trees to make a forest when the kids needed one, and two stone toilets where last summer Penny had taken off all her clothes and let some of the kids look at her, and where with lipstick she had drawn a picture of a naked woman on the wall and under it written her name and the phone number of the police station.

The other guys knew Penny. They were in the same grade with her and they didn't like her--over a year ago they nicknamed her Pigpen Penny. But since today was the first day of the new league, they needed some extra players so they let Penny play, and they also let a couple of the little kids play in the outfield, even though they didn't have gloves.

Penny and Danny weren't on the same side, and while Danny sat waiting his turn at bat he tried not to watch Penny--this was baseball and he had to pay attention to what his team was doing. But he couldn't help but look at her now and then. Playing second base, she stood on the bag with one foot, the other leg bent and its bare foot pressed against the calf of the other leg, and she took off Danny's glove and tossed it into the air and caught it without losing her balance. The other guys were watching her too. Now she was giving little tugs to the tight legs of her shorts. Suddenly she became very interested in the game. She started chattering, hopping around second base, barking encouragement to her teammates. Then the kid at bat hit a line drive at her and she turned and ran. The ball hit her on one of the round soft cheeks of her butt. Everyone laughed. They laughed so hard they fell down and rolled around. When they stopped, her team's pitcher took Danny's glove from Penny and gave it to the little kid, and sent Penny out to right field.

But Penny got bored in right field and wandered off to the girl's toilet and they were able to forget about her for a while. Then as if from very far away they heard her, her voice high and cool.

"Oh Danny. Yoo hoo. Dannnnn-y."

He tried to ignore her but everyone, even the little kids, got mad and started telling him to make her shut up.

"Shut up," he yelled.

But she kept it up. "Dannnnn-y. Yoo hoo."

Until his face was red and wrinkled, and he yelled so loudly he could have been heard clear to the swimming pool. "Shut up, damit. Leave me alone. You're a big fat stupid pig. I hate you."

And suddenly she was as cold as the stone walls of the girls' toilet. She stood looking straight ahead at the walls, the names, faces, the dirty words, the pictures of wonderful, horrible men and gaping witches, and she put on her clothes.

When she came out of the toilet she didn't look at them, but headed the other direction, though the forest, where she felt the same strange coldness, as if winter lurked here in the woods, watching the children. She walked to the swimming pool and some of the little kids came over to talk to her. But they were just little kids.

James was waiting for her when she came down the sidewalk, looking at the house as she walked along. It was a strangely silent afternoon, the only sound the whisper of the water sprinklers. She sat on the porch of the little house where she lived, and once she glanced up at James' window. And as she looked into his eyes, though she couldn't see him, James stared back at her, unblinking, and knew that for the first time in her life Penny was lonely: she knew as completely as she ever would that she would be a woman all her life, and she was stunned.

They played baseball all summer and they even got uniforms --polo shirts with numbers which their mothers sewed on. Danny --number 3--was the pitcher for one of the teams, and he pitched every game. At the height of the season they played four, five games a day, starting early in the morning and sometimes not stopping until suppertime--and then, likely as not, there was a game after supper.

And James and Penny were alone. She played bounce ball with the little kids in the block and rode double with them on their bikes, and sometimes she babysat Mrs. Clark's twins. At night Danny and Mike occasionally played hide and seek with Penny and the little kids. One night when they were playing, some junior high boys came around and Penny stopped playing and went down to the corner and talked to them. When they left and Penny came running back, Mike was still playing hide and seek, but Danny had gone home.

A tall, gaunt boy with long black hair--James never learned his name--came to see Penny about every night for a week. He played hide and seek with her and the little kids. He laughed a lot and Penny laughed at everything he said. And then one morning he came to see Penny and they went into her house. James knew what they did was what Penny had done with Danny, except James knew Penny didn't take her clothes off and let him look at her.

One afternoon Danny was up at the park playing baseball and a kid on the other team started talking about Penny and the tall, gaunt boy. They had got in her bed with their clothes off. The baseball game stopped and they listened. When the kid had told everything--and some parts twice--they all stood in silence. How had he heard it? The tall, gaunt kid, who would be a sophomore in high school next year, had told a bunch of guys, and now anybody in high school who wanted to could go over to Penny's and do it to her.

The game resumed. Danny pitched, concentrating, leaning into every pitch, sweating, not thinking, his team ahead 8–4, the endless afternoon safe from time, a fine dust and the smell of fresh-cut grass floating on the air, the sun high in the perfectly blue sky. . .

He turned from the batter, dropped the ball, and walked off the mound.

"Hey."

"What's the matter?"

He shook his head.

Several of them trotted after him.

We walked straight through center field, hearing now very clearly the kids at the swimming pool, and it occurred to him that never before when he was playing ball had he heard the kids at the pool, and he looked up at the sky, clear blue, blank.

Danny walked down the sidewalk, tossed his glove onto the front porch as he passed his house, and James from his window watched him coming down the street in his red shirt with number 3 in front, has faded red cap, his arms tanned smooth like dark stone. He walked not fast, not slow, as if he were on his way to the grocery store, but James knew, and in front of Penny's, Danny turned up the sidewalk, swinging his arms, not looking up, and he went up the steps, crossed the porch, and he didn't knock but opened the door and went in, shutting it slowly behind him with a quiet luminous click that James heard as he closed his eyes.

All the blinds were pulled and the house was dark. It had the smell of cigarettes and sour clothing. The front room was very small, smaller than Danny had ever noticed--and the ceiling seemed strangely low. The walls were brown, nearly black, and the chairs and lumpy sofa hunkered against the walls. As he passed through to the tiny hall joining the front room with the other three rooms of the house, he heard a drawer open, then close.

Wearing shorts and sleeveless yellow blouse, Penny was coming out of her bedroom. Her mouth fell open, but she didn't speak. They stared at each other, the hall, the entire house, narrowing to the tight lines of their staring, and Danny moved first, going toward her like a ship slowly turning to sea. "What. . .?" she started, and he stopped her, his face in hers, and he smelled her, and smelled her mouth, and saw deep into the slow swirl of her eyes, leaning forward until he was falling away, he was already into her and rising like gray smoke from the little boys' prison of innocence into weather that blew him toward life.

James watched the pink and white curtain of the bedroom. Once he believed it moved very slightly. But if it did, it didn't move again until it came down several months later when Penny's mother moved herself and Penny out with the help of a new fiance with a pick-up truck, and for years James watched the house and that window, sometimes covered by curtains, sometimes by blinds, and once the window had nothing over it and James could see in the narrow room a table piled with cardboard boxes.

In time he lost interest in the neighborhood and what they were thinking: he knew them too well. James spent most of his time watching television, soap operas, baseball in the summer, and for a year or so he avidly watched the wrestling matches. Now when he looked out the window it was either to watch for the newspaper boy, late in the afternoon, even after dark in the winter, or it was to look out at the sky through the limbs of the maple tree.

HOW IT WILL BE

by MARY LANE

from LUCILLE

nominated by LUCILLE

You will be rich, and we will fly off to meet for a week
at a tiny motel in the mountains. Or, you will be rich,
and you and your wife will invite me for tea. Or, you
will throw her into the roaring fire in the study and
send for me to keep house and take care of the twins.
                                                    We
will met at an international conference, sip sherry at
the Top of the Mark, pass each other in the glass elevators of the Hyatt-Regency, find ourselves in adjacent
seats at the Garden. And when Stevie Wonder sings, we
will soar encapsulated in an irridescent bubble, high
over the city, never coming down
                          until we reach the
Staten Island ferry. It carries us out, out, into the
dark Atlantic, past Provincetown, Nova Scotia, Iceland,
to the remnants of a lost civilization, vanished without
a trace in a mighty conflagration, all we see is the
ash.
    And rising from the center, two green leaves, and
perched on the slender stem, a lemon-hued bird with
dulcet voice. Singing, flames, and flying,
                            you will be
rich and telephone me long-distance, I will be rich and
wire you one thousand roses. We will order the chamber
orchestra back to their room and get tubas, trumpets,
kettle drums, harps, tall golden harps played by maidens
with silvery wings. We will skate on the ice, our coats
spread like broad sails to the dawn.

THE SLEEP

by PHILIP DACEY

from PRAIRIE SCHOONER

nominated by Joyce Carol Oates

In memory of Anne Sexton, 1928–1974

It is an answer, a going-into.
The soft helmet slowly eases over the head.
The limbs begin to believe in their gravity,
The dark age of faith begins, a god below
Draws down the body, he wants it
And we are flattered.
We are going to the level of water.
(Don't hold on. Drop fair, drop fair.)
This is fine seepage, we think,
Seepage ravelling to a river
To set ourselves upon. So
What is the price of dark water?
Where is the weight going?
The body powers the vaguest of shapes,
Pilot-boat, the falls collapse
And collapse upon themselves. We hear them
In time and imitate them.
We would turn to water that has lost
Its floor, water surprisingly
In space and beading,
A glittering disintegration.

Now, what was a bed
Rocks just perceptibly, this is a cradle
In search of a captain, the bone-cargo
Settles, the medium

Washes up over and across and fills
The spaces we have been keeping empty just for this,
The palpable black herein
Barbarian, riding us down.

                  There will be a level
We come to, will we know it?
A flat place with, look, a light.
It is a guess as our loins give way.
Already we are forgetting
Where we were
And left from, the human
Faces like sunglare hurting our eyes.
Did we even wave goodbye? Yet could there
Possibly be someone here now,
That this going down
Not be so sole, and sore,
A cup, a cupped hand, a basket,
These forms of containment
Forms of Person
Where, when we're water, we're caught?
Listen. It is the sound of ourselves,
This passage: a breath.
We are almost not here.
If we break up this softly,
We must be incomparably lovely.

THE MAN WHO INVENTED THE AUTOMATIC JUMPING BEAN

essay by "EL HUITLACOCHE"

from BILINGUAL REVIEW/LA REVISTA BILINGUE

nominated by BILINGUAL REVIEW/LA REVISTA BILINGÜE

M Y DAD INVENTED THE FIRST authentic wormless Mexican jumping bean with an empty Contac capsule and a ball of mercury he siphoned off a store-bought thermometer. He did it for potential profit in Ciudad Juárez in 1953 in a high-rise complex that the government built for *el pueblo* out of prefab concrete and reenforced plastic girders. They named it Huertas de Netzhualcoyotl after the Aztec poet-king.

It was a big seller all over Mesoamérica. I saw it in the heart of Aztlán, through the frosted glass of a candy store window in Alamogordo on Christmas eve. Big novelty! All-purpose wormless jumping bean! Never dies or runs out on you! Works on body heat! It was one of those candy stores that the Coca Cola company moves into in a heavy way. They put up all your signs for you. They tack up tantalizing murals of cheeseburgers and coke. Above the counter the name of the store and the proprietor is in lights with two psychedelic Coca Cola imprints on either side, like Christ between his thieves. They only let you sell Coke.

I saw them in the hands of *esquintles* on the Mexican *altiplano* and even in the capital. The jobbers on Correo Mayor sold them by the gross to the peddlers, hustlers and other street people. Years later on one of my wanderings I spotted them in the renowned Quetzaltenango market in Guatemala. An old Indian woman in her shawl had them stacked up in symmetrical mounds like *frijoles pintos*. She looked like one of those sibyline old *indigenas* from whom one might expect sage or psychedelic advice. I questioned her. "Mother! What do you sell here? Mexican jumping beans?" But she paid me no heed. She sat there, mute and sassy, receiving the indrawn vision.

Not that my old man made a *centavo* from his invention. That day in '53 he came home from across the border with only about fifteen Delco batteries in his pickup. Competition was getting brutal. And what with the invention of aluminum cans . . . He had himself two Carta Blancas, scratched himself here and there; then came an inspiration. From the souvenir shelf he took the miniature Empire State building that he had bought on Times Square after the War (fighting for Tío Sam was the thing to do in those days) and carefully removed the thermometer from the tower. Then he came out of the john with a Contac capsule that he had emptied. He split the thermometer and tapped the jelly-like mercury. He made a ball from the mercury and slid it into the capsule. He held the capsule tight between his palms. He looked like he was hiding a cigarette butt from the vicissitudes of the wind. Then he let it go on the table. Mother of God! Did it jump! My father, who was fond of scientific discourse (he could expound at length about the notion of sufficiency in scientific theory) explained that it was the heat of his palms that turned the mercury to frenzied bubbling and made the capsule bounce and teeter as if there were a drunken worm in it.

Two days later he produced a refined version with the capsule painted pretty like an easter egg. He showed it to this *compadre*, Chalo, who knew a jobber in El Paso. ¡*Qué amigazo!* They went to see the jobber. The jobber went to see a plastics manufacturer, a man with great metal presses and centrifuges to force molten plastic into little cavities.

There were endless delays, boredom, abulia. My father quickly got fed up with waiting and decided to invent something else. He put together a plastic submarine out of a Revell box, bored two holes into it and filled them with hoses. He pumped air in and out with a hand pump. The sub went up and down "like magic." With the other pump he fired a dart-like torpedo out of the submarine's hulk. The ship was not a total success. A little rough water in the bathtub and the sub would roll over like a dead bullhead on the Rio Grande. "It's the balance," my dad said. "The balance has to be perfect. The tolerances are too fine. After all, plastic weighs nothing. You'd have to be a *real engineer* to solve it."

My father didn't consider himself a "real" engineer. He was smart enough to know that he was some sort of claptrap genius, and also to know he had no credentials. Maybe he considered himself on a par with a "jailhouse" lawyer. He used the adjective "real" like a scourge and a vision.

About six months later we spotted my baby sister, Conchita, playing with one of those merry, lifeless beans. My dad turned from his domino game and glared at her with malevolence. "Where'd you get that!"

Conchita began to quiver. "I traded it at school for two clear marbles!"

"They have them at school!"

"Yes."

"Everybody has them?"

And so it was finished with the automatic jumping beans. Except for the *malestar* that it left in my father's gut. He didn't really care about the royalties that he had fantasized over. He just wished more people knew who the real inventor was. We never talked or told anyone else about it. We made ourselves forget.

That was one thing I couldn't tolerate about my father. We were witness to a succession of unprincipled ruses that were played upon my father's person to the discredit of the family honor. Part of it was that fatalism characteristic of papi's generation, that passive resignation and acceptance of "reality." That was difficult to stomach, yet certainly not unique; it was the norm, therefore tolerable. To this my father added a boundless and totally unfounded faith in people. He was an ingenue, a trusting child, a father to all his charges. And what's more, men, including confidence men, had confidence in him.

How my old man had faith! And he'd been in and out of so many operations. He had scoured the Southwest for old batteries to haul across the border to transform into lead ingots and sell back to the Americans; he had stamped out Jesus Christs on metal plate, struck Virgin Marys from rubber molds, learned the ins and outs of libraries in order to invent a process to detin cans; he had set diamonds, manufactured brass buttons for the armed forces, designed costume jewelry, set up a nickel-plating bath, run a route of gumball machines, managed a *molino de nixtamal* for tortillas, bought a chicken farm (without having read Sherwood Anderson), gone to school at the Polytechnic, bred rabbits, trained geese to be industrial watch dogs, raised a family and invented the automatic jumping bean. He trained scores of young men in the techniques of lathes, presses, files and baths. He was able to initiate not a few followers into the mysteries of the electro-mechanical creed. But after his accident with the sodium hydroxide he shut himself in. Now and then one of his former disciples would come over with a six pack to pay his respects. These men would be foremen at the mine at Smeltertown or supervisors of the toaster assembly line at the Magic Chef complex. Papi was pleased with his pupils but he used them as case studies—fox and crow style—to prove his point that my brother and I had to get college degrees as engineers. "There's no other way," my dad told us continually. "You have to have a passport."

In some circles my father was considered a soft touch. The chicken farm went broke after my father hired an *holgazán* with no experience "*y unos heuvos de plomo.*" A year after he convinced *el patrón* to get into the detinning business, everybody was privy and there were eight detinners in Juárez alone. Besides, they started coming out with the aluminum can. The geese functioned beautifully but he couldn't convince enough people to accept the idea. The War was over and nobody needed brass buttons. After a while his eyesight wasn't so good and he couldn't set diamonds. The big companies didn't like the idea of him moving into religious jewelry, so they muscled him out at the retail level. The United States customs officials raised the tariff on lead ingots. The gumballs got all sticky inside their machines in the Juárez corn dough. He never was able to graduate from the Polytechnic—after eight years of going at night he was doing an isometric drawing of a screw and he stopped and said he wouldn't. We ate lots of rabbit and someone went ahead and manufactured automatic jumping beans without informing my father.

I spent five years in college; for three of those I tried to be an engineer. Go be an engineer! Get thee to an engine! My father would pin my shoulders to the wall and lecture me with manic glee. Me and my younger brother would not only be engineers—but metallurgists! He feared for his poor Mexico-Americanized sons, alloys of detinned beer cans. Appreciable schizophrenes. Unable to speak a tongue of any convention, they gabbled to each other, the younger and the older, in a papiamento of street *caliche* and devious calques. A tongue only Tex-Mexs, wetbacks, *tirilones, pachucos* and *pochos* could penetrate. Heat the capsule in the palm of your hand and the mercury begins seesawing and the capsule hops. Those were his sons, transplanted, technocratic, capsular Mexican jumping beans without the worm. He believed in education and a free press. Would society listen to reason?

My father liked to walk in the barrio and as *hijo major* it was my privilege to be at his side. We'd walk down the main drag, past the *chicharroneria* (*"sin pelos, ¿eh?"*) where the pork rind hung to dry, and past the *molino de nixtamal* where at six in the morning you could queue up for the *masa* that came out like sausage from the funnel and was molded into a ball and sold like a pumpkin on a scale. Invariably we'd look at what was doing at the movies but we never went in. It would be either a Mexican flick like *Ustedes los ricos* or *Nosotros los pobres* with Pedro Infante or Jorge Negrete, or a World War II *gringada* with Spanish subtitles. John Garfield scowling like a Protestant moralist with a tommy gun emerging from his *vientre.* We would wind up at my father's favorite *tortera*, El Mandamás del Barrio. My dad would have a short beer and I'd wolf down some *nieve de mamey.* Then followed a half-hour rap between papi and the braggadocio owner, don Ernesto. They would share their mutual entrepreneurial visions. Going home my father could become very moody. He would compart his frustrations and his hopes. He made me feel like a true *varón* and I would listen to and guard his words jealously and, from the time I was twelve, with intense anguish. My father usually couched his ambitions in terms of money or some other material objective (*dólares* vs *dolores*). But it was transparent even to a youngster that his true goals were more intangible. He spoke of handing down an inheritance or heritage to his sons, a patrimony, a family business, the establishment of a new order. This pleased me. What I feared was his attribution of responsibility. His resentments had become self-directed; he blamed himself for his failures, he knew he was a brilliant man and yet, somehow his objectivity about the physical world had become perversely countervailed by a totally immoderate estimation of his position in it. Perhaps it was his pride and hunger for recognition that accounted for his overweening hunger for blame. Even his accident at the detinning plant he figured, along with the insurance companies, as some "act of God." My father had no sense of being suppressed, he believed in his freedom of action to a degree that, at the age of twelve, imbued me with fearful trembling for my own personal accountability. He pressed his sons hard on the school issue. School didn't matter to him particularly as a medium of factual knowledge (much less wisdom); he pushed it on us as a means of attaining the necessary credentials, *un pasaporte* was the term he used with blind naivete for the connotations of his choice. School, or rather, graduation and the diploma were a passport into America. It permitted the bearer to travel the road royal.

One evening as usual, my father was questioning me with meticulous detail about my schoolwork. I told him that tomorrow I would have to crucify a frog. It was for junior high biology and sad and dreadful. For two weeks Maestro Rodríguez, a maestro fiercely loved by me, had been methodically outlining with a piece of yellow chalk on a slate board, the life mechanisms of the green frog. I had committed the life to memory, consuming him organ by organ. Tomorrow I was to force him open. After the frog was dunked in anesthesia I was to nail him to a piece of plywood. That was the crucifixion part, his little limbs completely distended so that the torso would be exposed to the public, scientific eye. A disturbing image which my father relished; a frog pinned like a man or boy with arms and legs stretched out on the edges of a raft, belly up on the infinite green sea . . . And then I would use the stainless steel razor to cut the frog into twin symmetries. I was to remove and label the liver, the heart, the brain. I was required to identify the optic nerve.

That evening my father had more than one short beer at El Mandamás del Barrio and I had more than one *nieve* in order to sweeten my mouth. We were troubled and enchanted by the imagery of pollywog martyrdom. When we went home my father was more moody than usual. He looked like a sullen, pathetic victim. The honor in his jaw had softened and he almost seemed to be pouting. He transmitted to me an uncontrollable trembling and a fear for my life and integrity. The most dreadful thing was that none of it could hinder me or make a difference. In the morning I would put on my blue school uniform and go to my biology class and do what I must do.

One day in college I was staggering around the stacks and fell across Jung's *Psychology and Alchemy* and I had an inkling of what my papi's metallurgy was all about. Alchemy: The transformation of dross into gold and the fashioning of the gold into a higher, purer meaning. The goose that laid the golden egg. Out of your ass, man! I spent three years in college dunning the physical world for a sense of reality. I learned all about the acids, bases and salts. They took on a moral connotation for me. But I never could get much realization from the natural world. I preferred reading a novel or loving a woman. At that time my father was *semi-retirado*. His face had been disfigured by a geyser of caustic soda when the detinning bath blew. For over six months something had been going awry with the bath. Every three or four weeks there would be this awful rumbling and out of the tank 10 feet long by 10 feet wide would spout a geyser of boiling caustic soda and tin slush. My father was very concerned. The workers were coming on the job with heavy rubber tarpaulins close at hand. There was muttering that this was hazardous work and they should get a raise. My dad walked around with a yellow pad; he kept scribbling numbers. Every day he dropped his plumb line into the foul-smelling tank and took a reading of the solution level. He was convinced that the variation in the buildup of incrustation at the bottom of the tank had led to substantial variations in temperature within the solution. When the temperature differences became too extreme: the geyser effect. He advised that the tank be drained and that the incrustations be scraped from the bottom so that the solution would receive uniform heat. But *el patrón* wouldn't hear of it. There was too fierce a competition for the scarce tin cans. If they were out of business for two, three weeks, they'd never get back on beam. What they had to do was plumb the tank for all it was worth and when she blew, *¡que se joda!* If necessary they would go back to old batteries and lead ingots. One day my father was standing over the tank with his plumb line. He looked like a little bronze boy fishing in a vat of vaporous split-pea soup. Suddenly, without warning, the physical world spat up at him. He took a sop of alkaline base right on the head. Very funny! just like Laurel and Hardy. What the hell, there's only a finite number of tin cans anyway. Besides, my dad would never have to worry anymore that he was being discriminated against merely because he was Hispanic.

After the accident papi mostly stayed at home, although he was known to beat it out occasionally to Chalo's for *un partidito de dominó.* He gave up his vocation as *subpatrón,* a teacher, trainer and overseer of men. He claimed he wasn't up to breaking in new men with his face disfigured as it was. He wouldn't be able to face the *chisme* and derision of resentful ingenues. He had taken it on himself and it made him lose his confidence. Now and then he'd get an inspiration and rush to his closet which he had fashioned into a shop and work over a virgin hunk of metal with his press and files.

Chalito and I went to college where after many peripeteias I eventually majored in sociology. In the afternoon my brother and I ran the gumball route for *el patrón.* In our pickup we wandered through all the good and bad-ass neighborhoods of El Paso and Ciudad Juárez. Everywhere we stopped a horde of expectant *esquintles* descended on us. *"¡Ahí vienen los chicleros! Dame un chicle, ¿no?"*

My old man made it easier for the gumball business when he invented some kind of corn oil to spray on the gumballs so they wouldn't stick to the glass or to each other. On the other hand, it was our solemn duty to fix the charms to the glass sides of the machine so they couldn't fall down the gum slot and requite some grimy-pawed tot in his vision of hitting the *gordo* from a magnanimous vending machine. My dad even discovered that it was easier to give the storeowner's 15% cut of the sales by weight rather than having to count out all the money. Some storeowners were not so certain, however, about the reliability of mass in the physical world and they needed constant convincing that weight and count were equivalent. Every once in a while they'd "keep us honest" by making us count the money too.

It was a tolerable life and when I graduated from college my father was present in his dark blue suit and dark tie (the combo he reserved for a funeral) feeling proud and tender and somewhat ill at ease about his scarred, reprehensible face. He poured me a tequila with his own hand and made me lick the salt from his own wrist. "You've made something of yourself!" he told me. He was not too sure about the nature of these "social" sciences but he was confident that the degree would satisfy the contingencies of the "real" world. When he died, perhaps from boredom, loneliness and a thwarted imagination, he laid a heavy rap on me. He said I was the oldest and therefore I inherited the responsibilities. I should see to it that the family was kept intact, go about the unfinished business of establishing some solid, familiar enterprise, a patrimony.

If I did not forgive my father his naive belief in his omnipotence then I would have succumbed to his logic and in condemning him would validate his credo of an ultimate, personal accountability. The vicious circle; the double bind. It is better to forgive him and lay the blame on a myopic, racist society that would have granted a white Anglo of his talents an adequate station in life. This position too has its fearful hazards for it alienates me from my father's vision and his wishes. Pater noster. His love for and exuberant response to the world pose a momentous challenge. His younger son made it as an engineer. He works for General Dynamics where he helps design submarines.

He was a man who inspired confidence. . . I prefer to fix him as he was when I was twelve. It was long before the vat full of sodium hydroxide had turned eccentric and he was at his height of virility and joy. One golden afternoon after school I went down to the detinning plant and peered through the fence at the scrap metal yard. The yard was one square kilometer wide and filled to the brim with b illiant metal. It was a splendid day and my father had decided to do some physical work with his men. He sported a magnificent Zapatista mustache. He had taken off his shirt and his bronze chest and arms rippled with muscles as he dug into a mound 8 feet high of shimmering scrap and filled a massive wire cage. He looked like bronze Neptune with his trident or maybe like a revolutionary poster of an industrial worker emanating joyous aggression. The workers were laughing and marvelling as he filled the wire cage in six minutes and then attached it to the crane that hauled it to the tank of caustic soda. I wanted to go inside the yard but I was fearful because papi's trained geese honked militantly at me from the other side of the fence. At that time I was about the same height as these ferocious bull geese and a week earlier one had pecked me on the cheek. Neither the bruise nor the moral outrage had healed. Finally the geese became distracted by a stray dog and I made a dash for it. My father greeted me with delight as if I were a creature unique, a novelty. We went to the furnace where they melted the batteries. He knew the furnace fascinated me. He let some of the molten lead down the channel and into the ingot molds. Molten lead does not look base at all but rather like fine Spanish silver. We inspected the artisans who fashioned the soles for *huaraches* out of old rubber tires. We checked out the rabbits who also lived in the yard. There was a white fluffy one I enjoyed petting and laying on certain prepubertal fantasies.

During the break the young macho workers would place a narrow board 10 feet long by 10 inches wide across the steaming and bubbling vat of caustic soda. The brackish vat looked like a place on Venus where Flash Gordon might land and the machos liked to reassure themselves by walking over the board they had laid across the corrosive brew. My father did not approve of this practice. As a man of responsibility and devout observer of the physical world he believed to the utmost in the principles of safety. Unfortunately the young workers did not share his sense of caution and they played their little game. That day they invited a brand-new worker to walk his way across the board, just in order to verify his machismo. This worker did so without the slightest hesitation. He walked across once and was rewarded with the promise of a free beer. He walked over again and received another free beer. He was supremely confident. He went over again and stumbled into the vat. The worker had heavy rubber boots but before he could catch his balance he went in over the knee and the solution filled up his boot. The workers were hollering and my father came running with a fire extinguisher filled with neutralizer. They got the worker's boot off and a patch of skin from the man's calf came peeling off with the boot. My father foamed what was left of the leg and wrapped a blanket around it.

The ambulance seemed to never come. For me and perhaps for others present the young worker had somehow been transformed and transported to an inhuman category. He was no longer like me, he was something alien, revolting and mortifying, something with which I could no longer identify. But my father held him in his arms and comforted him. The young worker was in such intense pain and shock that he could not scream. He whispered to my father if he would be short a leg. My father was too committed a realist to deny it. He clenched the young man's hand in his own. He talked to the worker about the dignity of work. He told the worker that the leg didn't matter, that maybe he wasn't *el patrón* but he was *el subpat-rón* and after he was well he would see to it that there was work for him.

My question is: Why wasn't papi recognized as the inventor of the wormless bean and other joyous novelties?

from THE DUPLICATIONS

by KENNETH KOCH

from TRIQUARTERLY

nominated by TRIQUARTERLY

Note: This episode from *The Duplications* is part of one of the three or four main plots. Canada Dry and Schweppes are sponsoring a race across all the roads of Greece. There are two competing teams: Mickey Mouse and his associates; and Terence and Alma Rat. Mickey is the Canada Dry driver, Terence the Schweppes driver. The one who covers every road in Greece in the shortest possible time is the winner.—K. K.

Meanwhile in Nevada's
Gambling halls, the odds are five to four
That Mickey Mouse will conquer the White Protes-
Tant Anglo-Saxon rats who are his rivals.
The mice, both he and she, are better drivers,

The gamblers say; and many a bet is made
By those who can't afford it, kids in sneakers
With wistful looks, who all night long have prayed
For Disney's two to win this crazy Preakness
Through all the roads of Hellas. Undismayed,
Terence and Alma Rat have shown no weakness,
But, driving just as fast, with less support,
Intend to win. In Athens, in Earls Court,

And in the drowsy empires of the East
Interest is high, and television offers
Daily two-hour reports, a visual feast
To all who love the contest. Mickey proffers
A candy bar to Minnie. "Brewer's Yeast
Is all I'll eat today," squeaks she, but softens
And takes the bar and takes a bite. "My diet
Is less to me than keeping Mickey quiet

In mind and heart so he can be victorious,"
She thinks—while Donald in the back seat's dozing
As they pass Delphi, famous for its oracles,
Descend to Thrakis, famed for early closing,
Then speed with trembling wheels to Crete the glorious
Across the "Bridge of Spray," made by the hosing
Of people on the islands on the way;
This would not work in San Francisco Bay

Because there are no islands there to hold
The people spurting water; but there are
So many isles (twelve thousand five, all told)
Of Greece, there was no problem; so the car,
Supported by this water brave and cold,
Could brightly beam along, a daytime star,
Bearing two noted mice of black and one
Of yellow duck, whose name, you know, was Don.

O Donald Duck, if ever you could know
The destiny that waits for you in Crete,
You'd urge your best friend Mickey to go slow
And exercise the webbing on your feet
To leap into the blue sea air, for though
Your life with him and Minnie seems complete
Soon a most horrible wedge will drive between
You and your friends. Meanwhile the beckoning green

Of fair Heraklion with its Labyrinth
Spoke to them from afar. "Land, land at last!"
Said Mickey. Minnie said, "And it's a cinch
We'll all be glad this watery rise is past,
Although it was exciting!" "May the tenth:
Two thousand miles—eight hours." Don smiled and laughed
Then passed the book to Minnie: "Let Terence Rat
Just try to beat or even compete with that!"

And Donald's doom was on him in two days . . .
A Chinese gentleman named Hu Ching Po
Was interested in living different ways:
Spending the month on Crete, he wished to know
The black, the white, the intervening greys

Of all that happened there, Well, he was so
Surprised to see a duck walk up and speak
To him that he stared madly at its beak—

Or "bill"—men have a lot of names for noses:
"Schnozzola," "target," "ray-gun," and "proboscis";
And "implement for getting kicks from roses,"
Or "helpful, with the eyes, in winning Oscars";
And "Fresh air opens up what clothespin closes."
Whether by cows or beautiful young Toscas
Borne in the midst of face, it has the beauty
Of being both delicate and heavy duty:

We breathe all day and then we breathe all night—
Sometimes, it's true, the mouth takes over for it,
But mainly it's the nose, when sun shines bright
Or when stars gleam, that does, like Little Dorrit
More than it seems it ought to do. Our sight
Is veiled by lids, our hands in sleep lie forward
And do not touch, our ears the brain takes care of
By making dreams of sounds we're not aware of—

But nose, you go on breathing all night long!
What was I speaking of? Oh, Donald's bill.
Yes, well, an animal, chicken, or King Kong,
Will have a different nose than humans will,
A nose which on a girl might look all wrong
Would on a hen be beautiful; yet still
Our prejudice makes us think our type superior.
Don's was two darkish dots on orange near where your

Spectacles would usually rest.
A beak, I meant to say, sometimes we call
A human nose a beak, which is a test
To see if someone hits us, if at all
He hears what we have said, though if expressed
In honest love, our thought might really fall
Into the realm of flattery. "Bill," however,
Is rarely used for persons, perhaps never.

When Hu Ching Po, however, saw the beak
Of Donald Duck and heard him talk, he couldn't
Believe what he was seeing. In a week
They had him out of surgery, a wooden
Brain inside his head, and in his cheek
A "thinking cathode," which would help him goodn-
Ess know get through life's ordinary duties.
But now to Mickey and his "You too, Brutus"

Attitude toward Donald, for he found him
In Minnie's arms, with Minnie gently sighing!
"Minnie goddamn you've your two arms around him!
I see," cried Mick, "a duck will soon be dying!"
And seizing a huge rock, began to pound him
(Poor Donald Duck) to death. "I'm not denying
I hugged him hard, but good Lord, Mickey, listen!"
He stopped; he saw her eyes with teardrops glisten.

"Donald—I hope he's not dead yet—poor Donald—
Oh, Mickey, see, he's breathing! yes!" "Come tell me!"
The barely pacified Mickey screamed, "I've coddled
This duck enough! Don't try to overwhelm me
With sighs and tears. Goddamn, I feel dishonored!
What consolation are you trying to sell me?"
"Oh!" Minnie said; then, with a voice like bells,
"He was upset at hurting someone else.

It was the kind of thing we've gone through too—
Don't you remember, Mickey? Oh, you must!
Before the world got used to me and you.
Staring at my small shapely mousey bust
Full many a mariner would go cuckoo;
And you, you were not unaware, I trust,
How many of those who heard you speak your name
Went totally and hopelessly insane.

You know there is a hospital in Switzerland
With two pavilions, Mickey and Minnie Mouse,
For crazy people who go around insisting that
Rats and mice can speak. This crazy house

Has services and doctors both most excellent,
Yet no one's ever left it cured." A louse
Leaped through the air toward Mickey's ear but missed it.
Minnie took Mick's left hand in hers and kissed it—

Or, rather, kissed his white four-fingered glove
(These mice have clothing on their hands all year).
"Well, Donald drove one mad today. Oh, love,
Forgive him. And me, too. He felt such fear . . .
I was but pitying him." She kneeled. Above
Her head her lover gave her the all clear
By making spring-like signs of benediction.
Then both went over to Donald. "His condition
Is grave," said Mickey. "He may really die.
We've got to find a topflight veterinarian,
And soon!"

♨ ♨ ♨

THE TENNIS-GAME

fiction by PAUL GOODMAN

from NEW LETTERS

nominated by NEW LETTERS

(editor's note: "The Tennis Game is a chapter from a novelette-in-stories titled Johnson *written by Paul Goodman in 1932–33, just after he turned 21. It originally appeared in the City College of New York literary magazine* The Lavendar, *where because Goodman was no longer an undergraduate the editors hid his identity under the pseudonym L. Tovish. The Johnson stories heralded the start of Goodman's literary career. As New Letters editors point out: "While his friends took jobs (if they could find them) or went off to graduate schools, he stayed home to write. He was very ambitious, very daring, very confident. Trusting in his remarkable powers, he experimented freely—without imitating the fashionable avant-garde. His work was thus fresh and lively, developed rapidly, and was very uneven. Within the chapter-stories of* Johnson *itself one can see him boldly inventing, sometimes following his intuitions past sense or taste, sometimes achieving extraordinary effects, always learning. Among other things he was finding a means of integrating his life and his art . . .")*

THE PROCESS OF JOHNSON'S falling out of love was like fever and a quick death; and during the course of it his mind so thronged with a delirium of pictures that the most ordinary actions became impossible.

Striking the ground smartly, a tennis-ball bounded toward the level of his eye, while he raised his racket to strike.

Then he saw that the white ball, and his action, were in an infinite Receptacle of possibilities. He might strike it or not strike it, and fair or foul. There were many other things he might do with the ball. He might throw it into a field, or watch it bob on the waves of the sea (traveling there for that purpose), or skin it, or explode it by heating, or place it before a colored lantern; or he might think of it, as he was now, or think about thinking of it. He could annoy sleepers with it at night by tossing it against their windows; or write on it a rendezvous; or use the white sphere as an element in a mobile abstract-design; or with a sharp knife cut in the rubber a grinning face. And all of these to any degree or quality. . . . From the Receptacle was it all drawn. In the midst of a lake of relation he felt himself swimming—like a little beetle. . . . The ball began to emanate a halo of light such as painters place round a figure in the foreground to make it stand out from the canvas; and in this way, being a center of attention, the ball ceased to have relational existence at all, and became art. Or, on the other hand, it became all relations and altogether invisible, like the bundle of moves in the mind of a good blindfold-chess player who does not *visualize* the board as a plaid, sat on by wooden pieces with names, nor even geometrically, but a complex of moving formulae in a world of 64 units.

Bounding past him, the ball sang against the wire-net backstop. The player looked around, smiling a little shamefacedly at being so preoccupied in the midst of a game. The play continued with astonishing rapidity, he thought. A ball sped on a line into his service-box: he smartly sent it back up the alley for a placement-shot. But he had been caught almost altogether unprepared; and before he could really draw back his racket, crossed in front of his body from the drive he had just made, the game was again on. The reason every thing seemed so fast to him was that he lost quick control of his muscles and limbs; before he could bring them to any appropriate action—they were so heavy—everything had passed on.

From another point of view, however, the time of the game passed with incredible slowness, like a river so sluggish you can hardly tell whether it is flowing forward or backward. This was from the point of view of the speed of his thoughts. For his inner activity was so accelerated and so various that everything else, by comparison, seemed stopped dead. He saw images with the profusion of a nightmare. Among the troops of ideas that marched across his mind, the end one could always be that of returning the ball to the other side, and it would always arrive with time to spare; and there would still be an infinite number of thoughts between that one and the one that was really the last before hitting the ball, in which he could always make up his mind like Achilles catching the tortoise. "Thus," he thought, "I do not prepare to swing at the ball because it is never time; but when my arm moves to execute the swing, the ball is already flown by."

While he was deciding this, another ball sped by and sang against the wire net. He stabbed at it more than a second too late. Everybody laughed and the umpire said, "Game!"

"It really will not do," said Johnson, "to be so distracted. I really must keep a firmer grip on my thoughts, and keep my thoughts on the game. I cannot understand what has gotten into me; I am not feverish." This resolution to keep rein on his wandering thoughts was made with the perfectly lackadaisical manner of one already embarked on another day-dream. And it was a day-dream itself, for if his thoughts could really be gotten under control, as he wished, he would never think about it, any more than he would think about falling asleep. "I am not feverish," thought Johnson; "I used to be in love. I once knew a philosopher who said that if falling in love is blind, falling out of love is dizzy; for we are even more unfair now to the person we used to love, than we were partial at first. But it seems to be dizzy in a very literal sense as well, if it is what is happening to me now; if indeed I ever did love."

It was his service-game. But far from botching it, as he would any other situation—the hyperaesthesia that had possession of him gave him such accuracy of control as to terrify as well as exalt him. From a high place he seemed to dominate each little square of the field, so that if it were laid out with lady's-handkerchiefs, he could without difficulty hit any one of them and stain it with brown dust—for each one seemed big as a tennis-court to him. And he spun out like a rapid line in the air, in that graceful glittering curve that is only like itself, the flight of the ball to where it shot from an inside white line two feet from the corner, untouchable. He had more space to aim at than players ordinarily have. He served the balls deliberately; but they sped away with astonishing speed, for it was not the power of his muscles, but their synchronization, that was erratic. One time he missed altogether and dropped his racquet. This was because his eyes, following the ball he had tossed upward, were magnetized by the sight of many boychildren on some benches on the side, or seated on the ground. Many boy-children together, so that their combined gestures and scores of expressions formed a whole pageant of childhood, simple and fresh, yet because of their very numbers, various and interesting. For a single child is like a single beautiful note; there is a moment's pure joy and then you cannot listen any more, but must turn to an adult, corrupt, not nearly so radiant, but at least complex. But a group of children is a whole symphony, without sacrifice of purity. There were two in particular who caught his eye, 8-year olds, bare-kneed, dressed in grey shorts and roll-down grey woollen stockings and heavy grey sweaters with enormous collars that curled up over their chins and ears. They were seated on the ground leaning against the legs of a man Johnson at once took to be their father, and he began to seek out the family resemblance in their features and expressions. "What a projection into Time a face is that we see in both the son and father!" thought he. "A certain modern french romancer—Pierre Villetard?—has deplored the passing away of the old family-portrait, for it was, as he thinks the fugue-form of painting; there was an inner rhythm of meaning, richer than a rhythm of form, in the 8 or 9 heads subtilely resembling each other thru 4 generations. But in life this rhythm recurs in language, manners, gestures, in the inheritance of furniture and dress; in the Hapsburg lip and in the Bourbon mind; it is a whole chorale!—as well as in the grey-blue eyes of these boys and of their father. . . . But what am I thinking of? it is my friend Cleveland and not their father at all." At this, Johnson missed the service-ball he had tossed up.

He served a fourth ace, the ball seeming to be at the same time above his head and hitting a white corner many yards distant, as though there were a continuous glittering wire gracefully poised over the field; while everybody applauded, including his opponents. Several dozen people had come out to watch the practice. "What desirable children the two grey boys are!" he thought. "I am envious of Cleveland sitting above them, talking to them, instructing them in what is a good play, watching their teeth when they look up, he looking down reversed, into their eyes upside down. He is touching the hair of one: how dare he! . . . It is curious enough," he stopped to think, leaning on his racquet, "that among all the children these two seem so especially attractive to me that I am about to insult a lifelong friend on their account. . . . So, given any group of 10 children, or of the girls or nuns who live next door in the convent-school, there is always one with whom, immediately, I am in love. It is only later, when I have watched at my window for one to return home, or perhaps have even called out a name at night, in bed; when I have been undeceived a dozen times, by callousness, avarice, cruelty, mendacity—and still unwilling to learn; that I at last concede that there is nothing extraordinary about *this* one. (And even so, he or she is never just anybody, after.) For, what is it? it is perhaps only a dress or an outfit that catches my eye, or a certain ash-blonde color of hair, or a surly, unhappy face that may really be due to a toothache, or the fact that in a large group there are twins"—as a matter of fact, the boys in grey were not even brothers, but were dressed alike by the imitation natural to some friends—"or that one girl, when first I met them all, smiled at me more sympathetically than the others, because she was thinking of something else. . . .

"Then have I been truly in love these past two years, or has it been one of these?" Johnson asked himself anxiously. For he was in the peculiar position that, the first time in the past two years he could think coherently and without effort on this important question, it was beginning to make no difference whether he ever thought about it or not. He understood this himself. "The fact that I can doubt, proves I no longer love. For while actually I was seeing the great value, the qualities, of that person, this perception was so self-evident to me that, to deny it, I should have had to be insane (or out of love). But now it is easy. I must remember: there could be a sonnet:—

if I could doubt I loved, I should not love,
and that would be better—.

Suddenly he became altogether conscious of the tennis-game. Like a blinding sun it blotted out all his other thoughts, the past, himself, his love, into obscurity; and his whole mind became an act of pure contemplation. Up to now his thoughts had been, so to speak, corkscrewing in upon himself; now they leapt wholly into the environment, and were exteriorized. In a way equally abnormal, for there was still no relation between himself and the game, to enable him to act.

The sunlight inundated everything. The white field spread away before him as if it were on a globe that quickly vanished on all sides. The net, the markings of the field, were brighter lines, lit up, across the general whiteness. The duck-clad players leapt across the lines like naked angels. Back and forth sped the silvery ball. It sped from near him back across the field; and he was intrigued to see, flourishing and brandishing right before him, an angelic arm and a racquet with glittering strings (like the fiery swords of the cherubim before the gates of the garden of Eden). He could not perceive that this was his own arm and that he had just stroked a ball (there was a momentary twang, as of a guitar).

He was altogether dissociated. He saw, or rather contemplated, the game from far-off—the while he unconsciously made faultless strokes. Then, as he watched, everything became evident to him; all the rules and stylism of the game of tennis were standing about, invisible, but like so many real presences controlling the play. And they even began to be a little visible. He understood the Unity of the Form, of the ball bounding from side to side, of the leaping players, of the twanging of the guitar, of the muffled voices everywhere. Of the ball shooting towards him and away, and of the mysterious racquet that propelled it. Then, before his very eyes, this Unity floated into being and became almost a spirit, no longer made of matter and movement, but full of life and ghost, and the most beautiful thing that he had ever comprehended.

"I don't want to play any more, I want to look on!" he cried, hurling down the racquet he did not know he was holding. "Let some one else take my place."

"What's the matter with you, are you ill?" asked his partner anxiously, running over to him. The voice came from so far off.

"No, I want to talk to the game."

He walked over to where Cleveland and the children were, and sat down on the clay.

After a brief pause, the tennis-game at once began again, with a substitute player, for it was only practice; but try now as Johnson would to concentrate on it, the silvery splendor was gone. The field had reverted to its more usual color of dirty buff, the line of dirty white, the net gray; and the players garbed in loose-hung linen, the shirt-tail of one hanging outside his trousers. The ball dug up a puff of buff dust as it bounded skyward, not spinning, and scored with a visible stain like the cheek of dead, dragged Hector. The play was good; the drives low, fast, and angled. The players stood, or gained momentum across the field, with grace and ease. One volley of shots ended with so hard and angled a smash at the net that everybody applauded. But Johnson, whose perception had for a moment been wholly lost outside himself into that silvery work of art, and was not returning thru the normal experience of looking at a match of doubles from the side-lines, soon found himself again burrowing inward. He did not find the game interesting in itself, as a thing, but all manner of irrelevant thoughts distracted him, about the score, about the players, their tournament-ratings, for instance; about the spectators, about the boys in grey next to whom he was seated. It was all beginning again. By an effort of memory he recaptured the lines:

if I could doubt I loved, I should not love,
and that would be better.—

"Are you sure you are feeling well?" asked Cleveland, over his shoulder.

"Oh yes; I was a little tired."

"I should say you ought!" exclaimed Cleveland. "I have never seen such serving in my life."

"Gee, it was good," said one of the boys next to whom he was seated.

Johnson put an arm around his shoulders. "Are you two brothers?" he asked. . . .

"But I cannot doubt I was in love!" he cried to himself, "that for two years I was always oscillating between self-sacrifice and rage. I cannot doubt that there were in that person such qualities as compelled me to love, when once I had perceived them: such beauty, such fine-ness of grain, such erratic grace, such love of children. It would be easy now to maintain that I was deceived all that time and that the qualities I thought I saw did not exist; that it was only an ordinary person; that I was so eager to love anybody, that I found it easy to attribute any virtue at all to the first one to come along, just as I might now, for no reason, prefer one of these kids to another.

"But how could I deny that truth, it was so plainly so! Such mildness of manners, such precise uncertainty, such dignity in trouble! It was my *duty* to seek it out, to try to be near and contemplate it in an especial way; it was so plainly so. I confess I made no effort not to love, or to check my mind when it was not too late. But this is the duty of all who are naïve: when they see an undoubted value, to love it unhesitatingly, without regard to future pain or people's talk. . . .

"But what is this change for, then? Why am I not still in love?"

He smiled at the little boy distractedly.

"I cannot see it any more!" he thought. "If there is a change, it is in myself, not in what I saw. I used to be able to perceive a meaning in a certain body and soul; a splendor of form illuminated all its actions; but it is all gone; its walking, now, is only walking, and its moral beauty abstract, for I do not take fire altogether when I see, or shake inside like a tree full of wind (if I may say so), so as to understand it as this THING! For there is a special kind of perception in understanding a thing. . . . But the whole form, the moving form of my mind has changed, or I should still see it the same as ever. In respect to this at least, its sensitivity—its whole form, then, for it is a meaning and not a mere fact that is here to be perceived—has descended completely from one level to another, where it cannot see. There is as much difference as between the top of a mountain and the bottom. And this is why I have been so nervous, so hyperaesthetic these past days, for a revolution has been taking place inside me. This feverish movie-film of ideas in me, of the Receptacle, and how we think, and the boys who are twins, and the tennis-game, and how we fall out of love, so random and undisciplined—is really only my tumbling head over heels down the side of a mountain. Until I hit the bottom with a bang. And then there succeeds a time of apathy longer and more terrible than this delirium, until I become reacclimated.

"It is the meaning of death. The part of me that has perceived a value cannot any more, and there has been a real annihilation of an activity of the soul. There was an interior model of the one I loved, but it has died, and that one is a stranger.—"

Now Johnson began to cry, still seated on the ground. Tears streamed down his face and taking his arm from around the little boy's shoulders, he hid his face in his sleeve.

"I knew it!" said Cleveland, bouncing up, "he is really ill."

THEY SAID

by REG SANER

from DEMILITARIZED ZONES (East River Anthology)

nominated by East River Anthology

They said "Listen class attention before sorting
your blocks put the red ones in the tray
and yellow in the bowl." So most got all but one
or two of them right and drank paper cups
of pre-sweetened juice voting later to stuff
them nicely down the trash-clown on the way home.

They said, "Now color the Holy Manger brown
the Virgin Mary blue the Christ child pink
and St. Joseph anything you like." So this one boy
colored him polka-dot but was allowed to try again
on a fresh sheet getting a green paper star on his
second St. Joseph he colored him pink a suitable choice.

They said "Democracy is at the crossroads everyone
will be given a gun and a map in cases like this
there is no need to vote." Our group scored quite
well getting each of its villages right except
one but was allowed to try again on a fresh village
we colored it black and then wore our brass
stars of unit citation almost all the way home.

THE MONK'S CHIMERA

fable by TEO SAVORY

from **A CLUTCH OF FABLES** (Unicorn Press)

nominated by Unicorn Press

W HEN THE ABBEY was built, an old griffin came to perch on one of the flying buttresses. For centuries he sat there, watching the monks from his lidless eyes. After observing them for several generations, he realized that they never did anything different: prayers and penance, penance and prayers, the livelong day and half the night. True, there was some rather fine Gregorian chant coming out of the chapel, but after a few decades practice made it too perfect to be of interest. There was, of course, the activity in the distillery, after the lay brothers had gathered herbs in the meadows, when the monks made their profitable liqueur. But even that became, over the years, monotonously ambrosial. The griffin grew so bored he almost turned to stone.

He was thinking of flying back to Assyria when the mountebank, ragged and weary, arrived at the gates, breaking the even tenor of *ennui*.

The world of the open road and village square at carnival had not treated this poor fellow well. After finding haven with the monks, he stayed on, the humblest of the humble lay brothers. Then there was nothing of further interest until, one day, the griffin witnessed the miracle which occurred when the mountebank perfomed his juggling act for Our Lady. As we all know, the monks, educated persons of distinguished lineage, were able to offer up to her the fruits of their erudition, skill and industry, whereas this beggarly strolling player had nothing but an orange to balance on his nose while tossing two other oranges in the air—an indifferent act at best which this poor fellow, so the griffin thought, but indifferently performed. However, his lowly offering had evidently pleased Our Lady and she had smiled upon the mountebank.

The monks, when the miracle was discovered, were astounded. It was plain to the griffin that their noses, though unencumbered by oranges, were out of joint. The abbot was wise enough to make the best of it; the mountebank was soon made a monk, and later, when the abbey fell upon hard times, its liqueur having lost favor to that of a rival order, the new monk's accomplishment was put to good use. Previously the abbot had kept the mountebank's good tidings within the four walls of the cloisters. Now he let a few rumors seep out. On the following Sunday there was a small crowd from the nearby town, come to gape at the mountebank as he juggled for Our Lady. And soon there were large crowds, from town and city, weekdays as well as Sundays. Their offerings replenished the abbey's coffers, and the mountebank grew very tired. He searched for a solitary resting place, as far from the other monks, and from the scene of his labors, as could be found; by chance, the buttress he chose to lean upon was the one which the griffin occupied. One day the mountebank raised his eyes from the ground and, looking heavenward, cried out, "How long, O Lord?" But what he saw up there was not the Lord's benign countenance, or even the peaceful sky, but the griffin's stony gaze. "Who are you?" the mountebank asked in astonishment.

"*I* might better ask that question," replied the griffin "as I have

lived here much longer than you have." He looked down his nose in
a very superior way; still, he did not seem unfriendly and so the
monk replied, "If you have lived here so long, perhaps you have
seen my miracle?"

"Indeed, yes," the griffin answered. "You must be honored and
happy."

"Honored, but not happy."

"Not happy?"

"No, worn out. It was bad enough having to do my act once a day,
but now the crowds are so great I have to do it once an hour. Why,
it's worse than working the Fairs. I'm worn out, I tell you." A bell
rang. "Compline. If it's not one thing, it's another."

"Poor fellow." The griffin did not sound too sympathetic—
certainly he did not look it, with that stony face of his. Still, he was
more understanding than the monks. The mountebank fell into the
habit of spending a few minutes each day in converse with the
griffin. The griffin told him about his native perch, on a *ziggurat*
beside the Tigris, while the mountebank recounted the adventures
which befall a strolling player. Always these pleasant interludes
were cut short by a bell, summoning the mountebank to prayers or
to his labor of entertaining the public.

One day he said to the griffin, "Do you think it is quite right to
make the Smile of Our Lady into a sideshow?"

"Right, wrong—it seems to be the way of your world," the griffin
replied.

"But do you not feel that Brother Abbot is, well, exploiting the
goodness of Our Lady a trifle?"

"It would not be the first time," the griffin said, suppressing a
yawn.

The mountebank's voice dropped to a whisper. "Do you think
God approves?" he asked.

"How should a *Griffin* know anything of God?" the griffin retorted
in his superior way.

The mountebank's neck ached with craning upward, but he stood
on tiptoe (though that did not bring him much nearer) and craned
still more, staring at the griffin. "You sound like an unbeliever!" he
whispered, frightened. He had never noticed before how monstrous
the griffin looked. Who ever heard of a lion with *wings* . . .?

"The word can scarcely apply, for I am a Chimera," the
griffin said.

"Is that a name for a heretic?" The mountebank shrank down in his sandals. "God will strike you dead!"

"As God did not make me," the griffin said, "he cannot unmake me."

The mountebank was terrified and began making signs of the cross, wildly, into the air. "Begone, chimera!" he cried.

The griffin lashed his tail slightly. Boredom again, even from the mountebank! It was unbearable. Slowly he flapped his wings, grown heavy with so much perching, and right before the mountebank's astonished eyes, he flew away and disappeared over the edge of the horizon.

Brother Abbot had seen the mountebank in coversation with the griffin, and now not two days went by before its absence was noted. "What have you done with our griffin?" the abbot asked sharply.

The mountebank crossed himself. "He was a Godless monster," he whispered.

"Nonsense!" the abbot exclaimed. "He was part of our architecture."

When the papal legate came on a visit, Brother Abbot was severly reprimanded for losing a valued art-work. "You must ask Brother Mountebank about the disappearance," the abbot replied.

"Art-work?" the mountebank repeated in his uncultured way. "No, no. He was a chimera."

When the saintly head of the Order came to look into the matter, he accepted the mountebank's statement and soon it became known that what everyone thought they had seen had been but a chimera. Thus it came about that an ignorant mountebank gave a new meaning to a word, causing the griffin, from his more interesting perch in Paris, to break occasionally into sardonic laughter.

THE GARMENT OF SADNESS

by BARBARA SZERLIP

from GALLIMAUFRY

nominated by GALLIMAUFRY

She had been living her life so badly, wrapped in a dry sorrow that went on and on without ever making sense. I'll go to the seamstress, she thought, where things are made whole, piece by piece. There, bent over the dark stitching-arm, I'll sew and sew and be healed by the whirring and tonic of small machines.

Who had prepared her for life? She thought of childhood, how it was receding like a landscape. And her teachers, what had they offered? Waking governed by standards of sleep?

Smells of chili and fried fish from the kitchen,
followed by the seamstress' laughter. The twelve-
fingered man laughed also, working at a machine.
Each extra thumb perfect and useless, like the still-
born. She began to work slowly stitching sadness into a
garment, drawing it from her, cutting and shaping it
to a beautiful design

Once a young boy came, sat down with his cup of
tea, asked endless questions. Told her of the dangers
of swimming in the sea, of creatures who lived beneath
roofs of water. He's Moroccan, the seamstress said
later. Had she seen? The mark of Allah, the bluish
place on his wrist? The people prostrate themselves in
the street for the child, that's why the family had to
leave. Until he's old enough, until he's ready. Eight
miscarriages and he was born. Eight times trying to get
through, trying to match soul with seed, over and over
until it was right.

The garment was finished. The seamstress approved with a nod. Outside the city. January. It will be
all right, she thought, noticing how the night sky was
mirrored in the stitched cloth she carried. Noticing
how galaxies flew from each other like wishes someone
gave breath to.

🔥 🔥 🔥

the buickspecial

fiction by RAYMOND FEDERMAN

from TAKE IT OR LEAVE IT (Fiction Collective)

nominated by the Fiction Collective and Richard Kostelanetz

S O. THERE HE WAS ALL ALONE AGAIN. Broke now. But still on his
way to Camp Drum. Hoping that . . . . .

Hey listen! Would you mind if I told this part of the story myself? I
mean directly. Because you see we are now coming to the climax, I
mean the real juicy part, and it would be better, and also much more
suspenseful if I were to speak directly—first-hand!

I don't mind (I told him, when the time comes). But can you pull it
off? Can you handle it by yourself? I mean, remember, I am the one
who is supposed to recite this tale second-hand. And besides, it is

not legal, you know! What will our listeners say when they discover I've handed you the narrative voice?

Please let me try! Just for a while. For this one part. It really means a lot to me! You'll see, I'll do it right!

Okay!   Look! I'll sit here in that
                                           corner and if you need me
                                              for anything just call
Okay! Here I go:

I was on my way to Camp Drum (Upper New York State near the Canadian border) 1952. February 1952 to be exact. In the middle of a brutal snow storm.

Hey wait a minute! I've already told all that . . . . . .

I know, I know, but if I don't go over some of the details once more I'll never be able to push forward. I've got to step backward a few steps to be able to jump forward. So be quiet and listen!

Okay, get your froggish ass in gear and cancel away! I'll be quiet!

I was on my way to CAMP DRUM. Upper New York State (near the Canadian border). 1952. February 1952 to be exact. In the middle of a brutal snow storm.

Quite unexpected.

I was driving my old beat-up 47 BUICKspecial. Black. Doing about 12 miles per hour on a potholed icy road. In VERMONT. The shortest way to CAMP DRUM. I was assured.

Four in the morning.

There was a deep gully on my right. Very dangerous I tell you. Real precipice. It had been following the road for miles now. Visibility zero! Bald tires on my Buick. Lucky the heater is working. What an enormous banana wagon my Buickspecial! A tank. Radio isn't working. To keep awake. To take my mind off my troubles I'm whistling jazz tunes to myself. Improvising. To pass the time. And also not to think about that damn gully to my right.

Already four days on the road.

I was driving up to CAMP DRUM. It was because my outfit (the glorious gutsy spitshined 82nd AIRBORNE DIVISION) had been sent up there in the snows of Upper New York State to practice parachute jumps in the snow!

But me. I had been left behind. FORT BRAGG (Fayetteville, North Carolina—of all places!) In the fog. I was being shipped Overseas. Yes to the FAR EAST. (Korea to be precise.)

I had volunteered!

VOLUNTEERED! You're crazy man! All the guys in my outfit thought I was out of my mind. Some kind of a nut. A weak suicidal case. The nervous type. A psycho.

Bunch of hillbillies!

So when my outfit packed to take off on maneuvers (imagine that!) up in the snows of Upper New York State the Captain told me I wasn't going up with the rest of the regiment. To practice parachute jumps in the snow. Incredible!

No. Me, I had to wait for my travel orders. And then had 30 days (a whole month's vacation you might say) to get my ass to San Francisco. That's where you'll embark for the FAR EAST. The Captain explained.

And then they took off. The whole regiment. By trucks. In a cloud of dust at dawn. And I stayed behind (in the fog) at FORT BRAGG to wait for my orders. And finally my orders came. But they had goofed! They didn't have my travel expenses and also the one month's pay (the one month's pay in advance) they were supposed to pay me. Normal procedure. Those dumb bastards had sent my papers and my money (typical error!) up to the snows. All my payroll documents (that's what the fat sergeant at Headquarters called them) left for CAMP DRUM in that cloud of dust with the rest of the regiment.

I was screwed! The best thing to do (that fat nervous staff sergeant at Headquarters explained) is for you get your ass up to CAMP DRUM man to collect your dough. If not might take a good week or two for them damn papers to get back down here.

At most I had twenty bucks left.

That really bugged the shit out of me. But I had never seen that part of the country before. A little detour North I told myself before heading West. Why not! With my twenty bucks and my old 47 Buick (special) should be able to get that far. After that we'll see. It would be dumb of me to try crossing AMERICA without my money. And a month's pay in advance (plus travel expenses!) in those days (I was a corporal) that's almost 250 bucks. With or without my Buick I could have a nice cozy trip seeing the country. A marvelous vacation! Discovering the whole lay out Up and Down and Across. AMERICA!

So there I was! On this shitty narrow icy road in VERMONT. Four in the morning or thereabout. After four days' driving (in the rain mostly and now in the snow) with a quick stopover in New York.

A little rest so to speak. In Brooklyn to be exact. To get rid of all my civilian possessions which I'd left with Marilyn. My civilian junk. My half dozen books my jazz records (mostly 78's) my tweed sport coat with patches on the sleeves and my two pairs of trousers my three shirts my jockeys socks etc. All that piled in that black suitcase I've been lugging around for years. And my typewriter. Portable Underwood. Used of course. A whole life to dispose of. To hock in fact. But for the time being all that stored away in Marilyn's closets.

Suitcases and closets. That sums up a life. And typewriters too. And ultimately pawn shops. But for the time being all that shoved away in Marilyn's closets with her brooms and her vacuum cleaner.

Ah Marilyn! What a woman! She was Benny's wife. My former boss when I worked (full time) in his lampshade factory on Flatbush

Avenue before I got drafted into the Army. Marilyn! Wow what a gorgeous woman (29 years old). Beautiful body. Enormous boobs. Big black eyes. I was about 22 then. And quite naive.

What a set up we had. What a tremendous deal! Very sneaky. But I'll skip the details. A guy must have some decency. She was really sad. Even cried when I told her they're shipping me Overseas. But don't you worry I'll come back I swore to her. You don't think I'm going to let them shoot my ass full of holes! Be careful! She cried. And come back to me. She kissed me. Dearest love she said to me as I waved goodbye!

Anyway after that quick stop in Brooklyn just time to say goodbye (and all the rest) to Marilyn in a crummy motel room in Long Island there I was in the middle of the night in a incredible snow storm way up in VERMONT on my way to CAMP DRUM (near the Canadian border) to collect my money before heading out West across country across the Mississippi the great plains the rolling hills the Rockies the desert and California.

Wow what a vacation! Wow was I going to see things! Cowboys Indians perhaps gangsters in Chicago and rattlesnakes in the desert. Play crap in Las Vegas. See movie stars in Hollywood. Swim in the Pacific. Up and down and across. Discover the whole lay out. I had a hardon just thinking about it.

Okay I'll skip the details of all the adventures and misadventures I'd had since I left North Carolina. In my BUICKSPECIAL with my duffel bag. The unfortunate encounters and the unexpected incidents. Suffice to say that so far I had been robbed by an intellectual. Almost raped by an old pederast. Abused. Deceived. That I was dead tired and that my Buick was now dragging its ass on its last leg. At most I had a quarter tank of gas left (not even). And not a penny in my pocket. Out of cigarettes too and hungry like hell.

If I make it to CAMP DRUM I'll get rid of that damn jalopy. Should be able to get 25 bucks for it in a junk yard. After that we'll see. I'll bum rides along the way. Thumb my way across AMERICA like you thumb your way through a picture book.

Therefore everything is going well. So far! Except for the snow and the icy road. Visibility zero! Wow what soup out there!

Quarter past four. At least my watch is still working. No pawn shops around here.

So here I am on that stinking disgusting slippery road with twinkles in my eyes hanging on to the steering wheel with both hands. My windshield wipers screeching on the glass. Makes me nervous.

We'll go as far as we can. About three gallons of gas left. I estimate. Damn tank! Wow does it gobble up gasoline. And it puffs it farts burps like an old dying horse. Let's keep going though but without pressing too hard on the gas pedal. To save. To economize. I've got the steering wheel well in hand because this time it's really slippery. I'm almost out of control.

I'm going downhill now and there is a dangerous curve (that's what the sign said) can't see too well my Buickspecial (that old pile of junk) gets all excited and suddenly there she goes sliding sideways as I throw both feet on the brake pedal the damn boat hops to the left hits her ass against the snow embankment jerks rears bounces back in the middle of the road MERDE straightens up I've got my arms all twisted around the steering wheel trying to take the curve the rear tires skid and my wagon slides around in a full circle (almost a full circle) as though she wanted to go back uphill the motor whines into the night I give her a kick in the belly right there on the gas pedal she lets out a groan of pain the tires roar she lowers her front end and like a wild black panther there goes my BUICK leaping head first over the embankment diving full speed into the gully!

I had warned you about that dangerous precipice!

Here we go! That's it. I'm dead! I can feel my balls deflating. My blood rushing through my arteries for the last time. It's all over!

I wrap myself around the steering wheel fold my legs upward to protect my private parts. Normal reaction. My eyes are shut tight of course. So long life a little voice cries inside my skull!

CRASH!. . .BANG!. . .SPLASH!. . .SMASH! I feel atrocious
pains all over. Blood pissing out of my mouth. Nose. Ears. I feel the
taste of death under my tongue. A vision of my whole family (my
mother weeping my father shouting my sisters screaming) flashes in
my mind from beyond the grave . . . and everything stops!

But I'm neither dead nor at the bottom of the gully. I'm simply
suspended in a dead faint. In a pile of apples. Coniferous apples. For
in fact rising majestically from the bottom of the gully a giant pine
tree an enormous pine tree had spread its boughs to receive my
Buick in full flight and she had landed (head first) like an angel into
the salutary branches of that big beautiful Christmas tree well rooted
at the bottom of the gully.

At this very spot the gully must have been at least 100 feet deep. I'm
not exaggerating though it was hard to judge exactly in the darkness
and under the conditions of the present situation.

What a shock!

I had bells ringing in my head. Stars flying in my eyes. Butterflies
whirling in my stomach as I slowly regained consciousness. The
wheels of my Buick were still turning wildly into empty space. The
horn was stuck howling its cry of despair into the night.

The windshield was in pieces. But the blow of the accident had
jostled my radio back to life and for a brief moment a sad feminine
voice sang a blues into the night I'VE GOT YOU UNDER MY SKIN
and then went out. And now the gasping motor let out a final fart of
vapor at the very moment when my headlights extinguished themselves.

My BUICKSPECIAL recoiled upon itself. Twisted itself into a last
spasm of agony. Turned to junk on the spot. High in the branches of
this miraculous pine tree!

And then all was silence and darkness.

I felt blood still running on my face and neck. I'm torn to pieces.
Tattered. And my left shoulder is hurting like Hell!

But one must regain taste for life. Or at least one cannot remain
there suspended like a jerk or like an acrobat or as my friend Sam
used to say of similar situations suspended in this NIGHTMARE
THINGNESS into which I am fallen (or in this case he would have to
say into which I am risen) at four-thirty-seven in the morning
(needless to specify though I did manage to glance quickly at my
watch just as my Buick flew over the embankment—but now that
good old faithful time piece is also crushed to pieces). NO! I cannot
remain there like some nocturnal bird perched on a tree branch. The
wind could perchance make us tumble down from the height of this
great perch into the depth of this immense hole beneath where
certainly this time we would indeed leave forever whatever is left of
life in us.

And already I can feel a vague oscillation!

Quickly through the broken car window on the driver's side (since
the doors are jammed) I extricate myself from this twisted pile of
metallic junk.

I grab my big G.I. duffel bag from the back seat and find myself
in precarious balance like a night owl on a branch. An evergreen branch heavy with snow and dry pine cones. My heart
pounding madly after this frightening accident which could have
been fatal.

Can you visualize the scene? Can you imagine? Our story could have
ended there. The collecting of my money. The GREAT journey
West. The magnificent discovery of AMERICA. All that (and more)
could have ended in the bottom of that unfathomable precipice! Way
up in VERMONT. And you would never have heard the rest.

Therefore suspended on this bough. Arms spread out to better keep
my balance I glanced towards my Buick for the last time. A most
affectionate glance towards that beautiful Buick which had served
me so well up to this place but now reduced to a mere pile of buckled
metal and broken glass recoiling upon itself like a crushed snail
folded upon the remains of its glorious past existence as one of the
fine proud American cars but now just a pitiful stack of GENERAL
MOTORS junk (body by Fisher)!

The wind suddenly calmed down. And from behind the dark clouds the Moon sneaked out quietly to look over the scene.

For a moment I had a total vision of the situation and I will never forget it. My 1947 BUICKSPECIAL ass up in the air hanging in the evergreen branches stretched out like the arms of some saintly figure. Ah what a splendid tree I said to myself. What a divine tree! A true Pieta!

I managed to hook my duffel bag to a branch and slowly carefully painfully tiptoed towards the debris of my car like a tightrope walker on his wire arms outstretched. JESUS CHRIST! I screamed into the night. WHAT THE HELL AM I DOING UP HERE? And almost fell off.

When I reached my old Buick sprawled there like a clumsy baboon I gave her a kick full of affection and full of regret right there in the rear tire closest to me.

SO LONG YOU DEAR OLD BUICK I murmured with sobs in my voice. GOODBYE YOU BIG PANZER! FAREWELL SPECIAL BUICK! BARGE OF MY DREAMS! I sniffled a bit and then as I tiptoed away on my branch I said poetically: May angels guide Thee to Thy eternal rest in the Paradise of junk! FARE THEE WELL!

Well I'll skip the horrendous details of my ascension back up on the road where eventually I managed to scramble on all fours with my big duffel bag. My G.I. uniform torn to pieces. My teeth shattering. Blood stains all over. And where. Eventually. I sat down (collapsed rather) on a mount of snow with horrible pains all over my body. Pains which I hardly dare describe so horribly painful were they. My duffel bag rolled next to me at my feet like a wounded animal. It was full of blood and holes so much had it been tossed around during the accident. Torn pieces of pants shirts underwear socks were dripping out of it.

It was not a pretty spectacle! And even worse. Below me lost in the darkness now (her rear end up in the air) (tires torn to shreds) that heap of BUICKJUNK!

What a mess!

Alone on this lonely deserted road (up in VERMONT) Raped.
Abused. Deceived. And now without any means of transportation.
BUICKless. Pennyless. Arms and legs hurting. Frozen to the bones.
Starving. Alone. And not even a cigarette left (the last cigarette of
the condemned man). But nevertheless still on my way to CAMP
DRUM. I almost wept. Yes! I almost allowed myself this moment of
weakness. But I held back. It would have been useless in this
solitude.

Around me only emptiness. Nothing! Nothingness! Nobody! Only
the snow. The dark of night. And the cold. In other words Nature at
its worse. And so I waited
   I waited like that. Hurting all over. For hours. Two. Three Four.
I seemed to have lost the notion of time. And in fact I had lost it.

And also the notion of space. I was in total nothingness! In complete
LESSNESSness my friend Sam would say where nothing is even
less than nothing.

Yes I felt completely negated. If that's possible. That's approximately how I felt and where I was. I was (if I may say so —
metaphorically speaking) in SHIT up to my neck!

Useless to try walking (I decided) with my heavy duffel bag and my
terrible pains.

To pass the time. But especially not to freeze to death. I began
hopping from leg to leg in the middle of the road. I did all kinds of
gymnastics in spite of the pains and the bells still ringing inside my
head and also in spite of my left shoulder which I could hardly move
now.

I gesticulated. Capered about. Bounced around. Just to hang on. To
survive. If not I would die on the spot. Yes I could feel life quickly
abandoning me. Courage deserting me. And on top of that I was
hungry like hell. Anything for a cigarette!

If not I would die on the spot. Yes I could feel life quickly abandoning me. Courage deserting me. And on top of that I was hungry like hell. Anything for a cigarette!

It's all over! Finished! I felt humiliated. Must have been 10° below zero. I had a disgusting vision of myself frozen like a scarecrow in the middle of the road.

I was ready to give up. To renounce life when SUDDENLY   SUDDENLY in the distance   two beams of light gliding like fire on the snow probing the whiteness like the eyes of some giant monster rushing towards me   to devour me?
                                                                                A CAR!

AN AUTOMOBILE!   I jump in the middle of the road wave to that monster gesticulate shout scream stamp my feet enrage raise my arms and legs (in spite of the pain and the fatigue) hop leap rear roll myself on the ground crawl climb on top of a snow pile fall on my ass pull out my handkerchief (full of blood) wave it furiously cuff my trembling hands around my mouth to shout louder!
                                                                Stick out my thumb!

The car glides to a smooth stop in front of me without even skidding on the ice. It's an enormous car. A Chrysler. Golden. I notice that immediately. An IMPERIAL! I know my American cars. That one must have at least 420 horse power. The window slides down electrically and a head with splendid eyes appears (head of a woman useless to say at the stage where we are). An incredible beauty! Looks like a fairy queen or the heroine of a Victorian novel. Sensual deep blue eyes full of compassion. Compassionate enough to make you melt of love on the spot.

I lurch forward!

What is it young man? (A soft languorous voice).

An ACCIDENT! A TERRIBLE accident! Here come and see!

She steps out of her Chrysler wraps herself in a magnificent fur coat (mink of course). She's tall slim and svelte. Gorgeous legs to give you an erection on the spot. A delight to watch as she passes before the car's headlights. She hardly touches the ground. As though the snow did not exist.

She leans over the gully.

CAREFUL! I shout as I gently grab her arm.

Oh! is that funny! What's that in the tree? A car?

Yes . . . my BUICK!

She turns towards me and in the lights of the car sees that I'm wounded.

But you're wounded young man . . . young soldier! (She must have noticed my uniform. Or what's left of it). We have to take care of you immediately! Quick! Get in the car I'll take you to my doctor.

Blood must have started dripping again from my wounds. I suppose all that gymnastics I did to have myself noticed.

Hurry! Get in! You need medical attention.

I throw my duffel bag on the back seat (somewhat ashamed of its ragged condition) slide next to her on the front seat (the car seems perfumed) and she steps on the gas. The car floats on the snow like a speed boat on a smooth surface of water. She must have special snow tires because in spite of the speed (the female was doing 70 miles an hour) the huge car hardly skids.

My teeth were shattering like a pair of castanets.

You must be frozen poor dear one! How long were you out there?

I don't know. Hours! Maybe more. You know at this time of night and in such bad weather there isn't much traffic. Lucky you came along or else . . .

Poor boy! Yes lucky for you I was on my home. I was playing bridge at the house of some friends [at 4:37 in the morning! What a sneaky broad! Must have spent the night with some guy—her lover—but of course she didn't want to tell me and to be honest it's none of my business] You're a soldier?

Yes. A paratrooper! 82nd Airborne Division!

Oh! A paratrooper! That must be dangerous [damn right] . . . Are you Italian by any chance? You have a charming accent.

Italian! Me? No, I'm French. [They always pull that one on me. Because of my black hair I suppose and my big nose. They always take me for a lousy macaroni. I ask you! Do I look like an Italian?]

Oh a French paratrooper! She said. But what are you doing out here? What were you doing out there? In the middle of the night on top of a tree? Did you fall out of a plane?

I giggle a little but the giggle turns into a groan of pain.

Sorry. She says. But what are you doing in the American army any way if you're French?

Oh, it's a long story. I was almost ready to unload my whole sad story but I was so cold the words froze inside my throat.

But you're trembling like a leaf! Listen. I live just a few minutes away from here. Perhaps it'll be better if I take you home with me. At this time of night especially. We can always call the doctor from my house if necessary.

I was not going to argue with her. No. Especially since now (even though I was trying not to show it too much) my shoulder was hurting like mad. And then one never knows with such unexpected apparitions. Anything can happen.

Yes! Yes I think it's better. And quicker too. I said to this charming lady to make her understand that I agreed with her suggestion.

We arrive.

What a place! A castle! A place! A fantastic mansion! This time I'm really in a dream. A fairy tale.

We go in.

I'm stunned. Dumbfounded by the richness the vastness the elegance the luxury the splendor of this abode.

You live here alone? I finally dare ask.

No. With my husband, of course. He's a banker.

That cools me off a bit.

He's on a business trip. In Boston. Until tomorrow evening.

That warms me up a bit.

Yes. In fact that's why I was playing bridge with my friends. I hate to stay home alone when Joseph is away. [At 4:37 in the morning or thereabout in a weather like this! Wow that bitch's got nerve. Lucky for me though. Otherwise I would certainly have died out there like a dog on this lousy deserted road]

Do sit down, please. She said with a lovely hospital smile. No. Not there! Here. On the sofa.

I collapse into a brown leather sofa of maddening softness and depth. She disappears for a moment and comes back with a whole collection of little vials and some hygienic cotton. In the bright light of the room she's even more beautiful. More stunning than before. I rub my eyes to make sure I'm not dreaming. Even pinch my thigh to prove to myself that I'm not asleep or unconscious. She's standing next to me now. If she touches me I faint. Wow! is she gorgeous! Golden blond hair. Eyes blue like the ocean. Yes the Pacific. Skin soft white like sour cream. A real goddess! I'm ready to convert on the spot. About 32 at most. And so kind. So gentle. So full of warmth and delicate gestures. To give you confidence again in mankind.

She places one of her lovely hands on top of my head and with the other gently rubs my wounds with cotton. I let out a little groan. Does it hurt? Just a little I say. I know but I have to do it or else you'll get infected.

I give myself completely. She notices that my clothes are soaked and torn and that my left shoulder is bloody. You must take these off immediately she urges. I was not going to resist her.

Follow me!

We are in the bedroom now. She takes out a rich red silky robe from the closet. It's Joseph's she explains who is on a business trip in Boston. And she quickly unbuttons my paratrooper vest my shirt and all the rest and in seconds I find myself bare chested (but in my khaki G.I. drawers) standing in front of her. Trembling. I breathe deeply to expand my chest.

She's bandaging my shoulder now. Softly gently carefully and with a great deal of know-how. Funny! I don't even have a hardon. When she's finished with the shoulder she gives me a friendly tap on the back then leans forward and kisses my right shoulder softly kindly. It was as though a bird (a dove) had touched me lightly with the tip of its white wing.

I feel dizzy. Sort of split in half. No! That's not it. I feel soft and somewhat wobbly. She notices it because she asks don't you feel well? I say yes with my head.

Here. Why don't you stretch on the bed for a while.

No hesitation. I jump on top of the bed. KING size. An OCEAN of softness.

No no! Not on top of the blankets. Get inside. Rest for a while and warm up. I'll be right back. I just want to put on something more comfortable and then I'll bring you a nice hot grog to pep you up.

She disappears again and I sink into the waves of the delicious mattress and the current of the voluptuous sheets. In three minutes

I'm snoring like a dolphin and feel myself floating drifting into the kingdom of dreams.

SUDDENLY   SUDDENLY
is it a dream a nightmare (or a hurricane) but a long greedy white hand is toying with my private instruments which take a leap upward into gigantic dimensions? White sails stretched to the point of bursting by the blow of a stormy wind. And now that mythical hand pulls my nautical tools toward a vague mass of rocky flesh trying to guide it all down the corridor of a pair of narrow thighs at the end of which a gluttonous cave of fur gasps to swallow me. I hear a cry of distress inside my head. SHIP WRECK! *I'm going down. Sinking!* HELP!———S. O. S. *Though the water is tropically warm I struggle like a castaway body to remain on the surface.* MAY DAY! *I try to keep my eyes opened. And now I see her. Surrealistically. That beautiful charming blond siren soft and slippery (and naked) lying on top of me flinging herself about like a giant fishy creature in frenzy. She gulps shrieks whines howls sighs puffs. Lets out a stream of weird exotic cries: DO IT TO ME DO IT TO ME DO IT TO ME! A flood of fingers is pulling me down. GET IN she roars and I'm trying my best but the weight and furor of her slippery body is crushing me into the waves of this white sea of passion and its whirling foam. And now the nymph is pushing me down and under deeper and deeper with all her aquatic dexterity rowing paddling oaring slapping flapping the waters and eddies of this impromptu swim!*

Half of me has disappeared inside the whirlpool of her cavity. And when she's almost finished caving me in she starts all over again with even more appetite: *she gargles me up*
                                                      drains me down
                                                       mashes me up
                                                    gobbles me away!
                         Wow! What a cannibal! What a meal I make! Must have been shipwrecked for months and months on her deserted island of sexlessness!

I try to escape but now that flexible creature lifts me up into an arch (into a bridge) and slides my erected mast into her driveling porthole of a mouth swallowing it in one smooth stroke all the way down to my

inflated balloons. Then twisting her propeller-head in circular mo-
tions she bites & sucks & licks & chews (up & down & sideways &
obliquely) with wet little groans and moans and whispers and when I
let my material explode down her pipe she roars frantically and starts
spitting like a water dragoness all over the flaps and flips of my hot
belly and with her uncanny tongue she drags the sticky liquid all the
way down (I am not exaggerating) to my feet along the shores of my
legs and licks my feet my knees digs into my shivering thighs tongues
up my hips gets inside my cute belly button up my chest and under
my armpits. I start giggling embarrassingly while sinking ludicrously
and hopelessly to the bottom of this desperate licking. I hang on to
her with both hands as if she were a life buoy or a raft but she's the
one who climbs aboard me again (what the hell is going on?) *and with*
voracious fingers she grabs my loose paddle and stiffens it with jerky
strokes. It's too much I don't want to swim any more! Thumbs up!
Time out! Dammit it hurts like hell! Especially in my two blue sails.
Again I try to escape by plunging (head first) into the swirls of the
sheet to swim ashore but she grabs me firmly rigidly by the tip of the
bow-sprit with one hand and hustles three fingers of her other hand
into my stern I SCREAM (but in vain) as my poor splintered oar
plunges into her stormy port! It feels as though I have just sank into a
pool of honey. (Must be dessert time!) *And now she screws my tail*
(or what's left of the bloody thing) in all directions until in a last
stroke of rage and despair (a furious gasp of survival) I shout STOP!
. . .STOP IT! . . . I CAN't no more!

But she doesn't
hear me or else
pretends not to
hear!   True

her head is buried shyly inside my shoulder (the good one fortu-
nately). *Suddenly she leans backward*
away from me   and bursts
into hysterical inhuman laughter. I feel insulted vexed dejected
humiliated and quite repulsed. Get the fuck off! I scream as I try to
slide from underneath her. Get back down here! She replies as she
shoves me back into the water. Stop it! Please stop it! I plead.We're
going to capsize!
But she flops on top of me and wiggles herself into incredible posi-
tions to sail the rest of me. What suppleness!

I   *struggle.*   We   *struggle.   and*

SPLASH! We fall overboard onto the floor: me flat on my back her sitting on top of me her buttock against my crotch her back against my caving chest her long wavy hair (blond soft and wet) drowning my face in its silky net.

        We're like two swimmers doing a fancy aquatic ballet. Like two water-wrestlers trying to drown the other guy. If only there was a referee! No kidding! I assure you it's worse than a match of catch-as-catch-can!

I can't take it any more. I'm washed out. Dead crippled worn out. I'm empty crushed deflated. But she feels a remnant of an erection (a bit bloody no doubt) still wriggling against her derriere puffed like a pink cherub and she wants to take advantage of it. Gingerly (I can't believe it!) she tries to shove that scared piece of drift wood inside her rift. It won't go in. She crawls off me and dives across the room in the bathroom and bounces back in a shiffy with a little jar in her hand (just as I'm trying to slip under the bed) a pink jar. She catches me by one leg and throws me back into the waters of passion as she gets back into the sitting position on top of me. She must think I'm some kind of surfboard. (I'm on the verge of cracking up). She smears the cool goop from the jar (with two fingers) all over her anal passage (raising herself above me in an acrobatic posture) and piles a glut of the stuff on top of my frightened pinnula (what a mess) and SWISH there goes the panic-stricken needle of my compass slithering into her Northpole as if it were gooshy ice cream. This time it's not a joke we both howl in unison: me a sordid violent painful WHOOP she a roaring happy excited mewling of a WHAFF as we collapse together on the floor next to each other and roll on our stomachs limbs spread out like two bodies washed ashore by a furious tempest (it's all over I suppose)

Minutes later we manage somehow to climb the sides of the giant bed and fall inside the hull where we lie sweating puffing breathing sputtering coughing like two athletes who have just broken the world record for the 200 yard dash—no, rather, the 1500 meter free style!

           My darling
           My treasure
       My adorable paratrooper

how I adore you!   (Damn you!)

Wow you're delicious beautiful young strong superb and so juicy so hard so big so supple so delectable so voluminous so useful!

But me I rather feel ugly and small and weak and soft screwed up & down to the bone dried up useless abused deflated demolished pruned crushed!

But I'm not even listening to her any more as she goes on piling up her magnanimous mountain of adjectives on top of me. I'm drifting floating again downstream on my barge of exhaustion on my Medusa raft toward the kingdom of dreams wrapped in the chants of my snoring! ZzZzZzZzZzZzZzZzZz!

What would you guys have done in my place? I ask you! What a way what an incredible way to return to life after that terrible accident! What a resurrection! Call me Lazarus saved from the melting snows! I'm not kidding. What a swim! I ask you what would you guys have done had you to endure such a desperate such a brutal such an aquamonious salvation?

It was 4:30 p.m. when I woke up well tucked under the blankets of that king size bed. I had a lousy taste in my mouth and loud buzzing in my head. In fact my head felt like an empty box. A huge hole. A hollow sphere of darkness and forgetfulness. I felt rather weak (as if I had been blown out of existence by a stampede of buffalos!) and I couldn't remember a damn thing or at least it took me a good five minutes maybe more to realize where I was and what had happened to me in that storm!

In a moment of panic I thought of sneaking out through the window, but naked as I was it would be pure madness and this time for sure I would die out there in the cold of pneumonia. Better wait here and see what happens next. I looked around the room for my clothes. Just in case! Sonofabitch they're gone! A pain of anguish hit me in the chest. I'm kidnapped!

That's more or less how I felt and what I was pondering when the beautiful charming and smiling lady of the house walks in wearing a powder blue silky negligee and carrying a breakfast tray. For a moment (just in case) I thought of faking sleep but when I saw the sunnyside eggs & the bacon & the sausages the toasts jam (strawberry & marmelade) sweet butter coffee & two kinds of juices (orange & tomato) I propped myself against the fat pillows. What a feast! She had even brought me still unwrapped the Boston Globe. Not that I cared much that day about news of the world but it was a nice touch.

I eat the whole thing smartly dunking the yellow of the eggs with nice little pieces of toast. That's a good boy, she says as she watches me adoringly while sitting discretely on the edge of the bed her daringly sexy legs crossed outside her dishabille half opened all the way up to her perfumed crotch. I try to concentrate on my breakfast as she tenderly looks at me and from time to time leans towards me to touch with delicate hands the side of my face and then she kisses me with motherly affection on the cheek on the shoulder on the neck on the hands (as I steadily chew my delicious breakfast). She's really divine! Ah what femininity! No question about that. But we're not going to flop on top of each other again. Not at this unscheduled time of day. What am I? Some kind of amusement park? A toy? If she jumps me again, I scream! Or else I play sick and tell her I have horrible pains. I'm not going to let myself be abused (though after a breakfast like that . . . a guy could indeed . . .)

But if I were to talk to this charming hostess! Just to make a bit of conversation. After all we've hardly said three words to each other I must confess since she rescued me on the edge of that memorable precipice where indeed I should be lying dead now frozen (possibly devoured by wild starving animals) had she not appeared so unexpectedly to save me.

What's your name?
Mary!
Wow, you're beautiful Mary! And you have such lovely blond hair, such deep blue eyes!
It's because I come from the North. All my ancestors came from nordic regions. From Scotland originally. In fact do you know when they all came to this country? [No!] They all came on the Mayflower.

Yes way back at the beginning. That tells you how far back I go in the
glorious past of our great country.
That explains why you're such a fine navigator!
Yes, in a way they were all pioneers!

Shit! That really blew me off. Pioneers! Like me. That explains it
all. You guys realize. Me. I had just fucked (or been fucked
whichever way you look at it) what's best, what's most respected in
America today. ME. Poor lost paratrooper, poor wandering French
Jew (perhaps I should have mentioned that earlier) I had just wal-
lowed in bed without any scruple with all the glorious history of
America. This lovely WASP! This perfect WASP. This 100% American had landed her most distinguished ass, her historical ass on my
guilt-ridden circumcised dick without being aware of it. How proud!
How alive I suddenly felt, how relieved too! What luck! What
fantastic luck I had! Faced with this incredible revelation I suddenly
felt good and much better, tremendous in fact. I really felt great,
relaxed, secured, accepted, at home and free as I grabbed one of her
teats and reached subtly for her cunt her sophisticed ancestral cunt.
But she giggled (even blushed a bit around the eyes) as she pushed
my hands away gentle saying NONONO dearest love! We have to
hurry because she had to go and pick up Joseph [Oh yea] at the train
station and with such bad weather (it was still storming out there) it
might take a good 45 minutes to drive there. Therefore my dear wild
naked little ape hurry up! Let's take a quick bath together and get
dressed.

But what about me! What do I do? What happens to me now? I asked
anguishly.

You! I'll drop you at the train station with your duffel bag and you can
go on wherever you have to go.

[To CAMP DRUM . . .]

It's the most practical, my dear! There's nothing to do.

Just like that? And we'll never see each other again? Never!

I doubt it. But one never knows. Perhaps someday . . . by chance.

Yes . . . perhaps! In another journey. Another story. Yes! I would like that very much.

The train! I hadn't thought about that. Not a bad idea. Especially now that I'm carless. Buickless. A quick snapshot of my BUICKSPECIAL resting in the arms of that pine tree flashed through my mind and I felt a little pang of sadness.

Yes! the train. It's a good idea. Especially since I have to go to CAMP DRUM (because of my money) and CAMP DRUM mustn't be very far from here?

No. It's just about two hours from here by train. Direct in fact!

Things really work out well!

Yes, it's perfect. She says somewhat absentmindedly already thinking I suppose of Joseph's return.

Yes, but, I hesitate, the train, that's fine, but, you see, me, I'm, I'm completely broke, you understand, it's not my fault, it's because that old intellectual, yes a French-Canadian intellectual, he stole my wallet, and also a fine Cuban cigar I had brought in New York, for the trip, that was while I was driving through Massachusetts, way back, in another part of this story.

Why didn't you tell me before?

I didn't have a chance. And besides it's very long and complicated story. Do you want me to tell it to you?

Okay! If you want to but quickly while we're taking a bath.

And so while we're taking a bath and she's scrubbing my back with soap I tell her the whole sad story of my journey since I left North Carolina a good four days ago in the rain and in the snow in my old 47 Buickspecial back from beginning to end to this very moment I tell her about the chicken-shit 82nd AIRBORNE DIVISION and all the lousy hillbillies and the fat sergeant and the push ups give me 20 give me 25 give me 30 and on the double and the parachute jumps and

the butterflies in the stomach as she rubs my belly and the FAR
EAST and how I volunteered and the fucked up system and the goof
they made with my documents and my travel expenses up in the
snow of Upper New York State (near the Canadian border) and my
duffel bag and Brooklyn and my civilian stuff my jazz records my
half-dozen books my socks my shirts etc. my typewriter and my
black suitcase shoved away in a closet (nothing about Marilyn) and
my ambition my dreams my hopes my desires my departure and the
lampshade factory and Benny (but nothing about Marilyn of course)
as she shampoos my hair and that sneaky French-Canadian intellectual who read me the introduction to his doctoral dissertation right
in the middle of night as we drove through Massachusetts and how
after he left I found out he had lifted my wallet and my Cuban cigar
(that sonofabitch!) and then I plunged into the past my lousy childhood as she tickles my feet with her little bathbrush and the war the
occupation the Germans the Jews yes of course I'm Jewish do you
mind and the camps my father mother sisters uncles aunts and all the
cousins the whole family remade into lampshades exterminated
(X-X-X-X) and the farm where I worked so hard in the South of
France and the Liberation Victory V-DAY and the black market to
survive and the French ah the French with their acute sense of
patriotism LIBERTY EQUALITY FRATERNITY (Bullshit!) and
then AMERICA HERE I COME and my suitcase the black one
and loneliness homesickness starvation and the search for love and
despair and always broke and so on and so on ....

In other words I tell her the whole fucked up story of my life as she
keeps scrubbing me with her delicate hands and tears are running
down her cheeks and at the last moment just before she dries me off
with a thick towel she kneels at my feet to give me a farewell
blow-job (but this time gently kindly sadly even and with a great deal
of compassion in it because of all my sufferings) so that I won't forget
her she tells me and don't worry about the train I'll buy the ticket for
you it's the least I can do for you after all.

You couldn't do any better I was going to say [like 20 bucks or
something] but I didn't. I didn't because after all even though the
broad had screwed the hell out of me I had some decency left in me.
And besides. Besides I had slept well in her king size bed (their bed)
and even wore Joseph's lovely robe she had fixed me a delicious

breakfast. Even scrubbed me all over. A guy should be grateful for that much attention. Especially at the stage where we are for if one were to examine the situation carefully (in retrospect) it is quite obvious that at this very moment I ought to be dead. Yes frozen in the snow. A moribund lying alongside a deserted road way up in VERMONT had she not appeared in the picture to bring me back to life and thus permit me to continue my journey (by train now) and of course my story. Truly. Without her everything would have been finished. Don't you agree?

And so here we are again in her big golden IMPERIAL on our way to the train station both staring straight ahead at the road not talking to each other just staring blankly ahead beyond the road toward our future. Hers rich and happy. Mine still quite uncertain but certainly poor and doubtful.

We were both a bit sad now.

She had cleaned and mended my uniform nicely (though it was obvious that she was not very gifted for those sort of things) while I slept I suppose. Therefore I looked decent. And in fact one could say that I looked rather well. Healthy. Indeed I felt quite cheerful in spite of the brutal accident and the desperate storm I had endured during the night but through which I had survived. Nonetheless.

What time does Joesph's train get in? I finally asked just to say something.

6:15

What do we do if he sees us together?

Nothing! He won't see us because we'll arrive at the station before he does. A good twenty minutes. And your train leaves at 6:00 sharp. I called to make sure.

What a perfect hostess!

Things really work out well I said. But she was already somewhere else. In the arms of Joseph (figuratively speaking).

And at six o'clock sharp after touching but brief goodbyes there I was stretched lazily on the seat of an empty railroad car on my way to CAMP DRUM at last somewhat pooped I must confess but well fucked. Broke. Carless but nevertheless happy to be here. Happy to be back on my way. Anxious to push forward!

THE STATION

by MIRIAM LEVINE

from TO KNOW WE ARE LIVING (Decatur House Press)

nominated by Decatur House Press

In the high-ceilinged room
with the chandelier
we lay down to sleep with our father

not in the same bed
because there were no beds
and no goodnights

in fact, there were no words at all

Nothing we could bring
would be taken or eaten

we carried our hands

there were no drawers or shelves
not a ledge or a sill
or a hook or a bowl

not a chair or a table
or a sink or a toilet

Under the burning light
we lay down in our clothes
like refugees in a station

One by one we rose from sleep
and when we lifted the blue gauze
we saw the face of our father

He was smooth and calm as a baby
who would sleep the night
and would not cry or ask for anything

SONG

by JAMES SCHUYLER

from PROMISE OF LEARNINGS, INC.

nominated by John Ashbery

The light lies layered in the leaves.
Trees, and trees, more trees.
A cloud boy brings the evening paper:
The Evening Sun. It sets.
Not sharply or at once
a stately progress down the sky
(it's gilt and pink and faintly green)
above, beyond, behind the evening leaves
of trees. Traffic sounds and
bells resound in silver clangs
the hour, a tune, my friend
Pierrot. The violet hour:
the grass is violent green.
A weeping beech is gray,
a copper beech is copper red.
Tennis nets hang
unused in unused stillness.
A car starts up and
whispers into what will soon be night.
A tennis ball is served.
A horse fly vanishes.
A smoking cigarette.
A day (so many and so few)
dies down a hardened sky
and leaves are lap-held notebook leaves
discriminated barely
in light no longer layered.

The Poetry of Jack Spicer

LOWGHOST TO LOWGHOST

essay by ROSS FELD

from PARNASSUS: POETRY IN REVIEW

nominated by PARNASSUS: POETRY IN REVIEW

COME TO THE END of his first book, and there's Jack Spicer himself handing you a last message as you leave, that "It was a game made out of summer and freedom and a need for poetry that would be more than the expression of my hatreds and desires. It was a game like Yeats' spooks or Blake's sexless seraphim." And then, after one more poem's-worth of ado, you're out the door. This "game" that readers—and how many in 1957, could there have been of the small-press first edition of *After Lorca?* a hundred? two?—held in their hands consisted of 34 poems, six letters addressed to Federico Garcia Lorca beyond the grave, and a contemporary introduction by the same moldering Spaniard *in situ*. More like a joke. The poems were "translations"—the originals of some of which you could find and tag with your Lorca alongside, while others were half or more smudged away, and the rest of Lorca at all, pure Spicer. Through it all, meanwhile, back and forth, flowed tricky perfusions, flipped coins, compromised membranes: between Spanish and English, "real objects" and "the big lie of the personal," one dead poet and one live one. The letters were especially arresting, thick with the roots of a plain-spoken, strong, and cumulatively elegant aesthetic. A "game"—and here not only were the rules but also the Hall of Fame (Lorca, Yeats, Blake). Had it gone no further, had we been left only with this one strange book and not finally a total of twelve, *After Lorca* would have made for a spectacular artifact rather than an opus, a reputation. A twist of the poet's beloved lemon in our national drink—and we might have been forever intrigued but ultimately hazy about whether or not we wanted to play.

But there was an opus. Spicer's poems, in fact, got firmer, not slacker, as they went, and though wetting their lips there now and again, did not sit in precious pools or clever ones. How do we take them? We must decide.

Even in a self-conscious century, the fact of which we either embrace or avoid according to our (X-rayed) lights, no contemporary poet seems more art-occupied than Jack Spicer. Or more elusive. What he giveth in self-review he taketh away in a sort of holy thundering shyness that's more Jerome than Francis. What's more, self-consciousness leads also to sorrows, in particular loneliness— who else but me is looking?—and here also Spicer is no more fully satisfying: he's the poet's poet par excellence, no reference points except the very poem, yet he refuses to console us with homilies and buck-up, trade-union sermons. Wonderfully likable in his muscular, no-bullshit manner, and yet in a second he's gone, just as he originally intended. Is it, then, all worth it?

Yes. Spicer is something new and valuable, extremely so. He was the first poet to really *believe* the tradition that was being contemporaneously forged in American poetry in the 1950s. While others were busily crammed-mouth both with poems and announcements of the new in the making, Spicer was getting down to work, having accepted the clarion simply and at once. This is important to keep in mind. The hortatory, long-strided mode we indistinctly call the Black Mountain movement is eclipsed in subtlety by Spicer ten times over, but he is still of that widened-out mode. Clever, pithy,

brilliant, daring as he may be, Spicer was set from the start upon the
One Thing, larger-goaled even than Olson and his polis and
culture-straddling. Spicer wanted no less than to clear the totals on
poetry's machine, to introduce the proper multipliers and dividers.
Poem was all; and if so, what we made it from had to be more
perdurable, of more lasting and truer clay than we ordinarily
contributed. Spicer asked that it only be "objects," real things that
the poet, totally subordinate, could "disclose . . . to make a poem
that had no sound in it but the pointing of a finger." Ghosts, lemons,
seagulls, rocks, diamonds, baseball, God, radio, dead letters: they
are recurrently placed into the poems as *figuri*, as markers, as
shims—but above all as absolute quiddities, made realer than real
by a retrospective turn that Spicer would have both appreciated and
half as much rued. Arguing for collage in poetry, in *After Lorca*,
he says:

> But things decay, reason argues. Real things become garbage. The
> piece of lemon you shellac to the canvas begins to develop a mold, the
> newspaper tells incredibly ancient events in forgotten slang, the boy
> becomes a grandfather yes, but the garbage of the real still reaches
> out into the current world making *its* objects, in turn, visible—lemon
> calls to lemon, newspaper to newspaper, boy to boy. As things decay,
> they bring their equivalents into being.

A luminous, bracing, finally naïve incantation. The equivalents, of
course, never really do show; they knock on the door perhaps, but
when the poet comes to answer they hide, and he has to fashion
them himself in order to stand dumb at the jamb. Spicer may always
have known this—I would surely think he did—but not until the last
works did he really give up hoping that the original garbage, set into
the poem consciously, *dead-seriously*, would call up a metaphysical
rhyme: an anti-poem, the "thing language" he wanted so hugely
being neither an imagism or concretism but an anti-poetry. Spicer,
finally, is an anti-poet.

This isn't, please, fashionable, jacket-copy monickering. All devo-
tional poets are just that; their faith is in the things that are there, *out*
there; whether or not those things deign to join their words is all
accident. Spicer, by certain lamps, may look more trendily *meta-*
than *anti-*, which may explain some of whatever audience he has,
but not for long. The gradual, opus-long defeat of his own First

Principle shows us this, and conversely shores up his triumph. Accidents, Thomistic *and* highway variety, are both exciting and sad, and for a poet who embraced a Yeatsian sort of "dictation" that directed him at times to purposely misspell, duplicate poems exactly, shackle not only the literary will but also the emotive one ("you're trying to write a poem on Vietnam and you write a poem about skating in Vermont"), Spicer maintains a balance that's astoundingly sure:

> It does not have to fit together. Like the pieces of a totally unfinished jigsaw puzzle my grandmother left in the bedroom when she died in the living room. The pieces of the poetry or of this love.
>
> . . . The intention that things do not fit together. As if my grandmother had chewed on the jigsaw puzzled before she died.

Absolute, brave, alert, star of his own game. Yet in the end he must hand himself over to a tremendous irony: that a poet who tried so hard to write personality-less poems brings forth one of the language's strongest personalities. That if his poems could never quite point the finger in that "infinitely small vocabulary" he hoped they could lead the way with, he himself did. The world is, alas, perfect, and the poet moves further away from it with each effort. To read these collected books is to watch a fine poet get finer but lose every gain. But the directions remains. It is a moving, exhilarating, and expanding journey.

(Note: just to get it out of the way: A small cavil about this volume of collected books itself. It's equipped with a flagellum: half is biographical and documentary, the rest consists of a long essay entitled "The Practice of Outside" by Robin Blaser, Spicer's old, close friend and editor of this book. The essay, along its 55 pages, makes a number of cogent, illuminating points, among which are that in Spicer's work is posited an "outside" that "implies a world and a cosmology without an image. It is unknown and entering the time of language again"; and that these books assert "that it is among the powers, forces, and events of an outside that we live . . ." and not in our own poet-refineries, not as self-cherishing colanders of the real. Yet Blaser also overloads Spicer, unjustly, I fear, with large

Editors note: reference throughout is to The Collected Books of Jack Spicer, *Black Sparrow Press, 1975.*

and only approximately tailored gouts of Foucault, Heidegger, Coleridge—on the right road to begin with, he simultaneously grades and paves a whole clutch of parallel, unnecessary, and barely credible ones. The essay makes huge, Germanic claims, settles down a while and is forthright and trim, then luffs again. Published independently, say, in a book of critical studies or a magazine, an essay of this size, purpose, and feeling wouldn't bother me at all. Yet, as doubtlessly blessed, purely urged, and emotionally hard won as it may be, annealed to the completed bulk of Spicer's work, it does.

The documents, which include poems Spicer did not want included in his canon (which he dated from 1957 on) are often entertaining, fascinating, embarrassing, quenching, trivial, and as a reader of Spicer for years I found myself interested in them all. But again, not necessarily attached to the first edition of Spicer's collected works.

My point is simply this: that ignored poetry, like an ignored child, will take to its room to play hermetic and private games. Its own secrecy, self-congratulatory neatness, compensates for the attention it's not getting— and this it gives up unwillingly if at all. Most times, this works out; occulted art usually turns out to be ephemeral art. But with Spicer this isn't the case. He was an honest-to-goodness important poet, as his readers and contemporaries know, yet the volume at hand here has both a possessive and inadvertently trivializing aura to it that makes Spicer seem a package of time and place and death and effort that's totally self-contained. The editor's responsibility, here, I would think, is to allow the work its public specific gravity—which is considerable—and not wreathe it too memorially or grandly in its effluvia or in promises of artistic millenarianism. End of cavil.)

The letters in *After Lorca* (1957), the very first book, alert us uncannily to what we can expect from the next eleven; later on, there'll be no need to backtrack and beat the bushes for correlative glimmers. Spicer was set; he'd found his way. His aim was not to make beautiful *parts* of poems. If poems had to depend on the effect and not the actualities of their parts, they were better not written at all. And so, from here on, we discover poems that, faced with the assault of the personal or the affective, do away with themselves in whole or in part. These early Lorca translations and Spicer's own unmarked undifferentiated efforts are a case in point; while for the most part they're pretty good, it's the letters that haul the barge into open, fresh water:

> A poet is a time mechanic not an embalmer. The words around the immediate shrivel and decay like flesh around the body. No mummy-sheet of tradition can be used to stop the process. Objects, words must be led across time not preserved against it.

> I yell "Shit" down a cliff at an ocean. Even in my lifetime the immediacy of that word will fade. It will be as dead as "Alas." the word "Shit" will along with them, travel the time-machine until cliffs and oceans disappear . . .

> Words are what sticks to the real. We use them to push the real, to drag the real into the poem. They are what we hold on with, nothing else. They are as valuable in themselves as rope with nothing to be tied to . . .

> Things do not connect; they correspond . . .

The ideas are not mint; the devotion and purpose must perforce be. Though playing the didact, the poet isn't idly pamphleteering here, and despite the occasional humid excess, there's not the sense that the work has backed him into a corner out of which he can emerge only with the help of a bevelled aesthetic. A writer who offers so heavily camouflaged a first book simply isn't out to germinate a vast school. But nor did he think his intentions were tossed to the wind. In another letter, there's this:

> Dear Lorca,

> When you had finished a poem what did it want you to do with it? Was it happy enough merely to exist or did it demand imperiously that you share it with somebody like the beauty of a beautiful person forces him to search the world for someone that can declare that beauty? And where did your poems find people? . . .

> The quiet poems are what I worry about—the ones that must be seduced . . .

> When you are in love there is no real problem. The person you love is always interested because he knows that the poems are always about him. If only because each poem will someday be said to belong to the Miss X or Mr. Y period of the poet's life. I may not be a better poet

when I am in love, but I am a far less frustrated one. My poems have
an audience . . .

All this is to explain why I dedicate each of our poems to someone.

which is a strange mix: slightly mocking, also faintly febrile, like a
cross between Kafka's diaries and *Seventeen Magazine.* Both subtly
and guilelessly, it addresses a state of anxiety common to poets and
commonly hidden in one way or other. Spicer doesn't have an
answer, but a device. All the translations in the book, as he says, are
dedicated, which lets him, while still insisting on objects that will
excoriate "the big lie of the personal—the lie in which these objects
do not believe"—have it both ways. When personal contacts of the
poet's life intrude into the poem, they will be, he declares, "encysted" by the poet—"and the encysted emotion will itself become
an object, to be transformed at last into poetry like the waves and the
birds." Fancy footwork—but it's crucial: the tension and contradic-
tion of this very point go a long way in highlighting both Spicer's
attractiveness as a poet and also one of his major flaws. The personal
is made out to be not much better than a germ, yet its appearance is
relished for the sake of Spicer's controlling idea, which is leukocytic
and wants the workout. The poet's homosexuality is unconcealed,
and his poems have drawn a certain cultural nourishment—they
cruise, so to speak, ready to "encyst" friends, lovers, and personal
contact, at the same time chuting them into a world of objects. In all
his work, Spicer without explanation throws in names, direct addresses to lovers, an exacting, seamlessly specific "you." A later
sequence finally arrives at an utterance to limn the fact.

> One keeps unmentionable
> What one ascends to the real with
> The lie
> The cock in the other person's mouth
> The real defined out of nothing.
>
> Camp partly as the homosexuals mean it as private sorrow
> And partly as others mean it—lighting fire for food.
>
> (from *Lament for the Makers*)

but from the start it's apparent that Spicer required, to make his
poetry work, a gathering: real friends in a bar, real lovers, real gulls

on a pier or lemons on a tree. His poems are all "serial," they all are in "books" that are as insulated and close, raucous and definable as a crowd in a North Beach bar. The "I—never seen" is tacitly replaced with a "we"; the poems echo off each other, never lacking for a comforter, illuminator, extricator, foil. They speak best tribally and to the sentimentality of cognoscenti—be they homosexuals, baseballs fans, or, best of all, poets. Spicer the poet becomes a "character" who makes his point and then fades into the ensuing din.

Lorca, then, is more than a reasonable choice for Spicer to have picked as an interchangeable "pair of eyes and a lover" in his first book. Lorca, with his glossy non sequiturs, bell-jar ballads, and images lonely enough both in sense and ordinary poetic diction to hazily qualify as "objects." With one exception, a straightforward rendering of the "Ode to Walt Whitman," Spicer disdains the fabulous, the melony the plush of the Spaniard; he's used to better effect as backboard for the serious but playful letters that so fully introduce Spicer's distinctive sociability, honest, light-footedness.

The next sequence or book, *Admonitions* (1958), finds Spicer again cultivating an audience, cleaving to heroes, friends, acquaintances —each gets a poem, an "admonition." Specific personal references, hiding behind each one, are allowed their blinds and not coaxed out much. What has been faint and shy in the Lorca "translations" here is more confident; the style packs but never quite gets itself together enough to vault the so-so. And the poems suffer at the hands of lines like "People who don't like the smell of faggot vomit/ Will never understand why men don't like women" or Have guts until the guts/ Come through the margins/ Clear and pure/ Like love is"—a flip toughness that renders them precious and flyweight. But it's a start nonetheless of a bridgework, a pledge of allegiance to the serial poem, and Spicer establishing himself as the Poet, episcopal. Again there are letters (though, repeated, the device seems more mannered): "Poems should echo and reecho against each other . . . They cannot live alone any more than we can . . . This is the most important letter that you have ever received. Love, Jack." Even in these chummy and excessively clannish poems, it's this idea—that poems surround themselves not out of the orthodoxy of bulk or breadth, but much like people and animals in order to forge a reciprocity, a continuance, a humbling of the *one,* the *only*—that is forward-looking. So what looks pointless or crude to the first-time reader may often be this humility, though especially in relatively minor work like this, where the letters elevate the poet hieratically to a point where he needn't plead or demonstrate for trust but simply wills it, this is something hard to distinguish from a tight-spirited insouciance.

A Book of Music ("with words by Jack Spicer," 1958) is much better, less communally narcissistic than the "admonitions" and more direct. It is the first application of the aesthetic only through poems, and the message is there right off:

> The grand concord of what
> Does not stoop to definition

makes for the "true music." Anthologists' Spicer, every one of his constants is here either embryonically or fully birthed: Orpheus, who "points his music downward"; Eurydice, the poet's eternal noumenal quarry, who is "a frigate bird or a rock or some seaweed"; the moon; nursey rhymes. But, though striking, it's too sketchy a book. Almost in haste, the poems all take a dying fall—what the reader soon recognizes as a very Spicerian fall, an ironic thump—that here is yet to be completely convincing and seems more willy-nilly than eventual. This eagerness of their aggregate "points" makes the poems slightly too attention-directing to work effectively.

Billy the Kid (also 1958) has Spicer forsaking an investigation of the large for the small: his work will continually jump back and forth between verities we see clearly enough to either accept or try to civilize away (the world, the poem, God, language) and those that are incompletely revealed (mythology). Billy the Kid, who'd been one of those "admonished" in the earlier series, now returns to a greater range:

> Let us fake out a frontier—a poem somebody could hide in with a sheriff's posse after him—a thousand miles of it if it is necessary for him to go a thousand miles—a poem with no hard corners, no houses to get lost in, no underwebbing of customary magic . . .

and, in ten poems, Billy is dipped in and out of historical reality like a piece of incompletely developed photographic paper. Bathos melts down a large share of them, as does a soft-centered idealization à la Raymond Chandler (a problem Spicer would have up till the very last book). But here also is perhaps the best single poem he ever wrote, nestled, toward the end, between two over-ripe, hip parentheses—which makes you wonder about the soundness of the serial poem, wonder if finally it isn't *object* that devastates us with its lonely ardor and not *objects*. So I carefully peel back the rest of this book to lay open this one single poem, part IX:

> So the heart breaks
> Into small shadows
> Almost so random
> They are meaningless
> Like a diamond
>
> Has at the center of it a diamond
> Or a rock
> Rock.
> Being afraid
> Love asks its bare question—
> I can no more remember
> What brought me here
> Than bone answers bone in the arm
> Or shadow sees shadow—
> Deathward we ride in the boat
> Like someone canoeing
> In a small lake
> Where at either end
> There are nothing but pine-branches—
> Deathward we ride in the boat
> Broken-hearted or broken-bodied
> The choice is real. The diamond. I
> Ask it.

With "so" and "almost" clapping the mute on early, the poem pours, muttering, down the steps of its own stateliness, a decorum truly achieved only in the emotionally verifiable. Not only beautiful, though, it also gives an especially good look at two tendons flexing all of Spicer's work: one a persistent turn of phrase, the other, technique. "Like a diamond/ Has at the center of it a diamond/ Or a rock/ Rock" and then, five lines later, "Than bone answers bone in the arm/ Or shadow sees shadow"—we've seen the approximate locution before (the letter to Lorca: "lemon calls to lemon" etc.) and will see it again:

Promise to whatever is promised
Love to whatever is loved
Ghosts to whatever is ghosts

(*Homage to Creeley*)

The rhythm is deliberately repeated. Instead of the perfect metaphor, the thirsty image, Spicer is insisting that correspondences go beyond Baudelaire's descriptive Swedenborgianisms and lodge in the poem itself. Like Velcro, a fastening of tiny hooks and fiber eyes, the variously permuted thing-words make a matted, strong contact and are useless separated.

And, too, in the middle of the poem we get an unsheathed glance at what Spicer means by "dictation." "Being afraid/ Love asks its bare question—" and then all is broken off for the admission that

I can no more remember
What brought me here
Than bone answers bone in the arm
Or shadow sees shadow

—that knot of correspondence again, welded up in this particular poem into something like a bouquet, but also a public declaration of fealty not only to the false start, but the false middle, the false end; and then not only the false but the true as well—that that, too, may be broken in upon, that the poet's power and hold is far from absolute. As an exemplar of his whole drift and as an excellence itself, this poem is central in Spicer's work.

Fifteen False Propositions Against God (1958) leaves little doubt that what we're seeing is method, not just quirkiness. This series' first impulse is homage.

Beauty is so rare a th—
Sing a new song
Real
Music
A busted flush. A pain in the eyebrows. A
Visiting card.

The quotation is Pound, and is severed by dictation, which is God. The erasure, left rude, is gleaned from Williams*; Marianne Moore, too, puts in an appearance. It is clearly poets, then, who make the "false propositions against God," and though this series heralds that continuing Assumption, Spicer's own discretionary, non-manipulatory view of reality keeps it from going wild. Poets are always, rightly, going to get God-shivers from the proximity, but that doesn't mean there's more than one "King of the Forest." Whatever centering these poems make is individual, like the flattened bottoms of bowls, not re-alignments of the Scheme. Though not as accomplished as his later work along the vein in *Book of Magazine Verse*, they are still acute and satisfying, climbing careful sets of pitons—poets, trees, toys—to at last get close enough to make one more direct address, the ultimate and obvious one:

Dear Sir:
In these poems I tried to find the three-headed God I believed in
    sometimes both when talking to you and living with you. The abysmal
    toyshop
Intrudes.
(It is hell where no one
Guesses another. It is after
Every thing.)

Apollo Sends Seven Nursery Rhymes to James Alexander (1959), *A Red Wheelbarrow* (1959?), and *Lament for the Makers* (1961) seem more like run-throughs for later books than fully shaped achievements in themselves, though *A Red Wheelbarrow* experiments with a stark, daubed quality to the serialism that Spicer, perhaps unsatisfied, never used again. The seven "nursery rhymes" focus on Orpheus, warm him up, but are too occasional and ever so slightly swaggering. Aware, as he must have been, that he was writing at that moment like no one else, Spicer seems in these sequences to be skimming, less a pilgrim than a *flaneur*, holding off real advance.

That would arrive soon, and impressively. *The Heads of the Town Up to the Aether*, dated 1960–61, borrows its title from a Gnostic text, and Robin Blaser, in his afterword, tells us that Spicer thought of this triune work in terms of the classical division: Hell, Purga-

---

*The trees from "By the road to the contagious hospital" in *Spring and All;* and a nearly direct quotation from "The Last Words of My English Grandmother."

tory, Paradise—but this, like the title, is concealed and crepuscular, the erudition isn't plaited before our eyes. I can think of no book of American poetry quite like this one. It's Spicer's best work, I'd say, the most rigorous, most dilating, undeterred by any thought of the reader's meekness and caution. Its self-attention is so manifest and unflagging that the superficial sour tastes—the weak jokes, camp silliness, overly with-it lordliness—lie close to the surface, covered only by daring. Yet what he began with, that scorn of the "big lie of the personal" has by this time been thaumaturged and become sublimely beside the point. If there's any triunity about this book, it is in the stripped-downed annexing of poetry, poetry, and poetry—divined, discovered, and defined—and nothing else.

Homage to Creeley, the first part, surprises us with very short poems plus what Spicer dubs "explanations": lanky paragraphs that appear, after a good number of blank beats farther down the page, under a solid black line. It's to Creeley, at first glance, because of the poems' laconism; and then, as they progress and their figures materialize (scraped, most of them, from Cocteau's play/ film *Orphée:* poets, cars, messages, ghosts), perhaps also in recognition of an extraordinary reading of Creeley's early "I Know A Man" ("drive, he sd . . .")' a tooling on down to Hell. Now elusive and child-like, now pithy or spooky, the poems have a stunning adhesiveness which mortises them to their "explanation" without a wobble. Those "explanations" are of course the re-appearing correspondences—once again supplied by Spicer—and they work in turn to repurify the poems. Magically neither part is dislodged, even when silly to poignant or incantatory to wry. Maybe it's the tension of the last resort. Anyway, here are three, complete, to suggest the flavor:

> Strange, I had words for dinner
> Strange, I had words for dinner
> Stranger, strange, do you believe me?

> Honestly, I had your heart for supper
> Honesty has had your heart for supper
> Honesty honestly are your pain.

> I burned the bones of it
> And the letters of it
> And the numbers of it
> That go 1,2,3,4,5,6,7
> And so far.

Stranger, I had bones for dinner
Stanger, I had bones for dinner
Stranger, stranger, strange, did you believe me?

Orpheus was never really threatened by the Underworld during his visits there. In this poem they present him with a diplomatic note.

Honesty does not occur again in the poem.

The numbers do.

("Magic)

What is a half-truth the lobster declared
You have sugared my groin and have sugared my hair
What correspondence except my despair?
What is my crime but my youth?

Truth is a map of it, oily eyes said
Half-truth is half of a map instead
Which you will squint at until you are dead
Putting to sea with the truth.

This is a poem to prevent idealism—i.e. the study of images. It did not succeed.

Edward Lear was allowed to say this some time ago in his books for children. Actually The Poet thought of himself as "oily eyes." That is why The Poem could never prevent idealism (Idealism).

Orpheus and Eurydice are in their last nuptial embrace during this poem.

("The Territory Is Not The Map")

Dante would have blamed Beatrice
If she turned up alive in a local bordello
Or Newton gravity
If apples fell upward
What I mean is words
Turn mysteriously against those who use them
Hello says the apple
both of us were object.

> There is a universal here that is dimly recognized. I mean every-
> body says some kinds of love are horseshit. Or invents a Beatrice to
> prove that they are.
>
> What Beatrice did did not become her own business. Dante saw to
> that. Sawed away the last plank anyone he loved could stand on.
>
> ("Sheep Trails Are Fateful To Strangers")

Letters once were buttresses; here, as "explanations," they have
been integrally yoked to the poetic—a change. The prose paragraphs beneath are not only a wizardly half-light image of the Hell
motif ("Hell is where we place ourselves when we wish to look
upward"), but also a running meditation on the very reality of the
consciously recalcitrant poems. They are their ghosts, and own a
second, eerie sight; sometimes trivial, always compensatory for
corners and impossible fits. When the poems act up anticly, changed
dictationally in composition, the ghost-answers are cool and unflus-
tered; when the poems speak in the terrifyingly final rhythms of
children's verse (and a pleasure it is to watch Spicer's brilliant
perception of the nursery rhyme, that most supremely closed of all
poetic forms, used as a wedge to open up his own), the "explanations" aerate them. What comes through so strongly here is a sense
of the poet having calibrated his entire intellectual and sensible
voice; then coming away so gracefully with its pattern. Assurance, a
poet's most deadly affliction, is Spicer's pair of shears—with it he
snips, pins, trims, refuses to make the poem a cenotaph. Preferring
balsa to granite, he puts together mock-ups, and mock-ups are
investigatory. Is this what a poem is? Statements made? Questions?
Or perhaps questions-that are answers-that are questions again?
Where should the poet step in? Assuming the ghost persona, Spicer
might brazen out "Not anywhere," yet his written answer is
more like: In the flow, helpless, the poet as turnstile, listening for
echoes. Spicer has finally succeeded here in making his poetic a
poetry.

Then, hewing to the conventional profile, there's the sort of slump
even Dante experienced when the mid-ground, invisible matrix,
Purgatory, is reached. *A Fake Novel About the Life of Arthur
Rimbaud*, the second stage of the book, is as advertised: a faked

novel, cartoony and self-indulgent, a bar entertainment drawn out to nineteen pages. But the reader would be mistaken to ignore it. Interwoven through the campy prose are again the ghosts: Jim ("A private image. A poet demanding privacy in his poem is like a river and a bank unable to move against each other."), Rimbaud, the Poet. Spicer no longer is transferring himself, as he did into Lorca: the dead are conceded their distance. And Rimbaud is specially apt here. History hasn't offered a poet so disposable, a clearer or more brilliant example of start and stop. But built around him, this becomes an edgy book, uneasy; the style, modulating between the hard rustlings of *Homage to Creeley* and the concluding clipped prose of *Textbook of Poetry*, flickers, often wise-guyishly burning itself out. A chapter entitled "The Dead Letter Office," begins:

> If President Buchanan sent a letter to Cordell Hull (also dead) it would remain there. No thanks to the spirit of things. A dead letter is exactly as if someone received it.

The poem is a dead letter. What does that make the poet? Rimbaud.

> No way to turn except upward. Rimbaud will turn sixteen, invent what my shrewdness (our shrewdnesses) will not remember, come to a more usable concept of sex and poetry—a machine to catch ghosts . . .
>
> . . . Ghosts are not shrewd people. History begins with shrewd people and ends with ghosts.

Spicer is placed in a funny position: he wants to make the poet both something and nothing, Rimbaud, for all the talk of ghosts, assumes the mantle of Logos himself, as all poets will—and is absurdly successful at it. Describing metaphor as "something unexplained— like a place in a map that says that after this is desert. A shorthand to admit the unknown," is also to describe the poet-stenographer "playing leapfrog with the unknown." He can't quite square the poet being less and more. So Rimbaud may be the "dead-letter officer": meaningless, but he's also the "snark-hunter" and "whoever shares in the chase deserves the prize." Spicer, who always needs an ascendance, can't manage one here. Ground like this is too chronically shaky to build a hero on, and so this is a confused book. Earlier, in *Homage to Creely*, Spicer has admitted:

How can you love that mortal creature
Everytime he speaks
He makes
Mistakes

yet here he ends, sentimentally, with Rimbaud as "A cry in the
night. An offer. What the words choose to say. An offer of something. A peace."

Once the hero is let go, however, Spicer regains full confidence
and is less bewitched. *Textbook of Poetry*, the final section, begins
aggressively, brickishly prosed.

> Surrealism is the business of poets who cannot benefit by surrealism.
> It was the first appearance of the Logos that said, "The public be
> damned," by which he did not mean that they did not matter or he
> wanted to be crucified by them, but that really he did not have a word
> to say to them. This was surrealism.

Spicer's at top form when not mediate, when he's trailing
Eurydice in the opening section, and in this last one, when his eyes
are upward. "Metaphors are not for humans," he says, solving
Rimbaud. The poet is here always in small "p"; God replaces him as
the proper repository for the capital.

> "Esstoneish me," the words say that hide behind my alarm clock or
> my dresser drawer or my pillow. "Etonnez moi," even the Word says.
>
> It is up to us to astonish them and Him. To draw forth answers deep
> from the caverns of objects or from the Word Himself. Whatever that
> is.
>
> Whatever That is is not a play on words but a play between words,
> meaning come down to hang on a little cross for a while. In play.
>
> And the stony words that are left down with us great him mutely
> almost rudely casting their own shadows. For example, the shadow
> the cross cast.
>
> No, now he is the Lowghost when He is pinned down to words.

The book's theology is semi-Augustinian, positing a "city of chitter-
ing human beings." And Melvillean, reminiscent of Father Map-
ple's sermon in the Whaleman's Chapel:

We are all alone and we do not need poetry to tell us how alone we are. Time's winged chariot is as near as the next landmark or bus-station. We need a lamp (a lump, spoken or unspoken) that is even above love.

St. Elmo's Fire was what was above the ships as they sailed the unspoken seas. It was a fire that was neither a glow or a direction. But the business of it was fire.

Excepting perhaps the last poems (which, with its concept of "above love," it prefigures), this is Spicer's most moving work, going the route, like all the truest religious art, into elegy, acceptance, loss. The "textbook" is but one more counterfeit—the Lorca "letters," the haunted "explanations" of *Homage to Creeley*, the "faked novel" about Rimbaud—but here the second pressing is most clearly born of necessity. To "explain" that

It is fake. The real poetry is beyond us, beyond them, breaking like glue.

After this book, Spicer did not again use prose, as if satisfied that it had laid a strong enough foundation for his kind of poem, the one that's come to a profound peace with being "the noises alive people wear" and nothing more. Not many other books come to mind that are so liberating, that in early or mid-career send a poet onward so fortified. The reader who attends this daring and disturbing and least loveable of American masterpieces will come away from it tested and changed.

In his next book, Spicer returned to heroes. Categorically. "Magic," he mentioned in the *Textbook*, is "trying to hold onto people with your own hands"—what but the heroical would play more perfect position? Yet *The Holy Grail* (1962), consisting of seven sections, the Books of Gawain, Percival, Lancelot, Gwenivere, Merlin, Galahad, and the Death of Arthur, is a major disappointment. If Rimbaud's been cut out from underneath him, why this scrabbling for lesser, more secular adepts? That singlemindedness, the Logos/ poetry he previously fixed as the "circumference of a circle that has no point but the boundary of your desire" sneaks out for long stretches, replaced often by facile stylistic antinomies:

He has all the sense of fun of an orange, Gawain once explained to a
trusted friend.
His sense of honor is too much barely to carry his body
The horse he rides on (Dada) will never go anywhere.

The almost novelistic leisure that's permitted by having each character in his own book give the whole thing a malleability which offers
up a few good love poems, Christ poems, but in all it's too much the
private text, latter-day myth-construct sharing the fate of most such
projects. As if in dictational harmony, a secret, autochthonous accord, Spicer breaks the entire book off like this:

Something in God-language.
In spite of all this horseshit, this uncomfortable music.

Of all the books, it is perhaps *Language* (1964) that has received
the widest recognition. A linguist by training (the cover of the
orignial White Rabbit Press edition pictures a dim xerox of the
cover/contents page of the Linguistic Society of America's journal,
Language, circa 1952; and article by John L. Spicer with David W.
Reed entitled "Correlation methods of comparing ideolects in a
transition area" is the fifth contribution listed), Spicer came to the
focus with lumbering ease, the abdicated, passed-beyond expert.
Which may possibly account for the book's more than usual acceptance: poets often exhibit a continuing, tinkerer's fascination with
formal linguistics; and Spicer, lopping off technical corners as he
goes in order to make the thing fly, was articulating—most of the
time brilliantly—a well-historied grounding for poetry that no other
1965 ideology (or ideolect) was providing. Poetry, said Williams,
was "a small (or large) machine made out of words," and this book is a
Spicerian assent, parsed down to the cogs. In sections titled Transformations, Morphemics, Phonemics, and Graphemics, each
building-block is subjected to manifold tossings before being dropped into the poem's capacious bag. Even the section of love poems
concern themselves with said-love, quoted-love, the nub of expression (and one, beginning with a line of computerese, "Sable arrested
a fine comb . . . ," is really something). *Transformations*, for instance, presents an entire semiotic, the change from singular to
plural: it's made historical ("Troy was a baby when Greek sentence

structure emerged. This/was the real Trojan horse.") and then into a
harrowed nursery rhyme:

> This is the crab-god shiny and bright
> who sunned by day and wrote by night
> And lived in the house that Jack built.
> This is the end of it, very dear friend, this
> in the end of us.

Morphemics is no less cool and assured:

> Moon,
> cantilever of sylabbles
> If it were spelled "mune" it would not cause madness.
>
> the moon stays there
> And its there is our where

Phonemics plays with the telephone and Charlie Parker,
Graphemics writes of the scratches on iced-over Walden Pond, of
the ghostwriting of flames, sundials, postage stamps. The point the
book ends with has already been well taken.

> Love is not mocked whatever use you put to it. Words are also
> not mocked.
> The soup of real turtles flows through our veins. Being a [poet]
> a disyllable in a world of monosyllables. Awakened by the
> distance between the [o] and the [e]

Still, that pervasive consciousness of "a disyllable in a world of
monosyllables" mars the book. In the first part especially, which
contains some of Spicer's most sentimental work, there is poetry
speaking only to intiates, self-validating, congratulatory, insular.

> The trouble with comparing a poet with a radio is that radios don't
> develop scar-tissue.
>
> The poet is a radio. The poet is a liar. The poet is a
> counterpunching radio.
> And those messages (God would not damn them) do not even
> know they are champions.

The book begins with, and later repeats: "No one listens to poetry,"
which is true enough, of course—

                    The ocean
    Does not mean to be listened to. A drop
    Or crash of water. It means
    Nothing.
    It
    Is bread and butter

—and consistent with the thrust of the anti-poetry. But to equate
that with "no one"—clearly people, who are really the least of
it—and to grumble about scar-tissue strikes me as a step backward,
even though the impulse—Spicer's lack of recognition of much
understanding of what he was up to—is humanly cogent. Yet the
spleen and sorrow unmoors him. He comes to resolutions of problems he's always had ("Heros eat soup like anyone else. Sometimes
the kitchen is so far/ away/ That there is no soup. No kitchen. And
open space of ground/ recovered by/ The sky.") and then floats away
into marginalia such as baseball predictions, newspaper headlines,
his astrological sign. Which in turn is given the heel:

    We give equal
    Space to everything in our lives. Eich-
    Mann proved that false in killing like you raise wildflowers.

But the slight overtones, resistant and hectoring, nudge lines likes
these and poems like it distressingly into file with the same magus-
school wisdom-poetry Spicer in this very book takes off on: "'If you
don't believe in a god, don't quote him,' Valery once/ said when he
was about ready to give up poetry. The/ purposefull suspension of
disbelief has about the chance of/ a snowball in hell" and "Such/
Tired wisdoms as the game-hunters develop/ Shooting Zeus, Alpha
Centauri, wolf with the same toy gun." Spicer here has a toy gun of
his own—Kennedy's assassination, a hero's snuffing, directly referred to a few times—and, with it in hand, he seems both pusillanim-
ous and cocky, the same "snark-hunter" persona he developed for
Rimbaud taken totally to heart. Not only does he appear to be
writing with it all *behind* him—the thingness of the poem as pun to
the opaque thingness of things, the poet as "Lowghost"—getting

out to flower a hieratic bloom, a rose of manifesto, of prophetism
among poets; but one also suspects here that the serial poem has
failed, that its parameters are abused in weariness, that Spicer
cleaves to it out of loyalty and nothing else. The "idea" of the book
constricts more than frees. The "big lie of the personal" is flogged
weakly by weary reportage, some of the poems play to the grand-
stand, there's a nervousness, stuffiness, and brilliance that never
melds.

But *Book of Magazine Verse* (published, next, in 1966) recoups. It
is a posthumous volume, Spicer exiting in glory. In seven sequences
of extraordinary poems, the social edginess has become an almost
fearsome clarity. Real objects, the lemon of lemonness he began
with, have turned, in these last powerful words, into skin: all and
only what we can see—

> It's the shape of the lemon, I guess that causes trouble. It's
> ovalness, it's rind. This is where my love, somehow, stops.

The garbage Spicer proposed be set into the poem minus all per-
sonalization ("As things decay they bring their equivalents into
being") hasn't obliged. Strong hides have resisted the pinnings. It
was no more than the sentimentality that bruised the earlier poems
to think they could be, no more than a terrified dream:

> I saw the ghost of myself and the ghost of yourself dancing
>   without music.
> With
> Out
> Skin.
> A good dream. The
> Moment's rest.

The ghosts, played so dextrously so long, are, in this ultimate
shadow, "so far away." There was more to it than just the pointing of
a finger, or a radio message. That hopeful light in which lemon
would answer lemon has become a "darkness," one more covering to
break:

>   you need a clock that tells good time.
>   Something in the morning to hold on to
> As one gets craftier in poetry one sees the obvious messages
>   (cocks for clocks) but one forgets the love that gave them
> Time.

The love is patently Christian, though undeclared. Desperate and futile love—a crowning correspondence to the poem's. In this last book, Spicer has become as careful with the two as a man transporting beakers of acid. The erotic poems here are his best: hard, smooth, ungassy, the loved ones honored by not simultaneously being made objects—that's *a priori*. Spicer instead is very touching and valedictory:

> Our hearts, hanging below like balls, as they brush each other
>   in our separate journeys
> Protest for a moment the idiocy of age and direction.
> You are going south looking for a drinking fountain
> I am going north looking for the source of the chill in my bones.

These seven series of massively intelligent poems were ideally "for" different magazines; only one was submitted—those slated for *The Nation*—and it was rejected. In a realm of earnestness we could only wish that *The St. Louis Sporting News* had published theirs, or *Downbeat* theirs. But the realm of earnestness isn't Spicer's; this last counterfeit is sad and mightly proof of that. Sad, since the poem Spicer all his short life wished for, the one with the infinitely small vocabulary, like a boxscore, was still poignantly his dream, though failed. Mighty because the last irony is on us, the readers of his poetry, the ones who *did* listen to it: the magazines were our correspondences, and all were broken by his not submitting the poems.

Three of the series stand out. "Four Poems for Ramparts" (which, recall, took its first breath as a baby of the Catholic left in San Francisco) is Spicer's most cleanly vectored religious work, a terse re-writing of the *Textbook* for singed-soled quartet.

> "The shadows of love are not the shadows of God."
> This is the second heresy created by the first Piltdown man in
>   Plato's cave. Either
> The fire casts a shadow or it doesn't.
> Red balloons, orange balloons, purple balloons all cast off
>   together into a raining sky.
> The sky where men weep for men. And above the sky a moon
>   or an astronaut smiles on television. Love

For God or man transformed to distance.
This is the third heresy. Dante
Was the first writer of science-fiction. Beatrice
Shimmering in infinite space.

That distance is become abominable. The poems are more artless
than we're used to. "Get those words out of your mouth and into
your heart. If there isn't/ A God don't believe in him." Anti-poetry.
Humility upped a power.
The "Four Poems for The St. Louis Sporting News" are not only
classic American baseball art, but carry forward the other poems'
voices. In a poem about pitchers (who are "obviously not human"),
once more it is only love, the gesture, the delivered pitch, which,
successful or no, is unassailable.

the batter either strikes out or he doen't. You either
catch it or you don't. You had called for an inside fast ball.
The runners on base either advance or they don't
In any case
The ghosts of the dead people find it mighty amusing.

Emotion
Being communicated
Stops
Even when the game isn't over.

The world wins while we continue to apply love and mistake,
mistake and love. There's one final admonition, repeated in these
exfoliate, cranky poems: here it's for a rookie "sell-out" either in
baseball "or the name game":

"Learn
How to shoot fish in a barrell," someone said,
"People are starving."

After all the unashamed, consistent poetry talk, we're not unprepared for those first two lines, but the last one rocks us a little. The
bravado is gone.

God is a big white baseball that has nothing to do but go in a
curve or a straight line. I studied geometry in highschool
and know that this is true.

> I often thought of praying to him but could not stand the
>   thought of that big, white, round, omnipotent bastard.
> Yet he's there. As the game follows rules he makes them.
>
> I know
> I was not the only one who felt these things.

A whisper remains.

The last ten poems were meant for *Downbeat*, the jazz magazine. Singing over the chords of his life-long interest in folksongs (James Herndon in the biographical errata in this volume, recounts how Spicer hosted an FM radio progam in 1949 that he called "The Most Educational Folk-Song Program West of the Pecos," and on which he encouraged friends of his to sing his or their own "American" twentieth-century versions of old songs: "Skip, Skip you son of a bitch! instead of the usual refrain for Skip to My Lou."), the poems have wonderful things to say about California and our romantic sixties fetishism for guerillas. But more than anything they are about Spicer himself, much as the final *Cantos* are a totting-up of Pound:

> The poem begins to mirror itself.
>   The identity of the poet gets more obvious.
> Why can't we sing songs like nightingales? Because we're not
>   nightingales and can never become them. The poet has an
>   arid patch of his reality and the others.
> Things desert him. I thought of you as a butterfly tonight with
>   clipped wings.

The towel seems thrown in, thrown to those who from beginning to end have been closest at hand: other poets. In the very final poem, it's Allen Ginsberg who's addressed:

> At least we both know how shitty the world is. You wearing a
>   beard as a mask to disguise it. I wearing my tired smile. I
>   don't see how you do it. One hundred thousand university
>   students marching with you. Toward
> A necessity which is not love but is a name.
> King of the May. A title not chosen for dancing. The police
> Civil but obstinate. If they'd attacked
> The kind of love (not sex but love), you gave the one hundred
>   thousand students I'd have been very glad. And loved the
>   policemen. Why

Fight the combine of your heart and my heart or anybody's
   heart. People are starving.

The tone tells all. It didn't work, the collage didn't stick, things
remained stubbornly, goldenly discrete, and there was an absence
of answers. The moon, at the end of his life, comes to Spicer not
directed to by the poem but on televison, watching the astronauts:

    I can't stand to see them shimmering in the impossible music of
       the Star Spangled Banner. No
    One accepts this system better than poets. Their hurts healed
       for a few dollars.
    Hunt.
    The right animals. I can't. The poetry
    Of the absurd comes through San Francisco television. Directly
       connected with moon rockets.
    If this is dictation, it is driving
    Me wild.

The *there*, "shimmering," stays our *where*. It is time to also accord
Jack Spicer, dead eleven years, that distinction.

□   □

🔥 🔥 🔥

OLYMPIAN PROGRESS

by RICHARD KOSTELANETZ

from NUMBERS: POEMS AND STORIES (Assembling Press)

nominated by Assembling Press

10.8	15.1	21.7	42.4	48.2	55.1	1:51.9	3:16.6	3:35.8	14:36.6	30:20.8
10.8	14.8	22.0	42.2	49.6	54.0	1:53.4	3:22.2	4:01.8	14:55.6	31:45.8
10.6	15.0	21.6	41.0	47.6	52.6	1:52.4	3:16.0	3:53.6	14:31.2	30:23.2
10.8	14.8	21.8	41.0	47.8	53.4	1:51.8	3:14.2	3:53.2	14:38.0	30:18.8
10.3	14.6	21.2	40.0	46.2	51.8	1:49.8	3:08.2	3:51.2	14:30.0	30:11.4
10.3	14.2	20.7	40.0	46.5	52.4	1:52.9	3:09.0	3:47.8	14:22.2	30:15.4
10.3	13.9	21.1	40.3	46.2	51.1	1:49.2	3:10.4	3:49.8	14:17.6	29:59.6
10.4	13.7	20.7	40.1	45.9	50.8	1:49.2	3:03.9	3:45.2	14:06.6	29:17.0
10.5	13.5	20.6	39.0	46.7	49.3	1:47.7	3:04.8	3:41.2	13:39.6	28:45.6
10.2	13.8	20.5	39.5	44.9	49.6	1:45.1	3:02.2	3:35.6	13:43.4	28:32.2
10.0	13.6	20.3	39.0	45.1	49.6	1:45.1	3:00.7	3:38.1	13:48.8	28:24.4
9.9	13.3	19.8	38.2	43.8	48.1	1:44.3	2:56.1	3:34.9	14:05.0	29:27.4
10.1	13.2	20.0	38.2	44.7	47.9	1:45.9	2:59.8	3:36.3	13:26.4	27:38.4

2:36:54.8	6'4	12'11	24'11	48'5	50'4	145'1	179'7	198'11	6,162
2:32:35.8	6'4	12'6	23'6	47'7	48'7	146'7	173'6	215'10	5.970
2:41:22.6	6'6	12'11	24'5	50'11	48'3	151'5	174'10	206'7	6,668
2:32:57.0	6'4	13'9	25'5	49'11	52'1	155'3	168'8	218'6	6,770
2:31:36.0	6'6	14'2	25'1	51'7	52'7	162'5	176'11	238'7	6,896
2:29:19.2	6'8	14'3	26'5	52'6	53'2	165'8	185'4	235'8	7,421
2:34:51.6	6'6	14'1	25'8	50'7	56'2	173'2	183'11	228'11	6,326
2:23:03.2	6'8	14'11	24'10	53'3	57'2	180'7	197'11	242'1	7,731
2:25:00.6	6'11	14'11	25'8	53'8	60'11	184'11	207'4	281'2	7,708
2:15:16.2	7'1	15'5	26'8	55'2	64'7	194'2	220'2	277'8	8,001
2:12:11.2	7'2	16'9	26'6	55'3	66'8	200'2	228'10	271'2	7,887
2:20:26.2	7'4	17'8	29'3	57'1	67'5	212'7	240'8	295'7	8,193
2:12:19.8	7'4	18'1	27'1	56'11	69'6	211'3	248'8	296'10	8,454

A WOMAN WAKING

by PHILIP LEVINE

from POETRY

nominated by Michael Hogan

She wakens early remembering
her father rising in the dark
lighting the stove with a match
scraped on the floor. Then measuring
water for coffee, and later the smell
coming through. She would hear
him drying spoons, dropping
them one by one in the drawer.
Then he was on the stairs
going for the milk. So soon
he would be at her door
to wake her gently, he thought,
with a hand at her nape, shaking
to and fro, smelling of gasoline
and whispering. Then he left.
Now she shakes her head, shakes
him away and will not rise.
There is fog at the window
and thickening the high branches
of the sycamores. She thinks
of her own kitchen, the dishwasher
yawning open, the dripping carton
left on the counter. Her boys
have gone off steaming like sheep.
Were they here last night?
Where do they live? she wonders,
with whom? Are they home?
In her yard the young plum tree,

barely taller than she, drops
its first yellow leaf. She listens
and hears nothing. If she rose
and walked barefoot on the wood floor
no one would come to lead her
back to bed or give her
a glass of water. If she
boiled an egg it would darken
before her eyes. The sky tires
and turns away without a word.
The pillow beside hers is cold,
the old odour of soap is there.
Her hands are cold. What time is it?

♨ ♨ ♨

THE JUGGLER

by SIV CEDERING FOX

from KAYAK and THE JUGGLER (Sagarin Press)

nominated by KAYAK

I HAD PRACTICED FOR YEARS . Whenever I had a chance, I juggled with oranges, plates, pine cones, pennies. My uncle encouraged me, though my mother said: The boy should do something better. He should read. He should learn to make a living. She said: If your father was alive, he would show you. But I didn't stop. How could I stop? There was always some space above my hands calling me. Behind a tree, behind a tent, behind a truck, on the other side of the field, there was always this space where I could be God throwing the planets, or the wind commanding the leaves.

On the night of the first kiss, the air touched my hands in some new way. I juggled soft skin, Lena's lips, not quite open, her lapel, my own chin, the two pimples by my ear. My hands were clumsy. I almost dropped something, but caught it, just in time. I juggled NO, Well, Maybe, Yes. The director saw me. The boy is not so bad, he said. Give him some time in the third ring. I juggled lights. I juggled time. I juggled sound.

On the night I first entered a woman, the lights danced out of my hands. I juggled hair and lips and breasts and vulvas. I juggled small wet spaces that could suck me into some sweet oblivion I mastered. I juggled a soft curtain, a blood stain, my own large penis swelling. The music lifted me. I juggled applause and more applause. I juggled a soft voice calling me.

On the night my son was born, there was nothing to throw. My hands were empty, waiting. There was a strange fear inside me. The music was building, the lights were on me, but nothing happened. Until out of all that waiting, something came. I could reach my hand up into that waiting space, and suddenly, in my hand, there was a small shape, settling to the shape of my hand. My hand fell, rose, lifted high, fell again, and all things in the world were attached to my hand, rising, falling, holding, protecting.

On the night the girl died, my hands were some independent objects moving without me. A broken leg, a cut thigh, some blood stained clothing, a sequined ribbon, all tore out of my hands, pulling at the skin, exposing the bone, catapulting with a small scream out of my hands, to fall back to the space of my palms with a moan. The lights were on me, but I didn't juggle them, they juggled me. In the dark space of the tent, I bounced up and down, while the music of my own voice came from some strange distance, a slow heartbeat of sound repeating. No. No. No. No.

♨ ♨ ♨

THE LAST ROMANTIC

fiction by GERALD LOCKLIN

from THE CHASE (Duck Down Press)

nominated by Michael Hogan

the gymnasium was empty, all the chromed, expensive barbells neatly stacked along the wall, except for one man working on the bench press in the center of the room.

"hi," he said, as i approached, "you like to jump in for a set?"
"oh no," i said.
"i almost got 370 today."
"that's very good," i said.

his back and shoulders sloped severely and his head was almost bald. still he was obviously powerful, especially through the arms and chest.

"i've only got six weeks," he said.

"six weeks?"

"to make four hundred."

"why do you have to make four hundred in six weeks?"

"because in six weeks i'll be forty."

"oh," i said.

"i promised myself about two years ago that i would bench four hundred pounds by the time that i was forty."

"well," i said, "i hope you make it. i really do."

"i think i will."

"you work out often?"

"all the time. you might say that i live here now."

"no wife and kids?"

"oh yes," he said. "i haven't seen them in a year though. i finally saw that i would never make four hundred if i didn't give it all of my attention."

"how about," i said, "once you've reached your goal. you think you'll go on home then?"

"well," he said, "that's what i used to think. but now i'm not so sure i shouldn't try to get up to five hundred by the time i'm fifty."

"but look," i said, "five hundred won't be any kind of record. i mean, you won't be able to win any tournaments or anything."

"oh sure, i know," he said.

"you don't think maybe you could live at home and work out just enough to move up gradually . . . hold the line at least."

"at my age? no, young man, at my age there's no holding the line. you either go ahead or else you start the falling back. once the falling back starts, well . . ."

"good luck to you, old man, I said.

"you sure you wouldn't like to jump in for a set or two?"

BARRETT & BROWNING

by THOMAS LUX

from FIELD

nominated by Lynne Spaulding

Mr. Browning helped but I think poetry
and hatred
for her father made Miss Barrett decide
to live. I think

I believe this dire couple.
And for once I believe
scholars: *they loved each other.*

Elizabeth, of course, was smarter.
Robert, in the beginning, more ardent.
He was positive

and if his main inventions
were in a field
other than verse
he would have invented the wheelchair

and pushed her
relentlessly south and warmer.
I'm sure this was one reason why
she got up and walked alone. . . .

Love helped, thougn, and they did
love each other—bearing
one healthy but dull child
and many healthy poems,
which was probably not enough. . . .

𝄞 𝄞 𝄞

MINUTE STORIES

fiction by IAN MACMILLAN, DAVID OHLE, and
STEVE SCHUTZMAN

from TRIQUARTERLY

nominated by TRIQUARTERLY, *Clarence Major, and Mary MacArthur*

* * *

MESSINGHAUSEN, 1945—
THE UNKNOWN SOLDIER PASSES
by Ian MacMillan

Irmhild Stauffer walks down the dusty Messinghausen street lugging in her right hand the heavy container of milk, seeing by her shadow that her body is offset by its weight, and it seems to her that she has passed the entire war listening to her own footfalls. Only once did she see troops passing. And to where? She could not remember the direction. Brilon, to the north, where nothing of any value could be contested? Niedermarsburg to the south, where nothing of any value existed either? So went the first war too. Her husband, children, all had gone off, the men to die in both wars, and her daughter doubtless to a more sinful end in Duisburg.

She walks against the direction of the current of the stream which runs along the rail tracks, through the gorge from Brilon. She sees the little crowd coming in her direction, pointing down at the water, the men talking, the women covering their faces and retreating to the other side of the road. Some object in the water draws them along, makes the crowd increase in size as it approaches her. Old Mueller, who forty years ago was almost her lover, maintains his stern gait in the effort of walking so fast, and gestures at the sky with his cane.

She puts the can down. The object, she sees now, is an arm, with a military sleeve tightly containing it, with a bloated hand traveling always palm up, whirling slowly in the gentle eddies like a small ship in a sea storm. She stands still and lets the crowd pass, streaming by her. Mueller's cane brushes against her skirt. They continue on, discussing the bloated arm as it goes on its southward journey. She picks up the can and continues toward her house. When she reaches it, aching from the effort, she stands on the porch and watches the crowd, which is nearly twice the size of the one which briefly engulfed her a minute ago. It follows the arm out the other end of town. She leaves the milk on the porch and goes into the house to look one by one, and with close attention, at the many photographs of her husband and sons.

—nominated by TriQuarterly

* * *

THE BOY SCOUT
by David Ohle

The boy scout guides his wooden pedal car up the dirt road and parks it, in the shade of my turkey oak, without ceremony. The little car has tin-can headlights and a false grille. He approaches the steps and begins to climb, a box of rice cookies under one of his frail arms. It is a mystery how he crossed the bottoms in this handmade vehicle, how he avoided sinking in the soft mud ruts and being stung by the wasps in the sumac along the ditchbank. Twice the boy scout drops the box of cookies, backsteps to the ground, recovers it, and climbs up again. He knocks gently, the sound is as though his knuckles are made of hard rubber. I open the door and allow him in. He sits on the sofa with yellow eyes and looks at my feet and says nothing. I offer him a bowl of soy soup, which he declines, casting his glances on the floor. His face is ageless and simple, with precocious whiskers on the jaw. I build an oak fire in the woodstove and he warms his hands against the evening chill setting in. In the firelight I first become aware of the suggestion of a seam running down the front of him, over the nose from the khaki tip of the hat, across the lips and chin, into the neckerchief. He seems in the odd light to have been stitched together out of two unmatched bolts of cloth. His eyes are like coat buttons, the fists like ripe tomatoes. He smells of sodden laundry. Crickets bump against the tower window screens. The stink of pinesap and legustrum. The clack of crows in the sky. I take a cold chicken wing from the refrigerator and offer it to him. His head pivots, the lips emerge tubelike from the face. He says no. At least he has finally spoken. We don't want to sit here too long on the brink of conversation, like war figures behind plexiglas. Coffee? Does he want coffee? Cola? I move around the living room mechancially, under an odd influence from this boy scout, as though he were a planet and I his satellite, he earth and I moon. Threads of black yarn drape his forehead under the scout hat, a mockery of hair. He has a sewn-on eyebrow above one eye and nothing above the other one, and a faded disk of scar on the chin. I talk about the weather and he listens without comment. I ask him about a point of scout lore, and although his mouth opens and the dry tongue quivers, he says nothing. When he moves, which he seldom does, there is faintly audible rasp, as though his joints are dry of lubricant. I ask him if I might sample one of his cookies. He indicates no. I have to buy or not buy without tasting. I give him the required amount in National coupons. I eat one of the cookies, which have no taste and little consistency. I remember myself as a boy scout, driving my pedal car intricately through alleyways in the city, eating bruised fruit when I found it at the backs of government markets. In the rear compartment of the pedal car I kept a change of khakis and extra shoes. If night came on me I'd throw out my bag and sleep wherever I was. I've seen tumbleweed, or something similar, blowing past the house recently. A wild pig comes every night and snuffles around for any garbage I might throw down. I consider dropping something heavy on him from the roof, breaking the spine, dressing him out, cooking him over a fire pit. The boy scout has been here several days now. I've noticed a spider's thread from his shoulder to the windowsill. Two days ago he began an extended smile which has not yet broken. When the wind occasionally blows outside, the shiplap siding of the house gets to wailing in a high-pitched tone. The wind sock is full to the south, the awnings flapping. The fire in the stove belly has died hours ago, the sun's last yellow angle is narrowing on the tower walls. The old clock is ticking on the mantel. The evening wears on. I rebuild the fire as the night cools and wear my flannel robe and long johns. Before dawn I see an orange light in the pines, someone walking with a lamp. Morning again. An icicle has formed where the bathroom faucet dripped. The sun has come up in a haze. The boy scout is sleeping on the sofa. The wind sock is deflated and the day is warming up toward noon. By mid-afternoon I am perspiring in the humidity, wiping myself with a handkerchief. The boy scout remains dry and still. A slow drizzle now, hanging on three days. On the fourth day I see an egg of sun above the tree line. A katydid is dead at the bottom of my teacup. Overnight the weather turns cold again, and the drizzle becomes a wet snow. My mouth is sour, my toothbrush worn down to the plastic. It will be nice to chew salty pork meat, sometime, whenever I can kill the pig. I should raise the awnings before the snow collects and breaks through the rotted canvas. The wind sock is frozen stiff, pointing south. I·see the pig outside, standing in the white. He pisses and leaves a yellow circle on the snow crust. The pedal car is gone, tracks of the wooden wheels leading off down the road. The awnings are frozen and won't go up.

—nominated by Clarence Major

* * *

THE BANK ROBBERY
by Steve Schutzman

The bank robber told his story in little notes to the bank teller. He held the pistol in one hand and gave her the notes with the other. The first note said:

> *This is a bank holdup because money is just like time and I need more to keep on going, so keep your hands where I can see them and don't go pressing any alarm buttons or I'll blow your head off.*

The teller, a young woman of about twenty-five, felt the lights which lined her streets go on for the first time in years. She kept her hands where he could see them and didn't press any alarm buttons. Ah danger, she said to herself, you are just like love. After she read the note, she gave it back to the gunman and said:
"This note is far too abstract. I really can't respond to it."
The robber, a young man of about twenty-five, felt the electricity of his thoughts in his hand as he wrote the next note. Ah money, he said to himself, you are just like love. His next note said:

This is a bank holdup because there is only one clear rule around here and that is WHEN YOU RUN OUT OF MONEY YOU SUFFER, *so keep your hands where I can see them and don't go pressing any alarm buttons or I'll blow your head off.*

The young woman took the note, touching lightly the gunless hand that had written it. The touch of the gunman's hand went immediately to her memory, growing its own life there. It became a constant light toward which she could move when she was lost. She felt that she could see everything clearly as if an unknown veil had just been lifted.

"I think I understand better now," she said to the thief, looking first in his eyes and then at the gun. "But all this money will not get you what you really want." She looked at him deeply, hoping that she was becoming rich before his eyes.

Ah danger, she said to herself, you are the gold that wants to spend my life.

The robber was becoming sleepy. In the gun was the weight of his dreams about this momemt when it was yet to come. The gun was like the heavy eyelids of someone who wants to sleep but is not allowed.

Ah money, he said to himself, I find little bits of you leading to more of you in greater little bits. You are promising endless amounts of yourself but others are coming. They are threatening our treasure together. I cannot pick up fast enough as you lead into the great, huge quiet that you are. Oh money, please save me, for you are desire, pure desire, that wants only itself.

The gunman could feel his intervals, the spaces in himself, piling up so that he could not be sure of what he would do next. He began to write. His next note said:

Now is the film of my life, the film of my insomnia: an eerie bus ride, a trance in the night, from which I want to step down, whose light keeps me from sleeping. In the streets I will chase the wind-blown letter of love that will change my life. Give me the money, my Sister, so that I can run my hands through its hair. This is the unfired gun of time, so keep your hands where I can see them and don't go pressing any alarm buttons or I'll blow your head off with it.

Reading, the young woman felt her inner hands grabbing and holding onto this moment of her life.

Ah danger, she said to herself, you are yourself with perfect clarity. Under your lens I know what I want.

The young man and woman stared into each other's eyes forming two paths between them. On one path his life, like little people, walked into her, and on the other hers walked into him.

"This money is love," she said to him. "I'll do what you want." She began to put money into the huge satchel he had provided.

As she emptied it of money, the bank filled with sleep. Everyone else in the bank slept the untroubled sleep of trees that would never be money. Finally she placed all the money in the bag.

The bank robber and the bank teller left together like hostages of each other. Though it was no longer necessary, he kept the gun on her, for it was becoming like a child between them.

—nominated by Mary MacArthur

THE WEEK THE DIRIGIBLE CAME

by JAY MEEK

from THREE RIVERS POETRY JOURNAL

nominated by Mark Vinz

After the third day it began to be familiar,
an analogue by which one could find
himself in finding it, so whenever it came
outside the window what came to mind was how
marvellous and common the day was, and how expert
I'd become at dirigibles. And when
it stayed, one felt the agreeable confidence
that comes with having a goldfish
live four days. So I began to watch its shadow
passing through back yards, only once
looked at the tie-line swinging from its nose.
How much it seemed to want an effigy, a fish,
something that might save it from being simply a theory
about itself, and on the fifth day
old ladies came stomping out in their gardens
as the shadow passed under them,
and in the woods hunters
fired at the ground. The sixth day rained,
but morning broke clear and the air seemed grand
and empty as a palace, and I went out,
looked up, the sun crossing my nose
cast such shadows as sun-dials make,
and I knew whatever time
had come was our time and it was like nothing else.

THREE DAY NEW YORK BLUES

by JAYNE CORTEZ

from YARDBIRD READER

nominated by YARDBIRD READER

It's tuesday night
in ole possum face new york city sweet daddy
    spit upon sadness
in this fist of three vines of two dark lips of
sunken blisters in my need more need more
need more lovin sometimes baby please please please

And already it's wednesday mornin
in a deep end of my river
and like a woman
locked doors in a storm
    i got those mean wet kill me kill me
    stroke me baby do me tonight blues

May i present thursday
in moonshine of my weepin willow
in the lonesome road of my groanin
moanin sanctified dignified sweetsmellin
hoochicoo

Comes Friday
and this life beggin request
dead and gone
in noon time of my frisky whiskey money bag
cuttin mood

juice up new york   juice up

Cause i got a fine warm satisfying
  screaming   deep sea divin   good feelin papa
hoppin   skipping   jumpin   flyin
back home to me

THE FIRE AT THE CATHOLIC CHURCH

fiction by JOHN SANFORD

from ADIRONDACK STORIES (Capra Press)

nominated by Ben Pesta and Capra Press

FOREWORD TO THE BOOK

Several of the Characters in these stories, as well as much of the material and nearly all the locales, were come by in the summer of 1931 during a stay in the Adirondack Mountains in the company of Nathanael West. For some while prior, he'd been trying to complete the revision of his second book, "Miss Lonelyhearts," and I'd been trying to write "The Water Wheel," my first. The making of books in that period, though, was only our secondary occupation, our Sunday and sparetime things: West's everyday job was managing the Sutton, a hotel in mid-Manhattan, and mine was the practice of the law. We'd been complaining to each other for months about that self-division, and it was he who proposed finally that we quit the city for the summer and spend it in the woods, that we rent a cabin somewhere, or pitch a tent, or throw ourselves under a tree— anything would do as long as it was far from an office and further from home.

In an earlier year, I'd boarded for a few weeks at a farm near Long Lake, in the western part of the Adirondacks, and while there I'd met a game-warden whose name I've never forgotten. Beakbane, it was, and another oddity about him has proved to be just as memorable: he played Lalo one day on the farmhouse piano. I wrote to the man and told him what West and I were looking for, and he passed us along to a friend of his, one Harry Reoux of Warrensburg, saying that Reoux might be able to help us. Help us he did. Six miles out of War-

rensburg on the back road to Stony Creek, he owned upwards of twelve hundred acres wooded with pine and walnut, and in the middle of the double section lay a brook-fed pond that made a quarter-mile circle of open water within a half-mile collar of reeds; on the bank stood a seven-room hunting lodge, furnished right on down to corded wood and kindling. He helped us, Reoux did: he rented us that realm of his for $25 a month.

The lodge was so laid out that West and I, simply by closing a door, were able to make two suites for ourselves, each with a bedroom and a workroom, and all through July and August we wrote in the mornings (I could always hear a drone on my side of the wall; he had the habit of speaking his words as he put them on paper), and in the afternoons we knocked about the woods. In those days, there was still a good deal of sport going, and some of it we ranged for, and some we found near home: we fished for pickerel in Brant Lake, I remember, and for bass in the upper Hudson, and the pond (Viele Pond, it was called) was generally good for a mess of bullheads and now and again, where springs rose and the water was cold, a half-pound trout. Often, though, we chose to sit on the porch and fire .22-longs at paper targets, or we'd merely laze on the grass and smoke at the sky, talking of Pound and Eliot and Wyndham Lewis, of Perse and Apollinaire, of Sylvia Beach and Joyce and transition and that big guy, only a little older than we were, who loved to kill so dearly that in the end, still thirty years off, he'd even kill himself. Talking, I say, but it was West who did most of it, because he knew more than I did, and I who listened.

And then, too, there were times when we weren't doing any of those things, weren't writing, cooking, fishing, shooting at bull's-eyes or gray squirrels, or lying around in the grass, times when each of us, though rarely unaccompanied, was very much alone. What West dwelt on in those intervals I never asked and was never told, but my own thoughts were much on the two roads I'd been trying to travel at once. After Fordham Law School, after the Bar Examinations and the serving of a clerkship, there'd been a long dull stretch of reading my name backwards through the glass part of a door, and ahead there was only more of the same, more strife and spite, more dreary language poured out in sordid causes—with writing ever that Sunday and sparetime thing, I hated it that neither of my pursuits was getting my best, hated finding that each of my half-lives was failing—but that summer at Viele Pond happened to come in the *right period, and it was decisive. The Depression had been growing, and my clientele, always small, had shrunk, and more and more did every day seem to be Sunday and all time seem to be spare. There was no struggle, no anguish, there were no revelations or discoveries: the law quietly removed itself, that's all, and from then on, there was only the single road.*

On our return to New York in September, West invited me to put up at the Sutton—as a non-paying guest, of course—and of course I accepted. I remained there for the better part of six months, during which time the first five of these stories were written. Under my then name, Julian L. Shapiro, they were published in 1932, three of them in Pagany *and two in* Contact, *and apart from a few descriptive pieces that had appeared in the Paris vanguard magazines* Tambour *and* The New Review, *they're my earliest printed work. "The King of the Minnies," written in 1934, has never been published as a separate story.*

I've taken another name since those days, but I've not seen fit to tamper with the stories. It was many a year since I'd read them, but on preparing them for this edition, I found that they'd been brought off in a manner long lost to me—and lost, I must say, with regret. I do not write now as I did then. The plain aim is gone, the uncomplicated view, the ability to see and say directly, as if I were confronting a much simpler world—as indeed I was. I have changed after forty-five years, I suppose, we're all of us someone else, but the stories have not been touched.

JOHN SANFORD

Santa Barbara, Cal.
6 April 1976

✱   ✱   ✱

THE FIRE AT THE CATHOLIC CHURCH

Broadbent usually took the back road out of Red Bank. It wasn't paved, but it was hard fine dirt and sand and a car almost drove itself on stuff like that. The road went along the east bank of the Stone for a couple of miles; in some places, the bank went up and got to be a shoulder fifty feet higher than the water and from there Broadbent could see down into the holes where he sometimes went after a bass, riverbass, the green onepounders that put up such a good fight on a light line. On the way down that afternoon, Broadbent ran his car into a draw near one of the holes and sat for a minute wondering if he should get out and try for a bass, maybe only for an hour. The river looked good with the water bending around the hole just the way he liked it and it wouldnt be any trouble for him to rig up his pole and catch a few grassfrogs. After the fishing, he could get to Covington in plenty of time to see Doying. When Broadbent thought about Doying, he decided against the fishing and started up again for town.

Broadbent was a drummer and part of his regular route out of Utica was a stop at Covington once a month. Hed been making that circuit for years and got to know most of the people there pretty well, but the only one around Covington he couldnt exactly figure out was Doying, the man that ran the feed and grain store near the old iron bridge over Stone River. Broadbent had been thinking about Doying most of the way from Red Bank. The reason for that was not only because Doyings was the next stop, but also because the man there, Tolley, had asked him if hed heard the latest about Doying. Broadbent said no and wanted to hear, but Tolley said hed find out for himself fast enough when he got over to Covington.

While Broadbent was riding along, he thought about a part of the road hed have to pass in order to get to town. Four miles further on past the draw, hed come to the grounds of the Catholic Church. People said it had been built by the French when they first came down off Champlain. The church was small, no wider than a rod and a half across the front and except for the big gold cross on top of the steeple, youd hardly know it was Catholic. It looked to Broadbent like places hed seen when he once made a trip over Boston way. He liked the church and always stopped for a minute when he went by. Then hed think about the dreary look of the gold cross high up over the glossy white columns and walls; hed guess if you got your mind off the cross and just looked at the building, sometimes youd think of it like it was a girl in white linen standing up there on the hill, especially if there wasnt any wind and the dress came straight down in long round folds. But the drearylooking gold cross—Broadbent didnt like that.

It was winter the last time Broadbent went by way of church road. The dirty brown stubble, all that was left of the grass then, hadnt set the building off right; July was almost half gone now and the whitepainted walls and shining spire would stand out fine from the long brightgreen roll of the mound where the church stood. Four driveways went up the sides of the mound through shady alleys of evenset pines. They all met in a circle of trees around the church and made a cross with dipping arms. From the arched iron gate at the highway, you could see three of the arms. Back of the church, hidden behind the mound, there was a graveyard.

Broadbents car came past the end of a long cornfield that grew about seven feet high. Then Broadbent could see the church property. When he took a look up the mound through one of the alleys, he was so surprised by what he saw that he came near letting his car run into a ditch. Except for one blackened column still sticking up from the cavedin porch, the church was burned to the ground. The steeple with the gold cross, the other three fat white columns, the walls, the flight of steps leading up to the porch—all that was left of them was a tangled pile of ashes, charred beams and clumps of broken brick. To stop the fire from spreading, some of the trees in the circle had been chopped down. The others in the circle were as black as what was left of the church; all the pinegreen and most of the branches on the inside of the circle were burned off the trees, making them look like theyd been split in half.

For a little while, Broadbent just sat there looking up the hill out of his car; he still had his hands on the wheel and his lower jaw was hanging down like the trap on a hayloft. Afterward, he climbed out of the car and started walking slowly up the hill. On the way, he saw deep tracks crisscrossing the lawn where cars and trucks and maybe engines had gone up toward the top. The ground was ripped to pieces and all around Broadbent there were signs of the damage made by people that had tried to put out the fire. When he got up near the church, he saw there was even less left than hed supposed. The standing column hed seen from below was only half a column. He walked over and put his hand on it and it swayed like a good push would knock it over into the rest of the ruins. Then Broadbent thought about the steeple and the gold cross and looked to see if he could find any trace of them. There was a deep cut into the ground on the right side of the ashpile that made him think the steeple had gone off on that side and came down top first, but even though he kicked around in the cut, he couldnt find anything left of the cross.

Broadbent went around to the back of the church for a look at the graveyard. He couldnt make out why there wasnt a single stone left standing over the graves; it was hard to account for all the damage there because the yard was quite a way back of the church. There were tracks in the ground leading out of the yard down the back of the hill. Broadbent followed one of the tracks. Not far away, he came to a gravecross laying over on its side. He was kind of shocked to find that the stone had been abused and that a lot of people had done low things on it and all around it.

When Broadbent saw that, he didnt bother looking any more, but went back to the highway where his car was and drove off fast for Covington. Passing the Game Farm, he thought about Doying again and the funny way Tolley had acted when he asked Broadbent if hed heard the latest. Broadbent made up his mind to gamo right to Doyings.

Covington made a main street for itself out of the state road to Flagler. Part of the way up the street, near the middle of the town, a road went off west across the river and there it forked north and south. On the south, it ended in the woods at Clear Pond; there was only one farm that way, Jasper Darbys, and afterward long stretches of woods and marsh to the pond. North, where the river dropped over a twenty foot ledge, theyd built the sawmill and lumberyard. It wasnt handy to town, but thats where Doying had his store. It was in a long, low building set on the north fork of the road. The back of the building was on stilts and hung out over the water; the front came up to the edge of the road.

It was around two oclock when Broadbent got out of his car in front of the place and went over to the door. The shutters were closed on all the windows and there was a padlock hanging off hasps on the entrance. In the middle of the top panel, there was a notice saying that Doying expected to keep his place shut for some time, but he could be reached care of his Covington p. o. box. A date on the notice showed it was three days old.

Not finding anybody at Doyings, Broadbent figured hed be able to get the story out of Ed Smead, the sheriff, so he drove around to his office. When Smead saw Broadbents car out front, he came over to say hello. Broadbent said from what hed seen on the way down from Red Bank, thered been some big doings in town since the last time he was there. Smead said he guessed maybe Broadbent was right, but he didnt open up and talk about the doings any. Broadbent didnt feel like getting put off, so he spoke up plain and said Tolley, over by Red Bank, had made some hints about Doying, and now what was this with Doying shutting up shop, he wanted to know. And then about the church, too. Smead nodded his head in the direction of the office and said they had Doying in there now and in a few minutes theyd be taking him down to Stone River Junction on a warrant of arrest. But what was it all about, Broadbent said. What was everybody getting so tightassed for. Smead said he didnt have time to talk just then, but if Broadbent was so anxious to hear, hed tell him on the way down to Stone River; there wasnt any objection to Broadbents going along and Smead would ride with him and tell the news from beginning to end. Broadbent said fine and Smead went back to the office.

Broadbent sat in the car and smoked a cigar to kill time. Then a lot of people started coming out of the sheriffs office. First of all, there were a couple of deputies that Broadbent recognized; in between them was Doying. Then Smead, and after him the town banker and some others that were important around Covington. Among them were Father Jackman of the Catholic Church and Reverend Mister Titus, the local pastor. Broadbent got good looks at all of them. Doying, he thought was dopey and thinking about nothing. Smead had a long face that didnt show very much. The clergymen, even though they walked out together, didnt seem any too friendly. The men from the town were trying hard to look serious, but Broadbent could have sworn they all were like they wanted to bust out laughing.

By the time the crowd finished coming out of the office, half of Covington was around to watch. Broadbent looked up and down the road and noticed that there were more cars in sight than hed ever seen before in the town. Every kind of turnout that would roll—farmwagons, buggies, anything. All the cars and wagons were filled with people sticking their heads out, but there wasnt any noise at all. None of the rigs were moving and none of the people talking. All Broadbent could see was plenty of faces just looking and he was so stumped by the number of people that were interested that he could hardly wait for Smead to explain on the way to the county seat. The deputies and Doying went on ahead in another car, followed by the others that had been in the office. Smead climbed in with Broadbent and then they started off. Back of them came all the rest waiting in the street for how the case would turn out.

Near the south end of Covington, they passed the town church. It was painted white, same as the Catholic place, but it had no columns in front and it was square like a barn. The entrance was one step up from a gravel walk that went straight for the door from the road. The windows were small and plain and underneath each one, close up to the building, was a hydrangea bush in bloom, showing lavender colorballs against the white shingle. The roadfront had a rim of elms that made you look high up if you wanted to see the leaves. The trees were very old and many of them had gray concrete patches stuffing up holes in the trunks.

The trip down to Stone River was like a parade, only it really didnt start anywhere. It picked up as it went along. At every crossroad on the way, there was a new delegation and it fell in line when the others passed by. From the look of things, Broadbent thought the people were making a holiday out of the Doying matter.

Smead was talking. *Jackman and Titus had a lot to do with it.*

Had a lot to do with what, Broadbent said.

With Doyings setting the church on fire.

Doying burned down the church, the Catholic Church? Broadbent said very loud and high. Way down the road, his eye caught a clump of birch that went up white and together like stalks of celery. They made him think of the fat white columns. *Doying burned it down, did you say?*

Thats what I said. Three nights ago. And wed never have known who did it, except he came in my office the morning after the excitement and gave himself up. He didnt make any excuses. He just came in and said: I set off the church last night, boys; I guess you was wondering who did it.

What did you do when he said that? What are you so blamed tightassed for?

We locked him up. Thats what we did.

Smead stopped talking again. It began to look to Broadbent like hed have to go on asking questions till he got the whole story out of the sheriff. Smead was holding back. Hed speak up for a little and then stop again; he started and stopped like an r.f.d. horse.

Look here, Ed. You said it was the fault of the clergymen. I dont understand.

Broadbent got the car around a sharp turn and into a straight piece of road that ran along the foot of a steep ridge. The car was going south and the ridge was on the left; on the other side, there was another ridge that came down near the road, too, but in between there was a fastrunning brook half covered by trees sloping out over the water.

Smead was talking again. *Take Titus, for instance. He dont do his work right. Hes got a steady job, a home alongside the church, and a lot of people coming regularly to hear him once a week, that pay pretty well to get told whats wrong with them. Titus, hes never tried to find out whats wrong with himself. Hes been going on now for a long time thinking things is the same as they were when he got started. But all that time, or most of it since the priest came here after the war, Jackmans been getting in his dirty work. I criticize Titus for being lazy and too easy to fool, but Ive got a lot of hard words for Jackman, too. Hes a sneak. He dont work out in the open same as another man. He dont come right out and preach his faith, but he sneaks around and looks for folks that havent got much will power. Hes been playing on the weak ones, mostly the women. They got fooled by the show he put up for them whenever he could get them out to his church; even Mrs Doying went out there a lot. And its Titus thats been making it easy for him. Titus runs a hard church. With him, a mans got to be almighty righteous to get by, and even when he does, theres only a little by way of thanks because Titus sets a lot of store by goodness and tries to make out like goodness is the natural thing in a man. But Jackman; he took advantage. Hes a sneak. Both of them, Titus and the priest, most likely now theyll lose their jobs, but anyhow, we still got our church.*

Smead stopped again. Broadbent was driving pretty careful. Theyd passed the town limits of Stone River, but there was still a long winding hill to go down and it was dangerous on account of the way the road was built high in the middle and down at the sides.

I didnt know Doying was married, Ed.

Been married a long time. His wife used to be a right nice gal. Still is, far as I know. Pretty, too, but the quiet kind you cant tell what shes thinking. Shes had one child by Doying, a little girl thats five years old now and pretty just like her ma.

Smead got out a jacknife and started sharpening a pencil. He made out it was important to get the pencil fixed before he said any more and managed to take such a long time getting the right kind of point that by the time he finished, Broadbent was driving the car up the main street of the Junction. The town was where the river emptied into the end of Lake Henry and the County Court House was just past the ballfield, but on the left side of the road. A few hundred people were standing around the main entrance, waiting for the parade to come in sight. When the cars pulled up in front of the building, the Covington crowd got out and went upstairs to the courtroon. Everybody followed and there was a lot of excitement when more than half the people couldnt get in. Broadbent was way up front and had a good seat. All the other seats were filled and many people were in the jurybox, on the windowsills and radiators, and even on the floor.

Before long, the Judge came in. His name was Jessup, and he was captain of an automobile ferry that ran from the railroad dock on Lake Henry to a place across the way when the ice was off in the spring and summer.

As soon as the Judge sat down, the court attendant read a name off a paper he was holding and asked if the defendant was in court. Doying stood up when Smead gave him a poke. The Judge said he should go up front, so Doying went through a gate in the railing and stood there fiddling around with his hat like he didnt know what to do next. Smead went in after him and made him sit down at a long table in front of the Judges bench. Then the attendant read off the rest of the paper. It only took a minute or so. The charge against Doying was arson and the facts made out that some time on the night of July 7th, Doying had stopped his car at a filling station on the road out of Covington toward the Game Farm and bought two five-gallon cans of kerosene. Then he was supposed to have driven off in the direction of the church grounds. There was a fact in the paper that said when he got there, hed wet down the whole place with the kerosene and then set the fire going. The next thing in the paper was how Doying had confessed to Smead that he was responsible.

When the attendant finished reading, everybody in the courtroom started talking at once and it was a long time before the Judge could quiet them down. That gave Broadbent a chance to look around at the crowd, but even watching them he couldnt make out what the people were thinking. Over in a corner with Father Jackman, there was a small bunch that looked kind of serious, but the rest were just making noise and talking to each other and hollering across the room, so it was hard to tell what they had in mind. A woman was sitting across the aisle from Broadbent; someone told him she was Mrs Doying. Her face had the same serious kind of look that the people around Jackman had. Most of the time, she was staring at the back of her husbands head, but once in a while she turned around and looked over Jackmans way. Broadbent thought Smead was right; Mrs Doying was a pretty woman.

When the crowd stopped being so noisy, the Judge asked Doying what he had to say. He wanted to know if the confession was true. Jessup didnt say a word about the charge; he was just interested in the confession.

Doying had a lot to say. *She was always sticking them little crosses on the child. Crosses made out of brass. She never asked me for leave to do that. She just strung one up on a chain and put it around the childs neck. I got sick of seeing it there. The child didnt know what it was. She used to play with it in her fingers and when she wasnt thinking, shed hold it in her mouth and suck on it. Sometimes when I spoke to her, shed have the cross in her mouth and answer me like her mouth was filled with pebbles. She wore the thing all the time, day and night. I got sick of seeing it there around her neck like that, Whats the good of it, I said to myself; it isnt even pretty. So one day when I couldnt stand it any more, I grabbed it off the child and chucked it in the well. I must have scared the child because she started crying and ran in to her ma. The woman didnt say nothing, but next week the child was wearing another one of them crosses. Thats the way it went on for a long time, with me pulling off the crosses as fast as I saw them. I chucked them all in the well. The other night on my way back from the outhouse, I thought about all the crosses laying there in the water, so I went over and flashed down a light. There they were on the sandy botton; they stood out real clear in the light, a dozen if there was one. I got a spade and dumped in a lot of sand and then I couldnt see the crosses any more. When I got back to the house, I saw my wife there right next to the window. I asked her what she was doing out of bed that time of night, but she didnt answer me. Then I saw she had a cross in her hands, a big one made out of wood. I got mad and grabbed it away from her. If shed said anything, maybe it would have been all right, but she just went on praying and crying at the same time, so I hit her a clout on the jaw and she fell over on her side. I didnt pay any more attention to her, but I got dressed and went out to the barn. It was a nice night and I just drove around in my car without meaning to go any place or do anything, I cant remember what I was thinking about, less it was them little brass crosses in the well. All of a sudden, I found out I was in front of the Catholic Church. Then I got the idea, so I drove back to that gas station and bought the kerosene, just like that paper said I did. I did the rest, too. I burned down the church.*

Doying stopped there. That time, no one in the courtroom had anything to say. The people were looking back and forth from Doying to Jackman. Broadbent wondered what was going to happen next. Then he remembered what hed seen back of the graveyard eariler that afternoon, the dirtied gravecrosses. That was bad, he thought; the people neednt have done that.

The room stayed quiet even when Jessup asked Father Jackman if he felt like withdrawing the charge. Jackmans eyes got down to tight little knotholes in his face when he stood up. He started to talk, but Jessup wouldnt listen to him till he took off his hat. Jackmans face was a sight. His mouth was open, wide open like a bullheads, and back of his stuckout lips his eyes were still tiny round curls in his cheeks He started talking again, but the Judge cut him off a second time. Finally, Jackman took off his hat, so the Court listened to him. The priest said he insisted on seeing that the defendant got punished for the crime.

The Judge broke in and said, *What crime?*

Jackman said, *Burning down the church. Doying admitted it.*

The Judge said, *I dont believe him. Doying lied to Smead about that. I think its the wrong thing for a man to lie. He puts himself in a bad light. Why, a liars in a fair way to getting himself a character of being like to do most anything, but this is the first time I ever heard of Doyings telling a lie, so hes got to be excused. I dismiss the case.*

Mister Titus got up and tried to say something, but the noise in the room was so loud that no one heard a word come out of his mouth.

RETURN OF THE GENERAL

fiction by JERRY STAHL

from TRANSATLANTIC REVIEW

nominated by TRANSATLANTIC REVIEW

I DON'T KNOW IF YOU'LL believe this, but for a while my cock was the reincarnation of George Washington.

I still can't pinpoint exactly how I knew George's spirit had entered my meat. It may have been that the broad forehead—intelligent, a trifle restrained—took on some new dimension of nobility. Or it may have been the scent of wooden teeth. The point is, while venerable George inhabited my engine I had a problem. Did the ladies love me for *myself,* or were their thrills contingent upon the inspiring presence of the General? The question burned a hole in my flag, tore some seam in my soul, on those rare occasions when I stopped fucking long enough to think about it.

I wasn't the first to notice George's manly mug on my totem pole. Maureen—no resemblance to Martha, except for a certain plumpness to the thighs—made the heady discovery.

We had just been busy with a bit of wild Bicentennial balling. She lay on her back looking at the ceiling. Her eyes were misty, the way they always get after she comes and then lies back feeling kittenish and fat. I was standing by the bed. She wanted a Kleenex to mop up and I'd risen to get it in my own half-assed, chivalrous way. I had to take a leak anyhow, so it wasn't all charity work.

After I did my double-duty and came back scratching my balls (the dew had started to dry) she rolled her head in my direction and chuckled. Maureen occasionally had more than one chin, and a few of them now gathered under her face where her neck should have been. She was getting—I really shouldn't say it, anyone can look a bit off in the languid aftermath—maybe a shade too rotund. That was when she suddenly gawked at my cock and shouted: "Liberty Balls! It's him!"

"Who?" I cried, checking the windows for peepers. Maureen's chins quivered esctatically.

"George Washington, my hero!" she panted, salivating like the Potomac in spring thaw.

What could I say? In God I trust? My voice belied my squeamishness. "It *is* the Bicentennial that has you babbling like this . . . isn't it?"

Maureen harrumphed. "It is *not* just the Bicentennial," she assured me. "It's the way it hangs there: fat at the top, a little swollen, just the right powder-puff shade of pink. Washington *scrubbed his forehead,*" she tried to explain, but I didn't understand. "He wore a great white barrister's wig but underneath he was bald as an eagle. Like your cock there, droopy. If you put a wig on that crown you could pass it off on dollar bills."

I doubted it. "You've had too much to drink. Or too much sex," I added. That was the wrong thing to add.

She laughed outright. The post-coital mist evaporated from her brown Betsy Ross eyes as they rose mockingly to meet my own and then descended to taunt my impoverished pride once more.

I got pissed. "Do you know what it feels like to a man," I sputtered, "to have a woman laugh at him . . . right after, for Christ's sake! . . . Well, it's damned unpatriotic, if you ask me."

That was too much for a Daughter of the American Revolution to take. Maureen pouted. "I wanted to tell you that I *love* George Washington," she whined, either hurting in her heartland or acting up a storm. "I wanted to tell you that I fantasize about being the first President's mistress. That's all. And now you've spoiled it. Men are so fucking defensive."

I felt glum.

"You're kidding," I said, sounding weak even to me.

She pulled the sheets up to her chins. I considered slipping into her fort, but my musket wasn't loaded. I had to change strategies. "Well, if you're really the revolutionary kind you'll give sanctuary to the commander-in-chief. The head of a nation needs solace in these troubled times."

But there was nothing doing. Her civic resolve turned her into a lump. I suspected, though, from the slight troop movement under the covers, that she was dreaming of the Continental Army and diddling herself. I wondered whether to fling them back and catch her when a sudden flurry of activity made the decision moot. Blanket, sheet and bedspread flew from her body as if a Tory had snuck in and goosed her. Her legs splayed, her hands clawed in her snatch and her thighs spread wide as a capital Y. Maureen, my sweet, you looked ripe when you kicked your hot tent off and onto the rug.

Was I really the father of my country? I asked her straight out if it was my meat or her imagination that set her off.

"You don't *understand*," she wailed. "*It looks like George Washington*." Her expostulation echoed away dreamily. "George Washington, George Washington, George Washington . . ."

It was then that I started to believe it myself, probably because I've always been turned on by un-American things like the sight of diddling women. And Maureen was a diddler. At that moment, watching her head arch backward, her eyes strain shut, her powerful flanks open scissors-wide and writhe—my cock stood up and saluted.

There are good hard-ons and great ones. This was a great one— the kind you can walk around with, eat dinner with, shave and read the paper with, and still know that wherever, whenever, however you want to employ it, it will be there, ready to push through the slickest depths and spear you a treasure. I bided my time.

A flush of Yankee zeal accompanied each pulse of lust in my member. Her juicy cunt—*those damn British with their prissy red jackets!* The way her middle finger nudged her clit, rubbing the small bulb like a marble in oil, made me want to wear rags on my feet and suffer through a winter at Valley Forge. It wasn't natural. She muttered something that sounded like "Prez" and beckoned with dampened fingers.

My God, it was good, the first taste of her. My broad snout nuzzled up into her tube, lips snug and moist as sponge. She cleansed us both with her rousing, demented love of country. I didn't care now whether it was me or a phantom leader she was feeling. I knew my identity. The stoic Virginian bore into her heartland with vigor. It had been worse for George the first time out, much worse. Martha was a widow when he met her, and they produced no children. I think he enjoyed his second go-round more. Maureen gasped at the great, gorging strokes I was taking. Great men walk in giant steps. All is magnified by history. My cock felt worthy of its heritage.

When we were through—it didn't last that long—we lay together in a much richer mood. Maureen's breath stunk in my nostrils. A cloying sultriness filled me with calm. Still, I felt it beginning again. The creeping malaise had already begun its slow, inevitable ascent. What kind of game was Maureen playing. Was I encouraging her? Or was it *my* game?

But when my sombre paranoia reached its height and my flesh felt cold in her arms. I eased myself with the certainty that, yes, it was so after all. My cock and George Washington had struck up some irrefutable kinship, and that *was* something. How many could brag of it? Not more than a handful, I suspected.

Were there, in fact, any others out there, brothers in the cult of cock-identification? Perhaps another with my claim stalked his lady's treats at the very same moment. . . . But the thought had no real weight. I imagined others as one imagines life on another planet—simply because the universe is so large a place.

"My *dear* Mr. Washington," I caught myself thinking, as if the flesh between my legs were no more than a visiting companion. We'd had a good time together, George and I. He did the dirty work and I felt the explosions in balls and brain. Not bad. His was the labor that won nations, mine the profligacy that lived off that kind of sweat. Maureen's cheeks were rosy and a smile of sheer content-ment gave her face a beatific air.

Later, sadly, the spectre of my strange inheritance passed from glory to doom. To every lady I encountered I revealed the secret of the otherwise undistinguished member. "This may be hard to be-lieve, but my prick is George Washington."

How many gentle women simply met my announcement with a sneer! How many suspected some sort of ruse! In this jaded era, any evidence of the authentic or the wonderful is viewed with suspicion. But I always made my point with delicacy, careful not to mention the General until I had gotten a lady into intimate relations on my own merits. "Let others," I thought, "exploit their piece of the patriotic pie for commercial gain." I shared my secret—or so I was convinced—with those whose lusts I shared as well.

The others, after hefty Maureen, were a different breed. Cheer-leaders, stewardesses, apple-cheeked types with springy steps and spritely twinkles in their eyes. And weren't these supposed to be the sweethearts of quarterbacks?

I began talking to George, confiding to him in my most troubled moments. Once, after a particularly spicy session with a pom-pom girl from Duluth, I laid my cards on the table.

"For Christ's sage, George, no woman was ever as anxious to flash her gash as that blonde seemed to be . . ."

Pom-pom Peggy had literally walked up to me on the street and begun rubbing my belly, slipping her long, cool fingers in my crotch and whistling "God Bless America." She made me take her from be-hind in the first hotel room we could procure. To my surprise, Wash-ington cocked his head in my direction and eyed me mournfully. We were sitting on the bed, still sticky from the latest escapade.

"Son," he confided, lisping sightly from the splinters in his gums, "when you're the father of a country as grand and glorious as this one"—and here his voice lowered reverently—"you don't ask a lady why she wants you. *You just try to give her what she wants.*"

I closed my eyes, weighing the wisdom of his words. "What you're talking about, then, is duty. But don't you think you should fulfill yourself, too? As a military man, I should think you'd look to your own pleasure."

Though my argument made no sense (he was great in the sack, and I felt like a king when I watched pom-pom Peggy bite her lip clear through with passion), for curiosity's sake I wanted to know what was going on in his head. He was an organ of few words.

"Sex," sighed the President, "is a battle both sides should win. You don't chop down charries, you thrill them off the branches."

Emboldened by his frankness, I held him in my hand and asked the question that had been bugging me all along. "And Martha . . ." My voice faltered. "None of the history books say what kind of piece *she* was."

I felt him flush. His head turned deep purple. My nuts cracked together like colliding cannon balls and I nearly blacked out.

"Alright, alright," I cried, gasping with pain. "I take it back!" The nutcracker suite ground to a merciful halt. I took a breath. His words sounded distant now, almost inside my brain.

"I came back here, two hundred years later, to see if I could find a gal to beat my Martha. And, by God, none of your Bicentennial babes comes close to the original." He sounded all-powerful but comforting in his final pronouncement: "My advice to you, Son of the Second Century, is find one you really like and stick to her. *A good woman is hard to find.*"

So saying, he laughed a hearty laugh and left me to the sleep of the enlightened.

When I awoke, aware of his passing but in no way dissatisfied with the organ he'd inhabited, I felt myself again. In fact, I wasn't so sure he'd really left. All I knew was that I wanted my Maureen.

The urge to procreate possessed me like a mission. I wanted children—cities of them—and some sixth sense told me that she was the First Lady for me. Tired of the endless explaining to disbelievers, I cast my lot with dear Martha-Maureen and we were wed.

And now, as I record this story for the nation, I gaze at my belly and for the thousandth time read the words America's father left me. Here, faintly etched in an authentic facsimile of revolutionary blood, is the bit of graffiti which binds my wife and I forever in love and Patriotism:

GEORGE WASHINGTON SLEPT HERE

It will be something fine to show my grandchildren in the year 2000.

THE NEW CONSCIOUSNESS, THE NEA, AND POETRY TODAY

by FELIX STEFANILE

from BLACK ROOSTER

nominated by Harry Smith

(editors note: during the past years direct and indirect funding from The National Endowment for the Arts has enabled many small presses to survive. Here is another thought on the result of that funding. The opinions are the author's and do not necessarily reflect the views of Pushcart Press or our editors.)

THE NEW CONSCIOUSNESS of the Seventies is easier to sell than to define. We wallow in a soup of sales-engendered stimuli, as pervasive as the Muzak at the local Waffle House.

The words we all use are perhaps the best indication of the New Consciousness, for we trade them, like credit-cards, from counter to counter: feedback, interface, psychohistory, pansexualism, confrontation, ethnic, ecumenical, environmental, ecological, encounter (the e's do very well) advocacy, affirmative, awareness. Words count, in our society, even if only up to ten, and by using the same bureaucratized words, like awareness or encounter, over and over again, we can utilize our own lack of commitment in dealing with others, the Other, and avoid thought. Today words are our aspirins, our Valium pills. We keep the headache away, and we keep the exchange of words, our favorite activity, going. Activity, as we all know, is a splendid substitute for action.

When there is so much activity, so much murmuring going on, as contrasted with action, a need for categorization arises. The emphasis of activity, of exchange, is not on action or product, but on the relationship between exchangers. The game counts, not the goal. We come to baseball averages. We come to the budgeting of words. Thomas Sowell, in a recent issue of the *New York Times Magazine* (August 8, 1976) had this to say of exchangers in the service of the poor:

> . . . .championing the disadvantaged is not only an inspiration but an occupation. To be blunt, the poor are a gold mine. By the time they are studied, advised, experimented with and administered, the poor have helped many a middle-class liberal to achieve affluence with Government money. The total amount of money the Government spends on its "antipoverty" programs is three times what would be required to lift every man, woman and child in America above the official poverty level by simply sending money to them.

This categorical aspect of exchange is just as evident in that most slippery of the arts, poetry. With Government intrusion into the field, through the Literature Program of the National Endowment for the Arts (NEA), we now have a veritable team roster of poets, and a batting schedule, including lead-off hitters, clean-up men. Any analysis of federal grants being doled out to various little magazines and small presses reveals that, for fiscal reasons, (entering as "concepts" into the simplistic, topical jargon of New Consciousness critics and commentators) we now have the following categories of poets:

> Black Poets
> Chicano Poets
> Women Poets
> Native American Poets
> Third World Poets
> Ethnic Poets
> Gay Poets
> Lesbian Poets
> Prison Poets
> Senior Poets
> Children Poets
> High School Poets
> Regional Poets
> Asian American Poets
> Poet-in-the-Schools Poets

The category, by the on-going thrust of year-to-year budgeting, becomes inordinately important. It is a matter of utter fact that although the Literature Program has been handing out money for years it has not, since the failure of the early, original prize system, and except for one anemic effort--the Fels Awards--now in eclipse, succeeded in coming up with a clear, hearty system of "prizes" for poetry poetry. According to the NEA, poetry is just another Lebanon, with Moslem, Christian, Palestinian and Druse factions. Poetry, as such, is hardly an issue, because category, not essence, is what "counts," what can be *budgeted*. This is, perhaps, the most serious philosophical departure, for the New Consciousness, from the traditional values of the past.

Coincident with the bureaucratization of poetry comes the bureaucratization of the little magazine. Coordinators, panelists, directors, organizers of conferences, state arts councils, residents, executive secretaries, a massive infrastructure of top-level, middle-level and low-level employees and appointees created by the NEA, an infrastructure seething with its inevitable contingent of pols, society dames, and dilettantes, must today number, at the very least, in the several hundreds. The real activity of the NEA is activity, not art.

Government in the arts, and the present poetry fervor in the schools, feed on each other. Again, the emphasis is on activity. Some years ago, a large eastern institution, recognizing that creative workshops can be fun, and distinguishing between the fun to be had, and its own more literature-oriented, "advanced" workship, offered an evening course it called "Writing for Self-Expression." With that kind of handle, how can a course fail? The parade of would-be writers, non-writers, self-expressing writers, now forms, in all the schools, from semester to semester, and--with the help of the Poet-in-the-Schools program--from the third or second grade up. How can one object to the bringing of this form of delight to the children of our country? One does not object. But we need to be reminded, in our hasty enthusiasm, that there is a distinction to be made between what is going on in the classroom, and what poetry is all about. I am not at all certain we are raising a generation of poets, or poetry-lovers. I *am* certain a lot of half-truths are being splashed about in the school yard. Leaving the Philip Lopates aside, since for every Lopate we probably have ten duds in the system, we remain in danger of nurturing a brood of dilettantes permanently fixed and fizzled in their obsession that poetry is fun, which poetry certainly is, but then that's not all it is.

Today's little magazine editor gets to see a lot of these fun poems the kids probably first learned to write in high school a few years back: list poems, riddle poems, the I-wish-I-were-a-green-bee poems. Our mail is filled with these contraptions, and they are but another example of the kind of zany, futile activity being aided and abetted by the New Consciousness mob. In 1974 I played a small part in the seminar, sponsored by Government money and directed by A. L. Lazarus, which helped to establish the Poet-in-the-Schools program in the state of Indiana. My own suggestion was that we establish a method of helping *teachers* talk about writing and poetry. The suggestion seemed to fall on deaf ears then. Except for the new magazine at Indiana U., *Indiana Writes*, I know of no such program specifically funded by the NEA for this purpose. There are a few splendid organizations, like the *Teachers and Writers Collaborative*, which help do the job, and have probably received from time to time, Government help, but we have no ongoing system. Yet our teachers are the ones left with the debris in the classroom after the poet or non-poet-in-the-school has zoomed through. Given the opportunity the NEA will always opt for showmanship over thought.

A popular legend running through the little magazine movement is that we are going through a "great age" of poetry. Usually, in their euphoria, the propagators of this view cite chapter and verse--the category again--by rolling off a list of names, estimating the number of poetry magazines, and remarking on the popularity of poetry readings. In Indiana we say, "Anymore I wonder." I *am* sure we are also going through one of the *worst* ages of poetry. The publishing of a poetry magazine today is no longer the act of commitment it was a generation ago. It is remarkably easy, and Government grants make it easier, to put out a journal. We have reached a stage in alternative publishing where it is virtually impossible, this side of idiocy, for a person not to be published. Running the gamut from staid, old reviews like *Poetry*, or *Beloit Poetry Journal*, to the latest *Purple Commune* or *Butterfly Nights*, any individual with the patience to last the process through can be published, and quite frankly, any-body is. What we have, between our "great age" and our worst, between the fine poetic product and the crap, is a New Consciousness phenomenon, the Published Poem.

The Published Poem doesn't have to be good or bad; it is simply, as a matter of fact, there. It is our classic contemporary example, along with learning to play a few chords on a guitar, of "doing your own thing." Whether it's poetry or not, whether it's playing or not, ain't the point. The creative writing teacher, teaching his high-school mini-elective, manages to cadge seventy-five dollars from the "coordinator" at school, tells the children to bring in their haiku, and presto! a magazine is born, the Published Poem appears. A store-front social worker, skimming the latest guideline release from Washington, checks the grant possibilities for his project, applies for a few bucks, and presto! A community newspaper is born, peppered with Published Poems. I have no doubt that a great many sweet good things are happening, but in the schools, up hill and down dale, on the farms, the Publishing Boom that is going on is not necessarily one of them, nor the Published Poem. Given this immense heaven of activity, the blurring of lines between something we can call poetry and something we can call publication, culture is casualty. Culture has become sentimentalized. The fact of the matter is that the New Consciousness has given back to us, following on the demise of the New Criticism, a very old type: people who do not distinguish between the act of expressing oneself, and the art of writing. The next generation is going to have to fight that battle all over again. Precisely, the New Consciousness has become the new orthodoxy, and we have a breed of poet in our midst, the proper heir of the cultural "revolution" of the Sixties, whom the intellectual climate of the Seventies—the freedom, the enthusiasm, the cult of Expression—favors over all other kinds of poet.

He or she is usually young, not even thirtyish. (There are, of course, in the Seventies, permanently "young" and immortal people.) More often than not he has been through college, and may or may not have a degree. He travels a lot; the highway, or "wanderer" poem is a cliché of the New Consciousness imagination, inherited, and often copied, from pop music. He abhors rhyme as a poetic device, and his work—if he is any good—reveals an immense alertness to his immediate surroundings. New Consciousness people are film people, and the best work of the kind of poet I am attempting to describe is luminous with casually correct detail, the glow of a glass of water, the mist that fades away like smoke with the coming of the early morning sun. His ear, in contrast with his eye, and this has been remarked by many critics, is often defective. The lilt of words does not attract him. In his often litigious sense of loyalty to the spontaneous and the natural the concept of word-play, of phrasing, holds no glamor, and as a matter of practice he wants his poem to be urgent, rather than lively or pleasant. Because of this his plain speech will, too frequently not to be noticed, falter into talk and gab. He is not a well read person, and the influences he shows, as I imply above, are more generational than personal: a rhythmic line out of a song, an in-joke, like Dylan's about drugs. Allusion, though, is not his bag. He writes about sex the way his elders never did. The result is probably neither more nor less important that the dead dog theme of the Fifties. At his best, and in the best sense of the word, he is an utterly *personal* poet, by which I do not mean confessional, but solidly placed in consciousness, and, in his fear of abstractions and hypocrisy, stubbornly grounded in the narrow space of his confident ego.

I have described an attitude that fits most of the prevailing modes acceptable to the little magazines of the day. This "new" poetry is in some ways off to a better start than the young poetry of the Fifties, when tradition threatened to stifle thought. It will be interesting to see how these young men and women develop. A poetry is being formed; my reservations have to do with the fear that perhaps a poetry is being stalled. These people are growing up without reading, without any sense of the challenge of technique—the total banishment of meter and rhyme is only the tip of this iceberg— without any desire to encompass the larger statement, or say any of the things that art has traditionally said, and that has helped teach us to live our lives. Everyone is having a good time, everyone is having fun, but there is a sameness to the work, a lack of experiment, a cuddly anti-intellectualism always in danger of becoming trite and opaque, that makes for a homogenization in the pages I read that is sadly reminiscent of the homogenization, without the styles, of the Fifties. What will grow out of the Seventies? Not more NEA-sponsored fun and games, I hope.

More could be said, but I think I have proved my point. When the history of the little magazine of these times is finally written, it will not be noted, as a matter of prime scholarly importance, that Dylan Thomas stalked America, that Ferlinghetti published himself and Ginsberg, that Robert Bly—with no Government support—turned American poetry around with his magazine, *The Sixties;* it will be said that Government "supported" the small press, and became the prime element in alternative publication. This is not only a damn shame, but frightening. Those among us, surely a beleaguered minority in these days of happy times in Olympusville, who believe that art is fun, and dead serious as well, that whatever else art is, regardless of Government support or not, it is always artistic, have our work cut out for us. I don't think we ought to start writing sonnets to the chairman of the NEA. From what I hear sonnets won't work, sonnets aren't in, and the culture mob in Washington—as well as the boys and girls in California and New York—like things just the way they are. Of one thing I am sure: we must refuse to play the game; we must get on with the work. And we must protect our magazines and our ideals from the tender mercies of Government money.

"The American Revolution was not financed with matching funds from the Crown."
Eugene McCarthy

A LETTER HOME

by ADRIANNE MARCUS

from THE PAINTED BRIDE QUARTERLY

nominated by Naomi Lazard

"One Waits. One Waits."
—Weldon Kees

The island was not what I had imagined,
beach, trees, all sand and sun ready
to be walked, made into objects
for poems. Arriving in the fog, all
I could see at first was the shape
of water, but the fog lifted as we
docked and I saw:

marshes and grass, a white flickering
of distant birds. But then they
were gone.

We drove for a mile; palm trees
lined the dirt road. Beyond that,
wilderness. Came through the gates
to the one habitable house
with the clearing around it. Another
view:

a place where civilization is
accidental, requires constant
attention.

At dinner, the conversation avoids
these topics. We dress as survivors
might, with a sense of relief,
wearing items which can be commented
upon, pieces of jewelry brought
from exotic vacations, what we were
before we came. This permits us
to remember

names, to remember,
at least for now, what is not
with us, what we did not bring.

CRASH

By DAVID COPE

from THE STARS (Nada Press/Big Scream)

nominated by Allen Ginsberg

the cars lie, one on its side,
a rear wheel still spinning,
& the other upside down.
the bodies are scattered across the cornfield,
bent & broken on the frozen ground.
two ambulances pull up.
the attendants arrange & cover the dead.
cars pull over to the side of the road,
everyone shuffles,
eager to help, hands in pockets.

THEODORE ROETHKE
(a little memory)
by JAMES LEWISOHN

from GOLGOTHA (Greenfield Review Press)

nominated by Leonard Randolph

Come as summer woods
Worn with futures
That we lose
I see you strewn
Within the changing moth.
Teaching the smallest life
Its start, running with
Children after dark
To free things trapped
You kept love wise
Taking only what was there
And moving in and out of death
As flowers eat the air.
With you
The convolutions of the worm
Had pulse and speed.

It was discovery in what there is
Death   Love
Demands we stiffen or disclaim.
To keep alive
Despite
The daily dying forms
And searching under time
For mixtures folding and

Unfolding in the Islands
Off the bone, stitching
Gaiety into the rock.
Under casements in the heart
Of things
I always find a poem
Of yours.

IN IOWA

by CINDA KORNBLUM

from DENTAL FLOSS (Toothpaste Press)

nominated by Carole Dolph

In Iowa

          potatoes

are recognized

        not as a staple

but as an excuse

       for more butter

and so we are a sedentary people

     who value our property

and the fences

        or vessels

which mark

      the bounds

PREPARING TO SLEEP

by GREGORY ORR

from HARD PRESSED

nominated by Noel Peattie

Last of all, you remove
a tiny wooden box
from your chest, just under the heart.
It's a replica of your childhood
room. You place it under the pillow.
Naked, you lie down. Each night,
you dream of the future:
a huge desert
you will someday inhabit.

MENDING THE ADOBE

by HAYDEN CARRUTH

from THE GEORGIA REVIEW

nominated by Herbert Leibowitz

Sun dazzle and black shadow,
crow caw and magpie rattle
where I saw a pueblo woman,
dark and small, standing
on a ponderosa block
outside her home to smear
rich mud on the wall, red
and oily mud, using her
hands and a thin wooden
paddle. It shone smoothly,
and she left a swirling
pattern that I liked, although
I looked and said nothing.
When she stepped down for more
mud she said, "Sometimes
I fix it, sometimes not.
Mostly I fix it—now
in the dry time before rain.
That's good. But sometimes
I say the hell with it,
the rain will only wash it,
the frost crack it, the wind
blow it away. I'm not so
young no more. Well, but mostly
I fix it, I feel better
when I fix it—you know?
I remember my mother."

CONTRIBUTORS NOTES

JON ANDERSON has published three books of poetry and his work has appeared in *Back Door, Field, The Iowa Review, Lotus, Ohio Review* and elsewhere.

JOHN ASHBERY won both the *National Book Critics Cricle* Award and *The National Book Award* in 1976 for his poetry.

ANA BLANDIANA is a Rumanian poet translated into English by Peter Jay of Anvil Press, London.

JERRY BUMPUS is the author of the novel *Anaconda* and a collection of short stories, *Things In Place*.

ITALO CALVINO lives in Paris and has published widely in both literary and commercial presses. His latest book is *Invisible Cities*.

HAYDEN CARRUTH lives in Vermont and has published in many journals including poetry reviews for *The New York Times Book Review*. His books *The Bloomingdale Papers* and *Paragraphs 1–35* were published last year.

KELLY CHERRY is the author of the novel *Sick and Full of Burning* and has been published in *Commentary, Carolina Quarterly, Red Clay Reader, Aspen Leaves* and elsewhere.

DAVID COPE is an anti-war activist, and editor and publisher of *Big Scream*.

JAYNE CORTEZ lives in New York and has published much of her work independently.

DOUGLAS CRASE has been published in *Poetry, Paris Review* and *Partisan Review*.

PHILIP DACEY is director of the creative writing program at Southwest Minnesota State College and has published in *Poetry Northwest, North American Review, Esquire, Massachusetts Review, Shenandoah* and elsewhere.

STEPHEN DIXON has published short fiction in about a dozen small presses this year and lives in New York. A collection of his short fiction, *No Relief,* has just been issued by Street Fiction Press.

RUSSELL EDSON is the author of *The Intuitive Journey and Other Works*.

"EL HUITLACOCHE" is the pen name of Marco Antonio Cárdenas, who is an architect by profession, lives in Mexico and is at work on a novel about Zapata.

RAYMOND FEDERMAN is the author of three novels, two volumes of poems, two critical studies of Samuel Beckett and is editor of a collection of essays on contemporary fiction.

ROSS FELD is the author of *Years Out* and *Plum Poems*.

EDWARD FIELD's latest book is *A Full Heart*.

CAROLYN FORCHÉ's first volume of poetry, *Gathering of The Tribes* won the Yale Series of Younger Poets Award for 1975. She currently teaches at San Diego State University.

SIV CEDERING FOX published two poetry collections this year and lives in Rye, New York.

EUGENE GARBER lives in Bellingham, Washington and has published many stories in literary magazines.

PATRICIA GOEDICKE's most recent collection of poetry, *For The Four Corners*, appeared in the Spring of 1976. She lives in Mexico.

PAUL GOODMAN, who died in 1972, was a foremost social critic (*Growing Up Absurd*), novelist (*The Empire City*) poet (*The Lordly Hudson*), psychologist, literary critic and social planner.

JAMES HASHIM has taught at several universities in the United Sates and abroad and has published in *The Phoenix, New Voices* and elsewhere.

ALAN V. HEWAT has published in *Esquire* and elsewhere.

RICHARD HUGO is director of the creative writing program at the University of Montana and is the author of four books of poetry.

JOHN IRVING has published several novels and lives in Iowa.

ETHERIDGE KNIGHT has published three books of poetry and has received a National Endowment for the Arts Award and a Guggenheim Fellowship.

KENNETH KOCH's most recent book of poetry *The Duplications*, will be published by Random House this spring.

CINDA KORNBLUM's work has appeared in *Gum, Me Too, Typewriter, J Stone Press Weekly, The Spirit That Moves Us* and *Bandwagon* a book published by Toothpaste Press.

RICHARD KOSTELANETZ has published many experimental works, is the author of *The End of Intelligent Writing*, and is teaching at the University of Texas.

MAXINE KUMIN was awarded the Pulitzer Prize in 1973 for her collection of poems, *Up Country* and most recently published *House, Bridge, Fountain, Gate*.

MARY LANE lives and works in Chicago and has been published in *Open Places, A Hundred Posters, Poetry & * and other magazines.

CHRISTOPHER LASCH is the author of *The New Radicalism In America*, *The Agony of the American Left* and *The World of Nations*, and is completing a book on the bourgeois family.

BOB LEVIN practices law in San Francisco and has published in *Transfer*, *Folio* and *The New Republic*.

MIRIAM LEVINE's poems have appeared in numerous journals. She is the author of the chapbook, *Friends Dreaming*.

PHILIP LEVINE's latest collection of poems is *The Names of The Lost*.

JAMES LEWISOHN is the author of two collections of poetry, *Roslyn* and *Golgotha: Letters From Prison*. He is serving a life sentence at Maine State prison.

GERALD LOCKLIN is the author of four books of poetry, teaches at California State University at Long Beach and is "wardrobe consultant to Alfred Jarry."

PHILLIP LOPATE is the author of *Being With Children* and *The Eyes Don't Always Want To Stay Open*.

THOMAS LUX teaches at Sarah Lawrence College and has published two books of poetry, *Memory's Handgrenade* and *The Glassblower's Breath*.

SUSAN MACDONALD lives in suburbia with an ailing Fiat. *Dangerous As Daughters* is in its second printing and is her first book.

IAN MACMILLAN lives in Honolulu, Hawaii.

ADRIANNE MARCUS has published widely in literary journals and lives in California.

JAY MEEK's work has appeared in *Antioch Review*, *Paris Review*, *Poetry Northwest* and elsewhere.

HENRY MILLER is writing a second volume of his *Book of Friends*, describing pals from his Paris and Big Sur days.

HOWARD MOSS is poetry editor of *The New Yorker*.

LISEL MUELLER won the 1975 Lamont Prize for her second book of poems, *The Private Life*.

VICTOR MURAVIN, an emigre Russian merchant seaman living in the United States, has written a trilogy of his experiences in a labor camp in Siberia.

OPAL L. NATIONS has had over thirty books of his work published to date including *The Selected Writings of Opal L. Nations* (City Lights, 1974).

TIM O'BRIEN is the author of *If I Die In A Combat Zone* and *Northern Lights*.

DAVID OHLE lives in Austin, Texas.

GREGORY ORR lives in a farm house in Virgina. His latest book was *Gathering The Bones Together*.

OCTAVIO PAZ is well known for his poetry and essays, has authored several books and teaches at Harvard University.

JAYNE ANNE PHILLIPS grew up in Buckhannon, West Virginia and is working toward an MFA at The University of Iowa.

ALLEN PLANZ does not live on the Lower East Side. His home is East Hampton, N.Y.

T.E. PORTER, co-editor of *Falcon*, currently teaches at Mansfield State College in Pennsylvania.

JAROLD RAMSEY is the author of the poetry collection, *At Home With Strangers* and teaches at The University of Rochester.

MICHAEL RYAN lives in Waban, Massachusetts, and was a Yale Younger Poet.

REG SANER is author of *Climbing Into The Roots*, received The Walt Whitman Award and teaches at The University of Colorado.

JOHN SANFORD is working on a trilogy about American Literature to be published by Capra Press.

TEO SAVORY was born in Hong Kong, educated in London and Paris and is the author of ten published books.

STEVE SCHUTZMAN lives in San Francisco.

JAMES SCHUYLER is the author of three collections of poetry and two novels and lives in New York.

NTOZAKE SHANGE is the author of several books as well as the hit play *For Colored Girls Who Have Considered Suicide When The Rainbow is Enuf.*

JERRY STAHL is completing a novel, *Physical Education* and lives in New York where he works as a free-lance writer.

FELIX STEFANILE, with his wife Selma, is the editor and publisher of *Sparrow*, established in 1954. He received a National Endowment for the Arts grant in 1967 and is a Professor of English at Purdue University.

MEREDITH STEINBACH is writer in residence at Antioch College and is presently completing a novel. This is her first published story.

BARBARA SZERLIP, editor of *tractor*, has appeared in numerous journals, in *Four Young Women: Poems* and will publish a collection of her prose pieces, *Mata Hari* (Gallimaufry Press, 1977).

KATHRYN TERRILL teaches at Mt. Hood Community College, Gresham, Oregon.

MICHAEL VAN WALLEGHEN, associate professor of English at the Unversity of Illinois, has published *The Witchita Poems*.

MARNIE WALSH is a native Dakotan who received her M.A. in Creative Writing from the University of New Mexico and presently lives in a remote canyon in the Black Hills.

CHRISTINE ZAWADIWSKY lives in Milwaukee, Wisconsin and received a 1976 grant from the National Endowment for the Arts.

PAUL ZIMMER is associated with The University of Pittsburgh Press.

OUTSTANDING SMALL PRESSES

(These presses made or received nominations for the 1977–78 edition of *The Pushcart Prize*. See the *International Directory of Little Magazines and Small Presses*, Dustbooks, Box 1056, Paradise, CA 95969, for subscription rates, manuscript requirements and a complete international listing of small presses.)

Abattoir Editions, University of Nebraska, Omaha, NB 68155
Abraxas, 2322 Rugby Row, Madison, WI 65705
Act-Action Press, 710 Lodi St., Syracuse, NY 13203
Agni Review, Box 663, Cranford, NJ 07016
A Harmless Flirtation with Wealth Press, Box 9779, San Diego, CA 92109
Ahsahta Press, Dept. Of English, Boise State University, Boise, ID 83725
Aisling, Box 998, LeMargue, TX 77568
Akwesasne Notes, Mohawk Nation, Rooseveltown, NY 13683
The Alchemist, Box 123, La Salle, Quebec, Canada
Aldebaran Review, 2209 California, Berkeley, CA 94703
Aleph Magazine, 7319 Willow Ave., Takoma Park, MD 20012
Algol Press, Box 4175, New York, NY 10017
Alice James Books, 138 Mount Auburn St., Cambridge, MA 02138
Alphaville, Box 3424, Charlottesville, VA. 22903
American Scholar, 1811 Q St. N.W., Washington, D.C. 20009
American Poetry Review, Temple University, 1616 Walnut St., Philadelphia, PA 19103
Amnesty International, 200 West 72nd St., New York, NY 10021
Anima, 1053 Wilson Ave., Chambersburg, PA 17201
Ann Arbor Review, Washtenaw Community College, Ann Arbor, MI 48106
Antaeus, 1 West 30th St., New York, NY 10001

The Antioch Review, Box 148, Yellow Springs, OH 45387
Apple, Box 2271, Springfield, IL 62705
April Dawn Publishing Company, Box 4433, Falls Church, VA
    22044
Ararat, 628 Second Ave., New York, NY 10016
The Archive, Box 4665 Duke Sta., Durham, NC 27706
Arete, 830 Hyde, #6, San Francisco, CA 94109
Ars Poetica, 5548 North Sawyer, Chicago, IL
Ascent, University of Illinois, Urbana, IL 61801
Aspect Magazine, 66 Rogers Ave., Somerville, MA 02144
Aspen Anthology, Box 3185, Aspen, CO 81611
Assembling Press, Box 1967, Brooklyn, NY 11202
Athanor Press, 315 North Gibert St., Iowa City, IA 52240
The Atlantic Review Press, 40 Danbury St., London, England
Atlantis Editions, 4910 North 12th St., Philadelphia, PA 19141
Ausgabe, Rathausstrasse Ecke Konigstrs. 44, D-100, West
    Germany
Aura,% Brown, University of Alabama, University Sta., AL 35294

Bachy, 11317 Santa Monica, West Los Angeles, CA 90025
The Back Door Magazine, Box 481, Athens, OH 45701
Back Roads, Box 543, Cotati, CA 94928
Ball State University Forum, Ball State University, Muncie, IN
    47306
The B&R Samizdat Express, Box 161, West Roxbury, MA 02132
Bardic Echoes, 1036 Emerald Ave., Grand Rapids, MI 49503
Bartholomew's Cobble, 19 Howland Rd., West Hartford, CT 06107
Basement Workshop, 199 Lafayette St., 7th Flr., New York, NY
    10012
Bear Claw Press, 215 Bucholz Ct., Ann Arbor, MI 48104
Bellevue Press, 60 Schubert St., Binghampton, NY 13905
Beloit Poetry Journal, Box 2, Beloit, WI 53511
Berkeley Poets Cooperative, Box 459, Berkeley, CA 94701
Best Cellar Press, 118 South Boswell, Crete, NB 68333
Beyond Baroque Foundation, 1639 West Washington Blvd.,
    Venice, CA 90291
The Beiler Press, Route 2, Box 234A, Poynette, WI 53955
The Bilingual Review/La Revista Bilingue, York College, CUNY,
    Jamaica, NY 11455
Blackberry, Box 4757, Albuquerque, NM 87106

Blackberry Press, Box 186, Brunswick, ME 04011

Blackfish Press, 1851 Moore Ave., Burnaby, B.C., Canada

Black Rooster, 103 Waldron St., West Lafayette, IN 47906

Black Scholar, Box 31245, Sausalito, CA 94965

Black Sparrow Press, Box 3993, Santa Barbara, CA 93105

Bleb, 1918 So. 7th St., Minneapolis, MN 55454

Bloodroot, 316 Harvard St., Grand Forks, ND 58201

Blue Cloud Quarterly, Marvin, SD 57251

Blue Horse Publications, Box 6061, Augusta, GA 30906

Blue Leaf Editions, Box 857, New London, CT 06320

Blue Moon Press, University of Arizona, Dept. Of English, Tucson,
   AZ 85721

Blue Wind Press, 820 Miramar, Berkeley, CA 94707

Bogue Falaya Company, Box 20079, New Orleans, LA 70141

Bombay Gin / Naropa Institute, 1111 Pearl St., Boulder, CO 80302

Bonsai: A Quarterly of Haiku, 6227 North 13th Place #3, Phoenix,
   AZ 85014

Bopp Magazine, 542 West 112th Street #5F, New York, NY 10025

Brilliant Corners, 1372 West Estes #2N, Chicago, IL 60626

Burning Deck Press, 71 Elmgrove Ave., Providence, RI 02906

California State Poetry Quarterly, 22 Avon Rd., Kensington, CA
   94707

Calyx, Route 2, Box 118, Corvallis, OR 97330

Canadian Fiction Magazine, Box 46422, Station G, Vancouver,
   Canada 16R467

The Cape Rock, South East Missouri State University, Cape
   Girardeau, MO 63710

Capra Press, 631 State St., Santa Barbara, CA 93101

Caracol, Box 7577, San Antonio, TX 78207

Carolina Quarterly, Box 1117, Chapel Hill, NC 27514

Carpenter Press, Route 4, Pomeroy, OH 45769

Casa Editorial, 3128 24th St., San Francisco, CA 94110

Catalyst, 315 Blantyre Ave., Scarborough, Ontario, Canada
   M1N256

Cat's Pajamas Press, 423 South Humphrey, Oak Park, IL 60302

Cat's Paw Press, Box 19, Amenia, ND 58004

Center, 2920½ Wheeler, Berkeley, CA 94706

Centering, ATL, EBH, MSU, East Lansing, MI 48824

Chandler & Sharp Publishers, 5609 Paradise Dr., Corte Madera, CA 94925

Chariton Review, Northeast Missouri State, Kirksville, MO 63501

Chicago Review, University of Chicago, Chicago, IL 60637

Choomia, Box 107, Framingham, MA 01701

Chouteau Review, Box 10016, Kansas City, MO 64111

The Chowder Review, 2858 Kingston Dr., Madison, WI 53713

Chthon Press, 15 Hawthorne Village, Concord, MA 01742

CIE/Media Central, 628 Grand Ave. #307, St. Paul, MN 55105

City Miner, Box 176, Berkeley, CA 94701

Cleveland State University Poetry Center, Euclid at East 24th St., Cleveland, OH 44155

Cloud Marauder Press, 3051 Adeline St., Berkeley, CA 94703

Cocono, Suite 217, 564 Central Ave., Alameda, CA 94501

Cold Mountain Press, 4705 Sinclair, Austin, TX 78751

Coldspring Journal, Box 303, Cherry Valley, NY 13320

College English, Dept. Of English, Wesleyan University, Middletown, CT 06457

Colorado-North Review, University of Northern Colorado, Greeley, CO 80639

Concerning Poetry, WWS College, Bellingham, WA 98225

Concourse Press, Box 3268, Tallahassee, FL 32303

Confrontation, Long Island University, Brooklyn, NY 11202

Connecticut Fireside, Box 5293, Hamden, CT 06518

Contraband Press, Box 4073, Station A, Portland, ME 04010

Copper Canyon Press, Box 271, Port Townsend, WA 98368

Corduroy, Box 306, Jonesboro, TN 37659

Cosmic Circus, 521 33rd St., Oakland, CA 94609

Countryman Press, Taftsville, VT 05073

The Country Press, Box 482, Murfreesboro, TN 37130

CP Graham Press, Box 5, Keswick, VA 22947

Creative Arts Book Company, 833 Bancroft Way, Berkeley, CA 94710

Credence Press, 150 South Mantua St., Kent, OH 44240

The Crossing Press, Trumansburg, NY 14886

Cross Country Press, Trumansburg, NY 14886

Cross Currents, 103 Van Houten Fds., W. Nyack, NY 10994

CSP World News, Box 2608 Station D, Ottawa, Ontario, Canada K1P 5W7

Curbstone Press, 321 Jackson St., Willimantic, CT 06226

The Curveship Press, St. Andrew's College, Laurinsburg, NC 28352
Cut Bank, University of Montana, Missoula, MT 59801

Dacotah Territory, Box 775, Moorhead, MN 56560
Dark Horse, 262 Kent St., Brookline, MA 02146
Dark Tower, rm. 7, University Center, Cleveland State University, Cleveland, OH 44155
David Godine, Publisher, 306 Dartmouth St., Boston, MA 02116
Decatur House Press, Ltd., 2122 Decatur Place NW, Washington, D.C. 20008
December Press, 4 East Huron, Chicago, IL 60611
De Colores, 2633 Granite NW, Albuquerque, NM 87104
The Denver Quarterly, University of Denver, Denver, CO 80210
Desert First Works, 3870 Vine Ave., Tucson, AZ 85710
Diana's Bimonthly, 71 Elmgrove Ave., Providence, RI 02906
Dodeca, 11 Broadway, New York, NY 10004
Down River / World Publications, Box 366, Mountain View, CA 94040
Dramatika, 390 Riverside Dr., New York, NY 10025
Dryad Press, Box 1656, Washington, D.C. 20013
Duck Down Press, Box 2307, Missoula, MT 59801
Dustbooks, Box 1056, Paradise, CA 95969

EADS Street Press, 402 Stanton La., Crete, IL 60417
East River Anthology, 114 North 6th St., Perkasie, PA 18944
Echo, Box 728 Station A, Vancouver, B.C., Canada V6C 2N7
Edwardson Music, Ltd., 1 Serjeants Inn, Fleet St., London, England UK
Empire Building, 468 Wheeler Street N, St. Paul, MN 55104
Endymion, 562 West End Avenue #6A, New York, NY 10024
Energy/Black South Press, 2805 Southmore, Houston, TX 77004
English Publications, 357 Cockerell Dr., Abilene, TX 79601
En Passant Poetry Quarterly, 1906 Brandt Rd., Wilmington, DE 19810
Epoch, Cornell University, Ithaca, NY 14850
Eureka, 521 South Culver Avenue, Willows, CA 95988
Explorations Press, Dept. English, Illinois State University, Normal, IL 61761

The Falcon, Mansfield State College, Mansfield, PA 16937
Fiction Collective, Dept. English, Brooklyn College, CUNY,
Brooklyn NY 11210
Fiction International, Dept. English, St. Lawrence University,
Canton, NY 13617
Fiction Magazine, 193 Beacon St., Boston MA 02116
The Fiddlehead, Dept. English, University of New Brunswick,
Fredericton, N.B, Canada
Field, Oberlin College, Oberlin, OH 44074
Fighting Woman, 9 East 48th St., New York, NY 10017
The Figures, 2016 Cedar, Berkeley, CA 94709
Firelands Arts Review, Firelands Campus, Huron, OH 44839
First Person Press, Pallisades, NY
Five Trees Press, 660 York St., San Francisco, CA 94110
Floating Island, Box 516, Point Reyes Sta., CA 94965
Folk Frog Press, Box 15407, Salt Lake City, UT 84115
The Four Zoas, Box 461, Ware, MA 01082
Melvin Freilicher, % Wasserman, 210 West 109th St., New York,
NY 10025

Gallimaufry, 3208 North 19th Rd., Arlington, VA 22201
Garland Press Publishers, Box 933, Athens, GA 30601
Gay Literature, 723 Foerster St., San Francisco, CA 94127
The Georgia Review, University of Georgia, Athens, Ga 30602
Gerry de la Ree, 7 Cedarwood Lane, Saddle River, NJ 07458
Ghost Dance, ATL/EBH/MSU, E. Lansing, MI 48823
Glassworks, Box 163, Rosebank Sta., Staten Island, NY 10305
Gnomon Press, Box 1796, Lexington, KY 40501
Graham House Review, Box 489, Englewood, NJ 07631
Gravida, Box 76, Hartsdale, NY 10530
Graywolf Press, Box 142, Port Townsend, WA 98365
Great Society Press, 451 Heckman St., #308, Phillipsburg, NJ
08865
Green Earth Press, Box 339, Roseville, MI 48066
The Greenfield Review Press, Greenfield Center, NY 12833
Green Horse Press, Box 1691, Santa Cruz, CA 95061
Green Mountain Trading Post, Box 11, East Charleston, VT 05877
Greenwich-Meridian, 516 Avenue K South, Saskatoon, Canada
Grilled Flowers, University of Arizona Poetry Center, 1086 North
Highland Ave., Tucson, AZ 85719

Granite, Box 1367, Southampton, NY 11968
Grub Street, Box 91, Bellmore, NY 11710

Hand Book, 50 Spring St., New York, NY 10012
Hanging Loose, 321 Wyckoff St., Brooklyn NY 11217
Harbinger Magazine, Box 235 Annex Sta., Providence, RI 02901
Hard Pressed, 2830 Third Ave., Sacramento, CA 95818
The Harian Press, Ballston Springs, NY 12020
Happiness Holding Tank, 1790 Grand River, Okemos, MI 48864
Heirs, 657 Mission St., Rm. 205, San Francisco, CA 94105
Hofstra University Press, Hempstead, NY 11550
Hollow Spring Review of Poetry, Box 76, Berkshire, MA 01224
Holmgangers Press, 22 Ardith La., Alamo, CA 94507
The Hudson Review, 65 East 55th St., New York, NY 10022
Humble Hills Press, Box 7 Parchmont Sta., Kalamazoo, MI 49004

Icarus, Box 8, Riderwood, MD 21139
Icarus, N.W. State College, 4525 Downs Dr., St. Joseph,
    MO 64507
Images, Wright State University, Dayton, OH 45431
Impact, Box 61297, Sunnyvale, CA 94088
Indian Truth, 1505 Race St., Philadelphia, PA 19102
Inlet, Virginia Wesleyan College, Norfolk, VA 23502
Inprint, Box 329, Dobbs Ferry, NY 10706
Intermedia, 2431 Echo Park Ave., Los Angeles, CA 90026
Interstate, 4319 Airport, Austin, TX 78722
Iowa Review, EPB 453, University of Iowa, Iowa City, IA 52242
Invisible City, 6 San Gabriel Dr., Fairfax, CA 94930
Ithaca House, 108 North Plain St., Ithaca, NY 14850
Ithaca Press, Box 853, Lowell, MA 01857
ISAT Pragbhara Press, Route 1, Box 143-C, Houma, LA 70360
Island Press, 65 Beachcomber Ave., Bundeena NSW 2230,
    Australia

Jackpine Press, 3381 Timberlake La., Winston-Salem, NC 27106
Jam To-day, Box 249, Northfield, VT 05663
Janus, 1325 Cabrillo Ave., Venice, CA 90291
Journal of Black Studies, State University of New York, Buffalo, NY
    14226
Jungle Garden Press, 47 Oak Rd., Fairfax, CA 94930

Juniper Press, 1310 Shorewood Dr., La Crosse, WI 54601
J.Z. Press, Calais, VT 05648

Kansas Quarterly, Dept. English, Denison Hall, Kansas State
   University, Manhattan, KS 66506
Kayak, 325 Ocean View Ave., Santa Cruz, CA 95064
King Publications, Box 19332, Washington, D.C. 20036
Konglomerati Press, 5719 29th St. Ave. South, Gulfport, FL 33707
Kosmos, 130 Eureka, San Francisco, CA 94114

Lake Superior Review, Box 724, Ironwood, MI 49938
Lame Johnny Press, Box 66, Hermosa, SD 57744
Laughing Bear Press, Box 14, Woodinville, WA 98072
The Laurel Press, 1706 Nicholas Canyon Rd. #2, Los Angeles, CA
   90046
Lawrence Hill & Co., 24 Burr Farms Rd., Westport, CT 06880
Linden Publishers, 27 West 11th St., New York, NY 10011
Litmus, Inc., 574 Third Ave., Salt Lake City, UT 84103
Little Free Press, 715 East 14th St., Minneapolis, MN 55405
The Little Magazine, Box 207, Cathedral Sta., New York, NY 10025
Living Poets Press, 31 Eighth Ave., Brooklyn, NY 11215
Lodestar Press, Box 4657, Boulder, CO 80306
Long Island Review, 38 Weybridge Rd., Mineola, Long Island, NY
   11501
Long Pond Review, 533 College Rd., Seldon, NY 11784
Loon, Box 11633, Santa Rosa, CA 95406
Lowlands Review, 1305 Rosetta, Lake Charles, LA 70601
Lucille, 509 Terrace, Austin, TX 78704
Luna Bisconte Products, 137 Leland Ave., Columbus, OH 43214
Lunch, 220 Montross Ave., Rutherford, NJ 07070
Lynx House Press, Box 800, Amherst, MA 01002

Makar Press, Box 71, St. Lucia, Qld. 4067, Australia
Madness Incorporated/Radiant Zipper, 411 62nd St., Oakland, CA
   94609
Mana Publications, Box 5083, Suva, Fiji
Maneater, Box 2148, College St., Pullman, WA 99163
Many Smokes Magazine, Box 9167, Spokane, WA 99209
Massachusetts Review, Memorial Hall, University of
   Massachusetts, Amherst, MA 01002

Mati, 5548 North Sawyer, Chicago, IL 60625

Meanjin Quarterly, University of Melbourne, Parkville, Victoria, 3052 Australia

Menard Press, 23 Fitzwarren Gardens, London England

Micah Publications, 255 Humphrey St., Marblehead, MA 01945

Middle Earth Books, 1134 Pine St., Philadelphia, PA 10107

Midwest Quarterly, Kansas State College, Pittsburg, KS 66762

The Minnesota Review, Box 211, Bloomington, IN 47401

Mirror Press, 413 East 9th St., New York, NY 10009

The Mississippi Mud, 3125 S.E. Van Water, Portland, OR 97203

Mississsippi Review, University of Southern Mississippi, Hattiesburg, MS 39401

Modus Operandi, Box 36, Brookville, MD 20729

Mojo Navigator(e), 423 Humphrey, Oak Park, IL 60302

Momentum Press, 10508 W. Pico Blvd., Los Angeles, CA 90465

Montana Gothic, Box 756, Missoula, MT 59801

Montemora, Box 336, Cooper Sta., New York, NY 10003

Moondance, 1321 Swallow La., Memphis, TN 38116

Moons and Lions Tailes, Lake St. Sta., Box 8439, Minneapolis, MN 55408

Mosaic Press, Box 1032, Oakville, Ontario, Canda

Mountain Summer, Glen Antrim, Sewanee, TN 37375

Mountain Union Books, Antioch College, 107 Earwood St., Beckly, W. VA 25801

Mudborn Press, 209 W. De La Guerra, Santa Barbara, CA 93101

Mundus Artium, Ellis Hall, Ohio University, Athens, OH 45701

Mulch Press, Box 598, Northampton, MA 01060

Nada Press, 696 48th St. SE, Grand Rapids, MI 49508

Nantucket Review Press, Box 1444, Nantucket, MA 02554

Nausea / Russ Haas Press, Box 4261, Long Beach, CA 90804

Nemesis Press, Hindsboro, IL

Newedi Press, BGSU, Bowling Green, OH 43403

New Boston Review, 77 Sacramento St., Somerville, MA 02143

New Letters, University of Missouri, 5346 Charlotte, Kansas City, MO 64110

New Literary History, Wilson Hall, University of Virginia, Charlottesville, VA 22903

Neworld, 1308 South New Hampshire Ave., Los Angeles, CA 90006

New Orleans Review, Loyola University, N. Orleans, LA 70118
New Place Press, Box 266, Taunton, MA 02780
New Poetry, Box N110 Grosvenor St. PO, Sydney, NSW, Australia 2000
The New Poets Series, 541 Piccadilly Rd., Baltimore, MD 21204
New River Review, Radford College Sta., Radford, VA 24142
The New Renaissance, 9 Heath Rd., Arlington, MA 02174
Nobodaddy Press, 20 College Hill Rd., Clinton, NY 13323
Northwest Review, University of Oregon, 369 PLC, Eugene, OR 97403
Nostoc, 101 Nehoiden Rd., Waban, MA 02168

Obsidian, Dept. English, SUNY, Fredonia, NY 14063
Ohio Review, 346 Ellis Hall, Ohio University, Athens, OH 45701
Oink! 7021 N. Shridan, Chicago, IL 60626
Olivant Press, Box 1409, Homestead, FL 33030
Ontario Review, 6000 Riverside Dr., Windsor, Ontario, Canada N8S1B6
Open Places, Box 2085, Stephens College, Columbia, MO 65201
O Press, 138 Sullivan St., New York, NY 10012
Other Voices, 39 Oakwood, San Francisco, CA 94110
The Outland Press, Lewisville, PA 19351
Out Of The Ashes Press, Box 42384, Portland, OR 97424
Out There, 6944 W. George St., Chicago, IL 60634
Over The Garden Fence, 3960 Cobblestone, Dallas, TX 75229
OYEZ Review, Roosevelt University, Chicago, IL 60605

Painted Bride Quarterly, 527 South St., Philadelphia, PA 19147
Pale Horse Press, Box 109, New Philadelphia, OH 44663
PAN, Annex 21, U.N.O. Box 688, Omaha, NB 68101
Panache, Box 77, Sunderland, MA 01375
Padanaram, 52 Dunster St., Cambridge, MA 02138
Panjandrum Press, 99 Sanchez St., San Francisco, CA 94114
Parable Press, Box H., N. Amherst, MA 01059
Parabola, 166 E. 61st St., New York, NY 10021
Paris Review, 45–39 171 Place, Flushing, NY 11758
Partisan Review, Rutgers University, New Brunswick, NJ 08903
Paunch, 123 Woodward Ave., Buffalo, NY 14214
Parnassus: Poetry In Review, 205 West 89th St., New York, NY 10024

Pawn Review, 2806 Reagan, No. 204, Dallas, TX 75214
Peace & Pieces Press, Box 99394, San Francisco, CA 94109
Pembroke Magazine, Box 60, PSU, Pembroke, NC 28372
Penny Each Press, Thetford, VT 05074
Pentagram Press, Box 11609, Milwaukee, WI 53211
The Penumbra Press, Rt. 1, Lisbon, IA 52253
Pequod, Box 491, Forest Hills, CA 94931
Petronium Press, EWA Tower 1813, 1255 Nuuanu Ave., Honolulu,
    HA 96817
Phantasm, Box 3404, Chico, CA 95927
Phantasmicom Press, 1339 Weldon Ave., Baltimore, MD 21211
Phantasy Publishing, 19880 Lakeview Ave., Excelsior, MN 55331
The Phoenix. Morningstar Farm. RFD, Haydenville, MA 02133
Phone-a-Poem, Box 193, Cambridge, MA 02141
Pigiron Press, Box 237, Youngstown, OH 44501
Pilot Press Books, Box 2662, Grand Rapids, MI 49501
Pitcairn Press Inc., 388 Franklin St., Cambridge, MA 02139
Plantagenet Press, Box 271, Dobbs Ferry, NY 10522
Ploughshares, Box 529, Cambridge, MA 02139
The Poem Company, Box 3294, Vancouver, B.C., Canada
Poetry, 1228 N. Dearborn Parkway, Chicago, IL 60610
Poetry And, Box A3298, Chicago, IL 60690
The Poetry Miscellany, Box 175, Williamstown, MA 01267
Poetry Newsletter, Temple University, Philadelphia,
    PA 19122
Poetry Northwest, University of Washington, 4045 Brooklyn Ave.,
    Seattle, WA 98195
Poetry NOW, 3118 K. St., Eureka, CA 95501
Point Riders Press, Box 2731, Norman, OK 73070
Prairie Schooner, 201 Andrews, UN, Lincoln, NB 68508
Present Tense, 165 E. 56th St., New York, NY 10022
Promise of Learnings Inc., Apt. 7-F, 50 Riverside Dr., New York,
    NY 10024
Proteus Press, 1004 N. Jefferson St., Arlington, VA 22205
Provincetown Poets, 216 Bradford St., Provincetown,
    MA 02657
Puckerbrush Press, 76 Main St., Orono, ME 04473
Pulp, c/o Sage, 334 East 93rd St., New York, NY 10028
Puerto del Sol, Box 3E, New Mexico State University, Las Cruces,
    NM 88003

Quark Press, Box 193, Cambridge, MA 02141
Quarry West, University of California, Santa Cruz, CA 95064
Quartet, 1119 Neal Pickett Dr., College Sta., TX 77840
Quarterly Review of Literature, 16 Haslet Ave., Princeton, NJ
   08540

Raspberry Press, Rt. 6, Box 318A, Bemidji, MN 56601
Ragnarok Press, 1719 13th Ave., Birmingham, AL 35205
Rainbow Resin, 426 Pearl, Shell Beach, CA 93449
Raindust Press, Box 1823, Independence, MO 64055
Realitites, Box 453, Marina, CA 93933
Red Cedar Review, 325 Morrill Hall, MSU, E. Lansing, MI 48823
Red Dust Inc. 218 81st St., New York, NY 10028
Red Fox Review, Mohegan Community College, Norwich, CT
   06360
Red Hanrahan Press, Box 03527, Highland Park, MI 48203
Red Hill Press, 6 San Gabriel Dr., Fairfax, CA 94930
Red Weather, Box 1104, Eau Claire, WI 54701
Reed, Cannon and Johnson Co., 2140 Shattuck Ave., Berkeley, CA
   94704
Release Press, 200 Carroll St., Brooklyn, NY 11231
The Remington Review, 505 Westfield Ave., Elizabeth, NJ 07208
Review La Booche, 615 Paris Ct., Columbia, MO 65201
RFD, 4525 Lower Wolf Creek Rd., Wolf Creek, OR 97497
Rikka, Box 6031 Sta. A, Toronto, Ontario, Canada M5W1P4
River Bottom, 1212 W. 4th Ave., Oshkosh, WI 54901
Roadhouse, 900 West 9th St., Belvidere, IL 61008
Rook Press, 805 W. 1st Ave., Derry, PA 15627
Roots, Box 14645, Houston, TX 77021
Running Press, 38 South 19th St., Philadelphia, PA 19103

Sahara, 239 Mountain View St., Decatur, GA 50030
Sahner Publishing Co., Box 6817, Chicago, IL 60680
St. Andrews Review, St. Andrews College, Laurinburg, NC 28352
Salmagundi, Skidmore College, Saratoga Springs, NY
Salome, 5548 N. Sawyer, Chicago, IL 60625
Salt Lick Press, Box 1064, Quincy, IL 62301
Samisdat, Box 1534, San Jose, CA 95109
Sand Dollar, 1205 Solano Ave., Albany, CA 94706

The Saturday Centre, Box 140, Cammeray, NSW,
    Australia 2062
Scarecrow Books, 1050 Magnolia #2, Millbrae, CA 94030
Scotty MacGregor Publishing Co., 10 Pineacre Dr., Smithtown, NY
    11787
Scree, Box 761, Fallon, NY 89406
Seamark Press, Box 2, Iowa City, IA 52240
Second Back Row Press, 4/8 Victoria Parade, Manly NSW, Australia
    2062
Second Coming, Box 3124, San Francisco, CA 94131
Seems, Dept. English, Northern Illinois University, Dekalb, IL
    60115
Segve Press, 782 W. End Ave., New York, NY 10025
Seven Buffaloes Press, 20720 S. Fruit Ave., Riverdale, Ca. 93656
Seven Woods Press, Box 32, Village Sta., New York, NY 10014
Sewanee Review, University of the South, Sewanee, TN 37375
Shantih, Box 125, Bay Ridge Sta., Brooklyn, NY 11220
Shenandoah, Box 722, Lexington, VA 24450
Singlejack Books, Box 1906, San Pedro, CA 90733
SHY, Poste Restante, Hydra, Greece
Sipapu, Rt. I, Box 216, Winters, CA 95694
Skywriting, English Dept., W.M. University, Kalamazoo, MI
    49008
Slow Loris Press, Rapport Magazine, 6359 Morrowfield Ave.,
    Pittsburgh, PA 15217
The Smith, 5 Beekman St., New York, NY 10038
Snakeroots, Pratt Institute, Brooklyn, NY 11205
Snowy Egret, 205 S. Ninth St., Williamsburg, KY 40769
Solana, c/o Fogler, 11822 Kramper La., St. Louis, MO 63128
The Sole Proprietor, 2770 NW 32nd Ave, Miami FL 33142
Some, 211 West 91st, New York, NY 10024
Some Friends, Box 3395, Tyler, TX 75701
South Carolina Review, Clemson University, Clemson, SC 29630
Southern Exposure, Box 230, Chapel Hill, NC 27514
Southern Illinois University Press, Box 3637, Carbondale,
    IL 62301
Southern Review, Drawer D, Unversity Sta., Baton Rouge, LA
    70803
Southern Poetry Review, N.C. State University, Raleigh,
    NC 27607

Southwest Review, Southern Methodist University, Dallas, TX 75275

Spectrum Productions, 979 Casiano Rd., Los Angeles, CA 90049

Spirit That Moves Us, Box 1585, Iowa City, IA 52240

Star-Web Paper, Regents 509, NMSU, Las Cruces, NM 88003

Stonecloud, 1906 Parnell Ave., Los Angeles, CA 90025

Stone-Marrow Press, English Dept., University of Cincinnati, OH 45221

StoryQuarterly, Box 865, Ravinia Sta., Highland Park, IL 60635

Street Press, 1 Somerset Ave., Mastic, NY 11950

Sun, 456 Riverside Dr., New York, NY 10027

Sun & Moon, 4330 Martwick Rd. #418, College Park, MD 20740

Sunbury Press, Box 274, Jerome Ave. Sta., Bronx, NY 10468

Sunstone Press, Box 2321, Santa Fe, NM 87501

Swamp Press, 300 Main St., Oneonta, NY 13820

Sun Tracks, SUPO Box 20788, Tucson, AZ 85720

Tales, Box 24226, St. Louis, MO 63130

Taurean Horn Press, 601 Leavenworth #45, San Francisco, CA 94109

Tejidos, Box 7383, Austin, TX 78712

Telephone Books, Box 672, Old Chelsea Sta., New York, NY 10011

10 Point 5, 1035½ Ferry St., Eugene, OR 97401

Texas Center for Writers, Box 19876, 3015 Oak Lawn, Dallas, TX 75219

The Texas Slough, 151 S. Rester #111, El Paso, TX 79912

Third Eye Publications, 250 Mill St., Williamsville, NY 14221

Thorp Springs Press, 2311-C Wollsey St., Berkeley, CA 94705

Three Rivers Press, Box 21, CMU, Pittsburgh, PA 15213

Tidelines Press, Tannersville, NY 14850

Tin Tan, Box 1959, San Francisco, CA 94101

Toothpaste Press, Box 546, West Branch, IA 52358

Topia Press, Bradford, NY

Transatlantic Review, Box 3348 Grand Central Station, New York, NY 10017

Treacle Press, 4615 Cedar Ave., Philadelphia, PA 19143

Tree Books, Box 3005, Berkeley, CA 94703

TriQuarterly, 101 University Hall, Northwestern University, Evanston, IL 60201

Truly Fine Press, Box 891, Bemidji MN 56601

Truck Press, 1141 James Ave., St. Paul, MN 55105
Tundra Books, 18 Cornelia St., Plattsburgh, NY 12901
Turkey Press East, 42 Dana St., Providence, RI 02906
Turtle Island, 2845 Buena Vista Way, Berkeley, CA 94708
Tweed, Box, 304, Murwillumbah, NSW 2484, Australia
218 Press, Box 218, Village Sta., NY 10014

Unicorn Press, Box 3307, Greensboro, NC 27402
University of Windsor Review, Windsor, Ontario, Canada N9B3P4
University Press of Washington, D.C., University Press Bldg.,
    Riverton, VA 22651
Unmuzzled Ox, Box 840, New York, NY 10013
The Unspeakable Visions of the Individual, Box 439, California, PA
    15419
Uroboros, 111 N. 10th St., Orlean, NY 14760

Vagabond Press, Box 879, Ellensburg, WA 98926
The Vanity Press, Box 15064, Atlanta, GA 30333
Veins, Box 615, Middlebury, VT 05753
Vile, 1183 Church St., San Francisco, CA 94114
V.I.P. Books, 412 Lampson St., Victoria, B.C., Canada
The Voyeur, 301 Hicks St., Brooklyn, NY 11201

Walton Press, 22 Salmund Rd., Belfast, ME 02915
Waluna, 70 Wooster St., New York, NY 10012
Washout Publishing Co., Box 2752, Schenectady, NY 12309
Watermark, English Dept., UMSL, St. Louis, MO 63121
Webster Review, Webster Groves, MO 63119
West Coast Poetry Review, 11227 Codel Way, Reno, NV 89503
West Conscious Review, 1050 Magnolia #2, Millbrae,
    CA 94030
West End, Box 354 Jerome Ave. Sta., Bronx, NY 10468
The Westerly Review, 229 Post Rd., Westerly, RI 02891
Western Humanities Review, University of Utah, Salt Lake City,
    UT 84112
Wetlands, Box 252, West Islip, NY 11795
Whimsy Press, 1822 Northview Dr., Arnold, MO 63010
White Arms Magazine, Box 302, Howe, IN 46748
Whooly Names Press, Box 3853, Seattle, WA 98124
The Wind Press, RFD Rt. #1, Box 810, Pikeville, KY 41501

Wild & Woolley, Box 41, Glebe NSW 2037, Australia
The Windless Orchard, Purdue University, Fort Wayne, IN 46805
The Windmill Press, 1369 Linwood, Holland, MI 49423
Womanchild Press, 18 Walnut St., Ware, MA 01082
Woman Press, Box 59330, Chicago, IL 60645
The Women's Press, 280 Bloor St. W., Ste. 305, Toronto, Canada
The Woodbine Press, 4615 Cedar Ave., Philadelphia, PA 19143
Work/Shop Press, Box 56052, Atlanta, GA 30343
The Workingman's Press, 833 Bancroft Way, Berkeley, CA 94710
World Publications, Box 366, Mountain View, CA 94040
The Wormwood Review, Box 8840, Stockton, CA 95204
Writers' Resource Center, 12 Cooney St., Somerville, MA 02143

Xanadu, 1704 Auburn Rd., Wantagh, NY 11793

The Yellow Press, 2394 Blue Island Ave., Chicago, IL 60608
Yardbird Reader, 1718 Jaynes St., Berkeley, CA 94708

Z Press, % Elmslie, Calais, VT 05648
Zahir, Box 715, Newburyport, MA 01950
Zartscorp Inc. Books, 267 W. 89th St., New York, NY 10024
Ziesing Brothers Publishing, 768 Main St., Willimantic, CT 06226

CALEDONIA, the type in which this book was set is one of those referred to by printers, as a "modern face". It was designed around 1939 by W.A. Dwiggins (1880–1956) and it has been called "the most popular all-purpose typeface in U.S. history".

It is an original design, but, as from the beginning, fresh and exciting designs have often evolved from variations on the old, done by competent and disciplined hands. Caledonia shows marks of the long admired Scotch roman type-letters cut by Alexander Wilson in Glasgow in the 19th century. It also shows a trace from the types that W. Bulmer & Company used, cut in London, around 1790 by William Martin.

That Dwiggins was aware of the particular needs of our time is soundly attested to by the enduring good reception his "hard working, feet-on-the-ground" type has received from countless printers, authors and readers alike.

This book was designed and produced for the publisher, by RAY FREIMAN & COMPANY.